Teaching Manual for

World Religions

Teaching Manual for

World Religions: A Voyage of Discovery

Third Edition

Edited by Colleen Cichon-Mulcrone

Written by Jeffrey Brodd, Patrick Tiernan, Michael Wilt, and Jonathan Yu-Phelps

Saint Mary's Press®

The publishing team included Jerry Windley-Daoust, Jim Zellmer, and Christine Schmertz Navarro, consulting development editors; Lorraine Kilmartin, reviewer; manufacturing coordinated by the production departments of Saint Mary's Press.

Printed in the United States of America

1242

ISBN 978-0-88489-998-3

About the Authors and Editor

Jeffrey Brodd (author of the student text and coauthor of the teaching manual) received a doctorate in religious studies from the University of California, Santa Barbara. He has taught world religions at the College of Wooster, Ohio; Saint Mary's University of Minnesota, Winona; and Winona State University, Minnesota. He is now a member of the faculty of the Department of Humanities and Religious Studies, California State University, Sacramento.

Colleen Cichon-Mulcrone (editor and coauthor of the teaching manual) worked as a religion teacher and high school campus minister before she began freelance writing and editing for Saint Mary's Press. She holds a degree in English from Xavier University, Ohio, and a certificate in pastoral ministries from Saint Mary's University of Minnesota, Winona. Colleen recently taught in the English department at Queen of Peace High School, Burbank, Illinois.

Gregory L. Sobolewski (author of the foreword to the student text) received a doctorate in religious studies from Marquette University, Milwaukee. He is director of the Institute in Pastoral Ministries at Saint Mary's University of Minnesota, Winona, and teaches theology and interdisciplinary studies at the university.

Patrick Tiernan (coauthor of revisions for the third edition of the teaching manual) was an undergraduate double major in religious studies and philosophy at Merrimack College, Massachusetts, and holds master's degrees in theological studies and sacred theology from Boston University. He is currently a doctoral candidate at Boston College in educational administration, studying moral leadership in Catholic secondary schools. He and his wife, Anitza, reside in Waltham, Massachusetts.

Michael Wilt (coauthor of the teaching manual) received a master of arts degree in theological studies from the Maryknoll School of Theology, New York. He is an editor and writer currently living in Massachusetts.

Jonathan Yu-Phelps (coauthor of the teaching manual) holds a master of theological studies degree from the Weston Jesuit School of Theology, Cambridge, Massachusetts, and did graduate work at the Institute for Religious Education and Pastoral Ministry at Boston College. Recently Jonathan taught religion classes and served as a campus minister at Newton Country Day School in Massachusetts. He and his wife are currently serving as missionaries in Brazil.

Contents

Appendices

An Introduction to *World Religions*

The Academic Study of Religions

World Religions: A Voyage of Discovery is an introductory survey of religious traditions. Along with chapters on the major religions of the world, the text includes a chapter describing some representative small-scale, or primal, traditions: those of the Aborigines of Australia, the Yoruba of West Africa, the Native Americans of the Northern Plains, and the Aztecs of Mesoamerica. Another chapter presents the religions of ancient Iran, Greece, and Rome, partly to provide the background for Judaism, Christianity, and Islam.

This comprehensiveness is intended to allow you ample flexibility in course planning. Not all the chapters need to be covered to provide a balanced introduction to world religions. For instance, Jainism could be omitted if time is short; while it is a fascinating example of religious asceticism and the ethic of nonviolence *(ahimsa),* it has a relatively small following and is similar to Buddhism. Zen Buddhism could be considered within the larger scope of Buddhism, although its specific aspects and great appeal in the West recommend it for a separate presentation. The chapters can be read independently of one another, with the following exceptions: Jainism should be preceded by Hinduism and Buddhism; Sikhism should be preceded by Hinduism; and Zen Buddhism should be preceded by Buddhism.

The textbook chapters explain the main aspects of each tradition in a clear and equable manner. Peripheral aspects and overly sophisticated explanations are avoided. For students interested in further study, whether in college courses or through independent research, the text should be a helpful springboard. Appendix 3 of this manual, "For Further Reading," suggests additional reading materials for each chapter, most of which are suitable for high school students.

Two issues dealt with in chapter 1 of the text deserve some further comment here. The first has to do with each chapter's content. Chapter 1 charts the seven dimensions of religious traditions: experiential, mythic, doctrinal, ethical, ritual, social, and material. The text attempts to cover these basic dimensions evenly in its account of each religion. In some cases, however, such balance is not easily achieved, or even desirable. The chapter on Taoism, for example, focuses intentionally on philosophical aspects, and therefore emphasizes the experiential and doctrinal dimensions. The scheme of basic elements used in this course is similar to and much indebted to Ninian Smart's dimensional approach to the study of religions. For lucid and helpful discussions, see his *Worldviews: Crosscultural Explorations of Human Beliefs* or see the introductory chapters of his *World's Religions: Old Traditions and Modern Transformations and Religious Experience of Mankind,* third edition.

The second issue from chapter 1, dealt with briefly there, involves the perspective this course takes on the world's religions. In a word (mercifully left out of chapter 1) it is *Religionswissenschaft,* literally the "science of religion." *Religionswissenschaft* is the academic study of religion begun mainly in Germany at the end of the nineteenth century. As of the last three or four decades, *Religionswissenschaft* is a significant field in most universities and colleges throughout North America, Europe, and Australia. The field is now usually referred to as history of religions, comparative religion, phenomenology of religion, or simply religious studies.

Whatever its name, the academic study of religion attempts to approach the subject matter scientifically, through empirical observation and objective consideration, thereby striving to arrive at value-free descriptions of religious phenomena. In other words, it sets out to explain the truth *about* religion rather than the truth *of* religion. It is therefore not theology, or any other religious activity. Unlike theology, religious studies is a *second-order* approach because it is one step removed from its subject matter. In this sense it is analogous to political science, which endeavors to explain the truth *about* political systems and viewpoints rather than the truth *of* those systems and viewpoints.

This is not to say that religious studies is not concerned with theology or other religious activities. Indeed together those activities make up the subject matter that the student of religion attempts to understand and interpret. But the process of understanding and interpreting theology differs qualitatively from actually *doing* theology. A biologist studies nonhuman life-forms but does not attempt to be one of those life-forms, at least not in the capacity of biologist.

Because it avoids the *doing* of religion, this course—a religious studies approach to world religions—is not about interfaith dialogue or understanding other religions from the vantage point of Christianity. Rather, it attempts to present each religion from a position of neutrality. It is hoped that this approach has not stifled a sense of enthusiasm for the religions. To describe the religions enthusiastically seems appropriate owing precisely to empirically observable data, namely the many enthusiastic adherents of these religions through their often long and colorful histories.

Although the study of religions is *nonreligious,* it is by no means *antireligious.* The scientific study of religions should not intentionally violate or alter its subject matter. On this point a word of caution is in order: Religion, by its very nature, tends to be a deeply personal aspect of life. The study of religion, no matter how scientific, can and does affect the religious perspectives of those who undertake it. For most people, the study of world religions is a positive opportunity, providing both a healthy challenge to their own understanding of reality and a new set of possibilities for enhancing that understanding. For some people, however, the challenge might prove difficult.

A few words about the methodology of religious studies might shed some further light on the field's perspective. For one thing, religious studies is cross-cultural, or pluralist. The study of world religions is an especially helpful approach to understanding religion in general because it presents a rich array of religious phenomena from various cultures. For another thing, religious studies is polymethodic, drawing from several academic disciplines, especially history, sociology, anthropology, philosophy, and psychology. The pluralist and polymethodic nature of religious studies helps account for its growing popularity as an academic field. Through the multiple lenses of the humanities and social sciences, religious studies explores, across cultures and through time, the central human phenomenon of being religious.

The Contents of This Course

Course Goals

The goals of this course are as follows:

1. That the students strive to become knowledgeable about the answers each of the religions offers to the religious questions outlined in chapter 1 of the text
2. That the students become better acquainted with the basic dimensions of the world's major religions, through their study of abundant examples of each dimension
3. That the students emerge from this course with a greatly enhanced understanding of the people who adhere to the world's various religions

Major Concepts

The following major concepts correspond largely to the major sections in the chapters of the student text. This teaching manual is also organized according to these major concepts. This list serves as an outline of the course contents.

Chapter 1
Studying the World's Religions
A. The Nature of a Religious Tradition
B. Some Challenges and Rewards of Studying the World's Religions

Chapter 2
Primal Religious Traditions
A. Religion of the Australian Aborigines
B. An African Tradition
C. Religion of the North American Plains Indians
D. A Mesoamerican Religion

Chapter 3
Hinduism
A. Human Destiny
B. Hindu Society
C. Three Paths to Liberation
D. Hinduism in the Modern World

Chapter 4
Buddhism
A. The Life of Gautama
B. The Dharma
C. Three Rafts for Crossing the River

Chapter 5
Jainism
A. Makers of the River Crossing
B. Knowing the Universe
C. The Religious Life

Chapter 15
Religion in the Modern World
A. Modern Influences
B. New Religious Movements
C. Religion and Science

Multiple Intelligences Theory and This Course

Most world religion classes are composed of students with varying academic abilities and backgrounds. Multiple intelligences theory is an excellent tool for teachers to use in shaping classroom activities that will touch a diversity of students. That theory centers on Howard Gardner's belief that each person has a unique cognitive profile. In *Frames of Mind: The Theory of Multiple Intelligences* (New York: Basic Books), his 1983 book about how we perceive and learn, Gardner, a Harvard psychologist, proposes that there are at least seven types of intelligence: linguistic and logical-mathematical (the two traditional ones found in schools), plus bodily-kinesthetic, visual, musical, interpersonal, and intrapersonal. Gardner has also added an eighth type, naturalist intelligence.

Moving Gardner's multiple intelligences theory into methodology and strategies for the classroom is a dynamic and exciting proposition. It seems to go hand in hand with Saint Paul's teaching in First Corinthians: "Now there are varieties of gifts, but the same Spirit" (12:4). It recognizes that students are gifted in different ways.

The activities suggested in this teaching manual—particularly those in each chapter under the heading "Additional Activities" (that is, additional to the activities provided in the student text)—appeal to the varied intelligences that students have. By using an assortment of activities, you will give your students the opportunity to learn in meaningful, interesting, and challenging ways. Most important, you will offer them each a better chance to learn in the ways that are most effective for them. This can affirm your students and build a positive and interactive classroom.

Many of the additional activities in this manual are student centered. They employ active learning strategies, which is another way of saying they engage students through a variety of intelligences. It has become solid educational practice to design lessons and assessments that challenge students in more than a lecture or "paper and pencil" format. Of course, lectures and writing have their place, and this manual also employs those methods where appropriate. By tapping into the widely varied ways that students learn and know things, this course attempts to involve the whole person.

Tools for Teaching

During the brief explanation given here, you may find it helpful periodically to glance at one of the chapters in the text and its corresponding chapter in this manual to see examples of the teaching tools described.

Major Concepts

As mentioned earlier in this introduction, each chapter of the textbook and teaching manual is organized according to its major concepts. The major concepts for a given chapter of the text correspond to the thematic divisions within the chapter. Thus the major concepts are the organizing principle for teaching the material. Most chapters have two or three major concepts, and these can be helpful tools for scheduling and organizing your lessons.

At the beginning of each chapter in this manual, the major concepts for that chapter are listed and described, providing a summary of the chapter. Then each concept is treated in turn, with a major subhead accompanied by an icon identifying the related pages in the student text, followed by review questions and activities on the concept.

Review Questions

In this manual the review questions that end each chapter in the student text are repeated, and a suggested answer is provided for each question. The intent of the review questions is simply to check whether the students have retained the basic information for the given concepts. It is hoped that by using other course tools, they will go beyond that level to analysis, reflection, and application.

Student Text Activities

In the student text, lettered activities in the outside margins correspond with the accompanying text material. Those activities are repeated in this manual, and may be assigned as homework or as class work. Your students will not be able to do all the activities in a semester, the time normally allotted for this course, so you will need to select from those activities to fit the needs of your class. You might suggest that the students read all the text activities, even those that you do not assign for completion. Just reading a particular activity can help them see the accompanying text material in a new light—perhaps a more personalized light. The text activities should be viewed not as burdensome assignments but as intriguing reflection starters.

Additional Activities

For each major concept, you will find one or more additional activities. These are most often classroom activities that suggest small-group or large-group discussion. They occasionally require handouts that must be photocopied and then distributed to the students. Those handouts appear at the end of the respective chapters in this manual.

Appendices

Five appendices to this manual offer additional tools for teaching that can be used in many ways.

Appendix 1: Sample Test Questions. This appendix contains a bank of tests for each chapter of the student text. Objective and essay questions are included. You should pick questions from them to supplement tests of your own making. Test questions for this course and all other Saint Mary's Press high school courses are available online for downloading. Call 800-533-8095 for information about this resource.

Appendix 2: Audiovisual Recommendations. This appendix offers a chapter-by-chapter compilation of audiovisual resources. Most are nonfiction and documentary materials. You may wish to ask the students to write reports that highlight the religious traditions depicted in a video or film.

Appendix 3: For Further Reading. The resources recommended in this appendix can be of use for your own preparation as well as for student research projects.

Appendix 4: The Comparative Study of Religions. This appendix applies the comparative approach of studying religions to the traditions surveyed in the textbook. In doing so it exhibits the approach's usefulness for investigating and explaining the nature of a religious tradition and the phenomenon of religion itself.

Appendix 5: Worldviews: Religions and Their Relatives. It is commonly argued that modern worldviews such as nationalism and secular humanism have much in common with the traditional religions. Indeed scholars often categorize them with the world's religions. This article explores such modern worldviews, and points out how they answer questions that are similar to those addressed by religious traditions, and how they are composed generally of the same basic elements as established religions.

Other Resources from Saint Mary's Press. The student book and leader's guide for *Primary Source Readings in World Religions* (Saint Mary's Press, 2009) offer foundational readings in various world religions as guidance for looking at the readings with the students. *Teaching About Other Religions* (Saint Mary's Press, 2006) offers ideas and strategies for teaching about Judaism, Islam, Hinduism, and Buddhism in the classroom.

Strategies for Presenting the Course Material

Sometimes you may want to use a suggested lesson exactly as it appears in this manual. At other times you may want to skip, adapt, or even expand on a particular concept or activity. The following general ideas and suggestions may help you create meaningful experiences tailored specifically to your students' needs, abilities, and levels of interest:

Journal writing. A journal is a written record of a person's inner dialogue—the thoughts, feelings, questions, impressions, and connections that come to mind over a period of time. You may wish to direct the students to record their reactions in a journal as they study the world's religions. The text activities and ideas from the additional activities can provide starting points for reflection. Encourage the students to write in their journals not only what they understand about the course material but also what they think and feel about it. For example, does a particular religious practice or concept shed light on their own beliefs? Does it give them insight into the people of another tradition? Does it make them uneasy or cause them confusion?

Journal keeping is a deeply personal adventure. All of us are wonderfully unique, so journal entries, even about the same subject, will differ vastly from one person to another. Some students will jump into keeping a journal; others will write only grudgingly. In either case, they will be remembering, reflecting, analyzing, and sometimes creating. *In the process of writing, students can discover much about what they think, feel, and believe that they might never have recognized before.*

If the students are to be accountable for their journal assignments, you will need to collect the journals periodically to review them. This brings up the necessity of emphasizing to the students that their disclosures in the journals will be confidential—that their reflections will not go beyond you, the teacher. Be sure to mention one exception to this confidentiality: if students write about situations in which they or others are in danger, you will have to involve other professionals or school officials as needed for their protection.

It is recommended that you take time at the beginning of the course to emphasize the importance of the journal. Encourage the students to design a cover; for example, they could draw symbols of themselves, their interests, their relationships, and their faith (or who God is to them). Perhaps at the beginning of the semester, you could dedicate or bless the journals, also calling God to bless the thoughts, imaginings, and reflections of the students.

Discussion. Many of the additional activities in this manual provide questions designed to prompt discussion. In addition, although most of the text activities and several of the additional activities ask the students to respond in writing, you may tell the students that they can accomplish those activities through conversation. Here are some techniques for generating discussions:

Quiet collection of thoughts, followed by discussion. Ask the students to spend a few minutes thinking about the question or task presented in the activity, rather than writing about it. Giving them time to collect their thoughts beforehand often yields a more fruitful class discussion than would inviting off-the-cuff remarks. The follow-up discussion to the quiet time could be done in pairs, in small groups, or with the whole class.

Paired exchanges. Allow the students to quietly collect their thoughts or have them write down their response to the question or task. Then help the students pair up and discuss their reflections. After this initial sharing, a whole-class discussion could draw further insights from those who volunteer their thoughts. Before starting the whole-class discussion, caution the students not to bring up what their partner said unless the partner gives permission.

Thought museum. Write four or five quotations from various scholars on sheets of newsprint and post them around the classroom. Give each student two sticky notes. Direct them to write a brief comment or question about two quotations they find interesting or confusing. Have them post their notes on the newsprint underneath the quotations. Ask for volunteers to be curators for one of the quotations and instruct them to arrange the comments or questions in some particular order. They may choose to group questions together or to separate the comments based on their level of understanding. This activity allows every student to critically evaluate an idea or thinker in an anonymous manner while enabling a few to demonstrate their critical reasoning skills by organizing questions and comments and providing a summative explanation of how the quotation fits within the religious viewpoint.

Socratic seminar. Pose an open-ended question to the class that relates to a primary source from a religious tradition. Divide the class into two groups: active participants and non-participant observers. Members of the first group can provide possible answers to the question and ask for clarification from one another. They are not allowed to critique one another but are encouraged to cite the text to support their points and to assist one another. Members of the second group can monitor the activity of the other students by tracking what kinds of interactions occur. You might consider developing a guiding rubric to give the second group an idea of what to look for in the discussion and how to qualify the points being raised and the number of times individuals respond to one another. This type of class discussion encourages well-informed reasoning and rigorous critical thought. The teacher serves as a guide to redirect the focus to the reading and facilitate student-centered questions. The objective is not to present direct answers but to clarify the values and beliefs reflected in the writing. The students are given the opportunity to reflect on their course readings and written work during this seminar. A positive seminar environment is one geared toward creating meaning rather than mastering content. This type of discussion is more appropriate at the end of a unit, when the students will have more familiarity with the vocabulary and major themes of the tradition being studied.

Skits or role-plays. Activities that call for examples from the students' experiences might be extended into skits or role-plays. If those stagings are to be successful, you must have willing students who are comfortable with letting their experiences be the subject of dramatization. If you ask the students to portray their own responses to a dilemma, or a "what would you do?" incident, either the student who offered an example or another student could play the principal role and try to resolve the situation.

Some activities call the students to write imaginary dialogues between two persons. To heighten their impact, those dialogues could be composed in pairs and then read aloud by two students.

The students' dramatizations can be performed live; produced as radio or TV programs, documentary films, photo essays, and so on; presented on the Internet; or offered in some other format.

Art. Each chapter of the student text contains maps, photographs, and examples of art from the tradition being studied. Those selections are designed to invite the students into the material of the chapter. You might encourage the students to consider the graphic material and discuss its meaning before studying each chapter or upon completion of each chapter. You might also bring in your own visual examples.

Post images from a religious tradition around the classroom and allow the students to take notes on what they see and how the images reflect the particular religious and philosophical beliefs. Use a different part of the classroom for each type of visual you display. For example, you could have small groups in the class each examine a specific group of images, such as worship spaces, landscapes, deities, and ritual objects. When the groups are done taking notes, have someone from each group report to the rest of the class what the group observed and how the group sees the images within the context of the respective faith tradition. You may want to provide the students with a summary of the significance behind the images. You can then divide the class into another set of small groups where there is an informed leader from each category of images who teaches the small group the importance of the images. This jigsaw method allows the students to teach one another and allows the teacher to monitor discussions and answer questions.

Music. Music has a tremendous effect on human beings. Perhaps that is most evident during adolescence, when people feel that certain artists, groups, and songs can exactly express what they are experiencing. In this course, music can help the students further appreciate the religious traditions they explore. You may want to use a particular song or songs to introduce or conclude a chapter or concept. Or you might allow the students to bring in their own songs to use as part of prayer or to emphasize a point discussed in the text. Musically talented students could be invited to use their gifts.

Guest speakers. If you invite speakers to visit your class, be sure to prepare your students with some background about them and their topics. It may be helpful to introduce the topic during the class period before a speaker visits, and to direct the students to prepare questions to ask the speaker. Collect those questions and use them if needed during a discussion following the presentation. After the presentation and discussion, make time for the students to process what they heard.

Meditation. This manual includes a few reflection experiences, which you may present as directed or adapt for your class. Those meditations allow the students to become more self-aware by quieting their minds and focusing inward. They may also help the students tap into their religious imagination. The following directions can help you lead a successful meditation:

- Know your group of students. Some groups are simply too rambunctious to sit quietly for more than a few minutes. On the other hand, most students appreciate the relaxed, stress-free time allowed by guided meditations.
- Choose the appropriate time for the reflection. Meditations are best done when the students have been talking about and have received some input about a particular topic—when they have reached a point at which they need time to reflect, ponder, and integrate all the ideas into their own experience.
- Before a meditation, inform the students of its purpose.
- Consider using soft music to aid in relaxation. Several recording companies (including Narada and Windham Hill) produce reflective, stress-reducing music.
- Begin the meditation with a period of physical relaxation. Instruct the students to close their eyes, relax their muscles (you might lead them through this: start with their toes, ankles, and calves, and work up through the neck and face), and breathe deeply throughout the process. Do not overlook this part of the experience. An additional benefit of guided meditations is that they teach the students a means of stress reduction.
- Open the reflection with a call to focus. For example:
  Feel the warmth [or coolness] of the air moving around you. Listen to the sounds in the room. Listen to the even sound of [name the quiet, soothing sounds of the room, pausing after each and allowing the quiet to sink in]. Now listen to your own sounds, your even, relaxed breathing. Take a long, deep breath. Breathe in. . . . Breathe out. . . . Breathe in. . . . Breathe out. . . . [Repeat this breathing sequence until you sense that the students are at ease.]
- Read the meditation slowly and clearly, speaking in an even, restful tone of voice, pausing for a few moments after phrases or sentences as indicated. The flow of the meditation should be gentle so that the students can settle into a relaxed and reflective state.
- After the meditation allow some time for the students to write in their journals or discuss their insights. Ask questions related to the religious tradition you are studying, encouraging responses about feelings and other insights the students had during the meditation.

Cross-curricular connections. Often what is going on in one subject or class can have broader connections to another subject or class. You may want to speak to another teacher or other teachers about doing a cross-curricular lesson or unit. Because your students may not all take the same courses, and because the course sequences might not match, this can be difficult to do. Still, it can be valuable for students to see how insights from one subject area can affect one's understanding in a different subject area. For example, you might ask students how an issue raised in a novel for English parallels a topic you have been discussing in religion.

You may want to introduce students to various genres of literature from major religions. Reading different types of narratives allows the students to practice empathy across the various disciplines they are studying. Indigenous myths and native books from China or India, for example, can teach profound lessons through images and elementary ideas while reflecting the ways indigenous people learn about their faith.

The ideas and themes discussed in this course can easily be applied to history, geography, literature, and science. Making connections across subjects also encourages the students to go beyond mere comprehension to synthesis and application.

A Method of Planning and Scheduling

One attractive but potentially frustrating feature of this teaching manual is that generally more classroom strategies are offered than you can use in your teaching. Each chapter of this manual is set up like a smorgasbord from which you will need to select those activities that best meet the needs of your class. The need to make such decisions is a major reason for presenting here a method of planning and scheduling your teaching of the entire course. It is wise to do the planning at the beginning of the course and to set realistic goals, but each school calendar is different and has its own set of variables.

1. Identify the total number of class periods available for this course. If you are teaching the course within one full semester, you might start with approximately eighteen weeks, and then exclude vacations, holidays, special school functions, test days, and so on. Identify the days that are not available for teaching, and estimate how many weeks you have left for the course. Then estimate the number of class periods you have to teach during the semester. For example, if your classes meet in 50-minute periods, five times a week for sixteen weeks, you have eighty class periods to work with. With some schools using block scheduling, this may be altered because the classes typically last between 75 and 90 minutes and meet less often.

2. Assess for the entire course the approximate number of class periods needed for each major concept. To assist you in this step, the major concepts are listed and described at the beginning of each chapter of this manual. It may be immediately clear that some concepts will have to be treated briefly, perhaps in one class period or less. Other concepts may require several class periods.

If your school uses block scheduling, you will need to plan for 75- to 90-minute periods. When introducing new content in a block-schedule format, focus on depth as opposed to breadth. The additional activities in the teaching manual can help you plan meaningful and interesting lessons for your students.

You may decide to skip certain major concepts or even whole chapters. Such choices should be made at this preliminary stage of planning. The primary objective is to take a broad view of the course to ensure that you will cover all that you intend to cover. Consciously planning to omit parts of the student text is one thing; simply running out of time at the end of the course is another. This step of the planning should help you avoid such surprises.

3. Divide the course into approximately two-week blocks of time. In advance of each two-week block, make more specific decisions regarding which major concepts to present during that block. Determine how many and which class periods will be devoted to each of those concepts.

Right before each two-week block begins, you will be ready to make more immediate plans for your teaching. Attempting to look ahead more than two weeks in your selection of specific concepts and teaching strategies could reduce necessary flexibility. Your choices of what and how to teach a month from now will be based on your students' responses to material in the interim. One exception to this guideline applies to audiovisuals. A number of additional activities in the manual suggest video and sound recordings as teaching tools. You will need to order those materials well ahead of time if you are relying on national distributors or a diocesan resource office.

4. For each major concept to be taught during a given two-week block, select the pages of the student text that you will cover and the teaching strategies from this manual that you will use, keeping in mind the number of class periods devoted to that concept.

You may have two class periods available for teaching a major concept, but this manual and the student text offer enough material and strategies to fill several periods. How do you decide what to do?

Begin by considering these questions: What approaches have the students responded well to in the past? What kinds of strategies seem ineffective with them? How can you touch on all the different intelligences in the activities for this chapter? What are you comfortable doing in class? Which strategies feel right to you? How much time do you have? How much time is required by each available strategy?

5. After each class period, briefly evaluate for future reference your experience with the strategies selected. Ongoing evaluation may be one of the most talked about and least practiced virtues of effective teaching. We are usually so caught up with preparing for our next task that we simply do not take the time to look back on classes we have successfully completed—or maybe only survived! The task of ongoing evaluation can seem so tedious and time-consuming that we feel oppressed by it before even attempting it.

In this planning process, the step of evaluation is so simple that it can quickly and consistently be included in your teaching. For further explanation see point 6 of the next section.

A Lesson Planning Chart

On pages 22 and 23, you will find two copies of the lesson planning chart for this course: one includes examples of how the chart can be filled out, the other is blank and can be photocopied for use in your planning. You may want to complete the chart in pencil rather than pen, knowing that you will have to make at least minor adjustments, given the students' responses to the material, missed class periods, and so on.

This is how to use the chart:

1. In the first column, write the number or date of the class period. That is, identify the class periods in the semester from say 1 to 80, or specify each session by the date on which you will teach it.

2. In the second column, state the major concept that you will teach during the class period. Use an abbreviation of the concept title listed in this manual.

3. In the third column, list the pages of the student text that you will cover in class or that you will have assigned in advance as homework reading. If you are covering one complete concept in a class, simply copy the page numbers from the icon beside that concept in this manual. If you are teaching one concept for several class periods, identify the specific pages of the student text for each of those periods. (This point may become clearer when you read point 5, below.)

4. In the fourth column, specify the teaching strategies, or activities, that you will use during the class. Note that all the activities in this manual are either lettered (for example, activity A) or titled (for example, "Speculating on Religious Questions"). Use these letters and titles along with page references from this manual to complete the column. Also describe briefly any modifications or additions you make to a text activity. For instance, write, "Activity B as brainstormed with whole class" or "Activity C descriptions in paired exchange, with whole-class discussion following."

5. In the fifth column, specify the student text pages to be read, the text activities to be completed, or any other task that you want to assign as homework for the next class period.

6. In the last column, after teaching a class, jot down your evaluation of it, concentrating on the strategies you identified in the fourth column. You will likely develop a shorthand of your own for this. You might simply state, "Effective as described in manual; repeat next time." Or you might write, "Too much material; drop activity D." Statements such as these, brief as they are, may be all you need to refresh your memory when teaching the course in the future.

Sample Lesson Planning Chart

Date, Class	Major Concept	Text Pages	Activities	Homework Assignment	Evaluation
Mon. 9/7	Chap. 2: Intro	21–22	Provide basic overview of primal religious traditions.	Read pp. 23–26. Do text activities A and D in notebook.	Students seem to have lots of interest in this chapter after seeing film.
Tues. 9/8	Chap 2: A Religion of the Australian Aborigines	23–26	Go over review questions on p. 38 of text. Do activity "Understanding Taboo" (tm p. 37) to check understanding of concept.	Read pp. 26–28. Do text activity E in notebook.	Discussion of taboo went longer than expected; spend less time on review questions.
Wed. 9/9	Chap 2: B An African Tradition	26–28	Discuss text activity E in small groups; move to large-group sharing. Go over review questions on p. 38 of text.	Read pp. 28–32. Do text activities F and G in notebook.	Good discussion about worship of ancestors. Could be a good setup for "Día de los Muertos" activity.
Thurs. 9/10	Chap 2: C Religion of the North American Plains Indians	28–32	Go over review questions on p. 38 of text. Read handout 2–A (tm p. 47) together. Assign questions in activity "Outlawing the Sun Dance" (tm pp. 43) for written reflection and allow students to begin them in class.	Read pp. 32–38. Finish Sun Dance essay to turn in.	Some difficulty with concept of *axis mundi*; review in next session. Strong opinions about Sun Dance.
Fri. 9/11	Chap. 2: D A Mesoamerican Religion	32–38	Collect reflections on Sun Dance. Go over review questions on p. 38 of text. Discuss text activity I as large group. Begin activity "A New Aztec Ritual for the Head and Heart" (tm pp. 45-46). Plan to present rituals next Tues.–Wed.	Bring in items needed for rituals.	Reflection question difficult in large group—assign as homework? One session is not enough time for groups to settle into activity.

Lesson Planning Chart

Date, Class	Major Concept	Text Pages	Activities	Homework Assignment	Evaluation

Teaching Strategies

CHAPTER 1

Studying the World's Religions

Major Concepts

A. **The Nature of a Religious Tradition.** All human beings have the capacity for self-reflection. The world's various religions offer answers to life's fundamental questions about the human condition, spiritual perfection, human destiny, the nature of the world, and the nature of ultimate reality, or God. Some religions contend that spiritual perfection can be attained in this life, whereas other religions teach that perfection must await an afterlife. Nontheistic religions do not hold a belief in a relevant god or gods, but they do, like most other religions, teach that the ultimate reality is somehow revealed to human beings. Most religions share some basic elements, including experiential, mythic, doctrinal, ethical, ritual, social, and material dimensions.

B. **Some Challenges and Rewards of Studying the World's Religions.** Religion is grounded in mystery and presents many challenging questions about the nature of ultimate reality. To better understand the world's religions, we can compare the dimensions that the different traditions manifest and approach each tradition with empathy.

Pages 13–18

Concept A: The Nature of a Religious Tradition

Review Questions: The Nature of a Religious Tradition

Question 1. What issues do people usually address when they ask questions about the human condition?

Answer. What is our essential nature? Are we merely what we appear to be—physical bodies somehow equipped with the capacity to think and to feel? Or are we endowed with a deeper spiritual essence, some form of soul? Are we by nature good, or evil, or somewhere in-between, perhaps originally good but now flawed in some way? Why do we suffer?

Question 2. How does spiritual maturity or perfection relate to the quest for salvation?

Answer. Most religions teach that spiritual maturity or perfection is closely related to some form of salvation from the ultimate limitation that is imposed by the human condition: death.

Question 3. Briefly explain how religions differ over the question of destiny.

Answer. According to some religions, human beings face two possible destinies: eternal life in paradise, or condemnation. Individual destiny is linked to spiritual maturation: the degree to which one has achieved perfection corresponds to one's prospects for reward in the afterlife. For religions that teach that human beings live more than one lifetime, the immediate destiny after this life is generally not the final destiny, but another step toward it. Nevertheless, the need to seek spiritual maturity in this life remains vital, because the level of one's maturity tends to determine the nature of one's future life.

Question 4. Name some ways religions perceive the nature of the world.

Answer. The world may be real, or a cosmic illusion; living and sacred, or merely matter; a help or a hindrance to the religious quest.

Question 5. Describe the difference between theistic and nontheistic religions.

Answer. Theistic religions hold a belief in God or in multiple gods; nontheistic religions do not.

Question 6. How do most religions teach that the ultimate reality is usually revealed?

Answer. Through sacred stories or myths, or through various types of religious experience.

Question 7. Describe in general terms the religious experience of the theistic religions. Then briefly compare it with the religious experience of the nontheistic religions.

Answer. Generally speaking, in theistic religions God is experienced as a holy presence who is other. This presence evokes both fear and fascination. In nontheistic religions, religious experience usually takes the form of mysticism.

Question 8. Briefly explain the concept of myth.

Answer. Myths are nonhistorical and nonrational sources of sacred truth. Myths are also powerful, for they give meaning to life. Passed along from one generation to the next, myths set forth fundamental knowledge regarding the nature of things and the proper way to live.

Question 9. Identify at least two dimensions of religion, in addition to the mythic, doctrinal, and experiential.

Answer. [Any two of the following answers are correct:] Ethical, ritual, social, and material.

Text Activities: The Nature of a Religious Tradition

Activity A

Search newspapers, magazines, the Internet, and other sources for at least three stories that mention religion. Answer this question: How does religion affect people's daily lives in each example?

Activity B

The terms *spiritual* and *religious* often mean different things to different people. What does each term mean to you?

Activity C

Contemplate the human condition by comparing the situation of humans with that of a favorite animal (it could be a pet). Does the animal think or feel, like people do? Does it seem to have a spiritual essence or soul? Does it seem to be by nature good, or evil, or somewhere in-between?

Activity D

Summarize your personal cosmology—your own understanding of the nature of the world. Focus especially on the following questions: Where did the world come from? Is the world somehow a living, organic entity, or is it merely inorganic matter?

Activity E

Like the terms *religious* and *spiritual*, *faith* tends to mean different things to different people. What does *faith* mean to you?

Activity F

Myth is not as strong an element in the modern, scientific world as it was in earlier ages. Still, as the Creation story in Genesis suggests, some of our basic perspectives about life are derived from mythic sources. What other mythic truths—truths that are based on neither history nor science, but that give life meaning and direction—are prevalent in your society?

Activity G

Identify at least two examples of sacred entities, art, or architecture in your community. Compare the examples in terms of how they express religious ideas and provoke emotions.

1

Additional Activity: The Nature of a Religious Tradition

Speculating on Religious Questions

1. After the students have read the section of chapter 1 entitled "The Nature of a Religious Tradition," direct them to focus on the religious questions outlined in the text. Write those questions on the board, and direct the students to copy them into their notebooks:

- What is the human condition?
- What is spiritual perfection?
- What is our destiny?
- What is the nature of the world?
- What is ultimate reality, and how is it revealed?

2. Review the material that the student text presents on each question. Then give the students the following homework assignment:

- Choose two photographs or illustrations of artifacts, pieces of art, or architectural structures related to two of the world's religions. Your selections can come from the student text, library books, the Internet, or any other resources available to you. One of your choices should pertain to your own religion or the religion you know the most about. The other should pertain to a religion you know little about.
- Study the photographs or illustrations you have selected and then go through the list of religious questions and jot down what, if anything, the subject of each photo or illustration implies about that religion's answers to the questions. For example, a Catholic cathedral might imply a majestic view of God, which might lead to further insights on the Christian understanding of ultimate reality and human nature; a Japanese Zen landscape painting could imply great respect for nature and lead to additional insights on the Zen view of the world and human nature.
- After you have made some notes about the images, write a two-page essay explaining what you have inferred about each religion just by looking at its artifacts, art, or buildings. Observe your images actively and creatively.

3. Collect the essays, and evaluate them on the basis of the students' observations, not on whether their inferences are right or wrong.

4. When you return the essays, tell the students to keep them and to review them when the class studies the particular religions they worked with. The students may be interested to note the accuracy of their original observations after learning more about the religions.

Variation. Lead a class discussion about one particular piece of art. Examine an image of Paul Gauguin's painting *Where Do We Come From? What Are We? Where Are We Going?* (The same three questions are written, in French, in the upper left-hand corner of the artwork.) Allow the students time to observe the painting. Instruct them to write down the symbols they observe, how those symbols are used, and how the painting affects them personally. After an adequate amount of time, ask the class to share their observations and reactions. Point out that interpreting symbols and using one's imagination are powerful ways of communicating truths that are often larger than the words we have to explain them. Tell the students that this is a type of knowing that will be used throughout the course.

Concept B: Some Challenges and Rewards of Studying the World's Religions

Pages 18–19

Review Questions: Some Challenges and Rewards of Studying the World's Religions

Question 10. What is one benefit of using a comparative approach to study the world's religions?

Answer. Studying many religions of the world should enable us to know each one, including our own, more precisely.

Question 11. What is empathy, and how is it applied to the study of world religions?

Answer. Empathy is the capacity for seeing things from another's perspective.

Text Activity: Some Challenges and Rewards of Studying the World's Religions

Activity H

It is important to cultivate empathy—the capacity for seeing things from another's perspective when studying the religions of others. Try applying the saying about empathy, that we need to walk in another person's shoes, to a family member or close friend. What do you think life looks like from that person's perspective?

Additional Activities: Some Challenges and Rewards of Studying the World's Religions

The challenging issues and questions raised in this section of the chapter often inspire strong emotions, and sometimes those emotions impede productive discussion. In the following activities, the students explore two approaches to understanding religions. It is hoped that these exercises will help the students enter into the following chapters in a spirit of inquiry and openness.

The Comparative Model

1. Ask the students to select a random category with which they are reasonably familiar—such as food, cars, music, or clothes. Then issue the following instructions:

1

- Write your category at the top of a piece of paper or in your notebook. Just below it create three columns, writing the name of one item from your category at the top of column 1, writing "Both" at the top of column 2, and writing the name of a second item from your category at the top of column 3. In the first and third columns, list what is distinct about the item. In the middle column, list what both items have in common.

You might present this example:

Cars

Volkswagen New Beetle	*Both*	*Ford Explorer*
German engineering	Internal combustion engine	American engineering
Compact styling	Manual or automatic transmission	Large SUV styling
Two doors	Four wheels	Four doors

2. After the students have spent a few minutes working on their lists, have them pair up and share their answers. Then lead the group in a discussion about the strengths and limitations of the comparison model of learning, using the following questions as a guide:
   - What observations are easily made through this exercise?
   - What knowledge about your items does not surface from this exercise?
   - How might this model be helpful in learning about religions?
   - What might be limitations of this model?

Learning Through Empathy

1. Direct the students to think of a person they know well—perhaps a family member, a friend, or a coworker. Tell the students to imagine that they have to describe this person to a stranger. Instruct them to make a list of statements that sums up this person. Encourage them to include not only physical characteristics and general personality traits, but revelations about who this person truly is.

2. After the young people have had some time to work on their statements, invite them to review their lists while they ponder the following questions. You may wish to discuss these reflection questions in class, if time permits, or you may ask the students to complete them for homework.
   - With just this information, what kind of impression would a stranger have of this person?
   - Would that impression be accurate? Why or why not?
   - Is this information sufficient for knowing your person?
   - How is being told about someone different from actually meeting and interacting with them?
   - How effectively can we "walk in someone else's shoes"? Why might we try?

CHAPTER 2

Primal Religious Traditions

Major Concepts

A. **Religion of the Australian Aborigines.** All religions are rooted in the primal traditions of early peoples. The foundation of Australian Aboriginal religion is the concept of the Dreaming, when supernatural beings called Ancestors roamed the earth, shaping the landscape and creating various forms of life, including the first humans. The spiritual essence of the Ancestors remains in the various symbols they left behind and also within individuals. Totemism is common to many primal traditions, including the religion of the Australian Aborigines. Aboriginal religion is a process of re-creating the mythic past of the Dreaming in order to tap into its sacred power, primarily through rituals re-enacting myths. Aboriginal society is carefully structured on a foundation of taboos. Initiation rituals bring about the symbolic death of childhood to pave the way for spiritual rebirth.

B. **An African Tradition.** The Yoruba religion of Africa tries to maintain a balance between the human beings of earth and the gods and ancestors of heaven, while guarding against evil sorcerers and witches. The Yoruba believe that their supreme god, Olorun, is the original source of power in the universe, but the lesser gods—the *orishas*—are most significant in Yoruba religious life. Both the *orishas* and the ancestors (deceased humans with supernatural status) possess sacred power that can help or harm the living, and are worshiped through rituals at shrines. Esu, a trickster figure who is both good and evil, mediates between heaven and earth and is universally worshiped among the Yoruba. Trickster figures are common to many primal traditions. A number of Yoruba ritual specialists facilitate communication with a particular deity or ancestor. The Yoruba consider divination, through which one's future can be learned, essential for determining how to proceed in life.

C. **Religion of the North American Plains Indians.** The religion of the Plains is somewhat representative of Native American religion in general. The members of one large Plains tribe, the Lakota, call the supreme reality Wakan Tanka, whose name refers to sixteen separate deities. A trickster figure, Inktomi, mediates between the supernatural and human worlds. Inktomi taught the first humans their ways. The Lakota believe that four souls depart from a person at death, some of which may be reborn in new bodies. The vision quest is common to many primal traditions, and helps people purify themselves and access spiritual power. Another ritual common to all Plains tribes is the Sun Dance. The tribal members prepare for this ceremony by constructing a lodge around a tree—the *axis mundi*—which is the link between the earth and the heavens and represents the supreme being. The dancers tear their flesh as a sacrifice to the supreme being.

D. **A Mesoamerican Religion.** Aztec religion emphasizes the interrelationship between myth and ritual. The Aztecs built their civilization on the foundation of cultures that had come before them. They believed that the Toltec god Quetzalcoatl had presided over an age of prosperity and cultural brilliance, which his earthly devotee, Topiltzin Quetzalcoatl, had ruled as priest-king. The Toltecs provided the Aztecs with a mythic pattern for civilization. Aztecs identified the city of Teotihuacan as the origin of the cosmos. Aztec cosmology featured a close correspondence between time and space, and the Aztecs understood the universe to be built around four cardinal directions plus an *axis mundi.* The Aztecs also regarded the human being as an *axis mundi,* with two divine forces—one in the head and one in the heart—nurturing basic needs. Human sacrifice and mastery of language were two ways of fulfilling religious needs. Though the Aztec empire ended with the fall of Tenochtitlan to the Spanish army, aspects of Aztec culture survive today. In most primal religions, including those of Mesoamerica, the boundaries between the supernatural and the human worlds are easily crossed. The sacred and the secular are intertwined. Primal religions are constantly changing to adapt to modern life while retaining their ancient foundations.

Pages 23–26

Concept A: Religion of the Australian Aborigines

Review Questions: Religion of the Australian Aborigines

Question 1. Why are some forms of religion called primal? Describe some of the characteristics of primal religions.

Answer. Primal religions tended to come before other religious traditions. They do not depend on scriptures or written teachings; they pass down myths and stories orally from generation to generation; they tend to be the traditions of tribal peoples who dwell in villages, as opposed to large cities, although there are some exceptions; and they are diverse.

Question 2. What elements of the natural and human world did the Ancestors create or establish in the period of the Dreaming?

Answer. The Ancestors gave shape to the landscape and created the various forms of life, including the first human beings. They specified the territory each human tribe was to occupy, and determined each tribe's languages, social rules, and customs. They also left behind symbols of their presence in the form of natural landmarks, rock paintings, and so on.

Question 3. What survives in the symbols left behind by the Ancestors?

Answer. The spiritual essence of the Ancestors. The sites where the symbols are found are thought to be charged with sacred power.

Question 4. Explain the terms *totem* and *taboo.*

Answer. The term *totem* refers to the natural form in which the Ancestor appeared in the Dreaming. A totem may be an animal or a rock formation or other feature of the landscape. The term *taboo* refers to the system of social ordering that dictates that certain things and activities, owing to their sacred nature, are set aside for specific members of the group and are forbidden to others.

Question 5. Why is ritual essential if Aboriginal life is to have meaning?

Answer. It is only through ritual that the sacred power of the Dreaming can be accessed and experienced.

Question 6. How did Aboriginal rituals originate?

Answer. Aborigines believe that the rituals were taught to the first humans by the Ancestors in the Dreaming.

Question 7. What purposes are served by Aboriginal initiation rituals?

Answer. Aboriginal initiation rituals awaken young people to their spiritual identity with their totemic Ancestors, and at the same time redefine their social identity within the tribe. The rituals prepare the way for the spiritual rebirth that is a necessary step toward adulthood. Also, during the rituals, young people learn the essential truths about their world and how they are to act within it.

Question 8. Identify two acts of Dieri initiation rituals that symbolize death.

Answer. [Any two of the following answers are correct:] Circumcision, knocking out a boy's two lower middle teeth and burying them in the ground, and inflicting wounds intended to leave scars on a boy's neck and back.

Text Activities: Religion of the Australian Aborigines

Activity A

Empathy—seeing something from another's perspective—helps us gain the insight we need to understand and appreciate the diversity of world religions. Striving to understand the Aboriginal concept of a mythic geography offers a good opportunity for practicing empathy. Think of a favorite outdoor area, such as a place in the wilderness, a beach, a park, or your backyard. Imagine that every notable landmark has great religious significance and that your every move within the area is undertaken as if it were a religious ritual. Now describe the area and your experience of being there.

Activity B

Every society has rituals that re-enact origins, just as the Aborigines do. Some contemporary rituals are religious in nature, whereas others involve patriotism and other aspects of society. List as many such rituals as you can, briefly explaining how each is a re-enactment of an original event.

Activity C

To what extent does your society apply restrictions similar to those of the Aboriginal concept of taboo?

Activity D

What experiences have served as rituals of initiation for you, marking your passage from childhood to adulthood?

Additional Activities: Religion of the Australian Aborigines

Primary Source Reading

See *Primary Source Readings in World Religions* (Saint Mary's Press, 2009) for the selection titled "The Birth of the Butterflies," as well as the accompanying leader's guide for suggestions about how to use this reading in your study of Australian aborigines.

Choosing a Totem

1. Engage the students in a discussion of totems and totemism. Cover the following points in your own words:

- Think of ways that people in families or in society are seen as representatives of a predecessor. For example, a girl might be referred to as the spitting image of her great-grandmother, an environmentalist might be called a contemporary Thoreau, and a civil rights activist could be identified as a modern Martin Luther King Jr.
- Think of ways that your family members identify with an earlier generation. For instance, some families pass a wedding ring, Christmas ornaments, or recipes from one generation to the next, and American Protestants began a tradition of passing on Bibles with pages for recording births, deaths, and marriages.
- Maintaining such connections, which we often take for granted, has much in common with the ideas of totems and totemism (though it is by no means identical with those concepts).

2. Direct the students to complete the following tasks in class:

- Choose a relative or friend you know well, preferably someone at least ten years older than you. Spend some time thinking about that person and then list his or her qualities—for example, hot tempered, patient, wise, and silly. Next, think of an animal, plant, inanimate object, or feature of the landscape that seems to strongly represent the character of the person you chose. This will be that person's "totem." Write a detailed description of this totem next to your list of the person's qualities, taking care not to use any of the words from that list. In your description take into consideration the totem's behavior and surroundings—anything about it that gives it a clear identity—as well as its outward appearance.

3. Instruct the students to choose a partner and to decide which person in the pair will go first. Then tell the first partner to read her or his description of the totem aloud to the second partner. Explain that after listening to the totem description, the second partner is to list the qualities she or he believes might be part of the character of the person for whom such a totem was chosen. Ask the partners to compare their lists of qualities and discuss the similarities and differences noted. Then tell them to repeat the task with the second partner's totem description.

4. Emphasize that this exercise merely approximates the concept of totemism, but it may also make it clear that such a concept is not so far removed from the way we think about people, and their characteristics, in our everyday life.

Understanding Taboo

At first glance the students may consider the concept of taboo to be controlling or elitist. By using analogies of childhood, social, and religious restrictions the students have experienced, the following discussion can help them understand taboo as being protective and beneficial rather than restrictive and detrimental.

1. Ask the students to recall restrictions from their early childhood, such as rules about the use of scissors or sharp knives, limits on the hours spent viewing television, and orders that they not leave the backyard. Raise questions like the following ones:

- If you were a young child, how might you describe these restrictions? Would these regulations seem reasonable?
- From the perspective of your current age, how do you describe these restrictions?
- If you were a parent, would you place similar restrictions on your young children?

2. Broaden the discussion by encouraging the students to identify restrictions in social and religious contexts. Examples could range from regulations specifying roles that only an ordained clergy member can perform in some worship rituals, to rules identifying who can enter the stage door after a concert or play. Invite the students to evaluate these other restrictions using the insights gained from the discussion of childhood restrictions. Focus on two or three restrictions that have been experienced by many of the students, and pose questions like the ones that follow:

- How do you describe these restrictions? [Possible answers: elitist, protective, and respectful]
- Who, if anyone, directly benefits from these restrictions?
- If one benefits, should all?
- Do those who do not directly benefit from the restrictions receive any benefit at all? [For example, restrictions on who can enter the stage door after a rock concert benefit the audience indirectly, because they help prevent the stars from being mobbed and injured, thus enabling them to entertain fans at future performances. Also for example, though a clergy member may be the only one who can perform a particular act in worship, the entire worshiping community benefits directly by observing and responding to that act.]

Pages 26–28

Concept B: An African Tradition

Review Questions: An African Tradition

2

Question 9. In what part of Africa do the Yoruba live?
Answer. The western regions of central Africa—Nigeria, Benin, and Togo—mostly in cities.

Question 10. Why has the city of Ife always been the center of Yoruba religion?
Answer. The Yoruba believe it was there that the god Orisha-nla first began to create the world.

Question 11. Briefly describe the Yoruba understanding of the cosmos.
Answer. The Yoruba regard the cosmos as being divided into two separate worlds: heaven (the invisible home of the gods and the ancestors) and earth (the visible home of human beings, who are descended from the gods). Earth is also populated by a perverted form of humans, witches and sorcerers, who can cause disastrous harm if not controlled.

Question 12. Who is Olorun, and what is his role in Yoruba religion?
Answer. He is the supreme god of the Yoruba, the primary, original source of power in the universe, to whom all other life-forms ultimately owe their existence. He is distant and not involved in human affairs, so he is hardly worshiped at all, except in prayer.

Question 13. What are the *orishas?* Explain their significance in the religious life of the Yoruba.
Answer. The *orishas* are lesser deities who are sources of sacred power that can help or harm humans, depending on how well the rituals designed to appease them are carried out.

Question 14. Name and briefly describe at least two of the *orishas.*
Answer. [Any two of the following answers are correct:] Orisha-nla is the supreme deity who most Yoruba believe created earth. Ogun, the god of iron and war, was the first king of Ife. He occupies the borderline between the ancestors and the rest of the *orishas.* Esu, who is both good and evil, mediates between heaven and earth.

Question 15. What is a trickster figure?
Answer. A sort of mischievous supernatural being.

Question 16. Describe the two types of Yoruba ancestors.
Answer. (1) Family ancestors, who gained their supernatural status through having earned a good reputation and having lived to an old age, and (2) deified ancestors, who were once important human figures known throughout Yoruba society.

Question 17. Describe the role of Yoruba ritual practitioners.
Answer. They mediate between the gods and ancestors in heaven and human beings on earth.

Question 18. What is divination, and why do the Yoruba regard it as essential?

Answer. Divination is learning or interpreting someone's future. It is considered essential for one to determine how to proceed with life.

Text Activity: An African Tradition

Activity E

Deceased ancestors are worshiped in many religious traditions. Are they worshiped in any way in your society? Explain your answer.

Additional Activity: An African Tradition

Primary Source Reading

See *Primary Source Readings in World Religions* (Saint Mary's Press, 2009) for the selection titled "Creation Myth," as well as the accompanying leader's guide for suggestions about how to use this reading in your study of the Yoruba.

The Art of Divination

1. Divination is an important aspect of Yoruba religion as well as of many other primal traditions. Explain that although divination takes different forms in different cultures, in most cases it is far removed from what we usually refer to as fortune-telling.

Ask the students what comes to mind when they think of fortune-telling. They are likely to respond with some negative impressions—it is inaccurate, performed by charlatans, not to be taken seriously. Then point out what the text says about Yoruba divination: "The procedure involves an intricate system of hundreds of wisdom stories, which the diviner knows by memory. The diviner determines which of those stories are relevant for an individual, and from those stories interprets the individual's future" (p. 28).

2. Give the students the following directions for an essay to be written as homework:

- Take some time to think about stories you have heard or read recently or as long ago as early childhood. Consider all kinds of stories—such as fiction, nonfiction, news, and family memories. Pick two or three accounts that you consider particularly relevant to you as an individual, and from which you might interpret something about your future. Your interpretation should include events you think might occur, the type of person you would like to become, the kind of life you would like to lead, and so on.

  In writing, briefly summarize the stories you have chosen. Then write a paragraph about each story, explaining why you believe it is relevant to you. Finally, write another paragraph about each story, describing how it relates to your future.

3. Evaluate the completed assignments, then return them to the students and engage the young people in a brief discussion of questions like these:

- Is the way you predicted your future the same as the way you might expect a typical fortune-teller to do so? In what respects are the two methods of prediction the same or different?
- What type of prediction would you be more likely to trust: that of a typical fortune-teller or that of a person who interprets life stories?

Pages 28–32

Concept C: Religion of the North American Plains Indians

Review Questions: Religion of the North American Plains Indians

Question 19. According to the interpretation of the latest evidence, when and how do scholars think human beings first came to America?

Answer. Scholars believe humans first came to North America some twenty thousand to thirty thousand years ago. They migrated from Asia by crossing over the Bering Strait (between Russia and Alaska), which at that time was dry land.

Question 20. Why is the religion of the Plains Indians of vital interest among native peoples throughout North America?

Answer. It serves as the model for pan-Indian religion, a recent and popular movement uniting many tribes from across North America.

Question 21. What is Wakan Tanka?

Answer. The Lakota name for the supreme reality, sometimes translated as Great Spirit or the Great Mysterious, but literally meaning "most sacred." It actually refers to sixteen separate deities.

Question 22. Who is Inktomi?

Answer. The Lakota trickster figure who mediates between the supernatural and human worlds. He taught the first humans their ways and customs, and he also serves as an example of how not to behave.

Question 23. Briefly describe Lakota beliefs regarding death and the afterlife.

Answer. The Lakota believe that four souls depart from a person at death, one of which journeys along the "spirit path" of the Milky Way. The soul meets an old woman who judges it and either allows it to continue on to the other world of the ancestors, or sends it back to earth as a ghost. Meanwhile parts of the other souls enter unborn children and are reborn in new bodies.

Question 24. What do individuals try to gain access to by going on a vision quest?

Answer. Spiritual power that will ensure greater success in activities such as hunting, warfare, and curing the ill.

Question 25. Briefly describe the structure and function of the sweat lodge.

Answer. The structure of the lodge, a sapling hut covered with animal skins to make it dark and airtight, represents the universe. Heated stones placed in the center and sprinkled with water give off hot steam, causing the participant to sweat profusely, which leads to both physical and spiritual purification.

Question 26. Describe a typical vision experienced by a person who undertakes a vision quest.

Answer. The vision arrives in the form of an animal or some other object or force of nature, and is often accompanied by a message.

Question 27. Among the Blackfeet tribe, who presides over the Sun Dance?

Answer. A woman of outstanding moral character.

Question 28. What is the *axis mundi* in general? What is the *axis mundi* in the Sun Dance?

Answer. In general, it is the center of the universe. In the Sun Dance, it is a cottonwood tree around which a lodge is constructed so that it represents the universe with its four directions.

Question 29. Why do some participants in the Sun Dance skewer their chests and dance until their flesh tears?

Answer. Because they believe that their bodies are the only things they truly own, the dancers regard bodily mutilation as the only suitable sacrifice to offer to the supreme being.

Text Activities: Religion of the North American Plains Indians

Activity F

Imagine yourself living in the open wilderness of the North American Plains. Why, do you suppose, did the Lakota understand their supreme reality as being closely related to the four compass directions?

Activity G

The Indians of the Northern Plains traditionally lived off the land, depending on hunting and fishing to feed themselves. What elements of the vision quest and Sun Dance rituals are related to that lifestyle?

Additional Activities: Religion of the North American Plains Indians

Primary Source Reading

See *Primary Source Readings in World Religions* (Saint Mary's Press, 2009) for the selection titled "On the Ghost Dance," as well as the accompanying leader's guide for suggestions about how to use this reading in your study of the Lakota.

2

The Vision Quest

1. Engage the students in a discussion of the Lakota vision quest. Be sure they have read, from the student text, the section on the vision quest as well as Lame Deer's account of his own vision. Focus the discussion on this part of the student text's description:

> A vision comes to the quester eventually, usually near the end of the stay. It arrives in the form of an animal or some other object or force of nature. A message is often communicated along with the vision. When the individual returns to camp, the vision and the message are interpreted by the medicine man. (Pp. 31–32)

2. When you feel that the students have a basic understanding of the vision quest, instruct them as follows:

- In this activity we will attempt to experience an event analogous to the vision quest. Because we can't spend days fasting on a mountaintop, we need to create another situation in which we receive a vision.
- Choose an animal or some other object or force of nature. This will become the vision of one of your classmates, so select something you know well enough to describe thoroughly. Provide a written description that contains a setting for the arrival of the vision, actions and movements of the vision, and the way the vision communicates.

3. When the students have finished writing, collect all the vision descriptions and distribute them randomly. If a student receives his or her own description, he or she should keep it and continue the activity with it. Next, give the class the following instructions:

- You are approaching a turning point in your life. It won't be long before you are no longer a high school student, but have moved on to higher education or the working world. In view of this turning point, what message might the vision you have received communicate to you? In answering this question, be sure to consider the vision's meaning as a symbol. Think about what sort of analogy it might provide about your future. Write a page-long essay interpreting your vision.

4. You can end the activity here and instruct the students to hand in their essays to be evaluated. Or you might extend the activity by inviting the students to choose partners. It may be best if the partners know each other fairly well, but that is not absolutely necessary.

Tell the partners to sit together and read to each other the vision descriptions they received, imagining that the other person's description is a second vision that is coming to them during a vision quest. Then direct the students to verbally interpret their second vision in the same light that they interpreted their first—as a message about the turning point that is approaching in their life. Next, instruct the pairs to read each other's interpretive essays and to discuss the differences and similarities between them. Finally, invite the whole class to discuss the experience, using questions such as these:

- In what ways was the activity helpful? not helpful?
- Did you learn anything new about your own desires and expectations for the future?
- Although this experience was merely an analogy for the actual experience of a vision quest, do you now have a stronger understanding of the goal of the quest? Describe your understanding.

Variation. In step 2, invite the students to draw the setting and the vision, instead of writing about them.

Outlawing the Sun Dance

Handout 2–A

The student text points out that the Lakota Sun Dance was outlawed for some time by the government in the United States. It was suppressed in Canada as well. Handout 2–A, "What Harm Is in Our Sun Dance?" contains the thoughts of an anonymous Blackfoot Indian in Canada, early in the twentieth century, regarding the restrictions against the Sun Dance. Distribute the handout and instruct the students to read it. Base a discussion or writing assignment on questions such as these:

- Do you believe that it was right for the U.S. and Canadian governments to outlaw the Sun Dance? Why or why not?
- Under what circumstances do you think a government might be justified in restricting a religious practice?
- How might you react if your government considered an aspect of your religion illegal?

Pages 32–36

Concept D: A Mesoamerican Religion

Review Questions: A Mesoamerican Religion

Question 30. In what two ways does the Aztec tradition defy the description of a primal religious tradition? In what ways is the Aztec tradition like other primal religious traditions?

Answer. The Aztec tradition differs from the typical primal tradition in that its people built a highly developed civilization with a population of about fifteen million people, and many Aztecs were urban. However, like other primal traditions, Aztec religion emphasized the interrelationship between myth and ritual, as its practice of human sacrifice makes vividly clear.

Question 31. What geographical area did Mesoamerica include?

Answer. Most of present-day Mexico, extending southward to present-day Honduras, Nicaragua, and Costa Rica.

Question 32. According to Aztec cosmology, what god created and ordered the world? What ancient city is the origin of the cosmos?

Answer. The creation and ordering of the world are attributed to Quetzalcoatl. Teotihuacan is the origin of the cosmos, in terms of both space and time.

Question 33. Who was Topiltzin Quetzalcoatl? What was his significance for the Aztecs?

Answer. He was the earthly devotee of Quetzalcoatl, and ruled as priest-king. He provided Aztecs with the perfect role model for their authority figures.

Question 34. What did the Aztecs call their present age? What did they anticipate its fate to be?

Answer. The Age of the Fifth Sun. They believed that four previous suns and their ages had already been destroyed, and a similar fate was anticipated for this one.

Question 35. How did the Aztecs understand the spatial world?

Answer. They understood the world as having four quadrants extending outward from the center of the universe (the *axis mundi*), which connected the earthly realm to the many-layered heavenly realm above and the many-layered underworld below.

Question 36. Why did the Aztecs regard each human being as a sort of *axis mundi?*

Answer. Two divine forces, one concentrated in the head, the other in the heart, were believed to nurture the human being with basic needs. The potency of these forces connected the earthly realm to the divine.

Question 37. What were the special religious capabilities of the Aztec knowers of things?

Answer. The knowers of things could communicate with the gods and make offerings through language, thus providing an alternative to sacrifice.

Question 38. What historical coincidence contributed to the fall of Tenochtitlan to the Spaniards?

Answer. Topiltzin Quetzalcoatl, who had disappeared from earth long ago, was expected to return, possibly in 1519. By an amazing coincidence, Cortés—wearing a feathered helmet—arrived in Mesoamerica that year. The Aztec King Moctezuma thought Cortés was the returning Topiltzin Quetzalcoatl, and welcomed him with gifts.

Question 39. How does the popular Day of the Dead show the survival of Aztec religious culture?

Answer. The celebration, held at the end of October and beginning of November, joins the living and the dead through rituals that are both festive and spiritually meaningful. The Aztecs also set aside a certain time each year to perform similar rituals devoted to the same basic purpose.

Question 40. What three themes are shared by the primal religions studied in this chapter?

Answer. (1) The boundaries between the supernatural and the human worlds are very thin, and easily crossed. (2) The secular and the sacred are not separate; rather, the universe is full of religious significance, and humans constantly draw on its sacred and life-giving powers. (3) The traditions themselves are constantly changing.

Text Activities: A Mesoamerican Religion

Activity H

The Aztecs looked back to the Toltec tradition as a kind of golden age, providing them with a mythic pattern for the ideal civilization. In what ways do you and your society look to past traditions for cultural ideals?

Activity I

The Aztec cosmology is marked by a deep pessimism regarding the future. How does your society view the future? What can human beings offer to "nourish" the present so as to ensure a sound future?

Activity J

Considering the Aztec ritual of human sacrifice offers a challenging opportunity to see things from another's perspective. Explain how human sacrifice is part of the Aztecs' ordered and sophisticated religious worldview, given their cosmology and understanding of the human condition.

Activity K

In your experience how has the mastery of language helped to convey religious power? How does the significance of speech in the Aztec tradition compare with the significance of speech in another religious tradition with which you are familiar?

Activity L

In general, primal religions understand the boundaries between the human and the supernatural realms to be thin and easily crossed. Drawing from the religious traditions of the Aborigines, the Yoruba, the Indians of the Northern Plains, and the Aztecs, identify as many examples as you can that illustrate this understanding.

Additional Activities: A Mesoamerican Religion

A New Aztec Ritual for the Head and Heart

In this exercise the students design a modern ritual (without human sacrifice) in which they symbolically offer their heads and their hearts for the betterment of the world.

1. Make the following points in your own words:

- The ancient Aztec ritual of human sacrifice demonstrated a belief in a powerful, inextricable connection between people and the universe. In the act of sacrificing their lives to nourish the sun, the Aztecs believed they were helping sustain the sun, ensuring that the current age would progress and life would continue to flourish.
- Today we are increasingly aware of the interdependence between human beings and nature. Unfortunately our modern world often harms nature through pollution, overconsumption of resources, and ever-increasing human population. And despite a growing awareness of the relationship between human beings and nature, individuals, communities, and nations still engage in practices that are harmful, wasteful, or even life destroying. It sometimes seems that modern society would rather sacrifice nature to feed its own desires, than sacrifice its desires for the good of the natural world.

2. Break the class into groups of two or three and tell the groups each to appoint a recorder. Instruct the recorders each to make two columns on a sheet of paper, one titled "Head" and the other titled "Heart." Direct the groups to brainstorm a list of ideas for the head, and attitudes for the heart, that are necessary for humans to enjoy a beneficial and interdependent relationship with the natural world. For example, under the title "Head," they might list, "Developing alternative fuels that preserve resources and reduce

pollution"; under the title "Heart," they might write, "Looking at my own transportation needs as an opportunity to respect the environment (by carpooling, walking, biking, and so on)."

After a sufficient amount of time, tell the groups to now think of symbols that may evoke those ideas and attitudes, and to write them down.

3. When the groups have had enough time to think of symbols, give them the following directions:

- Using the ideas, attitudes, and symbols you just discussed, design a modern ritual that symbolically offers your heads and your hearts for the betterment of the world. The ritual does not have to be long, but it does have to include the following elements:
    - Appropriate objects and symbols (for example, photographs, illustrations, a globe, objects from nature, incense, candles, and music)
    - Appropriate readings and symbolic movements or gestures (for instance, poems, prayers, and vows to avoid certain actions or to embrace a certain lifestyle)
    - Participation of the assembly (for example, through responses to readings, singing, movement, sharing of thoughts, and bringing in of a symbol)

You may wish to collect the rituals in written form, or schedule class time for each group to enact its ritual and explain the ceremony's meaning.

Día de los Muertos

To expand the students' understanding of Aztec rituals as they have influenced present-day religion in Mexico, you may wish to invite someone from your school's foreign language department or a guest speaker to come to class and discuss the celebration of Día de los Muertos (Day of the Dead). To extend the activity, encourage the students to create altars honoring the dead in their families, following the Mexican custom. You can find links to resources about Día de los Muertos at the World Religions course page on the Internet, which can be accessed from the Saint Mary's Press home page, *www.smp.org.*

What Harm Is in Our Sun Dance?

During the late 1800s, when many Native Americans were initially being placed on reservations, many of their rituals and customs were restricted by law. The Sun Dance was one such ritual, outlawed because Sun Dancers fasted for extended periods and cut their own flesh with sharp skewers. The dance was also thought to be politically dangerous, with the potential of encouraging Native Americans to rebel against the reservation system.

The Sun Dance became legal again in the 1930s. During the time it was outlawed, a Blackfoot Indian from the Canadian Plains offered the following argument in favor of the ritual:

> You have been among us for many years, and have attended many of our ceremonials. Have you ever seen a disturbance, or anything harmful, that has been caused by our Sun-dance?
>
> We know that there is nothing injurious to our people in the Sun-dance. On the other hand, we have seen much that is bad at the dances of the white people. It has been our custom, during many years, to assemble once every summer for this festival, in honour of the Sun God. We fast and pray, that we may be able to lead good lives and to act more kindly towards each other. I do not understand why the white men desire to put an end to our religious ceremonials. What harm can they do to our people? If they deprive us of our religion, we will have nothing left, for we know of no other that can take its place. We do not understand the white man's religion. The Black Robes (Catholic Priests) teach us one thing and the Men-with-white-neckties (Protestant Missionaries) teach us another; so we are confused. We believe that the Sun God is all powerful, for every spring he makes the trees to bud and the grass to grow. We see these things with our own eyes, and, therefore, know that all life comes from him. (Walter McClintock, *The Old North Trail, or Life, Legends and Religion of the Blackfeet Indians* [Lincoln, NE: University of Nebraska Press, Bison Books, 1968], page 508. Copyright © in the United States. Used with permission of the University of Nebraska Press.)

3

CHAPTER 3

Hinduism

Major Concepts

A. **Human Destiny.** Liberation, or *moksha,* is the ultimate goal for Hindus. *Moksha* is characterized by infinite being, awareness, and bliss. Hindus generally believe in monism, the doctrine that all reality is ultimately one. The essence of reality is called Brahman, and the ultimate reality within human beings is called Atman, the eternal Self. Hinduism is polytheistic; its many deities are all points of contact with the divine. Hindu cosmology is cyclical: the universe undergoes long periods of creation and destruction. Individuals are repeatedly reincarnated until *moksha* is achieved. *Karma,* the moral law of cause and effect, determines the particular circumstances of one's life. *Dharma,* or ethical duty based on the divine order of reality, is the complete rule of life.

B. **Hindu Society.** The Hindu social order significantly affects individual identity and *dharma.* Hindu society is traditionally divided into four main classes. A person's caste identity is determined by the *karma* of past lives, and caste determines the *dharma* that governs a person's actions. Hindu society distinguishes four stages of life, and those stages also help determine a person's *dharma.* In addition, Hindu society recognizes four legitimate goals in life, each of which helps determine a person's identity. The ultimate goal of Hinduism is *moksha.*

C. **Three Paths to Liberation.** Hinduism embraces three great paths to *moksha,* each based on particular human tendencies. For those who prefer an active life, *karma marga,* "the path of works," involves performing actions in accordance with *dharma*—doing the right thing simply because it is right. For those who are philosophical, *jnana marga,* "the path of knowledge," emphasizes attaining knowledge of the true nature of reality. *Bhakti marga,* "the path of devotion," is most suitable for those to whom emotional attachment comes naturally. Spiritual energy is directed outward, in worship of the deity through gods, goddesses, or *avatars.* Hindu devotional life includes household and village rituals, pilgrimages to holy places, and veneration of cows.

D. **Hinduism in the Modern World.** Today significant religious leaders nourish Hinduism. Decades after his death, Mahatma Gandhi continues to be revered as a great religious figure. His influence has caused the caste system to change in modern times; discrimination against outcastes is now officially forbidden. The role of women continues to evolve. Hindus and Muslims have long lived side by side in South Asia, but tensions persist between the two groups. Although Hinduism is most prevalent in India and Nepal, it has expanded beyond South Asia, owing in large part to the teachers Ramakrishna and Vivekananda. Vivekananda established the Hindu Vedanta Society in the United States in the late nineteenth century.

Pages 42–48

Concept A: Human Destiny

Review Questions: Human Destiny

Question 1. Explain the meaning of the term *moksha.*
Answer. *Moksha* is a Hindu term that means "liberation" or "release."

Question 2. What doctrine says all reality is ultimately one? Give an analogy that describes it.
Answer. *Monism.* All rivers, lakes, and even drops of water share a common essence, originating from the ocean and eventually returning to it.

Question 3. Define Brahman and Atman. How are the two related?
Answer. Brahman is the ground of existence and the source of the universe. Atman is the eternal Self. They are one and the same.

Question 4. What is the general function of Hinduism's many deities?
Answer. They provide accessible points of contact with the divine.

Question 5. Give a brief explanation of the doctrine of *samsara.*
Answer. *Samsara* is the wheel of rebirth; the individual soul is reincarnated from one life-form to another until *moksha* is eventually achieved.

Question 6. What is the name of Hinduism's most popular sacred text?
Answer. The Bhagavad-Gita.

Question 7. According to Hinduism, what are the two principles that connect the divine to this world? Briefly explain each.
Answer. *Karma,* the moral law of cause and effect, which says that every action produces a justified effect; and *dharma,* or ethical duty, which provides a standard by which to judge the rightness or wrongness of actions.

Text Activities: Human Destiny

Activity A

Imagine you are Svetaketu's father. Create another analogy that might answer the boy's question about the Self.

Activity B

Many religions and philosophers, including Plato, have believed in reincarnation, considering it to provide a logical view of human destiny. How might reincarnation explain who we are, what we know, what we look like, and how we act?

Activity C

In the right-hand column of a sheet of paper, write the main actions you have taken during the last twenty-four hours. In the left-hand column, write what caused you to take each action. Then answer these questions: Is it possible for an action to lack a cause? Why or why not?

Additional Activities: Human Destiny

Tell Me More About This Self

This activity should be done in conjunction with text activity A.

1. After the students have composed answers to text activity A, invite several volunteers to share their answers aloud. Allow discussion after each answer is read. Encourage the students to ask questions and make comments that help clarify the volunteers' responses to the activity. Then discuss how effectively their answers helped them understand the Hindu concepts of Brahman and Atman.

Handout 3–A

2. Distribute handout 3–A, "Tell Me More About This Self." Explain that the handout contains a passage from the Chandogya Upanishad, in which Svetaketu receives from his father several answers to his question about the Self. Direct the students to read the handout, either silently or aloud. Ask them to identify other analogies that are used to help explain difficult concepts, such as those used by teachers to illustrate a concept in a physics or math class, by coaches to teach a physical skill or sport, and by Jesus to tell his disciples about the Reign of God.

3. Give the students the following homework assignment:

- Between now and our next class, read the handout again. Then rewrite your own response to Svetaketu's question about the Self so that it satisfies Svetaketu's question even further. Bring your revised answer to our next class.

In grading this assignment, look for creativity as well as an understanding of the concept.

The Game of *Samsara*

In this activity the students develop board games based on Hindu cosmology. This task requires the students to understand the concepts of Hinduism. Knowledge of Indian history and geography also can be incorporated. These games can be based on material studied in the student text, or they can be the end result of a research project on Hindu deities, epics, stages of life, or yogas.

Before you introduce the game assignment to your students, review the required elements and evaluation criteria listed in the procedure steps and handouts. You may wish to modify those items to fit the needs of your students and situation.

1. Divide the class into pairs and give the students the following or similar instructions, perhaps in written form:

- With your partner, design a board game based on the concepts of Hinduism. The game should include reincarnation, *karma, dharma,* castes, *moksha,* and the various deities, and should demonstrate your understanding of those ideas.
- Your classmates will evaluate the game for how well it "plays." I will evaluate it for how well it incorporates Hindu concepts.
- Your game can be as complex as Life or as simple as Chutes and Ladders. Its objective must be clear. To be considered complete, your project must include the following elements:
  - Typed directions that can be understood without assistance
  - An appropriately decorated game board
  - Tokens or game pieces
  - A method for moving the game pieces around the board (such as rolling dice, drawing cards, or spinning a wheel)
  - A beginning
  - An end

In addition, it may be helpful to give specific requirements (for example, "Include at least four Hindu deities in the game").

Handout 3–B

2. Give each pair one copy of handout 3–B, "Teacher Evaluation: The Game of *Samsara,*" which explains the criteria for your evaluation. Emphasize these points in your own words:

- Games with the following features will get the best evaluations:
  - Originality
  - Accurate portrayals of Hindu concepts
  - Creativity in the incorporation of Hindu concepts and game board decorations
  - Clear directions
- Be sure to complete the first two lines of the handout, naming your game and listing your own names, and to submit the evaluation form with your game on the date assigned.

Handout 3–C

3. Devote a full class period to evaluation of the completed games. For each game, assign a pair of students (or more if needed) to spend 10 minutes or so following the directions (ensure that the students are not assigned to play the game they developed). When time is up, distribute handout 3–C, "Peer Evaluation: The Game of *Samsara,*" and ask each pair to evaluate the game it played. Then invite the students to rotate to a new game (also not their own). Meanwhile, move around the room and complete a teacher evaluation for each game.

3

Understanding *Dharma*

Handout 3–D

The Bhagavad-Gita is an excellent source for understanding the Hindu concept of *dharma.* Distribute handout 3–D, "The Fruits of Action." After allowing the students time to complete the handout questions individually or in pairs or small groups, lead the class through a discussion of their responses. As a homework assignment, you may wish to have them construct their own *dharma* scenarios involving the executive and the doctor.

If you will be incorporating a more detailed study of the Bhagavad-Gita into your curriculum, this activity may be used to introduce the philosophical nature of the work. The students could complete the handout before reading the sacred text. Or this activity could help to focus discussion on the second and third chapters of the Bhagavad-Gita after the students have read them.

Pages 48–53

Concept B: Hindu Society

Review Questions: Hindu Society

Question 8. Name the four classes of the caste system and describe the people who belong to each.

Answer. Brahmin: priests; *kshatriya:* warriors and administrators; *vaishya:* producers, such as farmers, merchants, and artisans; and *shudra:* servants and laborers.

Question 9. In the Bhagavad-Gita, why does Krishna encourage Arjuna to engage in war?

Answer. Krishna reminds Arjuna that his sacred duty as a *kshatriya* is to engage in battle.

Question 10. Identify and briefly explain the four stages of life.

Answer. (1) Student: characterized by study of the Vedas and other sacred literature; (2) householder: marked by pursuing a career and raising a family; (3) forest dweller: requiring retreat from worldly bonds to engage fully in the spiritual quest; (4) wandering ascetic *(sannyasin):* involving returning to society but remaining detached from social life.

Question 11. Name and briefly describe the four goals of life.

Answer. (1) *Kama:* pleasure is sought, but within the limits of *dharma;* (2) *artha:* material success is sought, along with social power and prestige; (3) *dharma:* harmony with *dharma* is the primary concern; (4) *moksha:* the goal is to achieve the infinite being, awareness, and bliss of liberation.

Text Activities: Hindu Society

Activity D

Hindu society is separated by caste identity. Is Western society separated in any ways that are similar to the caste system? Explain your answer.

Activity E

Who do you think should choose a person's marriage partner? How does your perspective on this issue compare with Vimla's? What aspects of Hinduism might help account for any differences in perspective?

Activity F

Describe the four Hindu stages of life, comparing each stage to a similar stage in Western society.

Activity G

Reflect on a major goal you have had and have achieved. Was the satisfaction of accomplishing the goal permanent? Did it cause you to desire to achieve new goals? From the experience, what did you learn about desire?

Additional Activities: Hindu Society

Supplemental Reading: The Caste System

Handout 3–E

When assigning the section "Doing One's Job: The Caste System" in the student text, distribute copies of handout 3–E, "The Master and the Untouchable." Direct the students to read both the textbook section and the handout, and to then write responses to the handout questions, using a separate piece of paper if necessary.

On the day the assignment is due, discuss the handout questions as a class. Focus first on the students' intellectual understanding of the material, then shift to their interpretations and personal responses.

If you wish, allow the students to revise their answers to the handout questions before turning them in for evaluation.

Variation. Encourage the students to read and discuss *The Death of Vishnu: A Novel,* by Manil Suri (New York: W. W. Norton and Co., 2001). This book about a man who lives and dies on the landing of an apartment house in Bombay vividly illustrates the tension between classes in modern India. The subject matter is most appropriate for adults and older teens. Before assigning the book, review it and determine if it is suitable for your students.

Character Sketch: The Four Stages of Life

Issue the following instructions in your own words:

- You are each to write a four-page character sketch of a person going through the four stages of life: student, householder, forest dweller, and wandering ascetic *(sannyasin).* Devote one page to each stage. Write the sketch as if the character lives in your own community. By doing this you will adapt your understanding of the four stages of Hindu life to your own time.
- The adaptation need not be a literal parallel to the Hindu understanding. For example, at the wandering ascetic stage, the person might be a retiree who pays little attention to his own needs, possessions, and so on, and who spends each day "wandering" the local hospital, comforting sick or dying children.

- The character may be you or someone you know, or a completely fictional person. The sketch should provide a look at a day in the life of the person at each stage, highlighting the activities particular to that stage.
- The character sketch is to be handed in and will be graded.

Variations. Offer the students the option of performing their sketches as monologues or even dances. Or allow the students to portray the four stages in a visual art medium.

Pages 53–61

Concept C: Three Paths to Liberation

Review Questions: Three Paths to Liberation

Question 12. Identify the three paths to liberation. Which type of person is best suited for each path?
Answer. (1) *Karma marga,* "the path of works," for those who prefer an active life; (2) *jnana marga,* "the path of knowledge," for those who enjoy philosophy, learning, and meditation; (3) *bhakti marga,* "the path of devotion," for those to whom emotional attachment comes naturally.

3

Question 13. What are the three most important schools of Hindu philosophy? What is the basic task that concerns all three?
Answer. Vedanta, Yoga, and Sankhya. Their basic task is the attainment of knowledge over the ignorance that binds the self to *samsara.*

Question 14. Identify three important gods or goddesses of Hinduism.
Answer. Vishnu, Shiva, and Kali.

Question 15. What is an *avatar?* Name two important Hindu figures identified as *avatars.*
Answer. An *avatar* is an incarnation, or living embodiment, of a deity. Krishna and Rama are *avatars.*

Question 16. What Hindu text is most closely associated with the *bhakti marga?*
Answer. The Bhagavad-Gita.

Question 17. Identify three aspects of Hindu devotional life.
Answer. Household and village rituals, pilgrimages to holy places, and veneration of cows.

Text Activities: Three Paths to Liberation

Activity H

"Do the right thing only because it is right." Must right actions be rewarded for people to want to do them, or should they be their own reward?

Activity I

What might be some differences between the knowledge sought by a Hindu on *jnana marga* and the knowledge sought by a student working on a college degree?

Activity J

Discuss the differences between your own experience of worship and the worship of a Hindu on *bhakti marga,* "the path of devotion."

Additional Activities: Three Paths to Liberation

Bhakti Marga and *Puja*

In this activity the students design their own prayer experiences using the format of a Hindu *puja.*

1. Offer the following introduction in your own words:
- The worship of Hindu deities is typically called *puja.* During *puja* a deity or some aspect of the deity is honored through a combination of images, objects, and actions. Bells are rung to invite the deity's attention. Lamps are lit and waved in front of the deity's image. Prayers are chanted. Water and food are offered to the deity for blessing, and consumed by the worshiper. Images of the deity may be symbolically bathed or clothed. Incense is usually burned, or flowers are used to perfume the air and decorate the display. In these rituals the worshiper nourishes a relationship with the chosen deity through all five senses.

2. If possible, show the film *Puja: Expressions of Hindu Devotion* (20 minutes, 1996), which explains how the senses are used in *puja.* After the film use these or similar questions to discuss the students' observations:
- Where does *puja* occur?
- What are the components of *puja?*
- What symbols are part of *puja?* How are they used?

The film and a corresponding teacher's guide are available from the Freer Gallery of Art/Arthur M. Sackler Gallery (see appendix 2). If you cannot obtain the film, you may wish to use information from the Freer Gallery of Art/ Arthur M. Sackler Gallery Web site, which is rich in material about Hinduism.

3. Tell the students that they will now have an opportunity to design their own ceremonies using the *puja* concept of engaging all the senses. Assign this project to be completed individually, in pairs, or in small groups. Make the following points, using your own words:
- You are *not* to simply reproduce a Hindu *puja.* You are to adapt the idea of a *puja* and create a unique ceremony that honors something that is sacred to you because of your own belief system.
- The ceremony should reflect your own beliefs, values, and experiences. It may focus on experiences you have shared with your classmates, or it may focus on a personal quality or virtue that you would like to honor. It may be religious, or it may reflect your ideals without any religious references.

3

Be sure that the students understand that this ceremony should not be a real Hindu *puja* unless the student developing it is Hindu.

You might require written outlines of the ceremonies, or complete performances of them. Another option is to require outlines, and ask for volunteers to present their ceremonies, perhaps for extra credit. If the ceremonies are to be enacted, consider assigning one or two a day for the coming weeks, perhaps to open and close your class sessions.

The outlines or ceremonies should demonstrate all the components of *puja* that the students noted in the film or in their research. However you decide to evaluate the *puja* rituals, be sure that the students understand the criteria you will be using. You might design a rubric, such as the one used for "The Game of *Samsara*" on handout 3–B.

(This activity is adapted from one developed by John Reine, Newton Country Day School of the Sacred Heart, Newton, Massachusetts.)

Jnana Marga and Meditation

This activity gives the students an experience of the kind of meditation found in the Hindu tradition. Some general guidelines for meditation can be found in the introduction to this manual, on page 18.

If you have no experience with meditating, it might be helpful to invite someone who does to visit the class for this activity. The students are likely to have questions and even some misunderstandings as to the purpose of meditation. Your own confidence that this is a worthwhile activity, or the confidence of your guest, can encourage the students to make the effort to meditate.

You may want to shorten or adapt this meditation, to better suit the needs of your class. This particular activity may be too long for those who have never experienced silent meditation.

This exercise will be most effective in a setting that is conducive to quiet reflection and that allows the students adequate distance from one another, such as your school's chapel.

Note: This activity is similar to the chapter 4 exercise "Sitting," on pages 73–74 of this manual.

1. In a calm voice, read the following meditation, which is reprinted from Fr. Anthony de Mello's guide to meditation, *Sadhana, a Way to God,* pages 13–15:

- "**The Riches of Silence**

"'*Silence is the great revelation,*' said Lao-tse. We are accustomed to think of Scripture as the revelation of God. And so it is. I want you now to discover the revelation that silence brings. To take in the revelation that Scripture offers, you must expose yourself to Scripture. To take in the revelation that silence offers you must first attain silence. And this is not easy. . . .

"I want each of you to take a comfortable posture. Close your eyes.

"I am now going to invite you to keep silence for a period of ten minutes. First you will try to attain silence, as total a silence as possible of heart and mind. Having attained it, you will expose yourself to whatever revelation it brings.

"At the end of ten minutes I shall invite you to open your eyes and share with us, if you wish, what you did and what you experienced in these ten minutes. [Allow 10 minutes of silence.]

"In sharing with the rest of us what you did and what happened to you, tell us what attempts you made to attain silence and how successful your attempts were. Describe this silence if you can. Tell us what you experienced in this silence. Tell us anything you thought and felt during this exercise. [Allow time for the students to respond.]

"The experience of people who attempt this exercise is infinitely varied. Most people discover, to their surprise, that silence is something they are simply not accustomed to. That no matter what they do they cannot still the constant wandering of their mind or [quiet] an emotional turmoil they feel within their heart. Others feel themselves approaching the frontiers of silence. Then they panic and withdraw. Silence can be a frightening experience.

"No reason to be discouraged. Even those wandering thoughts of yours are a great revelation, aren't they? The fact that your mind wanders, isn't that a revelation about yourself? It is not enough to know this. You must take time to *experience* this wandering mind. And the *type of* wandering it indulges in—how revealing that is too!

"And here's something encouraging for you: The fact that you were aware of your mental wanderings or of your inner turmoil or of your inability to be still shows that you have some small degree of silence within you, at least a sufficient amount of silence to be aware of all of this.

"Close your eyes again and become aware of your wandering mind . . . for just two minutes . . . [Allow 2 minutes of silence.]

"Now sense the silence that makes it possible for you to be aware of the wanderings of your mind . . .

"It is this minimal silence that you have within you that we [can] build on. . . . As it grows it will reveal to you more and more about yourself. Or, more accurately, silence will reveal yourself to you. That is the first revelation: your *self.* And in and through this revelation you will attain things that money cannot buy, things like wisdom and serenity and joy and God.

"To attain these priceless things it is not enough for you to reflect, talk, discuss. What you will need is work. Get to work right now.

"Close your eyes. Seek silence for another five minutes. [Allow 5 minutes of silence.]

"At the end of the exercise note whether your attempts this time were more successful or less.

"Note whether silence revealed something to you this time that you failed to notice last time.

"Don't seek for anything sensational in the revelation that silence brings—lights, inspirations, insights. In fact, don't *seek* at all. Limit yourself to *observing.* Just take in everything that comes to your awareness. Everything, no matter how trite and ordinary, that is thus *revealed* to you. All your revelation may consist of is the fact that your hands are clammy or that you have an urge to change your posture or that you are worried about your health. No matter. The important thing is that you have become aware of this. The content of your awareness is less important than the quality of the awareness. As the quality improves, your silence will deepen. And as your silence deepens, you will experience change. And you will discover, to your delight, that revelation is not knowledge. Revelation is power; a mysterious power that brings transformation."

2. Allow the students to share their reactions to the experience, and to ask questions of you or your guest.

Karma Marga: "The Path of Works"

Handout 3–F

Distribute handout 3–F, "*Karma Marga:* 'The Path of Works.'" Read the introductory paragraph with the students. Address any questions the students have, and allow the young people time to write their responses to the handout questions. After the students have completed the handout, lead them in a discussion about the subtleties of personal motivations, using these or similar questions:

- What motivates our actions?
- To what extent do we control our motivations?
- How (or when) do we recognize selfish motivations for our actions?
- How can we cultivate selfless motivations for our actions?

Krishna and the Love of God

The student text points out that the *avatar* Krishna is sometimes depicted as an amorous cowherd, often accompanied by adoring female cowherds, or *gopis*. The relationship between the women and Krishna is a symbol of human love for God.

Handout 3–G

1. Handout 3–G, "'The Dance of Love,'" contains a Hindu folktale about Krishna and the female cowherds. Distribute the handout and give the students time to read it. You may also wish to read it aloud, or recruit a student to rehearse it ahead of time and read it aloud.

2. Engage the students in a discussion based on questions such as the ones that follow. Or assign the questions as written homework, to give the students a better opportunity to delve more deeply into the story and its meanings.

- What is represented by the relationship between Krishna and the *gopis?* [Human love for God]
- Plot out the significant moments in the relationship of Krishna and the *gopis*. [Krishna's promise; Krishna's call of the *gopis;* the *gopis'* response; Krishna's first test—telling the *gopis* to go home; the *gopis'* firm declaration of love; Krishna's acceptance; the development of pride, leading to the second test, the loss of Krishna; the *gopis'* repentance, revealed through their exhausting search; Krishna's return and his instructions about how to keep him always with them.]
- Using the scheme that has been plotted out from the story of Krishna and the *gopis,* present a similar scenario in terms of the faith tradition in which you have been raised or with which you are most familiar. [This scenario need not conform perfectly to the story's scheme, as long as it echoes the dynamic of the story. You may need to guide the students if they get stuck. Here is an example of how the scenario might unfold: A young woman hears about God and God's promise of love. She responds by entering a relationship with God and giving her love in return. Her commitment is tested and shaken by the sudden death of a friend. However, the woman looks deep within and senses that God is still with her, and she recommits herself to the relationship. As time passes, her understanding of her faith becomes rigid and formal to the degree that she believes her way of being with God is the right way and the only way. Her intolerance is manifested when she opposes her

church's inclusion of several people with AIDS. This experience leaves her feeling empty; she believes that God has left her. She knows that she wants to feel God's presence again, but it takes months of prayer and soul-searching before she can finally say that her relationship with God is back on track. Through this experience she learns that her relationships with her fellow humans must be just and loving if she is to stay in a good relationship with God.]

- In the story about Krishna, notice the importance of pride. Krishna makes an example first of the *gopis'* pride, then of Radha's individual pride. What do you think the storyteller is trying to teach? [Perhaps the storyteller is criticizing the pride of the community that believes it has an exclusive hold on the love of God, and the pride of the individual who similarly places himself above others because of a faulty perception of his own importance to God. Perhaps Radha and the other *gopis* have forgotten that if God loves all humanity, then God loves all individuals equally.]
- Share any other insights, reflections, or observations brought to mind by "The Dance of Love."

Pages 61–64

Concept D: Hinduism in the Modern World

Review Questions: Hinduism in the Modern World

Question 18. How did Mahatma Gandhi influence Hinduism?
Answer. Gandhi's steadfast efforts to stand up to oppression through nonviolence and civil disobedience forever changed the nature of India, and of Hinduism. His work won Indian independence from British rule. His insights continue to fuel Hinduism's tendency to accept all wisdom as lighting the way to the divine.

Question 19. What significant changes in the caste system took place in the twentieth century?
Answer. The Indian government in 1948 officially forbade discrimination against outcastes. Governmental programs since that time, similar to affirmative action programs in the United States, have sought to further promote the economic and social rights of those people.

Question 20. What is *sati?* What is its status today?
Answer. *Sati,* the burning of a widow, is now forbidden.

Question 21. What significant development occurred in relations between Hindus and Muslims in 1947?
Answer. The Muslim community forced the partitioning of India to form the divided nation of Pakistan (the eastern part of which is now Bangladesh), thus providing a Muslim homeland. This turned into a bloody ordeal in which many followers of both religions were killed.

Text Activity: Hinduism in the Modern World

Activity K

The secular state of India and the traditional religion Hinduism tend to disagree over some important issues. How does religion relate to the secular state in your country?

Additional Activities: Hinduism in the Modern World

Issues in Hinduism Today

Assign the students individually or in groups to research issues facing Hindu society today. Some timely topics are the tensions between Hindus and Muslims, relations between India and Pakistan, disputes over sacred sites (such as the temple at Ayodhya), the evolving role of women, and changes in the caste system. Encourage the students to search both print and electronic sources for current articles on the issues they select. Suggest that they share their research with the class using a presentation graphics program or other means.

A Life of Poverty, but Not Impoverishment

This activity uses the movie *City of Joy* (132 minutes, Columbia Tristar, VHS 1992, DVD 2006, rated PG-13). Note that this film contains some offensive language. It is advisable to view the film in advance to determine if it will be suitable for your students.

1. Introduce the movie *City of Joy* by noting that it depicts life in India today. Encourage the students to take notes during the film, keeping in mind discussion questions like these:
   - What is the City of Joy? Describe the living conditions there.
   - Point out any evidence of the caste system in the film.
   - How are women treated? How is Kamla Pal both a traditional and a nontraditional woman?
   - In what way is Dr. Max Lowe "twisted around" when he first arrives in India? What is he seeking?
   - What are the three choices in life, according to nurse Joan Bethel?
   - What does Dr. Max Lowe say he believes in at first, and why? What does he believe in by the film's conclusion?
   - Which of the three choices does he make?

2. After viewing the movie, engage the students in a discussion of the questions listed in step 1. The conversation can be done in small groups, with a member of each group responsible for reporting the group's answers to the whole class. End the discussion with questions like these:
   - Hasari Pal, an Indian farmer, is quoted at the end of the movie as saying, "All that is not given is lost." Using the events and characters in the movie as examples, explain what might be meant by the quotation.
   - Why, do you think, was the neighborhood called the City of Joy?
   - In what way did this movie inspire you? In what way did it disturb you? What did you learn from it?

Gandhi: The Peaceful Fighter

1. Show the movie *Gandhi* (188 minutes, Sony Pictures, VHS 1982, DVD 2008, rated PG). Ask the students to take notes while watching and to keep in mind discussion questions such as these:

- What moved Gandhi to dedicate his life to fighting for India's independence?
- What steps did Gandhi take to gain freedom for India? What did he always insist on? Why?
- What sort of power did Gandhi's simple campaign for freedom bring to bear on the British Empire?
- Why, do you think, was Gandhi's fasting to end violence so effective?
- What did Gandhi think of other faiths? What did Gandhi's character in the film mean when he said, "I am a Muslim and a Hindu and a Christian and a Jew, and so are all of you"?
- What similarities and differences do you see between Gandhi and Jesus?
- What did Gandhi recommend to the Hindu man who confessed that after Muslims killed his son, he brutally killed a Muslim child? Do you think the man will follow what Gandhi called a way out of hell? How would you react in a similar situation?

2. After the class has viewed the entire film, lead the students to discuss the questions from step 1 in small groups and to then share their answers with the whole class. Then assign as homework a one- or two-page answer to the following essay question:

- Mahatma Gandhi said, "When I despair, I remember that, all through history, the way of truth and love has always won." Do you think this is true? Back up your answer with at least two examples from history and one example from your own experience.

Additional Resources from Saint Mary's Press

See *Primary Source Readings in World Religions* (Saint Mary's Press, 2009) for selections from *The Bhagavad-Gita,* stories of Vendanta Sages, and an excerpt from *All Men Are Brothers,* by Mahatma Gandhi, as well as the accompanying leader's guide for suggestions about how to use these readings in your study of Hinduism.

Teaching About Other Religions (Saint Mary's Press, 2006) offers guidelines and suggestions for creating a respectful and intellectually stimulating environment when studying world religions in the classroom. For ideas and strategies on teaching Hinduism, see chapter 4.

Tell Me More About This Self

In this selection from the Chandogya Upanishad, a young man named Svetaketu has asked his father to teach him about the nature of the Self. His father, Uddalaka, gives him several answers.

"As the bees make honey by gathering juices from many flowering plants and trees, and as these juices reduced to one honey do not know from what flowers they severally come, similarly, my son, all creatures, when they are merged in that one Existence, whether in dreamless sleep or in death, know nothing of their past or present state, because of the ignorance enveloping them—know not that they are merged in him and that from him they came.

"Whatever these creatures are, whether a lion, or a tiger, or a boar, or a worm, or a gnat, or a mosquito, that they remain after they come back from dreamless sleep.

"All these have their self in him alone. He is the truth. He is the subtle essence of all. He is the Self. And that, Svetaketu, THAT ART THOU."

"Please, sir, tell me more about this Self."

"Be it so, my son:

"The rivers in the east flow eastward, the rivers in the west flow westward, and all enter into the sea. From sea to sea they pass, the clouds lifting them to the sky as vapor and sending them down as rain. And as these rivers, when they are united with the sea, do not know whether they are this or that river, likewise all those creatures that I have named, when they have come back from Brahman, know not whence they came.

"All those beings have their self in him alone. He is the truth. He is the subtle essence of all. He is the Self. And that, Svetaketu, THAT ART THOU."

"Please, sir, tell me more about this Self."

"Be it so, my child:

"If someone were to strike once at the root of this large tree, it would bleed, but live. If he were to strike at its stem, it would bleed, but live. If he were to strike at the top, it would bleed, but live. Pervaded by the living Self, this tree stands firm, and takes its food; but if the Self were to depart from one of its branches, that branch would wither; if it were to depart from a second, that would wither; if it were to depart from a third, that would wither. If it were to depart from the whole tree, the whole tree would wither.

"Likewise, my son, know this: The body dies when the Self leaves it—but the Self dies not.

"All that is has its self in him alone. He is the truth. He is the subtle essence of all. He is the Self. And that, Svetaketu, THAT ART THOU."

"Please, sir, tell me more about this Self."

"Be it so. Bring a fruit of that Nyagrodha tree."

"Here it is, sir."

"Break it."

"It is broken, sir."

"What do you see?"

"Some seeds, extremely small, sir."

"Break one of them."

"It is broken, sir."

"What do you see?"

"Nothing, sir."

"The subtle essence you do not see, and in that is the whole of the Nyagrodha tree. Believe, my son, that that which is the subtle essence—in that have all things their existence. That is the truth. That is the Self. And that, Svetaketu, THAT ART THOU." (Swami Prabhavananda and Frederick Manchester, selectors and translators from the original Sanskrit, *The Upanishads: Breath of the Eternal* [Hollywood, CA: Vedanta Society of Southern California, 1948; reprint, New York: New American Library, Mentor Books, 1957], pages 69–70. Copyright © 1948, 1957 by the Vedanta Society of Southern California. Used with permission of Vedanta Press.)

Teacher Evaluation: The Game of *Samsara*

Name of the game: ______________________________

Names of the student designers: ______________________________

In the following chart, each circled number indicates your game's score for the corresponding category.

	Exceptional	Good	Acceptable	Needs Improvement
Organization	Game is extremely well organized; directions are easy to follow; game play flows smoothly; organization enhances effectiveness of game	Game is thoughtfully designed; organization is apparent, and most directions are easy to follow	Game is somewhat organized; ideas are not clearly presented, and transitions are not all smooth; faults in organization are distracting to play of game	Game is messy or confusing, or both; format is difficult to follow; flow of play is abrupt and seriously distracts players from enjoyment of game
	4	3	2	1
Content accuracy	Content is completely accurate; all facts are precise and explicit	Content is mostly accurate, with few inconsistencies or errors	Content is somewhat accurate, with more than a few inconsistencies or errors	Content includes many inaccuracies; facts are presented in a way that misleads players
	4	3	2	1
Creativity	Game is extremely clever and original, with a unique approach that enhances player enjoyment	Game is clever at times; design is well thought out and unique	Game includes a few original touches, but they are not incorporated throughout	Game lacks creative energy, is bland, and does not engage players
	4	3	2	1
Incorporation of Hindu Concepts	Concept is strongly incorporated, and is used correctly as an integral part of game	Concept is used adequately and correctly, and fits in naturally with game	Concept is weakly incorporated, and is used incorrectly or seems not to fit game	Concept is not included
Caste	4	3	2	1
Deities	4	3	2	1
Dharma	4	3	2	1
Reincarnation	4	3	2	1

Total number of points: ______

Comments:

Peer Evaluation: The Game of *Samsara*

Name of the game: ______________________________

Names of the student designers: ______________________

Names of the peer evaluators: ________________________

In each of the categories below, evaluate the game on a scale of **1** to **4**, as follows:

1 = not at all
2 = somewhat
3 = mostly
4 = yes; no problems!

In the space provided for comments, explain the reason for a mark, give praise, or suggest improvements.

Instructions: The instructions and the objective of the game were clear.
1 2 3 4
Comments:

Ease of play: Play progressed smoothly and fairly.
1 2 3 4
Comments:

Game design: The playing board and the game pieces reflect the Hindu tradition creatively and originally.
1 2 3 4
Comments:

Fun: This game is fun! It held my interest.
1 2 3 4
Comments:

The Fruits of Action

Read the displayed passages from The Bhagavad-Gita, and use their teachings to answer the questions.

Be intent on action,
not on the fruits of action;
avoid attraction to the fruits
and attachment to inaction!
(Bhagavad-Gita 2:47)

1. What fruits might each of the professionals in the following situations hope that their actions will yield?
   a. A business executive promoting an employee to a managerial position

   b. A police officer arresting a youth for selling drugs

   c. A doctor attending a patient who is ill

2. If their actions do *not* attain the desired fruits, how might these people feel?

3. How might remaining unattached to the fruits of action help these professionals follow their *dharma?*

Your own duty done imperfectly
is better than another [person]'s done well.
It is better to die in one's own duty;
another [person]'s duty is perilous.
(Bhagavad-Gita 3:35)

4. Imagine that one of the professionals in question 1 sees a need for an action that is not appropriate to her or his particular role. For example, suppose the police officer recognizes that the young person dealing drugs needs to be taught job skills if he is to earn an honest wage. It might seem to the officer that the need for that action (providing the youth with job training) is greater or more important than the completion of her own task (getting the youth off the street immediately). According to Bhagavad-Gita 3:35, why should the officer stay faithful to her own *dharma* in this situation, which would mean arresting the youth? Why is it important to remain true to yourself even when that means another need might go unmet?

(The excerpts on this handout are quoted from *The Bhagavad-Gita: Krishna's Counsel in Time of War,* translated by Barbara Stoler Miller [New York: Bantam Books, 1986], pages 36 and 46.

The Master and the Untouchable

Read the following information along with the material on the caste system in your textbook. Then answer the questions at the end of this handout, using a separate sheet of paper if needed.

It is well known that Mahatma Gandhi was not enthusiastic about the caste system in India. In fact people excluded by the caste system, referred to as outcastes and including the Untouchables, were given a new name by Gandhi. That name was *Harijan,* "God's children." Because of Gandhi's efforts, the Indian government outlawed discrimination against Harijan in 1948.

Much earlier in Hindu history, another revered master made a strong point in favor of the Untouchables. His name was Shankara. He was born in the year 788 and is renowned for his contributions to the school of knowledge known as Vedanta.

> One morning Shankara was walking to the Ganges to bathe. Along the way he met an Untouchable. This man had four dogs with him, and the dogs and the man together blocked Shankara's path. Prejudice against the lower castes and Untouchables was so strong in Indian society that even Shankara, a *brahmin* and a spiritual master, responded with hateful anger. He ordered the Untouchable to get out of his way. Rather than move, the Untouchable asked a question: "You teach that there is only one God. If that is so, why are there so many kinds of human beings? Why are there distinctions of religion or caste at all?" Hearing the question, Shankara felt ashamed. But even stronger than his shame was his feeling of reverence. He prostrated himself at the Untouchable's feet. Later, he expressed his reverence in a poem that has this refrain:
>
> Anyone who has learned to see the
> Oneness of all,
> That person is my master—whether
> brahmin or Untouchable.

(Adapted from Swami Prabhavananda with the assistance of Frederick Manchester, *The Spiritual Heritage of India* [Hollywood, CA: Vedanta Press, 1969], pages 281–282. Copyright © under the Berne Convention.)

1. Summarize the structure of the caste system. Include the names of the four major classes.

2. Does any structure similar to the caste system exist in your society? in your community? in your school? Explain.

3. What reasons might be behind the development of the caste system?

4. In contemporary world history, what civic or religious leaders might be compared to Mahatma Gandhi? Name at least one and explain the comparison.

5. Shankara experienced both shame and reverence when he faced the wisdom of a person considered an Untouchable. Have you ever learned an important lesson from an unexpected source? If so, describe the experience. If not, write a paragraph about what you imagine Shankara might have thought in the moments just after hearing the Untouchable's words.

Karma Marga: "The Path of Works"

Karma marga emphasizes not only doing good works but also undertaking those works in the right spirit, with the right motivations. A person following *karma marga* must ask, "Does the way in which I accomplish this act increase or decrease the illusions I have of myself?" Even outwardly good or seemingly neutral acts can contribute to an inaccurate self-perception when they are done for the wrong reasons.

1. For each of the following actions, write a *selfish motivation* and a *selfless motivation.* Responses have been supplied for the first action as examples.
   a. Sleeping
   Selfish motivation: I sleep late or excessively to escape my responsibilities, my problems, or other people.
   Selfless motivation: I sleep to give my body the rest it needs.

   b. Giving money to a stranger who asks for help
   Selfish motivation:

   Selfless motivation:

   c. Running for an elected position
   Selfish motivation:

   Selfless motivation:

   d. Eating
   Selfish motivation:

   Selfless motivation:

   e. Learning and studying
   Selfish motivation:

   Selfless motivation:

2. Have you done things that outwardly seemed to be good, but were motivated by intentions that undermined that good? If so, list two or three of them and explain.

"The Dance of Love"

Lord Krishna promised the young female cowherds, or *gopis,* that he would dance with them when autumn came. The *gopis* eagerly waited for the time to come. When it did, Krishna went out to the forest on a delightful full-moon night and played his flute. The *gopis* heard the flute and felt it calling them away from home, and after some time they threw off their family responsibilities and ran off to find Krishna. They knew the consequence of running off: to their husbands they were now as good as dead.

The *gopis* followed the sound of the flute and found Krishna in the forest. They stood and gazed at him, astonished by his loveliness. Krishna asked about their well-being and chastised them for leaving their husbands and families. Then he said: "You have seen the lush forest and the moonlit night and the beautiful riverbanks. Now go home to your husbands." These cruel words struck the *gopis* hard. Not knowing what to say, they sank into their own endless thoughts, while tears, like pearls from a broken necklace, fell from their eyes. Finally they discovered the words to reproach him: "Krishna, you are a bold deceiver. With your flute you led us away. You took our hearts, our minds, and our wealth. And now you strike us with cold unkindness that will be the death of us. We have abandoned our families and homes and husbands; we ignored the world's call for us to remain in our places. Now there is only one who can protect us, and that is you. Where else can we call home now that we are fully wrapped up in love of you?"

Krishna smiled and called them to come closer. He asked them to dance, and they were glad. With his special skill, he made a golden terrace on the riverbank, and the *gopis* dressed themselves up in long robes and jewels. They were intoxicated with love for Krishna, and began to think that he belonged only to them.

Krishna sensed that they were becoming filled with pride, so he took Radha, one of the *gopis,* and vanished. The rest of the *gopis* were frightened and sad, and they searched for him, calling, "Oh, Lord, why have you left us behind when we have given ourselves to you?" After a while they found his footprints, with Radha's beside them, and followed them, feeling miserable as they searched.

Meanwhile, alone with Krishna, Radha was thinking very highly of herself. She thought she must be the greatest of all, and became so proud that she asked Krishna to carry her on his shoulders. Just as she was about to climb up, Krishna disappeared, leaving her standing alone with her arms stretched out. Her radiant beauty made the ground around her shine, but Radha wept, and all the birds and animals and trees wept with her.

The other *gopis* found her there, embraced her joyously, and then continued their search for Krishna. Finally they sat down on the riverbank and cried for him until they were exhausted. But he did not appear.

Krishna saw that the *gopis* were dying for his love, so he came again into their midst. When he did, their loneliness disappeared and they were glad again. Krishna said: "I have tested you in this way, and you have not abandoned me but have given me your hearts. I cannot reward you enough."

So Krishna played and danced with the *gopis.* He multiplied himself and danced in a ring, each *gopi* thinking Krishna was by her side and holding her hand alone. They whirled around; they played their lutes and sang. Rapt in love of Krishna, mind and body were forgotten. Even the gods came down from the heavens to watch, and the wind and water stood still to listen.

But as morning approached, Krishna told the *gopis* it was time to go home. He said, "Meditate upon me always, and I will always be near you." The *gopis* were pleased, and returned safely to their homes, for no one knew they had been away. (Based on Ananda K. Coomaraswamy and Sister Nivedita, *Myths of the Hindus and Buddhists* [1913; unabridged republication, New York: Dover Publications by special arrangement with George G. Harrap and Company, 1967], pages 232–235.)

CHAPTER 4

Buddhism

Major Concepts

A. **The Life of Gautama.** Siddhartha Gautama, who became the Buddha, was born into the warrior caste, and his father ruled over a small region of northern India. Gautama led a pampered life, but the Four Passing Sights (an old man, a diseased man, a corpse, and a religious ascetic) turned him away from the pursuit of worldly power and pleasure, to seek enlightenment. In his search Gautama discovered the central Buddhist teaching of the Middle Way, which rejects extremes of sensual indulgence and asceticism. Through diligent meditation Gautama attained enlightenment and became known as the Buddha, the Awakened One. He and his followers formed the Sangha, or Buddhist community. Being a Buddhist means taking refuge in the Three Jewels of Buddhism: the Buddha, the Dharma (Buddhist teachings), and the Sangha.

B. **The Dharma.** Buddhist teachings are difficult to understand, but because they are based on the insights of a human being, they are potentially comprehensible by anyone. Buddhism emphasizes the development of wisdom rather than faith. Buddhism has much in common with Hinduism in terms of its cosmology, but the Buddha reacted against Hinduism in some important areas: he dismissed philosophical speculation, rejected the institutional form of Hinduism, and made sure that Buddhist teachings were available in an accessible language rather than solely in Sanskrit. The Buddha noted Three Marks of Existence—*anatta, anicca,* and *dukkha*—recognizing that there is no self, that change is constant, and that suffering is the result of *anatta* and *anicca.* The Buddhist doctrine of rebirth, or *samsara,* holds that because of the lack of a self, rebirth consists of the transference of a bundle of energy, which is patterned according to one's *karma. Karma* is a key element in Buddhist morality and personal identity. The Four Noble Truths, discerned by the Buddha on the night of his enlightenment, are the central teachings of Buddhism. Through these truths, the Buddha diagnosed humanity's disease, determined the cause, issued a prognosis, and prescribed a cure. *Dukkha,* or suffering, is the disease, and *tanha,* or selfish desire, is the cause. The cure is to follow the Noble Eightfold Path, which sets forth a life of moderation. The goal is *nirvana,* which awaits the death of the body and is preceded by living as an *arhat*—one who is awakened, transformed, and characterized by compassion.

C. **Three Rafts for Crossing the River.** Buddhism has divided into three rafts, or vehicles, by which Buddhists can "cross the river" from suffering to *nirvana.* Theravada Buddhism focuses on the teachings of the Buddha rather than on the Buddha himself. Adherents of Theravada practice the Noble Eightfold Path, which emphasizes meditation. In Theravada the ideal type are *arhats,* whom all strive to imitate. Mahayana Buddhism focuses on the Buddha himself, celebrating him as a divine savior. Salvation comes through the infinite grace of the compassionate Buddha. Vajrayana Buddhism "fights fire with fire," harnessing the energy of desire and turning it against itself to propel the individual toward enlightenment.

Pages 70–75

Concept A: The Life of Gautama

Review Questions: The Life of Gautama

Question 1. What was the name of the man who later became the Buddha and founded the religion Buddhism?
Answer. Siddhartha Gautama.

Question 2. What were the Four Passing Sights? Explain their significance to the origins of Buddhism.
Answer. An old man, a diseased man, a corpse, and a religious ascetic. These sights led directly to Gautama's giving up his life of power and sensual enjoyment for the austere life of a mendicant, which led eventually to his enlightenment and to the religion Buddhism.

Question 3. Explain the doctrine of the Middle Way.
Answer. This doctrine holds that just as a life of sensual indulgence will not lead to salvation, neither will extreme asceticism. It embraces the idea that contentment is a good thing.

Question 4. Describe the event of Gautama's attainment of enlightenment.
Answer. While meditating Gautama observed his previous lifetimes, acquired the ability to perceive the deaths and rebirths of all living beings, and discovered the Four Noble Truths. Thus he attained enlightenment and won salvation.

Question 5. What is the Sangha? Who are its members?
Answer. The Buddhist community, consisting of Buddhist men and women from all walks of life.

Question 6. What are the Three Jewels of Buddhism?
Answer. The Buddha, the Dharma, and the Sangha.

Text Activities: The Life of Gautama

Activity A

How are the facts of old age, disease, and death given meaning within your religious tradition or within the religious tradition with which you are most familiar?

Activity B

Imagine yourself in Gautama's place, a pampered prince or princess with all life's worldly joys at your disposal. What would it take for you to leave it all, as Gautama did?

Activity C

How might the doctrine of the Middle Way be relevant to the way you live? Reflect on the ways you follow (or do not follow) the Middle Way.

Activity D

Gautama discovered the truths of Buddhism solely by looking inward, through meditation. Take a few minutes to look inward, to contemplate who you are. What truths regarding your own nature are you able to discover?

Activity E

As one of the Three Jewels, the Sangha obviously plays an important role in Buddhism. Describe a community (religious or otherwise) in which you participate. What is the role of community togetherness and organization? What is the relationship between community and learning?

Activity F

"Work out your salvation with diligence." Use what you know about the Buddha's religious quest to elaborate on the meaning of his final words.

Activity G

Although clearly legendary, the life story of Gautama is meaningful and instructive, reflecting the issues and ideals that lie at the heart of Buddhism. Within the story identify examples of at least five of the seven dimensions of religion.

Additional Activities: The Life of Gautama

The Buddha's First Sermon

The Buddha's First Sermon at Deer Park near Benares, India, is an important event in the history of Buddhism. Like Jesus' Sermon on the Mount, recorded in Matthew's Gospel, the Buddha's First Sermon spells out his basic teachings clearly, concisely, and even dramatically. So rich are sermons such as these that a person could study them over and over and barely scratch the surface of their meaning. In this activity the students get an overview of the Buddha's teaching by reviewing his sermon.

Handout 4–A

1. Distribute handout 4–A, "The First Sermon at Deer Park," and introduce it using comments such as these:
   - The handout contains a rendering of the Buddha's sermon as translated and imagined by Thich Nhat Hanh, a Buddhist monk who has been an influential teacher around the world since he was exiled from his native Vietnam during the Vietnam War.
   - Much of the sermon's content will be covered in detail later in this chapter of the student textbook.
   - Nhat Hanh translates some terms a bit differently than the student text does. For example, he calls the last step of the Noble Eightfold Path right concentration, whereas the student text terms it right meditation. Such variations are common in the study of religions. Be attentive to the differences and ask questions for clarification.

2. Direct the students to read the handout as a homework assignment (or you may read it aloud in class). Use comments such as these to encourage the young people to put themselves in the context of the sermon:
   - Imagine that you are a seeker of truth, like the Buddha's actual listeners. You have spent years on the path of enlightenment, have listened to the wisdom of many saintly teachers, and have practiced meditation, fasting, and other disciplines. In the Buddha's sermon, you hear a teaching that is leaps and bounds ahead of all the other teachings you have encountered.
   - In the sermon the Buddha refers to the five aggregates. These are bodily form, feeling, perception, emotional reactions, and consciousness. To cling to the five aggregates means to identify these elements of personality as one's real "self."

3. After the students have read the handout, engage them in discussion using these or similar questions:
   - The Buddha tells his friends to "listen serenely with all your awareness." Have you ever listened to someone speaking, or to music, or to sounds of nature with all your awareness? If so, describe the experience. [You may wish to lead the class in a meditation exercise. There are instructions for this in the next activity, "Sitting."]
   - Why would Kondanna consider it an act of compassion for the Buddha to teach his listeners? What other ways do teachers show compassion toward their students?
   - The Buddha teaches that plunging into sensual pleasures, on the one hand, and depriving the body through austerities, on the other hand, both lead to failure. Describe what you think living according to the Buddha's Middle Way would be like.

- What does it mean to you when the Buddha speaks of "living in awareness"?
- We will learn more about the Four Noble Truths later in this chapter. For now what are your impressions of the Buddha's view of the human condition: that to live is to suffer, that the cause of suffering is desire, that suffering can be stopped, and that the way to stop it is to follow the Noble Eightfold Path?
- When the Buddha said, "Kondanna! You've got it! You've got it!" how did you react? What does the Buddha's outburst say to you about his character?
- Describe an experience in which you felt you had suddenly awakened to new knowledge or feelings or experience.

Allow the discussion to continue as long as it seems fruitful. The point is not to argue the finer points of the Buddha's teaching, but to enter into the experience of hearing such a teaching for the first time. Direct the students to keep the handout for reference later in the study of Buddhism. You may wish to repeat this activity toward the end of the second major concept of the chapter, "The Dharma." At that point the students will have read more about the Buddha's specific teachings, and the discussion may be more specific and critical.

Sitting

The two meditation exercises in this activity come from the writings of Thich Nhat Hanh. Either one can be used in conjunction with the preceding activity, "The Buddha's First Sermon," or can stand alone.

Each of the following exercises can be adapted for your needs. It can be done once, or it can become a regular exercise every time or every other time that your class meets. The students will benefit more from meditation if they do it regularly. Encourage them to meditate on their own as well.

Thich Nhat Hanh's *The Miracle of Mindfulness: An Introduction to the Practice of Meditation,* translated by Mobi Ho (Boston: Beacon Press, 1987), offers many suggestions for daily activities to bring mindfulness into our lives. This small, highly readable book may be a good one to assign the class. You will find more suggestions for the use of meditation on page 18 in the introduction of this teaching manual.

Note: This exercise is similar to the chapter 3 activity "*Jnana Marga* and Meditation," on pages 56–57 of this manual.

4

Meditation exercise 1. Here is a simple exercise that may be used to introduce the practice of meditation.

Settle your students for meditation. They may sit in a full- or half-lotus position, or in a chair with both feet flat on the floor, spine straight, and hands resting in lap. In a calm voice, read the following excerpt from *The Miracle of Mindfulness* (p. 83):

- **"Following the Breath**

  "Begin to inhale gently and normally (from the stomach), mindful that 'I am inhaling normally.' Exhale in mindfulness, 'I am exhaling normally.' Continue for three breaths. On the fourth breath, extend the inhalation, mindful that 'I am breathing in a long inhalation.' Exhale in mindfulness, 'I am breathing out a long exhalation.' Continue for three breaths.

"Now follow your breath carefully, aware of every movement of your stomach and lungs. Follow the entrance and exit of air. Be mindful that 'I am inhaling and following the inhalation from its beginning to its end. I am exhaling and following the exhalation from its beginning to its end.'

"Continue for 20 breaths. Return to normal [breathing]."

Allow the students to sit quietly for 5 minutes, and then repeat the exercise.

When it is time for the meditation to end, direct the students to stretch and to gently massage the muscles in their hands and then in their legs or lower backs. Invite the students to share their reactions to the meditation.

Meditation exercise 2. Here is a slightly more advanced mindfulness exercise.

Settle your students for meditation. Point out that the directions for this exercise say to half-smile. Explain that Nhat Hanh describes a half smile as "a smile which affirms that you are in complete mindfulness, a smile that nourishes that perfect mindfulness" (*The Miracle of Mindfulness,* p. 28). Then, in a calm voice, read the following excerpt from *The Miracle of Mindfulness* (p. 84):

- **"Breathing to Quiet the Mind and Body to Realize Joy**

  "Sit in the full or half lotus. Half-smile. Follow your breath. When your mind and body are quiet, continue to inhale and exhale very lightly, mindful that, 'I am breathing in and making the breath-body light and peaceful. I am exhaling and making the breath-body light and peaceful.' Continue for three breaths, giving rise to the thought in mindfulness, 'I am breathing in and making my entire body light and peaceful and joyous.' Continue for three breaths and in mindfulness give rise to the thought, 'I am breathing in while my body and mind are peace and joy. I am breathing out while my body and mind are peace and joy.'

  "Maintain this thought in mindfulness from 5 to 30 minutes. . . . The beginning and end of the practice should be relaxed and gentle. When you want to stop, gently massage [the muscles in your hands] and then massage the muscles in your legs before returning to a normal sitting position. Wait a moment before standing up."

Images of the Buddha

Direct the students to bring in as many images of the Buddha as possible. Such images can be found in books on art, religion, and history, as well as on the Internet. Along with locating images, the students should also research and report on the various ways that images of the Buddha are used in Buddhism.

You may wish to assign this project early in the class's exploration of this chapter on Buddhism, and invite the students to present their findings during their study of the last major concept of the chapter, "Three Rafts for Crossing the River." Images of the Buddha have various degrees of importance within the three rafts, or divisions, of Buddhism—Theravada, Mahayana, and Vajrayana. They are sometimes used, for example, as objects of devotion and as focal points for meditation.

Some possible research topics are ancient Gandhara art, Southeast Asian Buddhas, Chinese Buddhas, Tibetan Buddhas, Japanese Buddhas, the giant Buddha statues of Sri Lanka, and the Taliban's destruction of Buddhist art in Afghanistan after the army assumed control of the country in 1996. You might assign these topics to individuals, pairs, or small groups. If the technology is available, the students can create electronic presentations. When you evaluate the projects, consider the quality and appropriateness of the images, as well as the depth and usefulness of the information.

Pages 75–84

Concept B: The Dharma

Review Questions: The Dharma

Question 7. What features of Buddhist cosmology are shared with Hinduism?
Answer. Both Hindus and Buddhists believe that the universe is eternal, that many worlds exist, and that the ongoing cycle of rebirth can be escaped only through liberation.

Question 8. Describe the Buddha's reaction against early Hinduism.
Answer. He dismissed philosophical speculation on the nature of the world, the self, and the divine. He reacted against institutional Hinduism and the caste system, and he made Buddhist teachings available to all.

Question 9. Identify the Three Marks of Existence. How are they interrelated?
Answer. Anatta (no-self), *anicca* (impermanence), and *dukkha* (suffering). All three are based in the changing nature of reality, and *dukkha* is the natural result of *anatta* and *anicca.*

Question 10. What is the doctrine of *anatta?* How does it relate to the Hindu concept Atman?
Answer. Anatta means "no-self"—there is no ultimate reality within. *Annata* contradicts the Hindu concept of Atman, which holds that an essence underlies existence.

Question 11. According to the Buddhist doctrine of *samsara,* what is actually reborn? Explain the role of *karma* in the Buddhist understanding of *samsara.*
Answer. A bundle of energy, patterned according to one's *karma,* is reborn. The nature of one's rebirth depends on the status of one's *karma.*

Question 12. List the Five Precepts, which apply to all Buddhists. Then list the five additional precepts that apply to monks and nuns.
Answer. The Five Precepts, for all Buddhists: (1) Do not take life; (2) do not take what is not given; (3) do not engage in sensuous misconduct; (4) do not use false speech; (5) do not drink intoxicants.
Additional precepts for monks and nuns: (6) Do not eat after noon; (7) do not watch dancing or shows; (8) do not use garlands, perfumes, or ornaments; (9) do not use a high or soft bed; (10) do not accept gold or silver.

Question 13. What are some possible English translations of the term *dukkha?* Explain its meaning in your own words.
Answer. "Suffering," "frustration," "dislocation,"or "discomfort." *Dukkha* implies that things are not as they should be, that they are in need of repair.

Question 14. What is *tanha?* How does it relate to *dukkha?*
Answer. *Tanha* is desire, thirst, or craving. It is the cause of *dukkha.*

Question 15. List the steps of the Eightfold Path.
Answer. (1) Right views, (2) right intentions, (3) right speech, (4) right conduct, (5) right livelihood, (6) right effort, (7) right mindfulness, and (8) right meditation.

Question 16. What is the difference between the Buddha and other humans who attain enlightenment?
Answer. The Buddha did not require a model to provide teachings to lead him to enlightenment, as others do.

Question 17. Define and briefly describe the character of an *arhat.*
Answer. An *arhat* is enlightened, free from *dukkha,* and thus no longer attached to affairs of the world. *Arhats* are especially characterized by compassion.

Question 18. What is the literal meaning of the word *nirvana?* How does this help explain the concept *nirvana?*
Answer. "Blowing out." The meaning implies that all selfish desire has been extinguished, like a flame, leading to freedom from *samsara.*

Text Activities: The Dharma

Activity H

"The essence of Buddhism is, there is no essence." Discuss the meaning of that saying.

Activity I

As you observe the natural world, do you tend to perceive things as permanent or impermanent? Could the things that you perceive as permanent really be impermanent? Give some specific examples.

Activity J

The analogy of the flame being passed from one candle to another is the most famous one used to describe Buddhist rebirth. Invent a second analogy to help explain this doctrine.

Activity K

Some systems of morality, such as the Buddhist one, emphasize the intention of an action; other systems emphasize the outcome of an action. Which do you think has greater moral significance: intention or outcome? Explain your answer.

Activity L

Reflect on the Buddha's teaching to the woman whose grandson had just died. How do you feel about this teaching? How does it compare with your perspective on family ties?

Activity M

Have you ever performed a truly selfless act? Is such an act, completely free from any selfish motivation, even possible? (According to Buddhism it would be possible only after the actor attained enlightenment.) Explain.

Activity N

Make a short list of "truths" that summarize the human condition. For each truth describe why you included it.

Activity O

The final three steps of the Eightfold Path tend to be specifically Buddhist, whereas the first five are similar to teachings of other religions. What aspects of these first five steps strike you as being familiar? What aspects are strange to you, and how do you think they relate to Buddhist teachings in general?

Activity P

Contemplate the story of Prince Mahasattva and the tigress. What does it tell you about the nature of Buddhist compassion?

Additional Activities: The Dharma

No-Self

Direct the students each to bring in three photos: one of themselves as a baby or young child, one of themselves as a grade-school student, and one of themselves taken recently. Instruct the young people to place the photos in front of themselves and to write a page-long description of the changes in their outer appearance through the years. Then have them write a paragraph speculating about their appearance twenty years from now. Next, tell them to call to mind something that is important to them today—a style of music, a food, a person, faith—and describe in writing its importance to them now and at the times represented by the earlier photos, as well as what they believe its importance will be twenty years from now.

Conclude by inviting discussion and comments about the Buddha's teaching of *anatta,* or no-self. Ask if the writing exercise has strengthened the students' grasp of the Buddha's assertion that much of what we consider our self is changing and impermanent and is, in fact, no-self.

Impermanence

Help the students understand the Buddhist concept of *anicca,* impermanence, by using one of the following exercises. The students may wish to invent additional exercises on their own.

Writing. Tell the students to write a paragraph describing the place where they are sitting right now. Then direct them to imagine what this place might have looked like one hundred years ago and to write a paragraph describing it then. Then have them imagine the same place two thousand years ago and write a paragraph about it. Next, tell them to imagine this place one hundred years from now and two thousand years from now, and to write a paragraph about it at each of those times. Finally, instruct them to write a paragraph explaining their agreement or disagreement with this statement: This place is characterized by impermanence.

Sand painting. Provide sand of various colors and suggest that the students make sand paintings. These artworks can be created indoors on pieces of cardboard, to be taken outside later, or they can be created outdoors on a paved area. Explain that the paintings may be abstract or representational, and they are to be done with great care by dropping sand in different patterns onto the cardboard or pavement (no glue is to be used).

When everyone is finished, if the paintings have been made inside, direct the students to take them outside. If the wind is blowing, the paintings will naturally break up and begin to disappear. If the air is calm, direct the students to blow the sand away. They may protest, but insist that they follow directions. When the paintings are gone, follow up with a discussion comparing the impermanence of the sand paintings with the impermanence of, for instance, the school building, a mountain, or the ocean.

Demonstration. This suggestion incorporates the concepts of *dukkha* and *samsara.*

Give the students each a clear glass of warm water. Direct them to put a drop of food coloring in the glass and to describe what happens to the food coloring. They should note that it moves around, it disperses, and the intensity of its color changes constantly. Inside the glass, nothing is the same from one moment to the next. Explain that this is *anicca,* or impermanence.

Observe aloud that the water in one student's glass is a particularly beautiful color. Ask the other students how they might get their water to be that color. Then observe that another student's glass has a beautiful color pattern forming in it. The pattern in the water will immediately change; when it does, ask, "How can I get that pattern back?" Point out that the desire for the water to retain a particular color pattern and the disappointment of realizing that it physically cannot, are very much like the desire to hang on to certain life experiences and the disappointment that accompanies life's inevitable changes. Encourage the students to describe experiences of desire and disappointment from their lives. Explain that what they have been talking about is *dukkha,* or suffering.

Finally, have the students pour all the glasses of colored water into a large clear bowl, and ask, "Can you dip your glass in the bowl now and retrieve the same water that you poured in?" Explain that this part of the exercise has provided an analogy for *samsara,* the cycle of death and rebirth.

Jataka Tales: Background

The story of the hungry tigress, presented on page 84 of the student text, is an example of a Buddhist jataka tale. Jataka tales describe the earlier lifetimes of the Buddha, showing his long process of evolution toward his awakening.

The following essay provides background on the jataka story form, along with some insights into the theme of the hungry tigress story. The source of this material is the book *The Hungry Tigress: Buddhist Myths, Legends, and Jataka Tales,* by Rafe Martin, a storyteller, writer, and student of Buddhism. You may want to share this information with the students in a class discussion provoked by the jataka tale in the student text. It will also provide helpful background for the activity "Jataka Tales: Reading, Discussion, and Creative Work," which follows this background essay.

It is believed that jataka tales were first told by the Buddha himself. They continue to play an important role in the transmission of his teachings and "living example."

> Buddhists accept jataka tales as stories of the Buddha's own earlier births as he evolved, over the course of endless world cycles and countless lifetimes, towards full Enlightenment and Buddhahood. As such, they form the backbone of the literary and artistic traditions of Buddhist Asia. "[The Buddha's] words," writes Lama Govinda, "according to changing times may be interpreted in a variety of ways; his living example, however, speaks an eternal language, which will be understood at all times, as long as there are human beings." As the fundamental expression of that "living example," the jatakas empower and dramatize some of the deepest values and beliefs of the culture. (A compassionate reverence for all life as well as faith in the dynamic workings of cause and effect, or karma, are two such implicit values and beliefs that extend through the jataka tradition). (P. xv)

The main thrust of the jataka tales is to describe the character of the Buddha and the nature of enlightenment. The tales demonstrate that in all the Buddha's previous lives, whether he was "born as human or animal, spirit or god, he strove for perfection of character and deeper wisdom" (p. xvi). At the same time, the jatakas emphasize "that while the actual historical figure [known as the Buddha] was a person of extraordinary character and depth, he was a man, not a god" (p. xvi). He was not seen as better than others or as a perfect person. Like any human he had to work hard toward his chosen goal of enlightenment.

The jatakas also tell us much about the character of the enlightened person. They are "tales of compassion and of heroic self-sacrifice," and through them "the theme of Buddhism as a path of compassion emerges clearly" (p. xviii).

The jataka tales have long served as an effective means of teaching challenging Buddhist truths. Rafe Martin points out that the literary form of the jatakas is a key reason for their efficacy and longevity:

> If we approach the jataka tradition with an open mind and really look at it ideally and as a whole, we see that the jatakas explore the ultimate meanings of life and death. They reveal life's often hidden, deeply spiritual purposes. They present a vision of the unity of all life. They also raise the animal fable to unexpected spiritual heights. And they give expression to a powerful impulse towards compassion. Whether they were first told by the Buddha or whether they came into being later through the efforts of unknown sages, teachers, and wandering storytellers, the best of these tales ring true, opening the imagination to a coherent world teeming with life and energy, meaning and wonder. (P. xx)

The entertainment value of the jataka tales is also noteworthy:

> Jataka stories have traditionally been seen as entertainments of the highest order, bringing delight to listeners and imparting wisdom. They explore a wide range of Buddhist teachings and make them dramatic and particular. They do what all narrative art does—make their subjects *live.*

> Themes that might have remained abstract or philosophical become intimate, are clothed in flesh and blood, fur and feather. What might have been distant and conceptual now pulses with life, emotion, and personality. Scholar Giuseppi Tucci, travelling in Tibet prior to the Chinese invasion, relates how the roughest sort of men, the muleteers and horse traders of his caravan, would listen as jatakas were told around the campfires at night and weep unrestrainedly, like babies. (P. xxi)

The overall value of these traditional stories is to dramatize "deep ecology, which . . . gives equal weight to the needs of the nonhuman" (p. xxiv). Although the jataka tales are among humanity's oldest creations, "their perennial significance is renewed by contemporary need, and so they *become* current" (p. xxiv).

Referring specifically to the story of the hungry tigress, Martin says, it "is perhaps *the* classic jataka" (p. 224). Martin also offers the following insights on the story's theme of compassion, from a contemporary point of view, and the ability of the jataka form to effectively communicate the theme:

> In [this jataka], compassionate self-sacrifice for the sake of another being—not simply another human being—and the universality of suffering are vigorously upheld.
>
> This is, in part, what makes the jataka tradition so interesting, even unique. The tales dramatize Equality and give life to an awareness of the ultimate worth of each living thing—even of something which may directly threaten our own self-interest and safety. ("Tyger Tyger burning bright," chanted Blake—"Did he who make the Lamb make thee?") In this fundamental realm, not only does each thing have its necessary and meaningful place in the Whole, each thing *is* the Whole, the center of the Universe itself. How have, how do, and how shall we humans live with this? As natural habitats disappear and tiger (and other animal) populations are threatened, we can only find ourselves considering once again the deep message of this ancient tale.
>
> Which is *not* to recommend that we should literally offer our bodies to tigers! As this, and all jatakas, are literary forms, we can see in this story of the prince and the starving tigress an artistic effort to express, through story patterning, a universal language. Through that language of image and action, the heart's desire is given shape. Our deepest aspirations, normally impossible to reveal except perhaps in times of great emotion or of great focused purpose, are called forth.
>
> So, what does the mind of a bodhisattva look like? What does pure compassion look like? Feel like? What is a love that is not stained by likes and dislikes, appearances, desires, or self-interest? How deep does our kindness, our sense of kindred go? By its very extremity, this jataka throws its light here. (P. 224)

Jataka Tales: Reading, Discussion, and Creative Work

Handout 4–B

1. Distribute handout 4–B, "The Lion, the Elephant, and the Merchants' Cries." Explain that it presents a story from the same genre as that of the hungry tigress in the student text. Give the students time to read the handout (and to reread "The Hungry Tigress," if you wish). Then discuss questions like the ones that follow. Use the background material on pages 78–80 of this manual as needed to help the students understand the jataka form.

- What do the stories of Buddha's previous lifetimes suggest about his character?
- What is the theme of the stories?
- Were the stories meant to be understood as literally true? Why or why not?
- Are the stories dramatic? Why or why not?
- Does the drama of the stories affect you as a reader or listener? If so, describe the effect.

2. Direct the students to write jataka tales. They may work as individuals or in groups of two to four. Their tales should express the same elements found in the jatakas they have read: dramatic impact, as well as information about the character of the Buddha and about the compassionate nature of enlightenment. Ideally the students should have a few days to complete this task.

Encourage the students to present their jatakas in a variety of forms, such as skits, one-person theatrical performances, and straightforward readings. Require that a written version of each tale be handed in as well.

Follow each presentation with a brief discussion of how well the tale demonstrated the jataka genre. To keep the discussion from becoming a contest, try to ensure that each tale is discussed on its own terms and is not compared with the others.

Is Buddhism Atheistic?

The students are likely to raise questions regarding the absence of God from the Buddhist tradition. This is an important topic for discussion.

1. Background. Present the following background material, drawn from *Buddhism Made Plain,* by Antony Fernando, to help the students appreciate some of the affinities between the Buddhist "neglect" of God and the Judeo-Christian understanding of God.

Buddhism is often described as an atheistic religion. In studying Buddhism it becomes clear that "God is not part of Gautama's picture of human liberation" (p. 104). The Buddha believed that worshiping God, or even having a concept of God, is not necessary to achieve liberation. This idea made Buddhism radically different from the other religions of Gautama's day. However, as Fernando points out, "although the concept of God was excluded from his path to liberation, Gautama never argued against it" (p. 104).

Assuming then that Gautama was not antitheistic, Fernando wonders why Gautama would have gone so against the grain of the religious understanding of his time: in Hinduism God and gods play a large role. The answer lies in the religious practices of Gautama's contemporaries: "The worship of God had by that time so greatly deteriorated that it distorted what Gautama considered to be the basic element in any religion—namely, liberation" (pp. 104–105). Traditional Hinduism was demanding total acceptance of the infallibility of the Vedas. Ritual and ceremony had more and more importance, and correct practice of rituals was overemphasized. The result was a great deal of fighting among various teachers and schools of thought within the tradition. Gautama considered Hinduism empty and hollow. "According to Gautama, exponents of diverse forms of the worship of God tragically failed to focus attention on the liberation most urgently needed by humankind" (p. 105).

> Gautama's stand in regard to God is very clear in a discussion that took place between Gautama and a monk named Malunkyaputta. The monk asks Gautama why he did not care to give a specific reply to questions such as: Is the world eternal, or is it not? Is it finite, or is it not? Is life in the body, or in the soul? Do beings continue after death, or do they not?
>
> Gautama explained that if he did not speak of them, it was because they did not come within the ambit of his primary preoccupation. His concern was limited to a more urgent need for humanity. To explain his position he told a very forceful story. Imagine that a man is going through a jungle. Halfway through he is shot by a poisoned arrow. If the poisoned arrow remains in his body, he will die. The injured person says: "I will not pull out this arrow until I know who shot it, whether he is tall or short, fat or lean, young or old, of a high caste or a low caste." I tell you, Malunkyaputta, says Gautama, that man will die before he knows the right answers. (P. 105)

According to Fernando, Gautama's perspective on the existence of God does not justify referring to him as an atheist or an agnostic. Gautama was not indifferent to God, nor did he reject God outright. His concern was "not about whether God exists or not, but whether belief in God has any relevance to the immediate problems of humanity" (p. 105).

> There is thus a conspicuous difference between Gautama's objections to belief in God and those of the traditional atheist and agnostic. His argument against God is not leveled against religion. On the contrary, it is in the very name of religion, and as an attempt to save religion, that he omits the concept of God. Differently expressed, Gautama tells the believer in God: let us avoid the confusing and controversial concept of God, of divinity, and let us immediately work toward the divinization of humanity. (P. 106)

In his discussion Fernando reveals some important points of contact between the presence of God in the Judeo-Christian tradition and the lack of God in the Buddhist tradition. For the Hebrew prophets and Jesus, belief in God "was not a matter of rite and ritual or of external formal worship, but a way of righteous living" (p. 107). When speaking about God, Jesus and the prophets did not focus on trying to describe God's nature; rather, "they spoke of the *qualities of the true believer*" (p. 107). Passages such as Isa. 1:11–17 and Amos 6:21–24, as well as stories like that of the good Samaritan, provide helpful examples of the emphasis Jesus and the prophets placed on those qualities.

To take this a step further, we need to recognize that Jesus and the prophets were not "concerned about promoting a *conceptual knowledge* of God, or of creating in the minds of people a clear mental picture of God's appearance. What they promoted exclusively was a *behavioral acknowledgment of God*" (p. 108). True worship of God is evidenced not in worshipers' adherence to the rules of formal ritual and ceremonies, but in "the characteristics of their day-to-day behavior. The most central of course is loving care—concern—for those in need" (p. 108).

Fernando concludes his analysis by briefly comparing the outlook of Judeo-Christianity to that of Buddhism. He finds a "common bond" between Gautama and Jesus and the Hebrew prophets, a bond that is seen "in the stand each of them took against the theism of their day" (p. 109):

> Unanimously, they condemned the false theism that prevailed in the societies to which they belonged. The prophets, Yeshua [i.e., Jesus], and his fellow Jews, of course, did not go so far as Gautama in completely rejecting the idea of God, but all were at one in their conviction that there is

an utterly meaningless form of theism that is destructive to the personality. They were at one in affirming that the best and the most needed form of the worship of God is that expressed by sublimity of character or a life of goodness. (P. 109)

2. Discussion. With the background material in mind, generate a discussion with the students based on questions such as these:

- Can a person be religious if she or he does not believe in God? Why or why not?
- What do you think is more important: a person's outward behavior or inner beliefs? Explain.
- How would you describe God?
- Does God influence the way you act in daily life?
- From what you have studied so far, would you characterize Buddhism with terms such as *godless, atheistic,* and *agnostic?* Define those terms in your answer.

Pages 84–88

Concept C: Three Rafts for Crossing the River

Review Questions: Three Rafts for Crossing the River

Question 19. What are the three divisions of Buddhism?
Answer. Theravada, Mahayana, and Vajrayana.

Question 20. What is the main focus of Theravada Buddhism?
Answer. Meditation.

Question 21. What is the literal meaning of the name *Mahayana,* and what are the implications of this meaning?
Answer. The Great Vehicle. This meaning implies that Mahayana is superior and that it is Buddhism for the masses.

Question 22. How does Vajrayana Buddhism "fight fire with fire"?
Answer. It harnesses the energy of desire and turns it against itself.

Question 23. Who is the Dalai Lama? How is each Dalai Lama chosen?
Answer. He is the head of the hierarchy of Vajrayana clergy. Dalai Lamas are chosen through a line of descent based not on natural birth but on rebirth.

Question 24. What are the primary geographical regions of the three divisions of Buddhism?
Answer. Theravada: Cambodia, Myanmar (formerly Burma), Sri Lanka, and Thailand. Mahayana: China, Japan, and Korea. Vajrayana: Tibet, which is now claimed as a part of the People's Republic of China.

Additional Activity: Three Rafts for Crossing the River

Experiencing Sangha

This activity requires a good deal of preparation of the classroom; in fact it might work well in a different room altogether. The activity takes its name from *Sangha,* the Buddhist word for "community." In this case the term *Sangha* is used to designate a place in which the students can experience different aspects of Buddhist practice. The students are directed to rotate through various learning stations in small groups. Each station is self-contained and does not require any verbal instructions. The students go through the stations in silence, remaining at each one for 5 minutes.

Preparation. Decide which of the following stations you will include, depending on the number of students in your class and the resources available. If you have a large class, consider using more stations, which will allow for smaller groups. For each station you will need a presentation board, the designated handout, and the items listed (note that the Right Speech station does not require any objects). For help finding images, see the World Religions course page on the Internet, which can be accessed from the Saint Mary's Press home page, *www.smp.org.*

Handouts 4–C to 4–H

1. *Right Meditation.* Handout 4–C, and a statue or picture of the Buddha
2. *Right Speech.* Handout 4–D
3. *The Fasting Siddhartha.* Handout 4–E, and a replica or picture of the fasting Siddhartha, a famous Gandhara statue
4. *Objects Used in Tibetan Rituals.* Handout 4–F, and the following objects (These items may be found at Tibetan art and craft stores. If there is no such a store in your area, you may be able to order some of the objects over the Internet. Photos can work for these, but the actual objects are preferable so that the students can pick them up and try them.)
   - A singing bowl and striker (The metal bowl is used to produce sound, not for eating.)
   - *Mala* beads or rosary (The students may be surprised to find something similar to a Catholic rosary in another tradition.)
   - A prayer wheel (This is an example of how Buddhists employ motion in their meditation practice.)
   - A *vajra* (Sometimes called a *dorje,* this is a diamond thunderbolt used to destroy mandalas after they have been completed; it symbolically "cuts through" ignorance and attachments.)
5. *Monks.* Handout 4–G, and a picture of a Thai monk begging for food (In Thai society young monks beg daily for food, and laypeople commonly donate bags of food to monks.)
6. *Kuan-Yin.* Handout 4–H, and a statue or picture of the deity Kuan-yin (This figure from pre-Buddhist Chinese religion is regarded as a *bodhisattva* in Mahayana Buddhism.)

For each station, attach the corresponding handout to a presentation board. Then assemble the stations as far apart as possible, placing their instruction boards and items in such a way that the contents and activities of each station are concealed from the other stations as much as possible.

Procedure

1. Divide the class into as many groups as there are stations, and instruct the students to stay with you until they have heard all your directions. You might find it helpful to quiet the young people with a short meditative breathing exercise. Then tell each group where it will begin, and give the following instructions, using your own words:
   - For this activity, you will imagine that you are part of a Buddhist monastic community. The monks who live in this Sangha expect you to maintain monastic silence while you participate in a series of learning activities.
   - You will be traveling to various learning stations and following the directions you find there. You will need to carry paper and a pen or pencil, as you will be directed to write at the stations.
   - There is to be no talking or noise at the stations. Each station provides all the instructions that are necessary, so you should not need to ask anyone for help. If you have questions about the material that is presented, jot them down and we will address them after everyone has visited all the stations.
   - I will be the timekeeper and will use a bell [or a timer] to signal the end of your stay at each station. When you hear the bell, your group is to rotate to the next station [indicate in which direction the groups should move], maintaining complete silence.

   Make sure the students understand the instructions before proceeding.

2. Ring the bell to signal the start of the activity. Ring it again at 5-minute intervals until all the groups have visited all the stations.

3. Gather the students and ask for their impressions, using any questions they wrote during the exercise, as well as questions like these:
   - What did you learn?
   - How did it feel to be working and thinking in silence?
   - Which station was the most striking for you? Why?
   - Which station was the most difficult? Why?

Additional Resources from Saint Mary's Press

See *Primary Source Readings in World Religions* (Saint Mary's Press, 2009) for selections from *The Dhammapada* and an excerpt from *Freedom in Exile: The Autobiography of the Dalai Lama,* as well as the accompanying leader's guide for suggestions about how to use these readings in your study of Buddhism.

Teaching About Other Religions (Saint Mary's Press, 2006) offers guidelines and suggestions for creating a respectful and intellectually stimulating environment when studying world religions in the classroom. For ideas and strategies on teaching Buddhism, see chapter 5.

The First Sermon at Deer Park

The Buddha said, "Then please listen, my friends. I have found the Great Way, and I will show it to you. You will be the first to hear my Teaching. This Dharma is not the result of thinking. It is the fruit of direct experience. Listen serenely with all your awareness."

The Buddha's voice was filled with such spiritual authority that his five friends joined their palms and looked up at him. Kondanna spoke for them all, "Please, friend Gautama, show us compassion and teach us the Way."

The Buddha began serenely, "My brothers, there are two extremes that a person on the path should avoid. One is to plunge oneself into sensual pleasures, and the other is to practice austerities which deprive the body of its needs. Both of these extremes lead to failure. The path I have discovered is the Middle Way, which avoids both extremes and has the capacity to lead one to understanding, liberation, and peace. It is the Noble Eightfold Path of right understanding, right thought, right speech, right action, right livelihood, right effort, right mindfulness, and right concentration. I have followed this Noble Eightfold Path and have realized understanding, liberation, and peace.

"Brothers, why do I call this path the Right Path? I call it the Right Path because it does not avoid or deny suffering, but allows for a direct confrontation with suffering as the means to overcome it. The Noble Eightfold Path is the path of living in awareness. Mindfulness is the foundation. By practicing mindfulness, you can develop concentration which enables you to attain Understanding. Thanks to right concentration, you realize right awareness, thoughts, speech, action, livelihood, and effort. The Understanding which develops can liberate you from every shackle of suffering and give birth to true peace and joy.

"Brothers, there are four truths: the existence of suffering, the cause of suffering, the cessation of suffering, and the path which leads to the cessation of suffering. I call these the Four Noble Truths. The first is the existence of suffering. Birth, old age, sickness, and death are suffering. Sadness, anger, jealousy, worry, anxiety, fear, and despair are suffering. Separation from loved ones is suffering. Association with those you hate is suffering. Desire, attachment, and clinging to the five aggregates are suffering.

"Brothers, the second truth is the cause of suffering. Because of ignorance, people cannot see the truth about life, and they become caught in the flames of desire, anger, jealousy, grief, worry, fear, and despair.

"Brothers, the third truth is the cessation of suffering. Understanding the truth of life brings about the cessation of every grief and sorrow and gives rise to peace and joy.

"Brothers, the fourth truth is the path which leads to the cessation of suffering. It is the Noble Eightfold Path, which I have just explained. The Noble Eightfold Path is nourished by living mindfully. Mindfulness leads to concentration and understanding which liberates you from every pain and sorrow and leads to peace and joy. I will guide you along this path of realization."

While Siddhartha was explaining the Four Noble Truths, Kondanna suddenly felt a great light shining within his own heart. He could taste the liberation he had sought for so long. His face beamed with joy. The Buddha pointed at him and cried, "Kondanna! You've got it! You've got it!"

Kondanna joined his palms and bowed before the Buddha. With deepest respect, he spoke, "Venerable Gautama, please accept me as your disciple. I know that under your guidance, I will attain the Great Awakening."

The other four monks also bowed at the Buddha's feet, joined their palms, and asked to be received as disciples. The Buddha motioned his friends to rise. After they took their places again, he said, "Brothers! The children of Uruvela village gave me the name 'the Buddha.' You, too, may call me by that name if you like."

Kondanna asked, "Doesn't 'Buddha' mean 'one who is awakened'?"

"That is correct. And they call the path I have discovered 'the Way of Awakening.' What do you think of this name?"

"'One who is awakened'! 'The Way of Awakening'! Wonderful! Wonderful! These names are true, yet simple. We will happily call you the Buddha and the path you have discovered the Way of Awakening. As you just said, living each day mindfully is the very basis of spiritual practice." The five monks were of one mind to accept Gautama as their teacher and to call him the Buddha.

The Buddha smiled at them. "Please, brothers, practice with an open and intelligent spirit, and in three months you will have attained the fruit of liberation." (Thich Nhat Hanh, *Old Path White Clouds: Walking in the Footsteps of the Buddha* [Berkeley, CA: Parallax Press, 1991], pages 146–148.

The Lion, the Elephant, and the Merchants' Cries

Once, the Buddha was born as a fearless lion. Together with his friend, a great bull elephant, he often adventured, exploring the caves, forests, mountains, and seacoasts of his island home.

One day the lion and the elephant were walking at the jungle's edge, not far from the sea. The lion lifted his heavy, golden-maned head and sniffed the salty air. Gulls cried. Waves broke and foamed against the shore just beyond the screen of trees. Suddenly, above the crashing of the waves and the shrieking of the gulls, they heard the sounds of many voices screaming in terror.

The lion gave a great roar and leapt out of the jungle onto the sandy beach. The elephant, too, maddened by those cries, burst through the bushes and trees to follow his friend.

There on the shore, they found a group of shipwrecked merchants running for their lives. A huge and monstrous serpent, its long body still sliding from the sea, swayed over them. Its fangs dripped venom. Its shining scales and cold green eyes glittered like ice.

The lion leaped up on the elephant's domed head. Lashing his tail in fury, he roared a challenge. The elephant, trumpeting shrilly, pointed his tusks towards the great snake and charged, carrying them into battle.

The serpent's head rose up into the air, higher and higher. With a long, murderous hisssssssss it released the merchants, who ran at once for the shelter of the trees. Drawing itself, coil upon armored coil, up out of the foaming sea, the great serpent slid angrily along the beach towards its oncoming foes.

The battle was terrible. The lion's roaring, the elephant's trumpeting, and the serpent's hissing were so loud that they drowned out the crashing of the waves. The merchants, now hidden in the jungle, threw themselves to the ground and covered their ears with their hands. Clouds of blinding sand whirled up, darkening the sun. To the terrified merchants it seemed as if the world were coming to an end.

At last the sounds of the battle died down. Once again the murmuring of the ocean could be heard, and the screeching of the gulls. As the air slowly cleared the merchants peered out fearfully from among the trees.

There, belly up, lay the long body of the serpent, bloody now, and crushed. The once hard, bright scales were dull and torn. The cold green eyes were faded and glazed. It was dead. Beside it, too, lay the two fearless friends, the lion and the elephant, alive, but dying. The serpent's venom had done its deadly work.

Later, the merchants built a great funeral pyre on the beach and, with all honors, consigned the bodies of the lion and the elephant to the flames.

And they wondered, "Why did two wild creatures give their lives to save us?" Indeed, they could not have imagined two more unlikely saviors—a mighty lion and a great bull elephant.

Such spontaneous and heroic compassion, the merchants concluded, would remain a mystery. (Rafe Martin, *The Hungry Tigress: Buddhist Myths, Legends, and Jataka Tales,* completely revised and expanded edition [Cambridge, MA: Yellow Moon Press, 1999], pages 113–114. Copyright © 1999 by Rafe Martin. Used with permission of the author.)

Right Meditation

1. Here is a Buddha statue or picture. Sit quietly and stare at it. Meditate on it. Let it be a visual focus for your meditation. Learn from it.

2. Write any impressions, observations, or questions you have.

Right Speech

We do not begin this step by resolving to speak nothing but the truth. Although that is an admirable goal, it is not one that can be achieved immediately.

Part 1

First, we must begin to notice our own speech. Take a moment to think about the following questions and write your answers.

1. How often do I deviate from the truth in large or small ways? Why do I do this?
2. How often do I speak words that are unkind? What are my motives for doing this?

Part 2

Once we have observed ourselves, we can begin to make changes. Take a moment to think of concrete ways to improve your moral use of speech, and write your responses to the following questions.

1. We should seek to speak the truth. Why am I afraid of the truth? What does lying say about who I am?
2. We should seek to speak with kindness. Why am I interested in idle chatter, gossip, slander, or abusive words? What do my attempts to put down others say about how I regard myself?

The Fasting Siddhartha

1. Observe the statue or picture at this station.

2. Notice that it is probably different from almost any other image of the Buddha that you have seen.

3. Look closely and write down what you observe. How does this Buddha image differ from others you have seen?

4. What do you think the artist was trying to express about the Buddha?

5. It is said that while Siddhartha was seeking enlightenment, he practiced extreme asceticism. He used his enormous willpower to try to attain wisdom. "He ate so little that when he thought he would touch the skin of his stomach he actually took hold of his spine" (adapted from Clarence H. Hamilton, *Buddhism: A Religion of Infinite Compassion* [1952; reprint, New York: Liberal Arts Press, 1954], pages 14–15). He learned from this experiment that if you damage the body, your spiritual progress is impeded. He knew that between overindulgence and extreme asceticism lies the Middle Way of reason and simplicity, which is best for the spiritual path.

Objects Used in Tibetan Rituals

1. At this station are several objects. Some may look familiar. Gently pick up each object and examine it. SOME OF THE OBJECTS ARE FRAGILE. PLEASE HANDLE THEM CAREFULLY.

2. Write the following information about each object:

   a. What you notice about it

   b. Any questions you have about it

   c. What purpose you believe it has

Monks

1. Look at the picture at this station.

2. Write words that describe the actions that you see in the picture.

3. Write words that describe the relationships between people that you see in the picture.

4. In Thailand young monks beg by the side of the road and laypeople give them prepared food. All the food is brought back to the community, mixed together, and then eaten. What does this say about how the monks regard food? the experience of taste? communal life?

Kuan-Yin

1. Look at the statue or picture at this station.

2. This image depicts the deity Kuan-yin. Write words that describe this image.

3. Kuan-yin is a *bodhisattva,* and is commonly regarded as the deity of mercy and compassion. Kuan-yin's origins are in Chinese pre-Buddhist polytheism. Buddhism does not make a statement about the existence of God or gods. Why might Buddhists want to keep the image of this deity in their practice of religion?

4. Does this image symbolize some of the ideals of your religion? If so, how?

CHAPTER 5

Jainism

Major Concepts

A. **Makers of the River Crossing.** *Ahimsa,* the principle of nonviolence, and asceticism are the defining characteristics of Jainism. The name *Jainism* is derived from *jina,* which means "conqueror." The spiritual conquerors who have attained salvation are called *tirthankaras,* or "makers of the river crossing," referring to the crossing of a river as a symbol of the spiritual quest. The most important *tirthankara* is Mahavira, a contemporary of Gautama the Buddha. Gautama and Mahavira had some common characteristics, as well as two striking differences: first, Gautama embraced the Middle Way, whereas Mahavira held fast to the most extreme asceticism; second, Gautama learned the spiritual path on his own, whereas Mahavira learned it from others. Jain enlightenment, or *kevala,* is omniscience. Having attained *kevala,* one is free from the negative effects of *karma* and is thus released from *samsara.*

B. **Knowing the Universe.** Gautama spoke little about cosmology, but Mahavira described the universe in abundant detail. According to Mahavira the universe is a vast but finite space called the *loka.* Humans dwell in several worlds within the *loka's* Middle Realm. The soul has a chance to move closer to salvation only in those human worlds. The universe passes through cycles of gradual decay followed by cycles of gradual improvement. These cycles go on forever, and each cycle is divided into six ages. In each age, twenty-four *tirthankaras* appear. In the current cycle, Jains believe, salvation is no longer possible. The *loka* consists of *jivas,* or "souls," and the nonliving *ajiva,* which includes all forms of matter. *Jivas* are perfectly pure, and matter is impure. Souls become tarnished when entwined with matter; the quest for salvation is for the *jiva* to make itself clean. Human destiny is based on the duality of soul and matter. *Karma* is central to the destiny of the soul.

C. **The Religious Life.** Jain religious life is divided into two categories: that of the laypeople, and that of the monks and nuns (the ascetics). *Ahimsa,* the principle of nonviolence, is the central standard of conduct for both lifestyles. Jainism consists of different sects, the largest of which are the Shvetambaras and the Digambaras. Complete purification of the soul can be achieved only through an ascetic life. Deities and the *tirthankaras* cannot offer help. Ascetics are bound by the Five Great Vows. Central to these is *ahimsa:* Do not injure other life-forms. Jain laity are concerned with living a prosperous and moral existence, which leads to a good rebirth. Jain laity adhere to the Twelve Vows and participate in various forms of worship.

Pages 94–96

Concept A: Makers of the River Crossing

Review Questions: Makers of the River Crossing

Question 1. Explain the meaning and significance of the term *tirthankara.*

Answer. It means "maker of the river crossing." The crossing of a river is a significant symbol of spiritual accomplishment. It symbolizes a means of crossing over the realm of *samsara* to salvation beyond.

Question 2. Who was Parshva?

Answer. The twenty-third *tirthankara,* who lived in the eighth century BC.

Question 3. Summarize the life story of Mahavira.

Answer. He was born into the warrior caste, married, and had a daughter. He was restless in his luxurious lifestyle, so he joined a group of Jain ascetics. He practiced severe forms of asceticism and attained enlightenment. Then he preached to his followers for the rest of his life.

Question 4. Describe the important contrasts between the life story of Mahavira and that of Gautama the Buddha.

Answer. Gautama rejected asceticism in favor of the Middle Way, whereas Mahavira held fast to the most extreme asceticism. Gautama discovered on his own the true practices of Buddhism, whereas Mahavira learned the true practices of Jainism from others.

Question 5. What is *kevala?*

Answer. Jain enlightenment, which is perfect and complete knowledge, or omniscience.

Text Activity: Makers of the River Crossing

Activity A

As the last *tirthankara* to have appeared on earth, Mahavira is the most important person for Jainism. Still he is only one *tirthankara* among countless who have appeared before and who will appear in the future. From your point of view, how does the fact that Mahavira is one of many *tirthankaras* affect his status as a religious figure? In your answer try to draw on comparisons with other religious figures, such as Jesus Christ and Gautama the Buddha.

Additional Activity: Makers of the River Crossing

Primary Source Reading

See *Primary Source Readings in World Religions* (Saint Mary's Press, 2009) for an excerpt from the *Acaranga Sutra,* as well as the accompanying leader's guide for suggestions about how to use this reading in your study of Jainism.

A Biography of a Historical *Tirthankara*

1. Share the following background with the students in your own words:

- Although the *tirthankaras* of Jainism are not, for the most part, considered actual historical figures, biographies and stories about them have been written. The stories about the various *tirthankaras* have some unique aspects, but the content usually follows a common pattern. In volume 14 of *The Encyclopedia of Religion,* edited by Mircea Eliade, Colette Caillat provides this background (note that Caillat uses an alternative spelling of *tirthankara*):

  "The career of a *tirthamkara* conforms to a well-structured pattern, and traditional descriptions of the *tirthamkaras* provide very few or no distinctive individual characteristics. The biography of a *tirthamkara* is stereotyped, listing in an almost formulaic sequence the following information: (1) some details of his former existence, (2) the five *kalyanas,* or religiously significant moments of his life (i.e., conception, birth, renunciation, attainment of omniscience, *nirvana* [that is, physical death, which results in complete liberation of the soul]), (3) the names of his parents, (4) the number of his followers, (5) the duration of his life, (6) the color of his body (most are golden, but the twentieth and twenty-second are black, the eighth and ninth are white, the sixth and twelfth are red, the twenty-third and another . . . are blue-green), (7) his height, (8) his guardian divinities, and (9) the length of time elapsed since his predecessor's *nirvana.* All are born to princely families. . . . The conception of a *tirthamkara* is announced to his mother by a standardized succession of auspicious dreams" (p. 535).

  Despite this expected conformity, the stories of the *tirthankaras* reveal some unique characteristics. For instance, the first *tirthankara* "set the groundwork for civilization: first as a sovereign, when he organized kingdoms and societies . . . and later, when he renounced the world and became the first mendicant" (p. 536). The twenty-second *tirthankara* is said to be a relative of Krishna's. Legends tell that he was revolted when he saw the animals waiting to be slaughtered for his wedding celebration and so refused to marry. This event is the "subject of many narratives, songs, and paintings that illustrate the greatness of the doctrine of *ahimsa,* or noninjury" (p. 536).

  Mallinath, the nineteenth *tirthankara,* is controversial because the Shvetambaras claim she was a woman, while the Digambaras (who believe women must be reborn as men to attain *kevala*) claim she was a man.

Handout 5–A

2. Distribute handout 5–A, "The Biographies of the *Tirthankaras,*" which summarizes the elements of the life stories that are described by Caillat. Go over the handout with the students, making the following points in your own words:

5

- In this activity you are to follow the handout's guidelines to tell the story of a historical figure who, because of his or her own life experiences and spirituality, has been able to lead others. This historical *tirthankara* may be a well-known figure, or someone you know personally. Although the *tirthankaras* of Jainism are, with one controversial exception, depicted as male, your *tirthankara* may be male or female.
- The biography you write does not need to exactly follow the entire outline. You may use only one or two of the elements as the story's focal point. In any case your product should both conform to the general biographical pattern and show the unique qualities of the historical *tirthankara* you have chosen. The biography should especially show how this person is a type of spiritual leader, or a "maker of the river crossing," which is the literal meaning of the name *tirthankara.*

You may wish to invite some or all of the students to share their stories with the entire class before handing their work in to be graded.

Variation. Allow the students to represent their *tirthankara's* life in a collage, drawing, dance, piece of music, or other form of artistic expression. This may be especially effective if the student has chosen someone she or he knows. Display the pieces around the classroom.

Pages 96–99

Concept B: Knowing the Universe

Review Questions: Knowing the Universe

Question 6. In Jainism, knowledge regarding the universe and salvation is very important. Why?

Answer. Salvation of the soul depends on understanding the soul's predicament in the universe.

Question 7. Describe the *loka.*

Answer. The *loka* is a space that is vast yet finite. It is eternal. In the center is the Middle Realm, home to several worlds inhabited by human beings. Below are hells inhabited by hell beings, and above are heavens inhabited by deities. At the very top is a realm of liberated souls.

Question 8. What is the role of deities in Jainism?

Answer. They are believed to provide certain forms of material welfare, but cannot assist with the quest for salvation.

Question 9. Explain the Jain concept of upward and downward cycles. In terms of these cycles, where is the world presently?

Answer. The cycles are depicted as the turnings of a wheel. As they turn upward, the quality of the world improves; as they turn downward, things decay and eventually reach a state of utter destruction. Then a new cycle begins. The world is in the fifth of six ages of the current cycle, near the end of a downward turn.

Question 10. Identify and briefly describe the two categories of reality and their relationship to each other according to Jain cosmology.

Answer. *Jivas,* or "souls," are perfectly pure. *Ajiva*—which consists of space, time, motion, rest, and matter—is impure. Souls have become entwined with matter and are thus no longer pure. The quest for salvation is for the *jiva* to make itself clean.

Question 11. What is the Jain attitude toward all life-forms?

Answer. All life-forms, because they are inhabited by a soul, are to be regarded as fellow creatures worthy of respect and care.

Question 12. Describe the Jain quest for salvation.

Answer. Salvation occurs when the soul cleans all matter from itself and regains its original state of purity. *Karma* is of central importance in the quest for salvation, because every action tarnishes the soul in some way. Once *kevala* has been attained, the soul is no longer subject to the tarnishing effects of *karma.*

Text Activities: Knowing the Universe

Activity B

Jains depict the universe, or *loka,* in the shape of a giant man. Try drawing this. How does this visual representation help to illustrate the Jain teachings regarding the human condition and the quest for spiritual perfection?

Activity C

Compare the Jain concept of upward and downward cycles with your own understanding of time and the cycles of growth and decay of the universe.

Activity D

Jainism holds that plants and animals, and even some microbes, can participate to some degree in religious life. In your opinion might animals possess any form of spirituality? Discuss some specific examples.

Additional Activity: Knowing the Universe

Debating Cosmology

The student text points out that the Buddha spoke very little about cosmology, which he felt did not serve the real concern of attaining spiritual perfection. Mahavira, on the other hand, offered a detailed cosmology, maintaining that salvation of the soul depends on understanding its predicament in the universe.

Set up a discussion panel consisting of six students. A seventh student may be selected as moderator, or you may moderate the discussion yourself. The proposition to be discussed is, *It is necessary to have a way of understanding the universe if one is ever to attain spiritual perfection.* Three of the students are to take the point of view of the Buddha, while the other three are to take the point of view of Mahavira.

Give the students a few days to prepare for the discussion. They may bring to their arguments insights from faiths other than Jainism and Buddhism, as well as from science and philosophy.

The discussion may be as structured or as unstructured as you wish; just be sure the ground rules you choose are understood by all, including the class members who make up the audience. Allow time for the audience members to question the panelists.

Pages 99–104

Concept C: The Religious Life

Review Questions: The Religious Life

Question 13. Name the two largest Jain sects and explain their differences.

Answer. Shvetambaras and Digambaras. Shvetambaras use bowls for begging and eating, and believe that women can attain *kevala.* They also believe that once a person attains *kevala,* he or she continues to need food. Digambaras use their hands for begging and eating, and believe that a woman must be reborn as a man to reach *kevala.* They also believe that once a person attains *kevala,* he longer needs food. Male Digambaras go about naked, or "sky-clad." The two sects have slightly different scriptures.

Question 14. Describe the initiation ceremony marking the transition to an ascetic life.

Answer. The ceremony resembles a wedding. Rituals include repeating vows, receiving an alms bowl (this does not apply to Digambaras) and a whisk, pulling out five tufts of hair, and fasting.

Question 15. List the Five Great Vows of Jain ascetics.

Answer. (1) Do not injure other life-forms, (2) avoid lying, (3) do not take what has not been given, (4) renounce sexual activity, and (5) renounce possession.

Question 16. Briefly describe *ahimsa* and its importance to Jain ascetic life.

Answer. Ahimsa is the principle of nonviolence; Jains are not to injure other life-forms. *Ahimsa* is central to ascetic life and encompasses all its aspects. For instance, Jain ascetics are not allowed to build fires or dig in the ground, because such actions inevitably injure life-forms.

Question 17. What is the relationship between Jainism's ascetics and laity?

Answer. The Jain laity honor and respect the ascetics. They acknowledge the ascetics' authority and give the ascetics food and shelter.

Question 18. What is the main concern of Jain laypeople?

Answer. Leading a prosperous and moral life.

Text Activities: The Religious Life

Activity E

Imagine you are a young Jain who has decided to become an ascetic. As the day of your initiation ceremony arrives, what aspects of your former life will you miss the most? In what ways might being an ascetic improve your life?

Activity F

Identify some ways in which something similar to the Jain ideal of *ahimsa* is applied in your society. Do you think these forms of nonviolence stem from religious motives or from something else? Explain your answer.

Activity G

Jain ascetic practices tend to be directly related to the ideal of *ahimsa.* Make a list of ways in which denying yourself physical and material things might help to prevent violence toward other life-forms.

Activity H

Carefully consider the Twelve Vows taken by members of the Jain laity. Which, if any, are similar to your own religious and moral principles and practices? Which, if any, are foreign to you? How might you benefit from following the principles that seem foreign?

Additional Activities: The Religious Life

Ahimsa and Vegetarianism

In this activity the students examine how vegetarianism demonstrates Jainism's principle of *ahimsa,* or "nonviolence." Also the students are encouraged to consider how their choices as consumers reflect their personal beliefs about nonviolence.

1. Write the Jain principle of nonviolence, "Do not injure other life-forms," on the board. With the class brainstorm ways that a person can interpret and live out this principle of nonviolence, listing the students' responses. (You may want the students to record the list in their notebooks for later reference.)

If vegetarianism and veganism are not suggested, add them to the list and describe the differences between them (vegetarianism allows the consumption of eggs and dairy products; veganism does not allow the consumption of any animal food or dairy products). Then discuss questions such as these:

- Why do people practice vegetarianism and veganism?
- Why might their diets be considered healthful in a physical way? in a spiritual way? in a moral way?
- Is what we consume a reflection of our ethics? our character? If so, how? If not, why not?

2. Assign the students to research the relationship between vegetarianism and veganism, and Jainism's principle of nonviolence. Links to some resources on these topics can be found by visiting the World Religions course page on the Internet, which can be accessed from the Saint Mary's Press home page, *www.smp.org*. Explain that the information the students find is to be the basis of a one- or two-page reflection paper. Note that the paper should answer questions such as these:

- What is the Jain philosophy of vegetarianism?
- Jains do not actively seek converts to their religion, but they do encourage the acceptance of nonviolence and vegetarianism. Why?
- Have you ever tried, or would you ever try vegetarianism? Why or why not?
- What lifestyle choices do you make based on your beliefs? (For example, do you avoid buying products from certain companies, watching certain television shows, or listening to certain music?) Explain those choices.
- Do you feel that you are a role model for your beliefs—that the way you live reflects your beliefs? Explain.

3. When the students return to class with their completed assignments, begin by asking them to share what they have written. Help the students to synthesize the information from the earlier class discussion, their individual research, and their written papers. Focus the discussion on central questions like the ones that follow:

- What might living your beliefs imply about your personal choices as a consumer?
- How does the collective result of individual choices affect your community? your society? the world?
- How important is it to be consistent in what you believe is right and what you practice as a consumer?

Jain Business Ethics

1. Introduce this activity using comments like these:

- As the student text points out, the vast majority of Jains are laypeople who live according to the Twelve Vows. They also tend to be among the wealthiest citizens of India. They are active in environmental and peace movements, and they give generously to national philanthropic efforts.

  Jains in business feel that their strong ethical values, based on the Twelve Vows, lead directly to their success. They avoid businesses and business practices that they consider violent because they involve meat and other animal products. The highest objective of Jain laypeople is to serve the community and to foster a sense of cooperation instead of competition. Jains are critical of contemporary business practices that make profit and wealth more important than the welfare of employees and customers.

2. Explain that in this activity the students will work in groups of two or three to define, or redefine, businesses by applying the Twelve Vows of the Jain laity to the way the organizations function. Assign each group a particular company. You may designate generic businesses (for example, shoe manufacturer, building contractor, and landscaper), actual businesses from your community, or actual businesses from the national or international scene.

Direct the groups to write, in detail, how their companies will live up to each of the Twelve Vows. Some of the vows may seem to be only marginally applicable to the project, but press the students to apply each one, if not in terms of its specific statement, then in terms of its general principle. For example, vow 4, on avoiding unchastity, can be applied to occurrences of sexual harassment, and vows 10 and 11, on meditation and fasting, can be applied to policies about the religions and religious practices of employees.

3. When the groups have completed the task, invite them to present their work to the entire class. Use questions like these to discuss how business practices based on the Twelve Vows might affect business and society:

- How might these practices improve business and society?
- How might these practices detract from business and society?
- Do you think these business practices would be profitable?

Variation. Encourage the groups to convey their responses through another media, such as magazine ads, television ads, newspaper articles, television and radio interviews, posters to inspire employees, or Web pages. Choose one media for all the groups, or suggest a variety of media and allow the groups to select their own.

The Biographies of the *Tirthankaras*

The life stories of the *tirthankaras* of Jainism conform to a pattern. In Jain literature they provide the following information:

- Details about the *tirthankaras'* former existences
- The five religiously significant moments of their lives: conception; birth; renunciation of material life; attainment of omniscience *(kevala)*; and physical death, which results in complete liberation of the soul *(nirvana)*
- Their parents' names
- The number of followers they had
- How long they lived
- The colors of their bodies (not restricted to typical human skin tones)
- Their heights
- The identities of the divinities that guard them
- The time elapsed since the previous *tirthankara's* physical death and attainment of final *nirvana*

The stories of the *tirthankaras* also include unique aspects of their lives that especially demonstrate Jain teachings such as *ahimsa* and other ascetic ideals.

(Summarized from Colette Caillat, in Mircea Eliade, editor, *The Encyclopedia of Religion*, volume 14 [New York: Macmillan Library Reference, 1987], pages 535 and 536. Copyright © 1986 by Gale, a part of Cengage Learning, Inc. Used with permission of Cengage Learning, *www.cengage.com/permissions*.)

CHAPTER 6

Sikhism

Major Concepts

A. **The Development of Sikhism.** Sikhism attempts to reconcile the great differences between Hinduism and Islam. Guru, or spiritual teacher, is an important concept in Sikhism, which uses the capitalized term *Guru* in three ways. It is the title of Sikhism's founder, Guru Nanak, and his nine successors; it refers to Sikhism's sacred text; and it refers to God. Guru Nanak (1469–1539), having rejected traditional forms of Hindu worship, embarked on a spiritual search that resulted in the teachings of Sikhism. Although he probably did not intend to create a new religion, Guru Nanak developed a following, and the Sikh community was founded. After his death, each of Guru Nanak's successors contributed to the development of Sikhism. The fifth Guru, Arjan, compiled the Adi Granth (the Sikh scriptures). Arjan had political concerns that gave Sikhism a military dimension. The tenth Guru, Gobind Singh, brought about two innovations that changed Sikhism forever. He instituted the Khalsa, an order within Sikhism to which most Sikhs belong; and he installed the Adi Granth as his successor, ending the line of human Gurus. The Adi Granth is noted for its poetic excellence, spiritual content, and haunting melodies.

B. **Religious Teachings.** Sikhism teaches that the ultimate purpose of life is to attain complete union with God, and thus to escape the cycle of death and rebirth, or *samsara.* The experience of union with God is eternal bliss. God is the Formless One, and God's divine order is called *hukam.* God is immanent and approachable through loving devotion. God is referred to as Guru because God delivers humans from darkness to enlightenment. God dwells in every human being, but humans tend to be self-centered. *Haumai* (pride or egoism) is humans' insistence on making do on their own rather than acknowledge dependence on God. Salvation amounts to moving beyond all human shortcomings to a state of complete union with God.

C. **The Religious Life.** Guru Nanak and his successors instituted certain practices that define the Sikh way of life. Any building that contains a copy of the Adi Granth is a *gurdwara,* a Sikh house of worship. Worship includes singing hymns, reading from the Adi Granth, or telling a story about one of the Gurus. It generally ends with sharing a cake made of wheat and honey. The most vivid Sikh ritual is the ceremony of initiation into the Khalsa. The initiate must possess the Five Ks: uncut hair, a comb, a steel wrist guard, a sword or knife, and a pair of shorts. The Five Ks strengthen Sikh identity. The three principles that guide Sikh life are work, worship, and charity.

Pages 109–114

Concept A: The Development of Sikhism

Review Questions: The Development of Sikhism

Question 1. Explain the literal meaning of the term *guru*.
Answer. *Gu* means "darkness," *ru* means "enlightenment." A guru delivers people from the darkness of ignorance to a state of enlightenment.

Question 2. What is the literal meaning of the word *sikh?*
Answer. "Learner" or "disciple."

Question 3. List the three ways the capitalized term *Guru* is used in Sikhism.
Answer. It is the title of the ten historical leaders of Sikhism, it refers to the Sikh sacred scriptures, and it refers to God, the True Guru.

Question 4. Briefly describe Nanak's early life.
Answer. He was born to the Hindu warrior caste. He married in his teens and had two sons. Nanak was dissatisfied with typical forms of employment and Hindu worship. He sought out holy men from both the Hindu and the Muslim traditions, and came to a religious outlook that asserted the oneness of God and the need to move closer to God. Nanak composed hymns and was a spiritual leader.

Question 5. Summarize Nanak's statement upon returning from receiving God's revelation.
Answer. He said there is no Hindu or Muslim, and God is neither Hindu nor Muslim, so he would follow the path of God.

Question 6. What is significant about the township called Kartarpur?
Answer. It was the site of the first Sikh community.

Question 7. What is the term for the Sikh community?
Answer. The Panth.

Question 8. What is the name of the Sikh scripture? Who compiled it?
Answer. The Adi Granth, compiled by Guru Arjan.

Question 9. Who is revered as the greatest Guru after Nanak?
Answer. Guru Gobind Singh.

Question 10. What is the Khalsa?
Answer. An order within Sikhism that is based on the principle of loyalty.

Question 11. Identify Guru Gobind Singh's successor.
Answer. The Adi Granth.

Question 12. What makes the Adi Granth Sikhism's "greatest attraction"?
Answer. Its poetic excellence, spiritual content, and haunting melodies.

Text Activities: The Development of Sikhism

Activity A

Guru Nanak spent about twenty years journeying from place to place and developing his spiritual perspective. In your view how might travel to distant places and encounters with foreign forms of religion nurture spiritual growth?

Activity B

Although he probably did not intend to found a new religion, Guru Nanak's life and leadership proved so inspirational that his followers united to form Sikhism. Which three or four characteristics of Guru Nanak's or events in his life do you think were most responsible for the establishment of Sikhism? Describe how those characteristics or events might have inspired his followers.

Activity C

Guru Arjan initiated a long history of Sikh involvement in political and military affairs. Do you see any relationships between religion and political or military affairs in the world today? Try to describe two such relationships.

Activity D

Imagine yourself as a Sikh in a crowd celebrating an annual festival in 1699. Suddenly your leader, Guru Gobind Singh, challenges anyone who is willing to die for him to come forward. What are your thoughts as you decide whether to step from the crowd?

Activity E

The Adi Granth features written material and musical accompaniment. Imagine the lyrics of a favorite song without any musical accompaniment. How does this alter their impact? How might a sacred text like the Adi Granth be strengthened by musical accompaniment?

Additional Activities: The Development of Sikhism

The Ten Gurus of Sikhism: Background

Handout 6–A

Handout 6–A, "The Ten Gurus of Sikhism," lists the names and the birth and death dates of all ten Sikh Gurus. It also provides a brief statement about each Guru's main contribution as spiritual leader of the Sikhs. Distribute this handout as supplemental material. Emphasize that the students need not memorize the names and dates of the Gurus, and encourage them to read the handout to gain a broader understanding of Sikh leadership in the first two centuries of the tradition's existence.

Variation. Divide the class into nine groups and assign each group to research one of the Gurus following Nanak. Determine a date for the groups to make brief presentations to the class. For helpful research links, see the World Religions course page on the Internet, which can be accessed from the Saint Mary's Press home page, *www.smp.org.*

Sacred Sikh Sites

Divide the class into six groups. Assign each group to research one of the following Sikh *gurdwaras:*

- Sri Akal Takht
- Sri Harimandir Sahib (the Golden Temple)
- Takht Sri Damdama Sahib
- Takht Sri Hazur Sahib
- Takht Sri Keshgarh Sahib
- Takht Sri Patna Sahib

Links to resources can be found by visiting the World Religions course page on the Internet, which can be accessed from the Saint Mary's Press home page, *www.smp.org.* Instruct the students to find information about the specific sites, and to consider how the basic *gurdwara* design reflects Sikh beliefs (for instance, *gurdwaras* are different from Hindu temples in that they are open to every caste, are available to believers of any religion, and emphasize the spirituality of individuals). For evaluation, you may wish to have the groups turn in a written report, make an electronic presentation, draw a detailed diagram of the structure, or even construct a model.

Variation. This activity could be expanded over later chapters to include the worship structures of other religions. The students could compare how different types of buildings reflect the beliefs of the religious communities.

Pages 114–116

Concept B: Religious Teachings

Review Questions: Religious Teachings

Question 13. What is the name of the summary of Sikh theology that begins the Adi Granth?
Answer. The Mool Mantra.

Question 14. Explain what it means to say that God is immanent.
Answer. God is indwelling, which makes God personal and approachable.

Question 15. Why is God referred to as Guru in Sikhism?
Answer. Because God delivers humans from darkness to enlightenment.

Question 16. What is *haumai?*
Answer. Humans' insistence on making do on their own rather than acknowledge their dependence on God.

Question 17. Why is God's creation necessary for Sikh salvation?

Answer. God's creation offers people the potential to know God and to move closer to God. God reveals the divine purpose to humans through creation and thus leads them to salvation.

Question 18. Describe the state of spiritual perfection for Sikhism.

Answer. Salvation amounts to moving beyond all human shortcomings to a state of complete union with God. It is a blissful state forever beyond the cycle of death and rebirth.

Text Activities: Religious Teachings

Activity F

The image of God in Sikhism is in some ways similar to the image of God in Western religious traditions, and in some ways similar to the image of God in Hinduism. Describe the Sikh God in your own words, including references to those similarities.

Activity G

In Sikhism, God's creation can be a hindrance because of human attachment to it, but it is also necessary for salvation because it reveals God's will, or *hukam.* How does creation relate to your spiritual life? Is creation completely good? or does it present some problems?

Additional Activity: Religious Teachings

Stories of *Haumai* and Salvation

This activity uses creative writing in an attempt to deepen the students' understanding of the Sikh concept of *haumai* and of the Sikh perspective on salvation.

1. Direct the students to read and study the sections of the student text that explain *hukam, haumai,* and salvation. Take time in class to reinforce and discuss what they have learned from the text. Then give them this assignment, along with its due date:

- Write a story, parable, or fable that illustrates the concept of *haumai.* It may also illustrate the Sikh understanding of salvation, if you choose. Write your story simply, so that even an eight-year-old could follow it and grasp its meaning. Your story can use human, animal, or divine characters. It can be realistic or fantastical, but it must provide a clear picture of how humans get caught up in *haumai.* Your story must contain the following elements:
  - A central act illustrating *haumai*
  - Evidence of at least one of *haumai's* five accompanying vices
  - Human ignorance preventing the main character or characters from seeking God—and thus continuing the cycle of *haumai*
  - Eventual salvation from *haumai,* according to Sikh beliefs (this element is optional)

2. On the due date, invite the students to take turns reading their stories to the class. (If time is short or your class is large, divide the students into small groups and instruct them to make their presentations to their groups, so that a number of presentations can be made simultaneously.) Allow time for discussion after every few presentations. Guide the students to examine each piece on its own merits, rather than allowing the discussion to become a forum for judging which pieces are "better" than others. Collect all the stories for formal evaluation after they have been presented.

Pages 116–119

Concept C: The Religious Life

Review Questions: The Religious Life

Question 19. Briefly describe the Sikh *gurdwara*.
Answer. It is a place of worship, usually with minarets and chalk-white paint. The presence of the Adi Granth is the only requirement for the interior; the sacred text sits atop cushions and under a canopy.

Question 20. What does the preparing and sharing of food symbolize in Sikhism?
Answer. It symbolizes the unity of the community, regardless of the caste status of individual members, and provides food for those in need.

Question 21. Identify the Five Ks.
Answer. Uncut hair, a comb, a steel wrist guard, a sword or knife, and a pair of shorts.

Question 22. Why is the ritual of initiation into the Khalsa performed by five people?
Answer. To recall the original initiation of Guru Gobind Singh by the beloved five.

Text Activities: The Religious Life

Activity H

Compare Sikh worship in the *gurdwara* with the forms of worship that are familiar to you. What are the similarities? What are the differences?

Activity I

The Five Ks of the Sikh Khalsa primarily strengthen Sikh identity. What similar symbols do you see in your own religious tradition or the traditions of people around you? How do you think those symbols strengthen a sense of identity among the members of the religions that use them?

Additional Activities: The Religious Life

Religious Identity and Symbols

This activity is designed to help the students identify the meanings behind familiar symbols used by individuals and groups. It can also lay the foundation for discussion in the following activity, "The Khalsa."

Divide the class into five groups. Give the following directions in your own words:

- I am going to assign each group a specific symbol. We are going to imagine that the powers-that-be have decided to abolish this symbol because of its negative or divisive effect on people. Your job is to convince those decision makers that this symbol is important and worth keeping. Your group is to show the symbol's importance to both individuals and the community, its positive effects on people, and what would be lost if it were abolished. Regardless of your personal feelings, you will be arguing that the symbol must be retained.
- You will be invited to present your argument to the class. You may make a straight verbal presentation, incorporate visual aids or technology, perform a skit, or write and perform a protest song. Each person from your group is to be involved in the presentation. You are also to turn in a written outline of your presentation.

Give each group a slip of paper on which is written one of the following symbols (feel free to add to or change these examples):

- American flag
- Crucifix
- School mascot
- School uniform
- Sports team jacket
- Varsity letter
- Wedding ring
- Class ring

Inform the groups how much preparation time they will have, and determine a date for the presentations.

When the last presentation has been made, bring things to a close by pointing out the richness that symbols bring to peoples' lives, even if their meanings are not readily apparent.

The Khalsa

Handout 6–B

Handout 6–B, "The Sikh Khalsa," provides additional information about the Khalsa and its members. It highlights the significance of each of the Five Ks, as well as the code of conduct that members of the Khalsa are expected to follow.

You might use the handout to provide the students with additional information about the Khalsa, and even test them on its material. You could also use the handout to stimulate discussion about the Khalsa. Here are some suggested discussion questions:

- Given that Sikhs have at times been in conflict with surrounding religious groups, or been misidentified with members of other religions, why might the Five Ks and the code of conduct be practical?

6

- Throughout history Sikhs have continued to practice the Five Ks while some of their situations changed. How might historical changes have affected the meaning of the Five Ks? How might the meaning of the Five Ks continue to develop in the future?
- What difficulties might be encountered by Sikhs belonging to the Khalsa? What specific difficulties might those Sikhs face in the United States?

Use the discussion to make the point that although the Sikh emphasis on identity may appear extreme, the same emphasis exists to varying degrees in most traditions and should not be a cause for prejudice or discrimination.

Additional Resources from Saint Mary's Press

See *Primary Source Readings in World Religions* (Saint Mary's Press, 2009) for selections from "Events in the Life of Guru Nanak," *Japjî,* and *The Self Spirit,* as well as the accompanying leader's guide for suggestions about how to use these readings in your study of Sikhism.

The Ten Gurus of Sikhism

This list of the ten Gurus of Sikhism briefly summarizes the key contributions of each Guru.

1. Guru Nanak (1469 to 1539)
The Sikh tradition began with his teachings.

2. Guru Angad (1504 to 1552)
He compiled Nanak's hymns, which were the start of the Sikh scripture.

3. Guru Amar Das (1479 to 1574)
He divided the expanding Sikh community into distinct congregations.

4. Guru Ram Das (1534 to 1581)
He founded the city of Amritsar, which is considered the sacred center of the Sikh faith.

5. Guru Arjan (1563 to 1606)
He compiled the Adi Granth and built the Golden Temple in Amritsar. He altered the role of the Guru by being a worldly, as well as spiritual, leader.

6. Guru Hargobind (1595 to 1644)
Under him the military strength of the Sikh community developed and grew.

7. Guru Har Rai (1630 to 1661)
He was only fourteen years old when he became Guru. Throughout his reign Sikhs were preoccupied with the military threat of the Moghul Empire.

8. Guru Har Krishan (1656 to 1664)
He was just five years old when he became Guru, and he died three years later in a smallpox epidemic.

9. Guru Tegh Bahadur (1621 to 1675)
He was martyred for refusing to convert to Islam.

10. Guru Gobind Singh (1666 to 1708)
The last of the Sikh Gurus, Gobind Singh established the Khalsa and named the Adi Granth his successor.

The Sikh Khalsa

The information on this handout provides further insight into the nature of the Sikh Khalsa.

The Five Ks

The Five Ks are physical symbols of membership in the Khalsa. Each one signifies a particular aspect of Sikh identity.

1. ***Kes.*** The long, uncut hair of a Khalsa member symbolizes spirituality, and reminds the member that she or he should always follow the example of the ten Gurus.
2. ***Kangha.*** The comb symbolizes hygiene and discipline. Unlike many ascetics who characteristically neglect their matted hair, Sikhs are expected to wash and comb their hair regularly.
3. ***Kara.*** The steel bracelet (or wrist guard) reminds the Khalsa member to act with restraint and to remember God always.
4. ***Kirpan.*** The sword or knife symbolizes the Sikh commitment to the struggle against injustice. It is worn solely as a religious symbol, never as a weapon.
5. ***Kachh.*** The pair of shorts symbolizes chastity and self-control.

The Khalsa Code of Conduct

Members of the Khalsa follow a specific code of conduct. Here is a summary of some of the main requirements:

- Sikhs worship only one God—no gods, goddesses, idols, or statues are to be used in worship, and no human being is to be worshiped.
- The Adi Granth is the only religious book in which a Sikh may believe. Other religious books can be studied only for knowledge and comparison.
- Sikhs do not believe in the caste system or the status of untouchability, nor do they believe in magic, omens, astrology, and many other widely known superstitions and religious practices.
- Members of the Khalsa maintain their distinctness by the Five Ks, but they are to avoid hurting the feelings of others who believe in different religions.
- Sikhs are to pray before beginning any work.
- Sikhs must learn the language Punjabi and teach it to their children.
- Sikhs are forbidden to use drugs, alcohol, and tobacco.
- Men and women of the Khalsa are not to pierce their ears or noses. Women do not wear veils.
- Sikhs must give to the poor with the attitude that all they give goes to the Guru.
- Sikhs are to live by the earnings of their honest labor.
- Sikhs must not gamble or steal.
- Members of the Khalsa should dress simply and modestly.
- When one member of the Khalsa meets another, the two are to use this greeting: *Waheguru Ji Ka Khalsa, Waheguru Ji Ki Fateh,* which means, "The Khalsa belongs to God; victory belongs to God."

CHAPTER 7

Confucianism

7

Major Concepts

A. **Great Master K'ung.** Confucianism provides the ethical foundation of East Asia. Confucianism began with China's "First Teacher," K'ung Fu-tzu, better known throughout the English-speaking world as Confucius (551–479 BC). Born to a noble but poor family, Confucius was an exceptional student who later became a teacher and a government official. His teachings provided solutions to China's problems that contrasted with those of others: the Legalists, the Mohists, and the Taoists. Confucius's solutions centered on human relationships and drew from rulers and sages of ancient times. Confucius's followers continued to study and add to his ideas, causing Confucianism's influence to be felt throughout China and eventually the world.

B. **Learning to Be Human.** Confucius saw learning as more than a mere gathering of information; he viewed it as a means of discovering what it is to be human. He provided a perspective on specific qualities of being human: what it is to be mature, what the pinnacle of human virtue is, how best to behave, how to be a cultured person, and how to govern. Learning the Tao, or universal Way, is fundamentally important in Confucianism. The human ideal is the *chun-tzu,* or "mature person." A *chun-tzu* has such abundant virtues that he or she is able to contribute to the improvement of society. *Jen* is the supreme virtue, a perfect form of benevolence—doing one's best to treat others as one would wish to be treated. The term for proper behavior is *li,* which means both "rite," or "sacred ritual," and "propriety," or "behaving properly given the situation at hand." Proper behavior in any situation carries the significance of a sacred ritual. A cultured human being acquires skills of behavior broadly characterized as *wen,* the cultural arts. Confucius viewed the arts as a source of moral education. Good government comes about through the cultivation of *te,* or virtue shown through the power of example.

C. **Self, Family, Nation, Heaven.** Confucianism envisions a grand harmony of human relationships, with the self, the family, the nation, and the entire world of humanity all intimately connected. The self is a center of human relationships, and is constantly changing and growing toward maturity. Family relationships in Confucian society are well defined, which provides people with a clear sense of place and purpose. Filial behavior and respect for elders are prominent characteristics of family relationships. On the national level, good government is a central concern of

Confucianism. The ruler is one who has acquired the moral perfection needed to lead by power of example, and the subjects are to be filial toward their ruler. Heaven, which represents the ultimate moral force that guides and nurtures humanity, is also part of the Confucian vision of harmony of relationships.

Pages 125–128

Concept A: Great Master K'ung

Review Questions: Great Master K'ung

Question 1. Describe Confucius's family background.
Answer. His family was of noble lineage but was poor.

Question 2. At what profession was Confucius an apparent failure?
Answer. Public official.

Question 3. Using evidence from the Analects, name three adjectives that describe Confucius's character.
Answer. [Any three of the following answers are correct:] *Eager, diligent, joyful, cordial, stern, awe inspiring, respectful.*

Question 4. Identify and briefly describe the three schools of thought that responded to ancient China's problems with solutions different from those of Confucius.
Answer. The Legalists advocated a stern rule of law enforced by severe punishments. The Mohists taught universal love, even toward one's enemies. The Taoists believed that the path to human happiness lay in the individualistic pursuit of harmony with nature.

Question 5. What did Confucius believe about the power of tradition?
Answer. He was more concerned with transmitting traditional ways than with inventing new theories, and he believed that the power of tradition would ensure acceptance of the traditional ways.

Question 6. Who is considered the second founder of Confucianism?
Answer. Mencius.

Question 7. Who was Chu Hsi?
Answer. A Neo-Confucian philosopher who interpreted Confucianism.

Question 8. Identify the Four Books of Confucianism.
Answer. The Analects, the Book of Mencius, the Great Learning, and the Doctrine of the Mean.

Text Activities: Great Master K'ung

Activity A

The Analects show us that Confucius had a great reputation for learning and teaching; he has been revered for that in East Asia throughout the ages. Does your society revere good learners and teachers?

Activity B

Confucius believed strongly in the power of tradition as a means of improving Chinese society. In your society does the power of tradition play a part in improving life? or does tradition get in the way of improvement?

Additional Activities: Great Master K'ung

The Analects

In this exercise the students work directly with some of the written texts of Confucianism.

1. Before class write the following quotes on the board:

- "Shall I tell you what it is to know. To say you know when you know, and to say you do not when you do not, that is knowledge" (Analects 2.17).
- "Faced with what is right, to leave it undone shows a lack of courage" (Analects 2.24).
- "Give your father and mother no other cause for anxiety than illness" (Analects 2.6).

2. Introduce this activity with comments such as these:

- Most of Confucius's sayings are collected in a book called the Analects.
- In the Analects these are generally one- or two-sentence thoughts about how to conduct one's life.
- The passages listed on the board reflect three main concerns of Confucius's: learning (school and leadership), character (self), and filial piety (family).

3. Divide the students into small groups, and ask them to discuss what each selection means, and why people would need to be told this advice, which seems self-evident. Direct each group to think of an example illustrating the kinds of things that keep us from living out these principles. Invite the groups to share their responses.

Handout 7–A

4. Distribute handout 7–A, "Confucius Says . . ." Instruct the students to do the handout in pairs or independently, in class or for homework. Regardless of how you use the handout, be sure to review it in class so that the students may hear a variety of interpretations for each saying.

Research Project: Sayings of Confucius's

This project allows further research into the Analects; consider using it after the students have completed handout 7–A.

Direct the students to find additional excerpts from the Analects in a library or on the Internet, and to select two or three sayings that have a common theme. For a link to the Analects on the Internet, see the World Religions course page on the Internet, which can be accessed from the Saint Mary's Press home page, *www.smp.org.* Instruct the students to create a poster that includes the sayings along with either a drawing that illustrates the theme or a news account of people following the advice of Confucius. Discuss and display the completed posters.

Concept B: Learning to Be Human

Pages 128–133

Review Questions: Learning to Be Human

Question 9. According to Confucius what can one discover through learning?
Answer. What it is to be human.

Question 10. What does the term *Tao* mean for Confucianism?
Answer. The moral order that permeates the universe.

Question 11. What is a *chun-tzu?*
Answer. A person with perfect moral character.

Question 12. Identify and briefly describe Confucianism's supreme virtue.
Answer. Jen is a perfect form of benevolence—doing one's best to treat others as one would wish to be treated.

Question 13. Explain the notion *shu,* or reciprocity.
Answer. Shu is basically identical to the reciprocity taught by the Golden Rule—"Do unto others as you would have them do unto you."

Question 14. What is *li?*
Answer. Li, the Chinese term for proper behavior, means "rite" and "propriety." Confucianism combines those definitions, holding that behaving properly carries at all times the significance of a sacred ritual.

Question 15. What does the rectification of names mean to Confucians?
Answer. It says that proper behavior is largely dependent on one's place in society, so an emperor ought to behave in a manner befitting the name *emperor,* counselors ought to behave as proper counselors, and so on.

Question 16. Name at least four of the Confucian cultural arts, or *wen.*

Answer. [Any four of the following answers are correct:] Music, poetry, archery, charioteering, calligraphy, and mathematics.

Question 17. What is *te?*
Answer. Virtue as shown through the power of example.

Text Activities: Learning to Be Human

Activity C

Carefully reread Confucius's words regarding his own lifelong process of learning (see Analects 2.4). In Chinese society those words have long served as a model for lifelong learning. Are people in Western society encouraged to learn more deeply as they grow older? Discuss similarities and differences between these societies' attitudes toward learning.

Activity D

Confucius taught that one becomes a *chun-tzu*—a person of perfect moral character—through steadfast learning. Explore the relation between learning and the development of moral character. Explain why you agree or disagree with this statement: It is possible to learn to be a better person.

Activity E

Compare the Confucian doctrine of *shu,* or reciprocity, with the Christian teaching to love one's enemies.

Activity F

According to Confucianism the cultural arts, or *wen,* play an important role in ensuring the unity and continuity of East Asian society. Explore the role of the cultural arts in your society. First identify several art forms that you consider most relevant. Then explain how they help maintain the unity and continuity of your society.

Activity G

Confucius believed that *te,* virtue as shown through the power of example, is a more lasting means of improving society than is mere punishment of bad behavior. If you agree with Confucius, reflect on two situations in which the power of moral example has proved to be more effective than punishing bad behavior. If you disagree with him, reflect on two situations in which punishment has been more effective than moral example.

Additional Activities: Learning to Be Human

Rectification of Names

According to Confucianism, proper behavior is determined by one's role in society. This manner of thinking provides both order for society and guidelines for the individual.

Handout 7–B

7

1. Distribute handout 7–B, "Chinese Calligraphy," and markers, and invite the students to try their hand at creating Chinese characters. After the students have finished writing, direct them to cut apart the characters and to attach a piece of double-sided tape to each one. Three points that you can share with the class while they work are these:

- Calligraphy is the art of fine handwriting.
- Creating calligraphy on scrolls has been a revered art form in many parts of East Asia.
- It has been especially important for the study of Confucianism. It is associated with *wen*, the pursuit of the cultural arts, and was considered part of becoming a *chun-tzu* (gentleman). Confucius is said to have been a master at it.

2. Explain that as you read aloud each of the following quotes from the Analects, the students should write down what the passage is saying about being a good daughter or son. You may wish to read each passage more than once.

- "When your parents are alive, comply with the rites in serving them; when they die, comply with the rites in burying them; comply with the rites in sacrificing to them" (Analects 2.5).
- "Give your father and mother no other cause for anxiety than illness" (Analects 2.6).
- "Nowadays for a man to be filial means no more than that he is able to provide his parents with food. Even hounds and horses are, in some way, provided with food. If a man shows no reverence, where is the difference?" (Analects 2.7).

3. Ask the class questions such as these:

- According to Confucius, what makes a good daughter or son?
- What do you think Confucius would expect from a good sibling?
- What are some obstacles to treating family members with respect?

4. Invite the students to name five other roles that they might take on (such as those of team captain, student, friend, class officer, and employee). Write them across the top of the board. Next, call the students to name the qualities that are important for "proper behavior" in each role. Write the qualities they name under the appropriate headings on the board.

5. When the lists are complete, invite the students to come to the board with their calligraphy characters and to tape a character next to the one quality that they find most important for each role (note that the students may use any character to mark any quality; the characters are used only as markers here). Evaluate the results with the class, using questions like these:

- What qualities were chosen as most important for each role?
- Were any qualities seen as important for every role?

- Are we born with particular qualities, are they taught to us, or do we develop them on our own?
- What happens if people in these roles lack the qualities that are considered important?
- What happens if people in these roles have the qualities that are considered important?

6. Instruct the students each to choose one of the roles listed on the board, and to write a short saying that describes the proper behavior for a person in that role. Explain that their writings should be modeled on those found in the Analects. Ask volunteers to share their sayings with the class.

Being Human

This activity gives the students a chance to explore Confucius's five qualities of being human: *chun-tzu, jen, li, wen,* and *te.*

When you are satisfied that the students have begun to grasp the concepts *chun-tzu, jen, li, wen,* and *te,* explain that they are each to choose one of those concepts and prepare a creative presentation that demonstrates the meaning of the concept. Allow the students to select from the following ways of approaching the assignment:

- *Writing.* Invite the students to write a short story about a fictional person or an actual person who exemplifies the chosen concept. Or suggest that they write a poem that expresses the essential meaning of the concept.
- *Visual arts.* Direct the students to create a piece of visual art that illustrates the chosen concept. Explain that they may paint, sculpt, draw, make a collage, film a video, use computer graphics, or employ any other visual method to create the piece.
- *Performing arts.* Instruct the students to create a brief performance that illustrates the chosen concept. Note that possibilities include role-plays, monologues, interpretive dance, and music (either original or existing).

Explain that the writing, artwork, or performance can demonstrate the *success* or *presence* of the concept, or the *failure* or *absence* of the concept. For example, a role-play about an unresolved conflict could illustrate the absence of *jen,* or benevolence. Students who illustrate a concept's failure or absence should also be prepared to articulate the benefits of its success or presence. Instruct the students to limit their presentations to 3 minutes.

Emphasize that the students are to develop their projects alone. However, if they need help for their presentations, they may recruit classmates; for example, a person who writes a role-play for two actors may recruit a classmate to play one of the roles. Recruits are merely helpers, and are fully responsible for their own projects as well.

Determine a date on which the students are to present their projects to the class. Encourage the students to jot notes as they witness the presentations. Invite a brief discussion (no more than 5 minutes) after each presentation, or save 10 minutes at the end of the class period and discuss all the presentations for that day at once.

Pages 133–136

Concept C: Self, Family, Nation, Heaven

Review Questions: Self, Family, Nation, Heaven

Question 18. Summarize the doctrine of the Five Constant Relationships, naming all five relationships.

Answer. This doctrine is summarized in the Book of Mencius as consisting of "love between father and son, duty between ruler and subject, distinction between husband and wife, precedence of the old over the young, and faith between friends" (3A:4).

Question 19. How does Confucianism regard the self?

Answer. The self is a center of human relationships.

Question 20. What is the primary virtue in relating to one's elders? Explain the meaning of that virtue.

Answer. It is to be filial, to act in a way that is suitable for a son or daughter.

Question 21. Describe the Confucian ruler.

Answer. The ruler is a gentleman *(chun-tzu)* who has acquired the necessary moral perfection to lead by the power of example.

Question 22. What does Heaven seem to represent for Confucius?

Answer. A universal moral force, similar, if not equivalent, to the Tao.

Text Activities: Self, Family, Nation, Heaven

Activity H

Consider the two quoted passages about the relationships within the Confucian family. Critique the structure that they describe. Be sure to comment on the Five Constant Relationships and on the virtue of being filial. Is this a good structure for family relationships?

Activity I

In Chinese society the older people get, the more deeply respected they are. Answer the following questions:

- What differences do you see between the Confucian attitude toward aging and the attitudes of your society?
- In both societies what are the consequences for older people and for the rest of society?
- Which perspective on aging do you prefer?

Activity J

Explain the nature and role of government in Confucianism. Then describe your own opinion of the proper nature and role of government. Finally, compare the two.

Activity K

Some people have wondered whether Confucianism can really be called a religion. What do you think? Make an argument for your position, based on what you have learned from this chapter, as well as on the discussion of religious traditions in chapter 1.

Additional Activity: Self, Family, Nation, Heaven

Confucian Harmony, and Circles of Concern and Influence

Prepare for this discussion activity by becoming familiar with Stephen R. Covey's concept of circles of concern and circles of influence. Covey explains this concept in *The Seven Habits of Highly Effective People: Restoring the Character Ethic* (New York: Simon and Schuster, 1989; see especially pp. 82–85), which is available in most libraries and bookstores.

1. Explain to the students the concept of circles of concern and circles of influence. The diagrams in Covey's book can help you make the concept clear. Then call the students' attention to page 133 of the student text, pointing out the following quote about Confucian harmony, from the Great Learning:
   - "The men of old who wished to make their bright virtue shine throughout the world first put in order their own states. In order to put in order their own states they first regulated their own families; in order to regulate their own families they first disciplined their own selves" (quoted in Thompson, *Chinese Religion,* p. 12).

2. Invite two or three volunteers to come to the board and make diagrams that illustrate this directive from the Great Learning. When the diagrams are done, have the class critique them and suggest improvements. Then compare the students' diagrams with Covey's diagrams of circles of concern and circles of influence. Lead the discussion with questions such as the ones that follow:
   - What elements do the concepts of Confucian harmony and of circles of concern and influence have in common? How do those concepts differ?
   - Do you think Confucius would have understood the idea of circles of concern and influence? Why or why not?
   - What are some other examples of "modern" wisdom that may be based on the teachings of ancient religious traditions?

For the last question, suggest that the students draw from the religions they have already studied in this course or from other religious and wisdom traditions of which they are aware. Try to help the students understand that although ancient wisdom is often repackaged for modern eyes and ears, it is always valuable to consult the original sources to discover the depth and richness of the wisdom. You may want to have the students answer the third question as a homework assignment. If so, encourage them to consult parents or other adults who may be able to direct them to contemporary books and programs that contain elements of ancient wisdom.

Additional Resources from Saint Mary's Press

See *Primary Source Readings in World Religions* (Saint Mary's Press, 2009) for excerpts from *The Analects,* the Great Learning, and *Confucius—The Secular as the Sacred,* as well as the accompanying leader's guide for suggestions about how to use these readings in your study of Confucianism.

Confucius Says . . .

Read the following quotations from the Analects, and answer the questions about them.

Part A

> If one is guided by profit in one's actions, one will incur much ill will. (4.12)

1. Why would one "incur much ill will" for following profit?

2. What do you think Confucius would have said should guide one's actions?

Part B

> Cunning words, an ingratiating face and utter servility. . . . I . . . find them shameful. To be friendly towards someone while concealing one's hostility. . . . I . . . find it shameful. (5.25)

3. Why would someone act in the shameful ways described in this passage?

4. If someone feels hostility, how would you advise them to behave?

Part C

The Master told Ch'i-tiao K'ai to take [a government] office. Ch'i-tiao K'ai said, "I cannot trust myself to do so yet." The Master was pleased. (5.6)

5. Reread Analects 4.12, above. Ch'i-tiao K'ai was a follower of Confucius's; why, do you think, did he refuse to take office?

6. What would you consider a good motive for taking a leadership position?

Part D

Do not worry because you have no official position. Worry about your qualifications. Do not worry because no one appreciates your abilities. Seek to be worthy of appreciation. (4.14)

7. What is the difference between worrying about an official position and worrying about one's qualifications? (In this case, an official position can be any job or accomplishment—including earning high grades, making the varsity swim team, or being invited to the homecoming dance.)

8. If someone followed this advice, what would happen in the long term?

Chinese Calligraphy

Calligraphy is one of the cultural arts that was pursued in the process of becoming a *chun-tzu*. Try your hand at reproducing the Chinese characters below, drawing your versions in the space provided to the right of the characters. The family roles with more than one character are meant to be read from top to bottom.

家

Family

兒
子

Son

母
親

Mother

女
兒

Daughter

父
親

Father

CHAPTER 8

Taoism

Major Concepts

A. **Lao Tzu and Chuang Tzu.** Taoism dates back to about the time of Confucius, and its origins are shrouded in mystery. Lao Tzu, traditionally considered the founder of Taoism, produced the tradition's foundational text, the *Tao Te Ching*. The *Tao Te Ching* consists of many paradoxical and profound teachings on living in harmony with nature. Chuang Tzu, Taoism's second founder, is known for his humorous and profound lessons and stories, collected in a text known simply as the *Chuang Tzu*. One of its central themes is that all things are relative, and that answers to questions such as what is good, what ought to be done, and who we are depend on particular circumstances.

8

B. **The Philosophy of Tao.** Tao is both the ultimate source and the principle of order in the universe. It is the Way of nature, both transcendent and immanent. Tao has two components: yin, the negative, passive, feminine, earthly component; and yang, the positive, active, masculine, heavenly component. Yin and yang are complementary; neither is essentially superior to the other. Taoism regards moral values as relative, and avoids absolute moral judgments. Taoist literature says nothing of an afterlife, and it depicts death merely as one among nature's many transformations from one state to another. Humans are part of the grand harmony of nature, and to live in accord with Tao is the only way for the individual to thrive. The primary virtue of Taoism is *wu-wei,* which means "nonaction." To practice *wu-wei* is to be so perfectly in harmony with nature that its energy infuses and empowers one. The virtues humility and noncompetition, naturalness and naturalism, and nonaggression and passive rule all reflect the basic virtue *wu-wei.*

Pages 140–142

Concept A: Lao Tzu and Chuang Tzu

Review Questions: Lao Tzu and Chuang Tzu

Question 1. Name the two founders of Taoism.
Answer. Lao Tzu and Chuang Tzu.

Question 2. Which of the founders is considered the author of the *Tao Te Ching?*
Answer. Lao Tzu.

Question 3. Define the word *paradox.* Give an example of a paradox from the *Tao Te Ching.*
Answer. A paradox is a statement that seems illogical and contradictory on the surface, and yet contains deeper truths that are accessible more through intuition than through logical thinking. [The students may give as examples any of the quotes from chapters 1, 19, and 56 of the *Tao Te Ching* that are cited in the student text.]

Question 4. What is the *Chuang Tzu?*
Answer. It is the text attributed to Chuang Tzu, the second founder of Taoism.

Text Activity: Lao Tzu and Chuang Tzu

Activity A

Paradoxes are found in many religious traditions, as well as in literature and poetry. Explain a paradox you have come across in religion or literature, or invent and explain a paradox based on those quoted from the *Tao Te Ching.*

Additional Activity: Lao Tzu and Chuang Tzu

Understanding Paradox

1. The student text points out that the *Tao Te Ching* has a profound and enigmatic nature, and that many of its teachings are stated in the form of paradoxes. Review with the students the definition of paradoxes that is given in the student text: "Paradoxes [are] assertions that seem illogical and contradictory on the surface, and yet contain deeper truths that are accessible more through intuition than through logical thinking." Explain that a paradox encourages the reader to think about what is being said because of the contrast contained within it, which can be surprising and even shocking.

2. Ask the students to recall and share what they have learned about paradoxes in language arts classes, and to give examples of paradoxical statements. Write the students' examples on the board and invite the young people to describe how each statement stimulates their thinking through contrast. The following paradoxes and observations can also be incorporated into the discussion:

- The poet Wordsworth wrote, "The Child is father of the Man" ("My heart leaps up when I behold"). At first this seems illogical and impossible, but on further reflection we realize that our childhood experiences are very much a part of who we become as adults.
- Oscar Wilde wrote, "There is only one thing in the world worse than being talked about, and that is not being talked about" (*The Picture of Dorian Gray,* chap. 1). The two halves of this statement seem to be mutually exclusive. However, we often find that we want both recognition and privacy, and there is a tension between these desires. You may have gained special insights into Wilde's statement through experiences of peer pressure, the desire to have friends and be popular, and so on.
- Paradox is central to many statements Jesus made. For example, he said, "For those who want to save their life will lose it, and those who lose their life for my sake, and for the sake of the gospel, will save it" (Mark 8:35). It might seem impossible to save one's life by physically dying. But Jesus was saying that only when we die to selfishness and embrace a loving attitude will we experience life as God intended. Jesus' paradoxical statement invites his listeners to reflect deeply on this.
- Saint Paul also used paradox: "If you think that you are wise in this age, you should become fools so that you may become wise. For the wisdom of this world is foolishness with God" (1 Cor. 3:18–19). Paul's statement causes us to re-examine our understanding of the nature of wisdom and foolishness, leading to the realization that spiritual wisdom is far different from the wisdom of the world.

You might want to raise this question: "Why do religious traditions, poets, and authors use paradoxes? Why don't they just speak 'plainly'?" Make the following points in your own words:

- Many people, including the disciples of Jesus', have asked that question. Using a paradox helps us express something that is otherwise inexpressible—such as love, God, and Tao. It can open up in the listener or reader a recognition of the truth in what is being said.

3. Point out that paradoxes are at the heart of mystical religious traditions. Invite the students to agree or disagree with this statement, and to explain their response: "The religion I know the most about would have more meaning for me if its paradoxes were emphasized as much as its doctrines."

Pages 142–149

Concept B: The Philosophy of Tao

Review Questions: The Philosophy of Tao

Question 5. What is the literal meaning of the title *Tao Te Ching?*
Answer. "The book of the Way and its power (or virtue)."

Question 6. According to the *Tao Te Ching,* what is Tao?
Answer. Tao is both the ultimate source and the principle of order in the universe. It is the Way of nature.

Question 7. Define the terms *yin* and *yang.*
Answer. *Yin* and *yang* refer to the complementary components of Tao. Yin is the negative, passive, feminine, earthly component, characterized by darkness and weakness. Yang is the positive, active, masculine, heavenly component, characterized by light and strength.

Question 8. Why does Taoism insist that values are relative and not absolute?
Answer. Because no value could exist if it were not for its opposite, and all values are tinged by the presence of their opposite.

Question 9. What does Taoism teach regarding an afterlife?
Answer. Taoism says nothing of an afterlife, and describes death as a return from life back into the original unity of the Tao.

Question 10. What is the manner of living perfected by the Taoist sage?
Answer. The sage attains oneness with Tao through apprehension of its simplicity and natural unity.

Question 11. Define and briefly describe *wu-wei.* Use an analogy in your description.
Answer. *Wu-wei* means "nonaction" and refers to being so perfectly in harmony with nature that nature's energy infuses and empowers one. The person who practices *wu-wei* "acts without acting." *Wu-wei* is like water in a stream, which, by merely staying its course, can create a valley or canyon.

Question 12. List six Taoist virtues that demonstrate the basic virtue *wu-wei.*
Answer. Humility and noncompetition, naturalness and naturalism, and nonaggression and passive rule.

Question 13. What characteristic of Taoist naturalism distinguishes it from some forms of environmentalism?
Answer. Taoist naturalism resists the temptation to meddle with nature, whereas some forms of environmentalism strive to fix things through human ideas and efforts.

Question 14. What does Taoism advocate as being the best way to govern?
Answer. The good ruler takes a passive approach through the practice of *wu-wei.*

Text Activities: The Philosophy of Tao

Activity B

Taoists are the first to admit that Tao can never be completely explained in words. After reading the textbook section "Tao: The Way of Nature," describe Tao as completely as you can in your own words.

Activity C

Magnetism provides a helpful analogy for understanding Tao. Think of another helpful comparison from nature, art, or technology, and explain how it is like Tao.

Activity D

Draw your own symbol for yin and yang. Explain its meaning.

Activity E

Chuang Tzu points out the relativity of values in his story of the monkeys in Sung. For no apparent reason, the monkeys are furious with the first arrangement and delighted with the second. Think of a time you or someone you know got excessively distraught over a superficial distinction. What might have been the reason for that reaction?

Activity F

Compare Chuang Tzu's perspective on the death of his wife with your own perspective on death. In what ways do you agree or disagree with Chuang Tzu?

Activity G

Use your own observations to expand on what the textbook has to say about the "sagely" ways of the cat. In addition, choose another type of pet, and describe what it does or does not have in common with the Taoist sage.

Activity H

Reflect on the following topic: How might the Taoist virtue *wu-wei* be applied to the task of writing a one-page essay?

Activity I

Imagine a stream of running water (if possible, observe a stream or river). The *Tao Te Ching* uses the stream as the ideal image of the yin—weak, passive, and feminine. Reflect on how the stream embodies the characteristics of yin.

Activity J

State your own solution to the following environmental dilemma. Then state the likely solution of a Taoist. Compare the two solutions.

The U.S. government has offered bounties on wolves and has operated other extermination programs that have severely reduced the wolf population. This and other circumstances have led to a great growth in the population of deer, which are natural prey for wolves. Now many deer starve to death each winter because they cannot find enough food in their overcrowded territories.

Activity K

Consider carefully what chapter 17 of the *Tao Te Ching* says about good government. How does the government of your nation rate according to Lao Tzu's perspective? Do you think Lao Tzu's assertion that the best rulers are merely known to exist (and rule passively) is true for your own nation?

Additional Activities: The Philosophy of Tao

Opposites, Complements, and Balance: Yin and Yang

1. The student text compares Tao to magnetism, and mentions that like magnetism, Tao has two polar opposites, the yin and the yang. Direct the class to look at the yin-yang symbol in the student text, page 144. Review the text material on yin and yang with the students, and ask them to answer text activity C, which challenges them to think of another analogy for Tao.

After the students have had some time to work, invite several volunteers to present their analogies to the class. Briefly discuss the merits of each analogy, asking whether it effectively conveys the idea of an unseen, incomprehensible, ultimate source (Tao), with two opposite but complementary components (yin and yang).

2. Continue the discussion of yin and yang by focusing on the aspect of balance. Ask the students to identify several ways that balance is important in their life (for example, in their diet, in their physical and intellectual activity, in their commitments to family and friends, in their planning for the future and enjoyment of the present). With each example they give, ask if the apparent opposites involved actually oppose each other, or if they in fact complement each other. For example: Does planning for the future negate our enjoyment of the present, or does responsible enjoyment of the present help us plan for the future? Does commitment to family relationships negate our friendships, or does it enhance our friendships? In most cases it will be clear that the "opposites" are in fact complements—that what gives us joy today can become the basis of our plans for the future, and so on.

3. Direct the final portion of the discussion toward the actual characteristics of yin and yang. Write them on the board:

Yin	*Yang*
Negative	Positive
Passive	Active
Feminine	Masculine
Earthly	Heavenly
Dark	Light
Weak	Strong

Tell the students to think of a person they know fairly well—a family member or friend who is not in this class—and to write that person's first name on a slip of paper. Then ask the students to sit together in pairs. Without identifying the person whose name they have written down, have each student describe that person to his or her partner by using the characteristics of yin and yang. For example, in what way is the person passive, and in what

8

way is he or she active? One response might be, "He is passive when it comes to making new friends, but active regarding his after-school job."

4. When everyone has described for their partner the person they chose, give the class the following assignment:

- Just as you have described a person you know in terms of yin and yang, now, in writing, describe yourself in those terms. Then write a one-page essay agreeing or disagreeing with this statement: Describing myself in terms of the characteristics of yin and yang helps me learn about and understand myself. Be sure to provide clear reasons for your agreement or disagreement.

Who Is the Sage?

Handout 8–A

Review with the students the concept of the Taoist sage, the person who lives in accord with Tao. Then review the concept of *wu-wei,* or nonaction, and the virtues related to it. Next, distribute handout 8–A, "Who Is the Sage?" Direct the students to complete the handout according to the instructions on it.

When the students have completed the handout, go over the results with the entire class and address any questions or misunderstandings that have surfaced. The final task on the handout calls for the students to invent an additional situation like the others on the handout, and to draw a cartoon illustrating that situation. You may wish to give the students more time for this task by assigning it as homework. Call for several volunteers to present their completed situations and cartoons to the class. Discuss the answers to these additional situations.

The correct answers to the handout questions are 1: B; 2: A; 3: B; 4: B; 5: A.

Relativity

To understand Taoism the students will need to grasp the concept of relativity. It may be useful to draw the yin-yang on the board and refer to it during the following discussion. A diagram of the yin-yang is found in the student text on page 144.

Note: This activity explores the concepts of selfishness and selflessness, which are also covered in the exercise "*Karma Marga:* 'The Path of Works,'" in chapter 3.

1. Invite a student to read the following quote from the *Tao Te Ching,* found on page 144 of the student text. (The other students may wish to read along.)

When the people of the world all know beauty as beauty,
  There arises the recognition of ugliness.
When they all know the good as good,
  There arises the recognition of evil.

(Chapter 2)

2. Begin the discussion of relativity by asking about the students' experience of "the recognition of ugliness," using questions such as these:

- Once you know what fresh milk tastes like, can you tell when milk is spoiled? If so, how?

- Could you know that a glass of milk tastes fresh without knowing what spoiled milk tastes like?
- Does knowing what spoiled milk tastes like enhance your knowledge or appreciation of fresh milk?
- Refer to the quotation from the *Tao Te Ching*. Can you know beauty without also knowing ugliness? Likewise, can you know moral goodness without also knowing evil?

3. Point out that the yin-yang illustrates that our understanding of one absolute suggests at least a limited knowledge of its opposite. Note that yin has an element of yang in it, and vice versa. In your own words, explain the symbol, covering these points:

- The yin-yang represents the view that our experience of fresh milk or spoiled milk necessarily presupposes an experience of the opposite.
- The same principle can be applied to moral good and evil. Taoism rejects the possibility of absolute goodness, because goodness is tinged by evil, and evil by goodness.

4. Ask the students to think of hypothetical situations in which a person is performing deeds for the benefit of others but is also motivated by selfishness. List the situations on the board. Next, do the same with situations in which a person is performing deeds that are harmful to others but is also motivated by altruism.

5. When the lists are complete, direct the students each to select one of the situations and write a fictional story that explores it. You may wish to instruct the students to complete a final draft of the story for homework.

6. Arrange for the completed stories to be shared in pairs, in small groups, or with the whole class. As the stories are read, have the students who are listening pay attention to the signs of altruism and selfishness. Discuss the stories individually and as a whole, and conclude by asking the class if actions are ever wholly good or wholly bad.

Additional Resources from Saint Mary's Press

See *Primary Source Readings in World Religions* (Saint Mary's Press, 2009) for selections from *The Way of Lao Tzu (Tau Te Ching)*, *Chuang Tzu*, and *The Taoist Body*, as well as the accompanying leader's guide for suggestions about how to use these readings in your study of Taoism.

Who Is the Sage?

In each pair of situations below, one of the people described resembles the ideal of the Taoist sage, the person who lives in accord with Tao and practices the virtue *wu-wei.* Read each pair of situations and circle the letter next to the description of the person that most resembles the sage. Be prepared to give reasons for your answers.

1

A. She prepares for an exam by staying up all night right before the exam, reading all the assignments for the first time and comparing them with the notes she took in class, and memorizing the meanings of the important terms and concepts.

B. She prepares for an exam by reading assignments regularly and attentively, listening, participating, taking notes in class, and then briefly reviewing her assignments and notes for several nights before the exam.

2

A. When leading a group project, he allows each group member to give her or his input and to choose a preferred role in completing the task.

B. When leading a group project, he assigns roles and gives directions to others to ensure that the task is completed according to his standards.

3

A. When she catches a cold, she takes several types of medication so that she can continue with her busy schedule.

B. When she catches a cold, she takes any necessary medication and gets plenty of rest, even if it means altering her schedule.

4

A. In trying to become the team's starting quarterback, he throws many long passes, completing one of every four.

B. In trying to become the team's starting quarterback, he throws many short passes, completing three of every four.

5

A. An actor in a school play does not like some of her character's lines, but she speaks them as written.

B. An actor in a school play does not like some of her character's lines, so she changes them.

6

Make up a situation modeled on those above. Write it on a piece of notebook paper. Then, on the back of this handout, draw a cartoon that illustrates both the person who lives in accord with the Tao and the one who does not. Be prepared to present your situation and your cartoon to the class, and to explain which person is the sage, and why.

CHAPTER 9

Zen Buddhism

Major Concepts

A. **Transmission of Zen Teachings.** Zen is a form of Mahayana Buddhism that focuses on the experience of enlightenment. The word *zen* means "meditation," and the Zen tradition traces its origins to the Buddha himself. From India, Zen spread first to China and then to Japan, where two sects of Zen are most prominent. The Rinzai sect emphasizes sudden awakening, whereas the Soto sect emphasizes gradual awakening.

B. **Zen Teachings.** Zen is direct experience of truth, which is beyond the reach of thoughts and feelings about truth, and beyond the words used to express thoughts and feelings. Zen emphasizes experience over speculation. Its insights cannot be expressed in words. Zen is beyond logical thinking, which clutters the mind and prevents pure insight into the truth. Zen enlightenment is called *satori.* It is an impermanent state that recurs with increasing frequency and intensity, and leads to a new, enlightened perspective. *Koans* are an important tool in Zen training. These puzzles are designed to short-circuit the workings of the logical, rational mind and lead to direct insight into reality. Zen is often seen as a negative and world-denying religion, but its adherents find that to be untrue. Zen helps one attain a healthy, vigorous mind; it sees the everyday world as relevant, and cultivates full attention to that world; and it focuses on the here and now.

C. **Zen Life.** Zen prescribes a monastic lifestyle that is designed in every way to move the disciple closer to enlightenment. *Zazen,* seated meditation, consumes most of the monks' time, but menial work is also an essential part of monastic life. The Zen master *(roshi)* has almost complete authority over the disciple. The practice of Zen does not require one to become a monk or nun; it can be performed outside the monastery. Zen has had a significant influence on East Asian cultural arts such as painting, landscaping, flower arranging, swordplay, and archery. Haiku is a well-known poetic form that exemplifies Zen's influence on literature.

Pages 154–155

Concept A: Transmission of Zen Teachings

Review Questions: Transmission of Zen Teachings

Question 1. How do the terms *dhyana* and *ch'an* relate to the name *Zen?*
Answer. All three words mean "meditation." The Chinese word *ch'an* and the Japanese term *Zen* both derive from the Sanskrit word *dhyana.*

Question 2. Why did the Buddha choose Mahakasyapa as his successor?
Answer. Because Mahakasyapa's smile indicated that he understood what the Buddha was teaching by holding up a flower instead of speaking.

Question 3. What is the name of the Zen patriarch under whose influence Chinese Zen flourished?
Answer. Hui-neng.

Question 4. Identify the two primary sects of Japanese Zen.
Answer. Rinzai and Soto.

Question 5. Which Zen sect is known as the school of sudden awakening?
Answer. Rinzai.

Additional Activity: Transmission of Zen Teachings

Primary Source Reading

See *Primary Source Readings in World Religions* (Saint Mary's Press, 2009) for an excerpt from "The Platform Sutra of the Sixth Patriarch," as well as the accompanying leader's guide for suggestions about how to use this reading in your study of Zen Buddhism.

Seated Meditation

Seated meditation, or *zazen,* is a basic practice in Zen Buddhism. It is discussed under the major concept "Zen Life" in this chapter of the student text. This activity encourages you and the students to attempt a meditative practice that will provide insight into the experiential nature of Zen. Introduce this practice on the first day of your class's study of Zen.

Give the students these directions in your own words:

- Sit with your back as straight as possible, your feet flat on the floor, and your eyes half-closed. Count your breaths—inhale, "One"; exhale, "Two"; inhale, "Three"; and so on, up to, "Ten." Then begin again with, "One." Focus all your attention on the breathing and counting, putting aside as much as you can other thoughts that occur. When you lose count (and you will!), start again at, "One."

If possible, signal the end of the meditation period by ringing a small bell (the use of bells is fairly common in Buddhism).

Practice this technique for 5 minutes at the start of each class session on Zen. Encourage the students to apply the experience of this simple technique of seated meditation to what they learn from the student text and in class.

If you wish to explore Zen meditation further, see appendix 3 of this manual for two books that may be helpful: *Zen Mind, Beginner's Mind,* by Shunryu Suzuki, and *Zen Training: Methods and Philosophy,* by Katsuki Sekida. Because of the popularity of Zen Buddhism in the United States, there are many Zen meditation centers throughout the country. You may be able to find and contact one in your area, to schedule a field trip or a guest speaker.

Pages 155–161

Concept B: Zen Teachings

Review Questions: Zen Teachings

Question 6. For Zen Buddhists and the historical Buddha, what is the primary means of attaining enlightenment?
Answer. Meditation.

Question 7. Briefly describe these three characteristics of Zen: it is experiential, it is beyond words, and it is beyond logical thinking.
Answer. Zen is experiential: it insists on firsthand experience and rejects speculation regarding the nature of reality. Zen is beyond words: the insight of Zen cannot be expressed in words; it depends on direct experience of the truth. Zen is beyond logical thinking: as long as the logical reasoning process is at work interpreting reality, direct experience is impossible.

Question 8. What did Japanese master Nan-in mean by telling the university professor, "Empty your cup"?
Answer. He wanted the professor to see things as if for the first time.

Question 9. What is *satori?*
Answer. Freedom from the bondage of thought, feeling, and self-centered ego; a pure experience in which the true nature of one's being is known directly.

Question 10. What is the difference between *satori* and *nirvana?*
Answer. Nirvana is a permanent state of enlightenment, whereas *satori* is a temporary state that is experienced with increasing frequency and intensity.

Question 11. What is a *koan* designed to do? Give an example of a *koan.*
Answer. A *koan* is a puzzle designed to short-circuit the workings of the rational, logical mind. [The students may give as examples any of the *koans* cited in the student text.]

Question 12. What is a *dokusan?*
Answer. A *dokusan* is a session in which the Zen master and the Zen disciple meet formally to discuss Zen teachings and training. The disciple is also expected to offer an answer to an assigned *koan.*

Question 13. Identify the positive effects of Zen on the mind.
Answer. Zen is said to significantly enhance the mind's strength and vitality.

Question 14. How does the perspective of Zen alter one's view of everyday reality?
Answer. Zen is fully attentive to everyday reality, which it sees in a new light.

Question 15. What does Zen teach about the existence of an afterlife?
Answer. Zen neither affirms nor denies the existence of an afterlife, and so overcomes the duality of life and death.

Text Activities: Zen Teachings

Activity A

Because Zen is experiential, it cannot adequately be described in words. Such a problem is not unique to Zen. Describe the experience of eating your favorite food. Now repeat your description, comparing it with your memory of the actual experience. In what ways does your description fall short of adequately expressing the full experience?

Activity B

In their conversation about death, what kind of answer do you think the emperor expected from Gudo? What might the emperor have said to encourage Gudo to elaborate?

Activity C

Explore what you think D. T. Suzuki means when he writes that "Zen teaches nothing."

Activity D

The next time you are outside with some free time, observe a tree. Try to see it simply for what it is, without categorizing, affirming, denying, or speculating.

Activity E

Try to compose your own Zen *koan.* Reflect on why you find the task difficult or easy.

Activity F

What does the poem written by Master Shoun tell you about his perspective on death? on life?

Additional Activity: Zen Teachings

Zen *Koans:* Food for Intuition

Zen *koans* are a fascinating aspect of Zen practice. *Koans* may be described as puzzles or riddles designed to frustrate, or move the thinker beyond, the logical mind. In this way *koans* are unlike standard riddles, for which logical connections can be made. The answer to a *koan* lies in one's intuitive response to it.

The book *Zen Flesh, Zen Bones: A Collection of Zen and Pre-Zen Writings,* compiled by Paul Reps (see appendix 3), contains a popular translation of *101 Zen Stories,* which provides tales about Zen teachers and their students, covering a five-century period. Reading those may give you a feel for the pedagogical use of *koans* by Zen masters and their students.

Handout 9–A

1. Distribute handout 9–A, "The Riddler," and instruct the students to solve its riddles in pairs or small groups, either in class or at home.

2. When the students have used up the time allotted for solving the riddles, call for their answers, and compare their responses against the correct answers listed below. Let the young people know which riddles they solved correctly, and provide answers for any riddles that were not solved.

Answers for Handout 9–A

1. The wind	7. A shadow
2. An egg	8. Fire
3. Your word	9. A candle
4. Your breath	10. An icicle
5. A river	11. A chair
6. Silence	12. A coffin

Then raise discussion questions along these lines:

- What kind of thought process did you use to try to solve the riddles?
- Imagine a thought process that is the opposite of the one you used. Would that process have helped you to solve the riddles more effectively?
- How would you characterize the answers in relation to the riddles? Do they make sense? Are they logical or illogical?

This discussion is intended to make the students aware that solving the riddles required the use of their logic and intellect, and that the clues in the riddles, although tricky, lead logically to the answers.

Handout 9–B

3. Distribute handout 9–B, "*Koans:* Food for ~~Thought~~ Intuition." Instruct the students to read the handout, which contains several Zen *koans.* If they have already read the section on *koans* in the student text, they will be familiar with the concept. Direct them each to choose one of the *koans* on the handout and to answer it on their own, either in class or at home.

4. When the allotted time is up, invite volunteers to share their *koans* and their answers to them. Engage each volunteer in a brief dialogue to determine whether her or his answer is a product of logical thought or of a more intuitive process. Emphasize the following points:

- Answers based on logical thinking would be rejected by a Zen master, as would whimsical answers that merely mimic the "nonsensical" or illogical quality of the *koans* themselves.
- Even if no one in the class achieved what might be an acceptable answer to a *koan,* it should be clear that Zen strives to transcend normal everyday thought processes—which include the thought processes needed to solve the riddles *and* to complete a high school education!

Handout 9–C

5. Distribute (or read aloud) handout 9–C, "'The Sound of One Hand.'" This handout contains a Zen story that chronicles the attempts of Toyo, a young Zen student, to unravel Zen's most famous *koan.* After the students have read or heard the story, encourage discussion comparing the students' experience of *koans* with Toyo's experience.

Pages 161–163

Concept C: Zen Life

Review Questions: Zen Life

Question 16. What is the literal meaning of the word *zazen?*
Answer. "Seated meditation."

Question 17. What is the intent of the practice *zazen?*
Answer. To clear the mind and thereby attain insight.

Question 18. What types of tasks do Zen monks engage in as part of their monastic training?
Answer. The monks do everyday, menial tasks such as preparing food, tending fields, gathering firewood, and begging in local villages.

Question 19. How does Zen foster the impulse to correct social injustice?
Answer. Zen insight overcomes the bondage of self-centeredness, so that the suffering of others becomes one's own. Through this process Zen fosters the natural impulse to alleviate all suffering by working to correct social injustices.

9

Question 20. What is the most famous example of Zen influence in the visual arts?
Answer. *Sumie,* or black ink painting.

Question 21. Identify at least three other arts on which Zen has had a strong influence.
Answer. [Any three of the following answers are correct:] Landscape gardening, flower arrangement, swordplay, archery, and poetry.

Text Activities: Zen Life

Activity G

Imagine yourself practicing *zazen* in a meditation hall and getting hit in the back with an encouragement stick. Describe what it would take for you to feel actual gratitude, rather than resentment, toward the attendant who hit you.

Activity H

Zen acknowledges the spiritual benefits of work, especially menial tasks. How does work relate to your spiritual well-being?

Activity I

Describe an aspect of your own society that might benefit from Zen teachings.

Activity J

Compose your own haiku. In it try to capture something of the spirit of Zen.

Additional Activity: Zen Life

Writing Haiku

1. To introduce the idea of writing haiku, instruct the students to take a blank sheet of paper, fold it into quarters, unfold it, and in each quadrant list words pertaining to a different one of the four seasons. It is not necessary to tell the students that this is a haiku activity; in fact, the concept of haiku may be more appealing to them if they work with it for a while before you name it. Explain that the words they list do not need to directly reference nature—they could list *baseball* for spring, for example.

After several minutes tell the students to describe, on a separate sheet of paper, images that come to mind when they read each list of season words. Encourage them to write as many images as they can think of.

2. When everyone has written several images, explain that this exercise has been a warm-up for writing haiku. Ask the students what they already know about haiku. Supplement their knowledge with the information below.

- In Japanese, haiku consist of three lines: the first line contains five syllables, the second line contains seven syllables, and the third line contains five syllables, for a total of seventeen syllables. In English, haiku do not need to conform to this exact arrangement of syllables, but they do generally consist of three short lines. In those three lines an image is presented in a clear and direct way. The image is often connected with a season, and it is usually juxtaposed with another image. The juxtaposition and clarity of the images are the keys to a successful haiku. Haiku do not contain similes, metaphors, or rhymes.

Handout 9–D

You may wish to spend some extra time helping the students understand the idea of the juxtaposition of images. Distribute handout 9–D, "The Haiku of Basho." Using the first haiku on the handout, along with comments like the ones that follow, show the students how the separate images—including an "image" of sound—work together to make a striking whole:

- Basho begins with three words, "The old pond," which call to mind an image of a pond that is likely overgrown and not well maintained. This image provides a sense of quiet peacefulness. Then Basho introduces the movement of a frog, which suggests that it is springtime. The frog image is sudden and jarring in contrast with the peaceful image of the pond. Finally, Basho lets us hear "the sound of the water," and with this we sense not only sudden disruption but also the pond's return to its quiet state. We can almost see the ripples from the frog's splash as they smooth out and disappear—until the next incident of sudden movement.

Direct the students to choose another haiku from the handout and to analyze the way the images work together to create a successful haiku. This will help them prepare to write their own.

After the students have analyzed the second haiku, suggest that they read the introductory paragraph on the handout and enjoy the remaining poetry by Basho.

3. Tell the students to return their attention to the images they jotted down earlier, to focus on the three images they find most striking, and to begin the process of turning each of those three images into a haiku. Point out that the word *haiku* literally means "play verse." Encourage the students to engage in the creation of haiku with a playful spirit, writing in the way a child might write.

Mention that when they have written a haiku, they should not consider it done until they have honed it. Tell them to reread it and ask themselves: "Is every adjective and adverb in this poem necessary? Is every article needed? Does the punctuation, or lack of punctuation, help or hinder the poem?"

4. When the students have each written three haiku, direct them to choose the one they like best. Then invite the students, in random or prearranged order, to face the class and read their selected haiku aloud. Encourage them to read slowly and deliberately, and make sure they speak loudly enough for all to hear. If possible, arrange for them to display their haiku so that the class can read along. Ask the listeners not to comment on the haiku at this point.

5. When all have read their haiku, call them back to repeat their readings in the same order as before. Pause after each reading and invite the listeners to comment on the haiku. Focus their comments with questions like these:

- How does the haiku make you feel?
- Are the images clear?
- Is the juxtaposition of images striking?
- Do any words get in the way?
- Are too few words used for the haiku to be effective?

Take care that the discussion does not become a matter of deciding which haiku is best. Ensure that the students discuss each haiku on its own terms rather than in comparison with others.

You may wish to compile the class haiku into a booklet to distribute to all the students.

The Riddler

Working alone or with classmates, identify what is being described in each of the following riddles.

1

Voiceless it cries,
Wingless it flutters,
Toothless bites,
Mouthless mutters.

2

A box without hinges, key, or lid,
Yet golden treasure inside is hid.

3

You must keep it after giving it.

4

As light as a feather,
but you can't hold it for ten minutes.

5

Has a mouth but does not speak,
Has a bed but never sleeps.

6

You break it when you name it.

7

Though I dance at a ball,
I am nothing at all.

8

I am always hungry,
I must always be fed,
The finger I lick
Will soon turn red.

9

My life can be measured in hours,
I serve by being devoured.
Thin, I am quick,
Fat, I am slow
Wind is my foe.

10

The root tops the trunk
On this backward thing
That grows in the winter
And dies in the spring.

11

I have legs but walk not
A strong back but work not
Two good arms but reach not
A seat but sit and tarry not.

12

He who makes it needs it not
He who buys it wants it not
He who uses it knows it not.

Koans: Food for ~~Thought~~ Intuition

Read the following Zen *koans* two or three times. Choose one and answer or explain it.

A monk told Joshu: "I have just entered the monastery. Please teach me."
Joshu asked: "Have you eaten your rice porridge?"
The monk replied: "I have eaten."
Joshu said: "Then you had better wash your bowl."
At that moment the monk was enlightened.

A monk asked Tozan when he was weighing some flax: "What is Buddha?"
Tozan said: "This flax weighs three pounds."

Shogen asked: "Why does the enlightened man not stand on his feet and explain himself?" And he also said: "It is not necessary for speech to come from the tongue."

Goso said: "When a buffalo goes out of his enclosure to the edge of the abyss, his horns and his head and his hoofs all pass through, but why can't the tail also pass?"

Basho said to his disciple: "When you have a staff, I will give it to you. If you have no staff, I will take it away from you."

Sekiso asked: "How can you proceed on from the top of a hundred-foot pole?" Another Zen teacher said: "One who sits on the top of a hundred-foot pole has attained a certain height but still is not handling Zen freely. He should proceed on from there and appear with his whole body in the ten parts of the world."

Two monks were arguing about a flag. One said: "The flag is moving."
The other said: "The wind is moving."
The sixth patriarch happened to be passing by. He told them: "Not the wind, not the flag; mind is moving."

A monk asked Fuketsu: "Without speaking, without silence, how can you express the truth?"
Fuketsu observed: "I always remember springtime in southern China. The birds sing among innumerable kinds of fragrant flowers."

(These *koans* are from *The Gateless Gate*, by Ekai, called Mu-mon, translated by Nyogen Senzaki and Paul Reps [Los Angeles: J. Murray, 1934]).

"The Sound of One Hand"

The master of Kennin temple was Mokurai, Silent Thunder. He had a little protéjé named Toyo who was only twelve years old. Toyo saw the older disciples visit the master's room each morning and evening to receive instruction in sanzen *[dokusan]* or personal guidance in which they were given koans to stop mind-wandering.

Toyo wished to do sanzen also.

"Wait a while," said Mokurai. "You are too young."

But the child insisted, so the teacher finally consented.

In the evening little Toyo went at the proper time to the threshold of Mokurai's sanzen room. He struck the gong to announce his presence, bowed respectfully three times outside the door, and went to sit before the master in respectful silence.

"You can hear the sound of two hands when they clap together," said Mokurai. "Now show me the sound of one hand."

Toyo bowed and went to his room to consider this problem. From his window he could hear the music of the geishas. "Ah, I have it!" he proclaimed.

The next evening, when his teacher asked him to illustrate the sound of one hand, Toyo began to play the music of the geishas.

"No, no," said Mokurai. "That will never do. That is not the sound of one hand. You've not got it at all."

Thinking that such music might interrupt, Toyo moved his abode to a quiet place. He meditated again. "What can the sound of one hand be?" He happened to hear some water dripping. "I have it," imagined Toyo.

When he next appeared before his teacher, Toyo imitated dripping water.

"What is that?" asked Mokurai. "That is the sound of dripping water, but not the sound of one hand. Try again."

In vain Toyo meditated to hear the sound of one hand. He heard the sighing of the wind. But the sound was rejected.

He heard the cry of an owl. This also was refused.

The sound of one hand was not the locusts.

For more than ten times Toyo visited Mokurai with different sounds. All were wrong. For almost a year he pondered what the sound of one hand might be.

At last little Toyo entered true meditation and transcended all sounds. "I could collect no more," he explained later, "so I reached the soundless sound."

Toyo had realized the sound of one hand. (Paul Reps, compiler, *Zen Flesh, Zen Bones: A Collection of Zen and Pre-Zen Writings* [Garden City, NY: Doubleday and Company, Anchor Books by arrangement with Charles E. Tuttle Company of Boston and Tokyo, 1957], pages 24–26. Copyright © 1957 by Charles E. Tuttle Company. Used with permission of Tuttle Publishing, a member of the Periplus Publishing Group.)

The Haiku of Basho

Matsuo Basho was born in 1644 near Kyoto, Japan. As a boy he was already interested in poetry, and in his twenties he studied extensively with notable teachers of literature in Kyoto. He was acknowledged as a master of haiku by the time he was about thirty years old. During the last ten years of his life, Basho traveled a great deal, making pilgrimages alone or with companions. On these trips he visited famous places of Japan and met with other poets. He died during one of his pilgrimages, at the age of fifty. The following is a small sampling of Basho's haiku, from *Japanese Haiku: Two Hundred Twenty Examples of Seventeen-Syllable Poems,* translated by Peter Beilenson.

Ballet in the air . . .
Twin butterflies
until, twice white
they meet, they mate
(Page 9)

Seek on high bare trails
sky-reflecting
violets . . .
Mountain-top jewels
(Page 9)

Now that eyes of hawks
in dusky night
are darkened . . .
Chirping of the quails
(Page 10)

For a lovely bowl
let us arrange these
flowers . . .
Since there is no rice
(Page 10)

April's air stirs in
willow-leaves
A butterfly
floats and balances
(Page 11)

In the sea-surf edge
mingling with
bright small shells
Bush-clover petals
(Page 12)

The river
gathering may rains
from cold streamlets
for the sea . . .
Murmuring mogami
(Page 12)

White cloud of mist
above white
cherry-blossoms
Dawn-shining mountains
(Page 13)

(Mount Vernon, NY: The Peter Pauper Press.
Copyright © 1955–1956 by The Peter Pauper Press.)

CHAPTER 10

Shinto

Major Concepts

A. **"Way of the *Kami*."** Shinto is Japan's native religious tradition. Shinto emphasizes the ritual dimension over the doctrinal. The *kami,* divine ancestors of the Japanese and sacred inhabitants of the land, include deities and certain human beings, as well as natural elements like mountains and animals. Shinto has no sacred scripture, but it does have authoritative histories containing a cosmology and an account of human origins. Shinto considers nature in all its manifestations to be sacred, and this sacredness is worshiped in its embodied form of *kami.*

B. **Shinto in the Religious Life of Japan.** Shinto worship focuses on simple expression of respectful gratitude to the *kami,* and to the experience of unity with them. Worship can take place in the home, at shrines, or during large seasonal festivals. Shinto shrines have a natural beauty and are found throughout Japan. The shrine entrance is marked by an archway called a *torii,* which is recognized worldwide as the symbol of Shinto. The most notable Shinto festivals are the Great Purification and the festival of the New Year. Three main types of Shinto can be identified today: Shrine Shinto is an organized institution, with officially designated shrines and priests. Sect Shinto is also organized, but consists of a wide variety of separate institutions, or "sects." Popular Shinto includes many of the practices of the other types, but lacks any formal organization.

Pages 167–170

Concept A: "Way of the *Kami*"

Review Questions: "Way of the *Kami*"

Question 1. What is a general definition of *kami*?
Answer. Kami are any people or things that have evoked the wonder of the Japanese.

Question 2. What is contained in Shinto's authoritative histories?
Answer. A mythological account of the origins of Japan.

Question 3. Who are Izanagi and Izanami?
Answer. They are the primal male and female from the mythological account of the origins of Japan.

Question 4. According to the Shinto myth of origins, what is the nature of the ancestry of the Japanese?
Answer. It is divine.

Question 5. According to the great Shinto scholar Motoori Norinaga, a wide variety of things can be considered *kami.* List at least four of them.
Answer. [Any four of the following answers are correct:] The deities of heaven and earth, the spirits of the shrines, human beings, birds, beasts, trees, plants, seas, mountains, thunder, dragons, echoes, foxes, tigers, wolves, peaches, and a necklace.

Question 6. What do the ancient histories recognize when they say that the *kami* number "eight hundred myriads," or eight million?
Answer. They recognize that the islands of Japan abound with the sacred forces that the *kami* embody.

Text Activities: "Way of the *Kami*"

Activity A

Myths provide answers to fundamental questions about human life and history. Often they give those answers using symbolic images and events that do not have obvious meanings. With this in mind, carefully consider the Shinto myth. What fundamental questions does it answer, and how?

Activity B

The concept of *kami* is central to Shinto. After reading the descriptions and examples of *kami,* close your textbook and describe *kami* in your own words.

Additional Activity: "Way of the *Kami*"

The Nature of the *Kami*

As the student text points out, understanding the nature of the Shinto *kami* is such a difficult task that it even humbled the great Shinto scholar Motoori Norinaga. One way to approach understanding the *kami* is to engage the students in a discussion about the feelings of holiness and awe that can be inspired by particular natural and human-made objects.

1. Lead the class in brainstorming a short list of things and places that might inspire a holy feeling, and jot that list on the board. If the students need help getting started, suggest examples such as these:

- Autumn leaves
- Ocean waves
- Majestic mountains
- Flowers
- A newborn baby
- Rosary beads
- A Bible
- A work of art
- A chapel
- A grove of evergreen trees

2. Invite the students to call out objects that have actually evoked a sense of holiness or awe for them. Or, if you think the class would prefer an anonymous method of sharing, ask everyone to write the names of such objects on slips of paper and to pass the slips forward. Add these objects to the list on the board. Also encourage the students to describe their sensations of the sacred in the presence of a particular object or place.

3. Mention that the holiness of nature is a consistent theme in world literature. Consider reading aloud the following brief examples:

- "Every day is a god, each day is a god, and holiness holds forth in time."
  (Annie Dillard)

- "And yet, there is only
  One great thing,
  The only thing:
  To live to see in huts and on journeys
  The great day that dawns,
  And the light that fills the world."
  (Inuit song)

- "There is religion in everything around us,
  A calm and holy religion
  In the unbreathing things in Nature."
  (John Ruskin)

- "In Your goodness You have made us able to hear
  the music of the world. The voices of loved ones
  reveal to us that You are in our midst.
  A divine voice sings through all creation."
  (Jewish prayer)

- "Wherever you are is home
  And the earth is paradise
  Wherever you set your feet is holy land."
  (Wilfred Pelletier and Ted Poole)

- "When you walk across the fields with your mind pure and holy, then from all the stones, and all growing things, and all animals, the sparks of their soul come out and cling to you, and then they are purified and become a holy fire in you."
  (Hasidic saying)

- "Where I sit is holy,
  Holy is the ground."
  (Anonymous)

Ask the students if they recall any similar pieces of literature, perhaps from English classes. You might also instruct them to bring in an additional example of literature that celebrates the sacred in creation, or to turn in a written account of their own experience of a sense of holiness inspired by a certain object or place.

4. Note that in Shinto the recognition of the sacred in nature and human-made objects is taken further than it generally is in Western society. The sacredness is not simply admired or respected—it is worshiped, celebrated, and prayed to in its embodied form of *kami.*

Pages 171–176

Concept B: Shinto in the Religious Life of Japan

Review Questions: Shinto in the Religious Life of Japan

Question 7. What is the *kamidana?* Briefly describe how it is used.
Answer. It is the small altar that is the focal point of Shinto worship in the home. It contains a variety of objects that are regarded as symbols of the presence of *kami.* Worship at the *kamidana* is simple and commonly occurs daily. Worshipers purify themselves by washing, then they present offerings, clap their hands to signify their presence to the *kami,* and say prayers.

Question 8. What is the *torii?*
Answer. An archway formed by two upright pillars and a cross beam, marking the entrance to a Shinto shrine.

Question 9. What is a *kami* body, and what is believed to happen to it during worship?
Answer. A common object that is extremely sacred and is kept in the sanctuary of the shrine. The *kami* of the shrine is believed to descend into the *kami* body during the worship ceremony.

Question 10. Identify the grandest and most famous of all Shinto shrines.
Answer. The Grand Imperial Shrine at Ise.

Question 11. From the Shinto perspective, why do humans need to undergo frequent acts and rites of purification?
Answer. Purification is needed to allow the light of humans' divine essence to shine through with its true luster.

Question 12. What measures did Japan's imperial government take to preserve Shinto as the national tradition after the appearance of Buddhism?
Answer. The government recorded Shinto's mythology, organized its priesthood, and began caring for its shrines.

Question 13. What was the Meiji Restoration? What religious transformation took place during that period?
Answer. It was a crucial project that transformed Japan into a modern nation. During that period Buddhism lost state support, while Shinto gained it.

Question 14. How did Japan's defeat in World War II affect Shinto?
Answer. State support of Shinto, which had been misused as a tool to fan the flames of extreme nationalism and militarism, ended in disaster.

Question 15. How did sect Shinto come about?
Answer. When the government recognized shrine Shinto, it categorized the leftover elements of organized Shinto as sect Shinto. These sects were designated as religions, along with other faiths like Buddhism and Christianity.

Question 16. Which type of Shinto defies classification? Why?
Answer. Popular Shinto, because it has never been organized.

Text Activities: Shinto in the Religious Life of Japan

Activity C

For Shinto, purification is necessary to allow the light of one's inborn divine essence to shine through. Think about the purification rituals of other religions, and explain why religions practice purification.

Activity D

Until the end of World War II, Shrine Shinto was involved with nationalism to an extreme degree. Such involvement, usually on a smaller scale, has been common throughout world history. What kind of connection do you detect between your nation and religion? What forms does this association take? In general, what do you think should be the relation between religion and a nation?

Additional Activities: Shinto in the Religious Life of Japan

The Purification Experience

1. Remind the class of the importance of purification for Shinto. Review text activity C, particularly the purification rituals of other religions. Explain to the students that this activity entails planning a purification ritual of their own.

2. Divide the class into small groups and direct the groups to discuss questions such as these:

- What specific faults or sins, in you and in your family, classes, parish, and society, need purifying? Make a list.
- What elements might be used in purification rituals? [Water, fire] What actions might be performed to indicate a desire for purification? [Fasting, washing]
- What sorts of rituals would be appropriate for purifying people of the faults and sins you just identified? Describe a specific ritual for at least one of those faults or sins. [For example, if the sin is overconsumption, the students might bring something they have acquired but do not need, and donate it to a collection for needy people. Then they might pour water over their hands while praying that they will consider others' needs whenever they spend money.]

3. Invite the groups to share with the class their answers to the discussion questions. List their ideas on the board. Then vote on one or two purification rituals for the class to enact. To help the students refine the ritual, pose questions like the ones that follow:

- What will be each person's role in the ritual?
- If anything is said during the ritual, who will say it? Will someone write it down ahead of time or read it from a book? Should music be part of the ritual? If so, who will provide it?
- What materials are needed?
- Where will the ritual be performed? How long will it take?

After the ritual has been planned, select a day to perform it.

4. On the appointed day, invite the students to perform the ritual reverently. Allow time afterwards for them to reflect, either in writing or through a class discussion, on their participation. Raise questions such as these:

- What were your expectations going into the ritual?
- How did you feel during it?
- Do you think it will make any difference in your life?
- How did it affect your understanding of purification rituals in general?

Nature Walk: Encountering the Divine

As a prelude to inviting the students to take a nature walk, remind them that Shinto considers nature sacred. Its shrines are usually found in natural places. People of all faiths often feel the presence of the divine in places of natural beauty, and find their spirits refreshed there.

Take the students to a place of natural beauty, such as a park, a garden, or a body of water. Spend most of the time walking, but also allow time for them to stop and to pray or meditate. Some may wish to focus on a natural object, such as a flower or a blade of grass.

When you return to the classroom, invite the students to discuss their experience and respond to this question: "Did being outside in a beautiful place help you feel closer to the divine (or God)? Why or why not?"

Handout 10–A

End the exercise with a recitation of the excerpt from "The Canticle of Brother Sun," by Saint Francis of Assisi, on handout 10–A. Point out that while Saint Francis does not say that nature in itself is divine, and Shinto does not say that God is "behind" nature, both emphasize that creation reveals the sacred. You might distribute the handout in advance to all the students or to a group of students, and ask them to prepare a group recitation of the canticle. Or you might invite one student to do a solo presentation of the canticle.

Additional Resources from Saint Mary's Press

See *Primary Source Readings in World Religions* (Saint Mary's Press, 2009) for a Shinto Creation Myth, "The True Tradition of the Sun Goddess," and "The Meaning of *Kami*," as well as the accompanying leader's guide for suggestions about how to use these readings in your study of Shinto.

"The Canticle of Brother Sun"

by Saint Francis of Assisi

Praised be You, my Lord, with all your creatures,
especially Sir Brother Sun,
Who is the day and through whom You give us light.
And he is beautiful and radiant with great splendor;
and bears a likeness of You, Most High One.
Praised be You, my Lord, through Sister Moon and the stars,
in heaven You formed them clear and precious and beautiful.
Praised be You, my Lord, through Brother Wind,
and through the air, cloudy and serene, and every kind of weather
through which You give sustenance to Your creatures.
Praised be You, my Lord, through Sister Water,
which is very useful and humble and precious and chaste.
Praised be You, my Lord, through Brother Fire,
through whom You light the night
and he is beautiful and playful and robust and strong.
Praised be You, my Lord, through our Sister Mother Earth,
who sustains and governs us,
and who produces varied fruits with colored flowers and herbs.
. . . .
Praise and bless my Lord and give Him thanks
and serve Him with great humility.

CHAPTER 11

Ancestors of the West

Major Concepts

A. **Religion in Ancient Iran.** The region surrounding the western part of the Mediterranean Sea is commonly referred to as the cradle of the West. The religion of ancient Iran, Zoroastrianism, is one of the world's oldest living religions. Zoroastrianism began to flourish throughout Iran during the Persian Empire, which was at its height in the fifth and fourth centuries BC. Zarathustra, its founder, most likely lived during the sixth or fifth century BC. He preached the radical message of monotheism to his polytheistic society. Zarathustra recognized the one true God as Ahura Mazda, the Wise Lord, who is eternal and universal goodness. Ahura Mazda is opposed by the Lie, an evil, cosmic force. For Zarathustra, the universe was a cosmic battleground of good and evil forces, depicted as angels and demons. According to Zarathustra, humans must choose between truth and the Lie, and the choice has eternal consequences. After death each individual will undergo judgment. The good will enter paradise, and the evil will be cast down into an abyss of torment. Good and evil alike will be bodily resurrected and will undergo a test by fire and molten metal; the evil will burn, while the good will pass through unharmed. Worship practices include prayer and the fire ritual, which celebrates the perfect purity of Ahura Mazda. Few Zoroastrians live in Iran today; most, known as Parsis, live in India.

B. **Religion in Ancient Greece.** The Greek classical period began with the epic poet Homer, around 750 BC, and ended with the death of Alexander the Great in 323 BC. Judaism and Christianity were strongly influenced by the Greeks. Homer's epic poems contain important religious teachings, most notably their portrayal of the Greek pantheon. Homeric religion is polytheistic. Its gods and goddesses are anthropomorphic. Lofty theology regarding the pantheon is found in the work of the Greek dramatists, in which the pantheon takes on more dignity. The deities were worshiped through prayers and words of praise. They relished receiving gifts, especially sacrificial ones. Worship also occurred at festivals such as the Olympic Games. The gods communicated their desires and intentions to mortals through direct conversation with heroes, through dreams and ominous signs, and through sanctuaries called oracles. In an oracle a particular god would communicate in some manner to visitors. The Homeric view of the afterlife left little room for optimism in the face of death. The afterlife was a dark and dreary underworld where souls remembered their earthly lives with regret and longing. Mystery religions offered alternatives to the dark Homeric view. These religions also worshiped deities, though they tended to stress different ones than Homer did, and emphasized three basics aspects: individuals chose to become adherents and underwent an initiation ritual; initiates experienced a personal encounter with the deity; and initiates could hope for a better afterlife and spiritual renewal. Orphism is a school of thought holding that humans possess a dual nature: the evil, bodily aspect, and the good, spiritual aspect. Plato embraced this notion, which strongly influenced Christianity. Worshipers' relationship with the god Asclepius, believed to be a physician and healer, resembled Christians' relationship with Jesus.

C. **Religion in the Roman World.** Roman religion was based on the notion that life is restrained by the numerous divine powers inhabiting the world. Roman gods and goddesses had counterparts in the Olympian pantheon. The deities belonged to a larger category known as *numina,* which were supernatural powers, each with a specific function. *Numina* inhabited a wide variety of spaces. The Roman pantheon is recognizable today in the names of seven planets and the month January. Mystery religions were especially popular in the Roman world. The two main rivals to Christianity in the later Roman Empire were mystery religions—Mithraism and the cult of the goddess Isis. Emperor worship was another facet of Roman religion. Some emperors chose to be worshiped by declaring their divinity; later emperors encouraged worship of their genius, or guardian spirit, which actually focused worship on Rome.

Pages 180–185

Concept A: Religion in Ancient Iran

Review Questions: Religion in Ancient Iran

Question 1. When and where did Zoroastrianism begin to flourish?
Answer. Zoroastrianism began to flourish throughout Iran during the Persian Empire, which was at the height of its power and influence in the fifth and fourth centuries BC.

Question 2. How did Zoroastrianism spread beyond its place of origin?
Answer. After Persia was conquered by the Greek general Alexander the Great in 328 BC, aspects of Persian culture, including Zoroastrianism, spread far and wide.

Question 3. Briefly describe the religious experience Zarathustra had at about age thirty.
Answer. An angel appeared to him and brought him before Ahura Mazda, the Wise Lord and one true God.

Question 4. Name the sacred text of Zoroastrianism. What is the oldest material in this text, and who wrote it?
Answer. The sacred text of Zoroastrianism is the Avesta. The oldest material in it is the Gathas, which are hymns that were written by Zarathustra.

Question 5. Summarize the characteristics and actions associated with Ahura Mazda.

Answer. He is eternal and universal goodness, controlling the cosmos and the destiny of human beings.

Question 6. What is ethical dualism?

Answer. The belief in universal forces of good and evil.

Question 7. What is the Lie, and how does it relate to Ahura Mazda?

Answer. It is the evil force of the universe. One of the offspring of Ahura Mazda chose the Lie instead of truth.

Question 8. What must humans choose between in the Zoroastrian cosmic scheme?

Answer. Truth and the Lie.

Question 9. Summarize Zarathustra's understanding of human destiny.

Answer. After death each individual will undergo judgment. The good will enter paradise, and the evil will be cast into an abyss of torment. Good and evil alike will be bodily resurrected and will undergo a test by fire and molten metal; the evil will burn, while the good will pass through unharmed.

Question 10. What are the general ethical demands of traditional Zoroastrian life?

Answer. One is to lead a simple life, always telling the truth and doing what is right. Great care should be taken to avoid those on the side of evil.

Question 11. Who are the Parsis, and where do most of them live today?

Answer. They are modern Zoroastrians, and most of them live in India.

Text Activities: Religion in Ancient Iran

Activity A

Review the Gathas passage on Ahura Mazda. To what extent does this strike you as a familiar description of God?

Activity B

Does the Zoroastrian explanation for the existence of evil account for the evil you have experienced and observed? Why or why not?

Activity C

Fire is often used as a symbol. Recall several ways you have seen fire used as such. Then think about what fire represents for you personally. How does this relate to what fire represented for the Zoroastrians?

Additional Activity: Religion in Ancient Iran

A Zoroastrian Symbol

Handout 11–A

Handout 11–A, "A Zoroastrian Symbol," contains a picture and an explanation of the Faravahar, a symbol of Zoroastrianism. The handout instructs the students to use a graphic medium and a written statement to create and explain a symbol of their own faith or their own understanding of human nature and destiny. The handout suggests that the students each share their symbols with one other student. However, if you feel that your students will not be intimidated by sharing with the larger group, ask them to make presentations to the entire class.

Pages 185–193

Concept B: Religion in Ancient Greece

Review Questions: Religion in Ancient Greece

Question 12. What are commonly regarded as having been the Bible of the ancient Greeks?
Answer. Homer's *Iliad* and *Odyssey.*

Question 13. Explain the meaning of this sentence: The gods of the Olympian pantheon are anthropomorphic.
Answer. The gods have human attributes. They have specific talents, functions, and limitations. Also, their moral behavior is much more humanlike than godlike.

Question 14. What was Aeschylus's main contribution to the understanding of the gods of the Olympian pantheon? Give an example.
Answer. In the work of Aeschylus, the pantheon takes on a new dignity. Zeus, for example, is no longer merely a god of tremendous power; he is now the source and enforcer of universal moral principles.

Question 15. What is an oracle? What is the most famous oracle of ancient Greece, and why was it consulted?
Answer. An oracle is a sanctuary favored by a particular god, who communicated in some manner to those who visited the site. The oracle at Delphi, where the Greeks sought the wisdom of the god Apollo, is the most famous one. It was consulted on issues ranging from private matters to far-reaching public concerns.

Question 16. Briefly identify the three basic aspects of the mystery religions.
Answer. (1) Individuals had to make the choice to became initiates, and went through some form of initiation ritual; (2) initiates experienced a personal encounter with the deity; (3) initiates could hope for a better afterlife, along with the spiritual renewal gained through participation in the religion.

Question 17. What mystery religion honored Demeter and Persephone?
Answer. The Eleusinian mysteries.

Question 18. What is the god Dionysus associated with, and how is he often depicted in Greek art?
Answer. He is a god of fertility and vegetation, specifically the vine. He is often depicted with vines and grapes.

Question 19. Name the goal of the ascetic practices of the Orphics.
Answer. The goal was for the soul to escape from the body and fully realize its divine nature.

Question 20. What is Plato's theory of knowledge?
Answer. Plato theorized that we know things in this life partly because we have experienced them in previous lives. Knowledge, therefore, is recollection.

Question 21. What is Platonic dualism?
Answer. Truth exists independently of any bodily, or material, evidence, consisting of Forms, or Ideas, which are eternal and perfect. Wisdom lies in identifying oneself with the truth of the Forms, rather than with the material world.

Question 22. Why did Jesus seem to have much in common with the ancient Asclepius?
Answer. Both were called Savior, and the intimacy of the worshipers' relationship with Asclepius bore a strong resemblance to the relationship with Christ celebrated by Christians.

Text Activities: Religion in Ancient Greece

Activity D

Religions of ancient cultures were primarily polytheistic. Think about the gods and goddesses of the Olympian pantheon, and speculate as to why polytheism appealed to people of ancient cultures.

Activity E

Today's emphasis on sports makes athletes into heroes, and awards them with fan adoration and large sums of money. Some scholars of religion have even suggested that sports are a religious phenomenon. Discuss the similarities between sports and religion that might have led to this suggestion.

Activity F

Suppose you were to travel back through time to ancient Greece and visit the oracle at Delphi. What question would you ask? Given your modern perspective, what concerns would you have regarding the oracle's accuracy?

Activity G

The theme of life arising from death, celebrated in classic fashion by the Eleusinian myth of Demeter and Persephone, is universal. It is being expressed all around us, sometimes in myth and other literary and artistic forms, sometimes in nature, and sometimes even in our own personal and social worlds. Think of three ways you have seen this theme expressed. Briefly describe each.

Activity H

The influence of Plato, especially of his dualism of body and soul (or mind), is deeply ingrained in Christian thought, and in Western culture generally. Reflect on Plato's notion of the body as being distinct from the mind. Do you tend to look at yourself as Plato would have? Do you think this is necessarily the correct perspective? Why or why not?

Activity I

Ancient societies normally viewed the healing of the body as a religious concern. In primal cultures healings were (and sometimes still are) typically performed by a witch doctor, medicine man or woman, shaman, or other religious figure. Do you think modern Western society treats the healing of the body as a religious concern?

Additional Activity: Religion in Ancient Greece

Greek Gods and Goddesses

Assign each student one of the Greek gods or goddesses from the following list: Gaia, Kronos, Demeter, Hades, Hera, Poseidon, Zeus, Apollo, Ares, Artemis, Athena, Dionysus, Hephaestus, Hermes, Persephone, Aphrodite, and Eros. Direct the students to use the library, the Internet, and other resources to find stories about their gods and goddesses. If someone at your school teaches Greek mythology, you may be able to borrow materials from them. Instruct the students to use the stories they find to interpret the characteristics of their gods and goddesses, and to write descriptive sketches of the deities' personalities. Also have the students complete one of the following assignments:

- Choose a story about your goddess or god and rewrite it as if you were the deity. Be sure that the story reflects the personality elements you described in your sketch. Then assume the character of the goddess or god and tell the story to the class as a performance monologue.
- Create a drawing, painting, or sculpture of your god or goddess. Your depiction can be realistic or abstract. In either case it should reflect the personality elements you described. Present your work to the class.
- Write a short story that parallels one of the stories you found. In your version, however, present the goddess or god as a human character in a contemporary setting. It may help to think of contemporary situations on TV shows, in the news, or in literature, and to use them as the context for your story. Read the story to the class.
- Use the music from a contemporary song to create a ballad about your god or goddess. (A ballad is a poem that tells a story, often dramatic or tragic, and traditionally is intended to be sung.) Rewrite the lyrics to tell a myth in which your god or goddess plays a central role. Turn in a recording of the music with your new lyrics.

Allow the students to do the last two options individually, in pairs, or in small groups. You also might give them the choice of making a video to hand in, or performing their pieces for the class.

Pages 193–197

Concept C: Religion in the Roman World

Review Questions: Religion in the Roman World

Question 23. What were *numina,* and what sorts of things were they thought to inhabit?

Answer. *Numina* were supernatural powers, each in charge of a specific function. They inhabited a wide variety of spaces, such as fields, streams, trees, doorways, altars, and shrines.

Question 24. Who was the most powerful Roman deity?

Answer. Jupiter.

Question 25. Identify the six planets of our solar system that are named after Roman deities.

Answer. Jupiter, Venus, Mars, Neptune, Mercury, and Saturn.

Question 26. Why did the Roman state consider it essential to maintain official worship practices?

Answer. It was believed to help ensure the welfare of the Roman state.

Question 27. Which mystery religions were the main rivals to Christianity in the later Roman Empire?

Answer. Mithraism and the cult of the goddess Isis.

Question 28. Briefly summarize the Egyptian myth of Isis and Osiris.

Answer. Isis's husband, Osiris, was killed and hacked into pieces by his evil brother. Isis searched far and wide, finally finding Osiris's body parts. She mummified him, which brought him back to life. Osiris became god of the underworld.

Question 29. Briefly describe the sort of emperor worship encouraged by Augustus.

Answer. He encouraged worship not of himself but of his genius, or guardian spirit. This actually focused worship on Rome, because the emperor's genius was thought to guard the welfare of the state.

Question 30. Why did Christians and Roman rulers clash over emperor worship?

Answer. Christians refused to worship on behalf of the emperor; doing so would have contradicted their belief in one God. The Roman rulers were suspicious of the Christians because of their refusal to worship on behalf of the emperor, which implied that they did not support the state.

Text Activities: Religion in the Roman World

Activity J

The initiates of the mystery religions were forbidden to reveal the secrets of their rites. Apuleius's description of Lucius's moments within the inner sanctuary is therefore especially intriguing to specialists attempting to discover the secrets of the cult of Isis. You have read about the Greek and

Roman mysteries, as well as Apuleius's brief—and intentionally sketchy—account of the rites of the inner sanctuary. Now come up with your own description of the rites. Include the elements described by Apuleius, but add details you think Apuleius may have left out. Use your imagination!

Activity K

Roman worship of the genius of the emperor was really a means of expressing one's devotion to the state. In other words, it was a form of patriotism. What forms of "emperor worship" do we practice today? Would you label such forms of devotion "religious"?

Additional Activities: Religion in the Roman World

Greek and Roman Gods Today

Handout 11–B

The students may be surprised to discover how often the names of Greek and Roman gods and goddesses are used in contemporary contexts. Handout 11–B, "Greek and Roman Gods Today," contains a chart with the names of many Greek gods and goddesses side by side with their Roman equivalents. Adjacent to each name is a space for the students to jot down anything they associate with that name, whether from contemporary culture or from history. Suggest that they cite titles of songs or TV programs, brand names, places, months, planets, and so on. Allow them to work alone or in small groups, or together as a class. You may wish to encourage them to bring in visual references such as advertisements, photos, and news articles, and post those on a bulletin board. Use this activity to spark conversation about the endurance of the names of the Greek and Roman gods and goddesses. For the most part, though, allow the students to have fun with the activity.

Here are a number of ways that the names of some of the deities are used today:

Greek Names
- *Apollo.* Names of U.S. spacecraft (for example, *Apollo 13*), name of theater in Harlem, euphemism for a young man of great physical beauty
- *Gaia.* Earth goddess, associated with the environmental movement
- *Hermes.* Brand of typewriter, brand of silk scarves
- *Poseidon.* Title of movie *(The Poseidon Adventure)*

Roman Names
- *Venus.* Name of planet, sobriquet for *female,* symbol of feminine beauty or sexuality, name of plant (Venus's-flytrap)
- *Mars.* Name of planet, name of month (March), name of candy bar, sobriquet for *male,* root word for *martial* (which means "warlike")
- *Cupid.* Name of Valentine's Day character, symbol for falling in love, name of popular song from the 1950s
- *Pluto.* Name of a dwarf planet, name of Disney character
- *Vulcan.* Name of *Star Trek* planet, name of company that makes construction materials, brand of motorcycle
- *Juno.* Name of e-mail program
- *Hercules.* Title of TV series, title of Disney movie, brand of airplane, root word for *Herculean* (which means "requiring tremendous effort")

- *Mercury.* Name of planet, brand of automobile, name of spacecraft, name of florist, name of chemical element, trademark for Goodyear Tire and Rubber Company (winged foot)
- *Saturn.* Name of planet, brand of automobile, name of spacecraft, root word for *saturnine* (which means "sullen or grave")
- *Neptune.* Name of planet, brand of fishing gear
- *Jove, or Jupiter.* Name of planet, part of exclamation ("By Jove!")

News from Ephesus

The student text points out that Christians in the Roman Empire were often in conflict with the Roman state over their refusal to worship the emperor. In the Acts of the Apostles, Luke tells a story in which Christians clash with non-Christian Romans over the Christians' belief in only one God and the Romans' economic interest in making and selling images of the Roman gods. In this activity the students can explore the reality of the conflict between such different belief systems in a way that is both fun and enlightening.

The story of the riot of the silversmiths at Ephesus (Acts 19:23–41) has a contemporary ring to it. One way to promote the story's modern feel is to treat it as if it actually were a contemporary event. The students' job is to produce a classroom newscast about the incident. You will need to assign the following roles to students:

- News reporters and analysts (number may vary)
- Demetrius (a silversmith)
- Gaius, Aristarchus, and Alexander (Paul's companions)
- The town clerk and various other officials
- Bystanders (for person-in-the-street interviews)

The newscast should include the following elements:

1. A detailed retelling of the event, based on the account in Acts
2. Interviews with the principal participants: Demetrius, Alexander, and the town clerk (The account in Acts seems to indicate that Paul was not available for comment afterward. The students can decide if he in fact was or was not.)
3. Interviews with secondary participants: Gaius or Aristarchus, other officials, and bystanders
4. News analysis: commentary by "experts" regarding the issues behind the uproar—religion, economics, conflict resolution, and so on

The participants should feel free to mention any current events that might be comparable to the conflict at Ephesus. The idea is not to pretend to be living in the first century, but to see this first-century event in a modern context.

The riot at Ephesus was a challenge to the status quo. As the students are developing their newscast, be sure that they keep in mind questions such as these:

- What are some groups that use demonstrations or other public protests to challenge popular ways of thinking and often end up angering people?
- What economic motives make people want to protect the status quo?
- Do you think economic concerns should stand in the way of preaching about one's religion?
- Do you think concern for the religion of another should stand in the way of preaching about one's own religion?

A Zoroastrian Symbol

The illustration on this handout is the Faravahar, a symbol of Zoroastrian faith. The Faravahar may have originated as a royal insignia, but throughout the centuries it has been interpreted in many ways by Zoroastrians. Although these interpretations are not based on the Zoroastrian scriptures, some are used to illustrate aspects of the faith, especially for children.

According to one such interpretation, the bearded man in the central circle represents the human soul. One hand is extended in blessing, providing a reminder to keep in mind the path to heaven. The other hand holds a "ring of promise," reminding Zoroastrians always to keep their promises. Each wing has three layers of feathers, which symbolize good thoughts, good words, and good deeds. The central circle represents eternity. The two ribbonlike shapes that extend from the circle symbolize the two choices humans face—good and evil.

With the example of the Faravahar in mind, create, on a separate sheet of paper, a symbol that represents your own religious faith or personal understanding of human nature and destiny. You may incorporate symbols from your religious tradition, or you may create something completely original. Use any materials you wish: markers, pens, pencils, paint, construction paper, glue, scissors, magazines, and so on. Then write a brief description of your symbol and of the meaning behind each of its elements. Present your symbol to a classmate and explain the intention behind it. Then listen to your classmate's explanation of her or his symbol.

Greek and Roman Gods Today

Next to the name of each god or goddess in the chart below, jot down any person, place, object, time, program, or product with which you associate the name. You may also note titles of songs or TV programs or other works. For example, the names of some gods are used to identify planets (such as Mars) and products (such as Hermes scarves).

Association	Greek Name		Roman Name	Association
	Apollo	/	Apollo	
	Aphrodite	/	Venus	
	Ares	/	Mars	
	Artemis	/	Diana	
	Athena	/	Minerva	
	Dionysus	/	Bacchus	
	Eros	/	Cupid	
	Gaia	/	Tellus	
	Hades	/	Pluto	
	Hephaestus	/	Vulcan	
	Hera	/	Juno	
	Heracles	/	Hercules	
	Hermes	/	Mercury	
	Kronos	/	Saturn	
	Poseidon	/	Neptune	
	Zeus	/	Jove, or Jupiter	

12

CHAPTER 12

Judaism

Major Concepts

A. **Judaism's Central Teachings.** Judaism can be summarized in several ways. It is the Covenant between God and the people, in history and in the present. The basic theological statement of Judaism is the Shema: "Hear, O Israel! The LORD is our God, the LORD alone" (Deut. 6:4, Tanakh). *Torah* literally means "instruction" and is also loosely translated as "law." The term also refers to the first five books of the Bible. The "written Torah," the Hebrew Bible, contains a variety of forms of writing that present laws, prophets, prayers, and stories of Judaism. The Mishnah and the Talmud constitute the "oral Torah," transmitted by the great rabbis of antiquity. This material complements the written Torah and addresses the continually changing situations of the Jews in a world that is also always changing.

B. **The History of the Chosen People.** Originally the Jews were the descendants of the ancient Israelites (or Hebrews). History has great significance for Judaism because God is believed to be directly involved in guiding and caring for creation. Judaism of the classical period, from the end of the first century AD through the seventh century, remains the standard for Jews down to modern times. In the medieval period, owing to the Diaspora, Jews were scattered and lived under various political and social conditions. Jews were often successful in business, but they were also resented for being "sons of the crucifiers" who rejected Christ. This resentment led to open and violent persecution, causing many European Jews to migrate eastward, especially to Poland. Moses Maimonides represents the Jewish masters who continued interpreting Torah throughout the medieval period. He applied the philosophy of Plato and Aristotle to the biblical tradition. Whereas Jewish philosophy emphasizes reason, Jewish mysticism, or Kabbalah, teaches that God can best be known with the heart, through love. Hasidism draws from Jewish mysticism, emphasizing personal relationships with God and the community. *Zionism* refers to the support of Israel. Faced with anti-Semitism, some Jews were convinced that the only way to ensure their safety was to have their own nation. The Holocaust, from 1933 to 1945, in which six million Jews were senselessly murdered, is the most horrific tribulation suffered by the Chosen People. The State of Israel, established in 1948, provides a great deal of unity for Judaism. The three modern divisions of Judaism are Reform, Orthodox, and Conservative. Reform Judaism holds that as society changes, so must Judaism adapt to it. Orthodox Judaism maintains that Torah is the standard of truth, and that life within society must always conform to it. Conservative Judaism occupies a middle position between Reform and Orthodox.

C. **The Sanctification of Life.** According to Judaism, life is sanctified through the moment-to-moment observance of Torah. Judaism is far more concerned with correct practice than with correct belief. Observing Torah requires not only worshiping God but also leading an ethical life. The predominant form of daily worship is prayer. The home and the synagogue are the two centers of Jewish worship. Rules based in Torah govern family relationships. The social and religious center of the home is the dinner table. Synagogues are centers for prayer, study, and fellowship. The Sabbath is both the religious and the social high point of the week. Along with being a day of rest, the Sabbath is also a day of worship and celebration. The annual observance of holy days ensures both the unity of the Jews and the continuity of their religious tradition. Judaism prescribes rites of passage marking life's major changes. The rites for the birth and naming of a child, the coming of age of young people, marriage, and death and mourning demonstrate how thoroughly Judaism deals with life's transitions.

Pages 202–205

Concept A: Judaism's Central Teachings

Review Questions: Judaism's Central Teachings

Question 1. Define the term *covenant* in relation to the Jews.
Answer. Covenant refers to the agreement established long ago between God and the ancient Israelites.

Question 2. Why do observant Jews avoid pronouncing the divine name? How is the name written?
Answer. It is considered too holy to be spoken by human beings. The name is written in the Hebrew equivalents of the letters *YHWH.*

Question 3. What is the Shema?
Answer. Judaism's basic theological statement: "Hear, O Israel! The LORD is our God, the LORD alone" (Deut. 6:4, Tanakh).

Question 4. Identify the three related meanings of the term *Torah.*
Answer. It means "instruction" and refers to the will of God as it is revealed to humankind. It also means "law," referring to the Jewish Law, which guides proper human conduct. And it refers to the first five books of the Bible.

Question 5. Why is the Hebrew Bible also known as the Tanakh?
Answer. The Hebrew Bible is divided into three parts: the Torah, the Prophets, and the Writings. In Hebrew the words *Torah, Nevi'im,* and *Ketuvim* begin with the letters *T, N,* and *K,* respectively, so the Bible is referred to as the Tanakh, from *T-N-K.*

Question 6. What is the Pentateuch?
Answer. It is the Torah, or the first five books of the Bible.

Question 7. Who is traditionally regarded as the author of the Torah? How many specific commandments is the Torah thought to contain?
Answer. Moses. 613.

Question 8. What is the literal meaning of the term *prophet?*
Answer. "One who speaks for."

Question 9. What is the oral Torah? How is it thought to complement the written Torah?
Answer. The oral Torah is the material taught and transmitted by the great rabbis of antiquity, written down in the Mishnah and the Talmud, among other texts. It complements the written Torah by addressing the continually changing situations of the Jews in a world that is also always changing.

Question 10. When was the Mishnah written, and what does it contain?
Answer. The Mishnah was written in about AD 200. It contains teachings that were formulated and transmitted orally by the rabbis of the preceding four centuries.

Question 11. What do the rabbis comment on in the Talmud, and how do they support their arguments?
Answer. They comment on small portions of the Mishnah, and support their arguments by citing biblical passages.

Text Activities: Judaism's Central Teachings

Activity A

The term *Torah* has three meanings: "God's revelation (instruction)," "the Law," and "the first five books of the Bible." One of the books of the Torah is Leviticus. Read chapter 19 of Leviticus. List several of the specific laws given. Then discuss how those laws of the Torah might also convey God's revelation.

Activity B

Read at least the entire first chapter of the Book of Jeremiah. Explain how the prophet Jeremiah is one who speaks for God. Also describe the sorts of messages Jeremiah delivers.

Activity C

Choose a discipline or subject area that interests you, such as music, science, mathematics, or literature. Then choose a specific activity from that discipline and describe the concentric rings of creation and interpretation that surround it. For example, a certain scientific theory is formulated by one person, studied and commented on by another, revised by yet another, applied in a practical way by someone else, and so on. Be specific.

Additional Activity: Judaism's Central Teachings

Rings of Interpretation

This activity demonstrates the dynamic of Judaism's rings of interpretation, in which one teacher interprets or explains a passage from the Bible, then another expands on those comments, another expands further, and so on. Each commentator sheds new light on the passage as it applies to the time and place in which he or she lives. In Judaism, the Torah, the Mishnah, and the Talmud are the three main rings of interpretation.

Handout 12–A

1. Divide the class into groups of three to five students. As much as possible, the groups should have equal numbers. Give each student a Leviticus passage cut from handout 12–A, "Rings of Interpretation," making sure that the members of a particular group each receive a different passage. Announce directions in these or similar words:
   - Read the passage from Leviticus that you have been given and think quietly about it for a few minutes. Then, on a clean sheet of paper, describe how the Bible passage applies as a law for how to live in our school. This description will serve as the first interpretation for your passage. Pass your description to another person in the group, who is to read the Bible verse and your interpretation and then add to the paper her or his own expansion of your comments. The second interpreter is to pass the paper to a third interpreter, and so on, until everyone in the group has interpreted the passage and the preceding comments on it.
   - In your interpretations, you may include examples, stories, other biblical verses, and even humor to support your points. These elements should be used to help clarify the directive given in the original passage from Leviticus as it applies to our school.
   - Your group's result is not likely to closely resemble the Talmud, but that is not the point of the exercise. Rather, the idea is for you to experience being involved in a process similar to the rings of interpretation that are characteristic of Jewish teachings.

   You can conduct the interpretations in class, or assign them as homework. If you conduct them in class, ensure a smooth flow of the activity by determining how long each student can spend commenting, and alerting the students when they have reached their time limit. If you assign the interpretations as homework, allow the students, in turn, to take their groups' interpretation sheets home and write their commentaries. This alternative gives the students more time to think about their passages and writings.

2. When all have written their interpretations, direct the groups to review their work. (If possible, photocopy each completed sheet so that all the members of a group can look at it simultaneously.) The group members should discuss their overall and individual interpretations among themselves, raising questions like these:
   - Does our overall interpretation cover enough specific circumstances to make this passage helpful as a law for how to live in this school?
   - Does our overall interpretation respect and retain the spirit of the Bible passage?
   - Are our individual interpretations consistent with one another, or do they contradict one another? Is consistency a strength? Is contradiction a weakness? Explain.

3. If time permits encourage the groups each to make a decorative poster, with their Torah passage in the middle and their various commentaries surrounding it. Photographs of Jewish manuscripts may serve as helpful examples as the students design their posters. You may wish to post the completed artwork in the classroom or in the prayer space the class uses.

Example. The following example shows how the students' work on this activity might appear after all have written their comments:

- *Bible passage.* "You shall not steal; you shall not deal falsely; and you shall not lie to one another" (Lev. 19:11).
- *First interpretation.* "No student should ever take anything that belongs to another student. If someone steals someone else's lunch, then someone goes hungry. It would be better to ask for a loan to buy lunch at the cafeteria.

  "I think dealing falsely means making a promise and then not keeping it—like if you say you'll meet with your project partner after school, you can't just blow it off and go out with some friends instead.

  "When people lie they just start digging a deeper and deeper hole for themselves, and sooner or later they'll find they can't get out of it."
- *Second interpretation.* "The part about not stealing applies not only to students but to teachers too, and to ideas as well as material things. Last year my friend Jim made a really good comment in literature class, and the teacher was impressed. But later she shared the comment with another class without giving Jim credit. She acted like it was her thought. That's as bad as taking someone's lunch.

  "I think sometimes it's okay to lie, but only to avoid hurting someone's feelings. I mean, if your friend looks dumb with her head shaved, you don't want to tell her that, so you just say, 'Oh, it looks okay,' and just hope she grows it back. But it's her life."
- *Third interpretation.* "Yes, but I think as a general rule it's better to say, 'Never lie.' Of course there will always be exceptions, but that's all a matter of personal conscience and personal judgment.

  "There should be some sort of punishment for stealing, especially in school. Because if you can't trust people in school, who can you trust? We're stuck here all day, so we might as well try and work things out. If someone steals, they should not only give back the stolen goods when they get caught, but they should also have to do something as punishment, like stay after school and sit in a place where everyone will see them and know why they are there.

  "Anyone who doesn't keep a promise (except because of an emergency, which I could understand) doesn't deserve to have friends. They'll never get a partner for a project again, and it serves them right."
- *Fourth interpretation.* "Well, I think punishment should be productive. Not just staying after school, but doing something helpful, like cleaning a classroom or raking the lawn or something. And maybe the person should write an essay about why he or she stole, and talk about it with a guidance counselor or something, because maybe he or she has a problem that needs attention.

  "I think everyone still deserves friends, no matter what they do wrong—as long as they don't hurt somebody really bad. I've broken a few promises before, but my friends got over it; they forgave me. Sometimes I have to cut them some slack too. I think if we respect one another enough we won't steal, break promises, or lie too much to begin with. And if we do, then we should be able to work it out productively."

Pages 205–213

Concept B: The History of the Chosen People

Review Questions: The History of the Chosen People

Question 12. Rather than describing them as a single "race" of genetically related people, what is the most accurate way to think of the Jews?
Answer. The Jews are an ethnic group that shares a common history and religion.

Question 13. What does it mean to say God is providential?
Answer. It means that God is directly involved in guiding and caring for creation.

Question 14. Why did the Pharisees emerge after the destruction of the Second Jerusalem Temple in AD 70 with their religious ways intact?
Answer. Because they focused more on the study of Torah than on the rituals observed at the Temple.

Question 15. What is the Diaspora?
Answer. The Diaspora, or Dispersion, is the situation in which Jews live away from their homeland and yet maintain their religious identity.

Question 16. In what areas of the world did medieval Jews live under Muslim rule? under Christian rule?
Answer. Muslim rule: Africa, Spain, and the Near East. Christian rule: most of Europe.

Question 17. Briefly describe the situation of medieval Jews in Poland.
Answer. Jews living in Poland enjoyed a large degree of governmental autonomy, and lived in relative safety and prosperity. Polish rabbis made remarkable intellectual achievements. But even here the threat of persecution loomed.

Question 18. What does the Kabbalah teach?
Answer. That God can best be known with the heart, through love.

Question 19. What is believed about the *zaddik,* the leadership figure in Hasidism?
Answer. That he has an especially close relationship with God, and that through his teachings and mere presence, Hasidic Jews are able to move closer to God.

Question 20. What is Zionism?
Answer. Zionism was originally a movement that was committed to the re-establishment of a Jewish homeland. Since the establishment of the modern State of Israel, the term *Zionism* refers generally to the support of Israel.

Question 21. When did the Holocaust occur? What does the Hebrew term *Shoah* mean?
Answer. The Holocaust occurred from 1933 to 1945. *Shoah* means "mass destruction."

Question 22. Briefly describe Reform Judaism.

Answer. Reform Judaism holds that being Jewish and being completely involved in modern society are compatible. As society changes, so must Judaism adapt to it.

Question 23. How is Orthodox Judaism distinguishable from Reform Judaism?

Answer. Orthodox Judaism maintains that Torah is the standard of truth, and that life within society must always conform to it. Jewish life should change very little, for Torah is unchanging. Compared with Reform Judaism, Orthodox Judaism is deeply traditional.

Question 24. What are the distinguishing characteristics of Conservative Judaism?

Answer. Conservative Judaism is quite strict regarding observance of traditional Jewish practices. Worship is in Hebrew, and laws regulating diet and behavior on the Sabbath are strictly observed.

Text Activities: The History of the Chosen People

Activity D

Consider the reasons behind the persecution of medieval Jews. In general, why, do you think, did certain groups of people harass other groups? Try to name at least one example in today's world of a group persecuting another group. What seem to be the reasons behind this harassment?

Activity E

Might the philosophy of Maimonides and the mysticism of the Kabbalah be used as two complementary approaches to God? Describe how the two approaches could work together.

Activity F

In "The Precious Prayer," the rabbi learns that "while humans see what is before their eyes, God looks into the heart." Compare this insight about prayer with that offered by Jesus in Matthew 6:5–6.

Activity G

Review the opening section of this chapter, beginning with the passage from Abraham Joshua Heschel. What challenges do you think the Holocaust presents to this understanding of Judaism?

Activity H

For some two thousand years before 1948, Jews endured without a national homeland. Imagine what your life would be like if your nation did not exist in a physical location and you were living in exile in some foreign land. What important things would be missing? How would this situation affect your religious outlook? In general, how would it affect your priorities?

Additional Activities: The History of the Chosen People

God's Communication in History

The student text points out that God is providential, or directly involved in guiding and caring for creation. In this exercise the students read and discuss biblical passages in which God communicates with the Jews of biblical times.

1. Divide the class into five groups. Make each group responsible for reading and discussing one of the following sets of passages from the Old Testament:

- Gen. 12:1–7; 17:1–12,15–19
- Exod. 3:1–10; 19:16–19; 20:1–17
- Isa. 1:11–20; 6:1–13
- Jer. 1:4–10; 31:1–4,31–33
- Ezek. 1:1–28; 36:24–38

2. Instruct each group to prepare a report on its assigned readings, answering the following questions:

- With whom is God communicating?
- How does that person experience God's presence? What image of God is represented?
- What does God promise, if anything?
- What does God demand, if anything?

3. When the groups report their findings, record the information in abbreviated form on the board. The groups' findings should be along these lines:

For the Readings from Genesis

- God communicates with Abram, whose name is later changed to Abraham as a sign of God's choosing him.
- God speaks to Abraham, but the Scriptures do not say what form God takes.
- God promises to bless Abraham, to make him great, to give him a land. Abraham will be the father of many nations; he and his wife, Sarai (now to be called Sarah), will have a son named Isaac.
- Abraham's descendants must be faithful to God.

For the Readings from Exodus

- God speaks first to Moses and later to all the Israelites.
- God appears to Moses in a burning bush. God's presence is revealed to the Israelites by thunder, lightning, trumpet blasts, a cloud, and fire.
- God promises to free the people from their slavery in Egypt.
- The people must keep the Ten Commandments.

For the Readings from Isaiah

- God communicates with Isaiah.
- God is seated on a throne, guarded by angels.
- God promises that the people will eat good things.
- The people must convert, stop their evil ways, and love and serve others.

For the Readings from Jeremiah

- God communicates with Jeremiah.
- The hand of God is probably visible, because it touches Jeremiah's lips and puts God's words into Jeremiah's mouth.

- God promises to rebuild Israel and to make a new covenant with the people.
- The people have to abide by the covenant.

For the Readings from Ezekiel
- God speaks to Ezekiel.
- God appears in a whirlwind, a cloud, and fire.
- God promises to deliver the people from their captors, to give them a new spirit, and to let them dwell in their own land.
- The people have to repent their old ways and keep the Commandments.

4. Discuss with the students the recurring pattern of promises and demands found in ancient Jewish history. Refer to the quote from Abraham Joshua Heschel that begins this chapter in the student text. Heschel says, in part, that Judaism "is not a doctrine, an idea, a faith, but the *covenant* between God and the people" (*Man's Quest for God,* page 45; emphasis added). Invite the students to discuss this notion of Judaism as covenant, in reference to the biblical passages they have just explored. Use questions such as these:

- From what you have read in the student text and these Bible passages, how would you now explain the meaning of the term *covenant?*
- In your opinion what is most important in the keeping of a covenant: belief, worship, action, or something else? Explain your answer.

Hasidic Wisdom

Handout 12–B

Handout 12–B, "Wisdom from a Hasidic Master," contains a number of sayings from Rebbe Nachman of Breslov, a Hasidic master who lived from 1772 to 1810. You may wish to distribute the handout for the students' own supplemental reading and edification, or as the basis for the following activity.

1. Give the students ample time to read the sayings on handout 12–B. Then have the students pair up and discuss their impressions of Rebbe Nachman's teachings. Also direct them to select the saying that most impressed them and to tell their partner why that particular saying stood out for them. This informal conversation need not last more than 5 minutes.

2. Instruct the students to return to their individual places, and to choose one of the sayings from the handout and write about it. Explain that they may select the saying they just discussed, or another one, and they are also to select one of the following writing options:

- *Option 1.* Think of a friend or relative who is experiencing, or has experienced, some sort of distress for which she or he might seek your help or advice. Write the person a letter that centers around the saying from Rebbe Nachman that you have selected. (Avoid identifying the person you are writing to in the letter you hand in.)
- *Option 2.* Write a short story in which the saying of Rebbe Nachman provides the turning point for a character in a conflict. The conflict may be an external one with another character, or it may be an internal one, such as a crisis of conscience.
- *Option 3.* Write an essay interpreting the saying you have chosen. In the essay answer questions such as these: What does this saying mean to me? How might I apply Rebbe Nachman's words to my life and to the lives of people in my family and community?

3. Determine a due date for this assignment. On that date collect the papers and invite the students to discuss questions such as these:

- While you were working on your project, did your understanding of the saying change? Explain.
- Do you think wisdom such as that of Rebbe Nachman is useful in today's world? Why or why not?
- How might you apply the wisdom of Rebbe Nachman in actual situations?
- If you could ask Rebbe Nachman a question, what would it be?

Voices from the Holocaust

1. Prepare for this conversation about the Holocaust by creating a handout that contains quotations from different Holocaust survivors or witnesses. (An Internet search using the keyword *Holocaust* yields links to the United States Holocaust Memorial Museum, which offers many multimedia options as well as print resources. Other sites also have firsthand accounts.)

2. Engage the students in discussion to ascertain their level of knowledge and understanding about the Holocaust. Many of them may be familiar with the film *Schindler's List,* the book *Anne Frank: The Diary of a Young Girl,* or any of the many other films and publications related to the Holocaust. Mention these and others to stir the students' memories about the Holocaust.

3. Distribute the handout. If time allows, have the students read it silently in class. Then direct them to take the handout home, read it again, and write a two-page essay sharing their reactions to Wiesel's experience. If time does not allow for reading the handout in class, tell the students to read it at home, and encourage them to find a quiet, private time in which to read it slowly and thoughtfully.

Pages 213–219

Concept C: The Sanctification of Life

Review Questions: The Sanctification of Life

Question 25. According to the Mishnah, what sustains the world?
Answer. The Law, or Torah; Temple service, or worship; and deeds of loving-kindness.

Question 26. What is the predominant form of daily worship in Judaism?
Answer. Prayer.

Question 27. What are the two centers of Jewish worship?
Answer. The home and the synagogue.

Question 28. What does every synagogue contain?
Answer. A scroll of the five books of the Torah.

Question 29. When does the Sabbath occur? What are the two main aspects of its celebration?

Answer. The Sabbath begins at sunset on Friday and lasts until sunset on Saturday. Its two main aspects are rest and worship.

Question 30. What is celebrated on Rosh Hashanah?

Answer. The new year.

Question 31. What is emphasized on Yom Kippur?

Answer. Repentance through confession of sin.

Question 32. What does the festival Passover commemorate?

Answer. The Exodus of the Jews from bondage in Egypt.

Question 33. What is signified by the rite of passage that marks the birth of a child?

Answer. Entrance into the Jewish community.

Question 34. What are the bar mitzvah and bat mitzvah?

Answer. Bar mitzvah (for boys) and bat mitzvah (for girls) are ceremonies marking the point at which Jewish children take on the religious responsibilities of adults.

Question 35. What symbols and events highlight the Jewish marriage ceremony?

Answer. The bride and groom stand beneath the *huppah,* or bridal canopy, which creates a special, sacred place. Seven blessings are read over a cup of wine. The groom breaks a wine glass with his foot, a reminder that marriage involves difficulties along with joy.

Question 36. What is the kaddish?

Answer. A prayer of mourning.

Text Activities: The Sanctification of Life

Activity I

People often tend to think of religion as primarily a matter of believing in certain doctrines. Drawing from your own experiences, list several examples of religious practices. In your opinion are these practices meaningful if they are independent of beliefs?

Activity J

Read Deuteronomy 6:4–9. Identify parts of this passage that relate to the Jewish worship practices you have read about in this section of your textbook. Describe how you think the Shema (Deuteronomy 6:4) relates to the rest of the passage.

Activity K

On the Sabbath Jews celebrate the creation of the world by avoiding labor in order to rest and to worship. Do you reserve time in your life for that kind of celebration? If so, describe what that time is like. If not, reflect on what benefits it might bring.

Activity L

Judaism carefully observes rites of passage, as can be seen in the details involved in its mourning of the dead. How does Judaism's approach to mourning compare with secular society's approach?

Additional Activities: The Sanctification of Life

The Sustenance of the World

1. As your class begins to study the final major concept in this chapter of the student text, call their attention to the sentence from the Mishnah quoted under the heading "Ethics." The Mishnah points out that the world is sustained by three things—the Law, or Torah; worship; and deeds of loving-kindness. (Recall that the Law is the revelation of God's will.) Engage the students in a brief discussion of this sentence from the Mishnah, using questions along these lines:

- What are some examples of law, worship, and deeds of loving-kindness that you might encounter in your daily life?
- Do you think that examples such as these have the power to sustain the world? Why or why not?

2. After the discussion divide the class into three approximately equal groups. Designate one group as law, another as worship, and the third as deeds of loving-kindness. Give the groups the following instructions, in your own words:

- For the next week, look for articles and stories that illustrate the aspect you have been assigned—law, worship, or loving deeds. You may search for these examples in newspapers, magazines, books, TV programs, films, Internet resources, and so on. You may choose fiction or nonfiction items, and you must choose at least one article or story. For example, an article about a court case that has upheld a law protecting the environment would show how law sustains the world, and a review of a CD in which an artist sings about her relationship with God would show how someone worships.

  When you have found and read an article or a story, think about it for a few minutes. Ask yourself, "In what way does what happens in this article or story sustain the world?" Write a brief reflection on the article or story, relating how it made you feel as you read it and how it is significant for the world.

Set a due date for this assignment.

3. On the due date, have the students bring in both their articles and stories, and their written reflections. Before these materials are handed in, direct the students to pair up with someone from another group. Instruct the partners to share their articles and stories (they may summarize to save time), as well as their thoughts about how the events of those items sustain the world. Next, tell the students to find another partner, also from another group, and repeat the sharing. Do this as long as time allows. Then ask the students to hand in their articles, stories, and reflections to be evaluated.

Variation. After your evaluation, hang the articles and stories in a central location, perhaps on a bulletin board. Allow the students to add instances of people sustaining the world. Encourage them to catch people in the act of sustaining their local and school communities, and to post local or school newspaper articles or photos, or even index cards on which they have written examples of neighbors and classmates doing acts of law, worship, and loving-kindness.

Miriam's Shabbat

This prayer service is modeled after the traditional Jewish blessing over the Sabbath lights. Recalling the faith heritage that Jews and Christians share, it honors Mary both as the mother of Jesus and as a woman of faith in the tradition of her female Jewish ancestors. This particular prayer service focuses on women; however, feel free to adapt it by including Joseph, Miriam's husband, and the patriarchs of the faith (Abraham, Isaac, and Jacob) in the prayers and final blessing. You may find *The Book of Blessings: A New Prayer Book for the Weekdays, the Sabbath, and the New Moon Festival,* by Marcia Falk (Boston: Beacon Press, 1999), a helpful resource.

1. Set up a prayer space in your room. You will need enough challah for your students, a pitcher of grape juice, cups, and two taper candles and holders. Flowers may be used to decorate and perfume the prayer space. You can recruit students to bring in the objects (they may need assistance finding a place to purchase challah). Arrange these items on a table.

Handout 12–C

2. Recruit four students ahead of time for the readings. Provide them with handout 12–C, "Miriam's Shabbat," and allow them time to prepare. Point out the Hebrew translation of each prayer, and the pronunciation that follows it. Practice with them so that they read their prayers slowly and calmly, first in Hebrew and then in English, and are comfortable extending their hands in blessing over the objects. You might also ask the students to hold the objects while they say the blessing, so that the class may see the items.

3. Begin the service by distributing handout 12–C to the entire class and gathering the students in the prayer space. You may wish to have soft instrumental music playing in the background. Invite the students to place themselves in God's presence. When the class is ready, ask the first reader to light the candles and begin.

4. After the final blessing, conclude the prayer service by inviting the students to share the bread and the juice. You may want to lead students into a discussion that encourages them to reflect on the theme of life's holiness. You might also ask the students how the Hebrew translation affected their experience of this service.

(This prayer service is adapted from one developed by John Reine, Newton Country Day School of the Sacred Heart, Newton, Massachusetts.)

Additional Resources from Saint Mary's Press

See *Primary Source Readings in World Religions* (Saint Mary's Press, 2009) for chapters 19–20 of Exodus and excerpts from *Pirke Aboth: Sayings of the Fathers* and *The Family Markowitz,* as well as the accompanying leader's guide for suggestions about how to use these readings in your study of Judaism.

Teaching About Other Religions (Saint Mary's Press, 2006) offers guidelines and suggestions for creating a respectful and intellectually stimulating environment when studying world religions in the classroom. For ideas and strategies on teaching Judaism, see chapter 2.

Rings of Interpretation

Photocopy this handout and cut it apart along the dashed lines.

When you reap the harvest of your land, you shall not reap all the way to the edges of your field, or gather the gleanings of your harvest. You shall not pick your vineyard bare, or gather the fallen fruit of your vineyard; you shall leave them for the poor and the stranger. (Leviticus 19:9–10, Tanakh)

You shall not insult the deaf, or place a stumbling block before the blind. (Leviticus 19:14, Tanakh)

Do not deal basely with your countrymen. (Leviticus 19:16, Tanakh)

You shall not take vengeance or bear a grudge against your countrymen. Love your fellow as yourself. (Leviticus 19:18, Tanakh)

When a stranger resides with you in your land, you shall not wrong him. The stranger who resides with you shall be to you as one of your citizens; you shall love him as yourself. (Leviticus 19:33–34, Tanakh)

You shall not falsify measures of length, weight, or capacity. You shall have an honest balance, honest weights. (Leviticus 19:35–36, Tanakh)

Wisdom from a Hasidic Master

Rebbe Nachman of Breslov was born in 1772 in the village of Medzeboz in the Ukraine. His great-grandfather, Rabbi Israel Baal Shem Tov, was the founder of Hasidism. As a teacher, Rebbe Nachman had a large and devoted following that consisted of people from all walks of life, from scholars to workers. He taught about the depths of Jewish mysticism, and at the same time offered down-to-earth tales and sayings that have made him one of the most studied and quoted Jewish teachers in history. Rebbe Nachman died in 1810 at the age of thirty-eight, but his influence continues to this day. The samples on this handout reveal that Rebbe Nachman's wisdom can be applied to many people in many situations, whether they seek profound spiritual insight or they look for simple advice to help them get through the day.

Know! A person walks in life
on a very narrow bridge.
The most important thing
is not to be afraid.
(Page 15)

Everything in the world—
whatever is and whatever happens
—is a test, designed to give you
freedom of choice. Choose wisely.
(Page 17)

When asked how things are,
don't whine and grumble about
your hardships. If you answer
"Lousy," then God says,
"You call this bad? I'll show you
what bad really is!"
When asked how things are and,
despite hardship or suffering,
you answer
"Good," then God says,
"You call this good? I'll show you
what good really is!"
(Pages 34–35)

Talk to God as you would talk
to your very best friend.
Tell The Holy One everything.
(Page 92)

The most direct means for
attaching ourselves to God from
this material world is through
music and song.
Even if you can't sing well, sing.
Sing to yourself. Sing in the
privacy of your own home.
But sing.
(Page 50)

Better to be a fool who believes
everything than a skeptic
who believes nothing—
not even the truth.
(Page 67)

As often as you can, take a trip
out to the fields to pray.
All the grasses will join you.
They will enter your prayers
and give you strength to sing
praises to God.
(Page 86)

Always remember:
Joy is not merely incidental to
your spiritual quest.
It is vital.
(Page 99)

Finding true joy is the hardest of
all spiritual tasks. If the only way
to make yourself happy
is by doing something silly,
do it.
(Page 101)

Miriam's Shabbat

Blessing over the Sabbath Lights

Reader 1:

בָּרוּךְ אַתָּה יְיָ אֱלֹהֵינוּ מֶלֶךְ הָעוֹלָם

אֲשֶׁר קִדְּשָׁנוּ בְּמִצְוֹתָיו וְצִוָּנוּ לְהַדְלִיק נֵר שֶׁל שַׁבָּת.

BAH-ROOK AH-TAH, AH-DOH-NAI EH-LOH-HAY-NOO, MEH-LEHK HA-OH-LAHM,
AH-SHER KIH-DE-SHAH-NOO BE-MIHTS-VOH-TAHV VE-TSIH-VAH-NOO
LE-HAHD-LEEK NAYR SHEL SHAH-BAHT.

Blessed are you, LORD, our God, ruler of the universe, who has sanctified us by your commandments and commanded us to kindle the Sabbath light.

Blessing over the Kiddush Cup

Reader 2:

בָּרוּךְ אַתָּה יְיָ אֱלֹהֵינוּ מֶלֶךְ הָעוֹלָם

בּוֹרֵא פְּרִי הַגָּפֶן.

BAH-ROOK AH-TAH, AH-DOH-NAI EH-LOH-HAY-NOO, MEH-LEHK HA-OH-LAHM,
BOH-RAY PE-REE HAH-GAH-FEN.

Blessed are you, LORD, our God, ruler of the universe, creator of the fruit of the vine.

Blessing over the Challah

Reader 3:

בָּרוּךְ אַתָּה יְיָ אֱלֹהֵינוּ מֶלֶךְ הָעוֹלָם

הַמּוֹצִיא לֶחֶם מִן הָאָרֶץ.

BAH-ROOK AH-TAH, AH-DOH-NAI EH-LOH-HAY-NOO, MEH-LEHK HA-OH-LAHM,
HAH-MOH-TSEE LEH-KEHM MEEN HAH-AH-REHTS.

Blessed are you, LORD, our God, ruler of the universe, who brings forth bread from the earth.

Reading: Isaiah 61:10

Reader 4: A reading from the prophet Isaiah:
I will greatly rejoice in the LORD,
my whole being shall exult in my God;
for he has clothed me with the garments of salvation,
he has covered me with the robe of righteousness,
as a bridegroom decks himself with a garland,
and as a bride adorns herself with her jewels.
The word of the LORD.

Prayer

All: Yeshua, sun of justice,
Reader 1: Miriam was the white dawn announcing your rising:
grant that we may always live in the light of your coming.

All: Yeshua, eternal word,
Reader 2: you chose Miriam as the ark of your dwelling place:
free us from the corruption of sin.

All: Yeshua, heart of generosity and love,
Reader 3: you gave Miriam as a mother to your beloved disciple:
help us to live as worthy children of so noble a mother.

Blessing over One Another

[Readers extend their hands in blessing over their classmates.]

All:

יְשִׂימֵךְ אֱלֹהִים כְּשָׂרָה רִבְקָה רָחֵל וְלֵאָה.

YE-SIH-MEHK EH-LOH-HEEM KE-SAH-RAH, RIV-KAH, RAH-KAYL, VE-LAY-AH.

May God inspire you to live in the tradition of Sarah and Rebekah, Rachel and Leah.
May you be mindful of God's holiness within you and around you. Amen.

(This handout is adapted from one developed by John Reine, Newton Country Day School of the Sacred Heart, Newton, Massachusetts. Used with permission.)

13

CHAPTER 13

Christianity

Major Concepts

A. **Christ.** Christianity is the world's largest religion. Christians acknowledge Jesus Christ as Son of God and savior, believe in the doctrines of the Incarnation and Trinity, and belong to the Church. Jesus was a Jew living under Roman rule. He seemed to hold an apocalyptic perspective. During Jesus's two-year ministry, he attracted disciples and large crowds. The Gospels portray Jesus as an exorcist and healer who often taught in parables. He focused on two interrelated themes: the imminent coming of the Kingdom, or Reign, of God, and the urgent need for ethical transformation through loving all people. By order of the Roman procurator, probably in AD 30, Jesus suffered crucifixion, a manner of execution reserved for those condemned as political threats to the Roman Empire. Christianity really began after the Resurrection, when Jesus's followers first experienced him as the risen Lord. The Christian message is often called by the name *Gospel,* which means "good news" and refers specifically to the Good News regarding Jesus Christ. The Gospel of Matthew presents Jesus as the revealer of the new Torah, the Gospel of Luke presents him as a role model for the perfect way to live, and the Gospel of John presents him as the Son of God who has become fully human in Jesus Christ while remaining fully divine. Paul emphasizes that through the sacrificial death and Resurrection of Christ, human sin and death have been overcome, and all people are saved through the grace of God and faith in Jesus Christ.

B. **Creed.** The Apostles' Creed, in use since the second century, sets forth the foundations for two of Christianity's central doctrines: the Incarnation and the Trinity. Both the Apostles' Creed and the Gospel of John emphasize that Jesus is fully human and, at the same time, fully divine. The first chapter of John establishes the basis for later formulations of the doctrine of the Incarnation. The doctrine of the Trinity states that the three Persons of God are distinct from one another, yet have the same essence or substance. The creed developed at the Council of Nicaea in 325 states that Jesus the Son and God the Father are "one in Being." The Nicene Creed also precisely states the distinctive features of the three Persons of the Trinity. God the Father is creator and judge; God the Son is redeemer, begotten by, yet coeternal with, the Father; and God the Holy Spirit is reconciler and sanctifier, proceeding from the Father and the Son.

C. **Church.** Although the Church is meant to be a unified body of Christian believers, many differences exist among Christians. After the Resurrection an organized Church gradually took shape. Paul was a zealous Pharisee who at first persecuted Christians. Then he experienced the risen Christ and became an Apostle. Paul's leadership helped free Gentile Christians from the requirements of Torah. Early Christians lived with few constraints within the Roman Empire, but conflict did occur. By the end of the fourth century, Christianity was the empire's only legitimate religion, thanks in large part to Emperor Constantine. After the fall of the Roman Empire, a gradual split took place between the Christianity of the East and of the West, resulting in Eastern Orthodoxy and Roman Catholicism becoming independent of each other in 1054. The Protestant Reformation began in the sixteenth century with Martin Luther, who challenged corrupt Catholic practices and was excommunicated from the Church. Other reform movements took place throughout Europe, resulting in many new Christian denominations. Today Christianity remains divided primarily into Roman Catholicism, Eastern Orthodoxy, and Protestantism. One distinctive characteristic of Catholicism is its dependence on both the Bible and Tradition as the means of God's revelation of Christ. The bishops and the popes are successors of the Apostles, and they carry on and clarify anew in every age the Tradition passed on to them. The patriarch of Constantinople is acknowledged as the head of Eastern Orthodoxy. He has no special doctrinal authority; that authority is held instead by the entire Church body. Eastern Orthodoxy limits its doctrines to those reached prior to the year 787. For Protestants, the Bible is the primary means of knowing Christ. Protestants believe that faith is central; as long as one has faith, good works will naturally follow. The movement known as ecumenism promotes worldwide Christian unity.

Pages 224–230

Concept A: Christ

Review Questions: Christ

Question 1. How much of the world's population is Christian? Where is Christianity the dominant religious tradition?
Answer. Nearly one-third. The Americas, Europe, and Australia, with significant followings in Asia and Africa.

Question 2. Define Christianity's two core doctrines.
Answer. The Incarnation asserts that Christ is both fully divine and fully human. The Trinity holds that God consists of three Persons—God the Father, Jesus Christ the Son, and the Holy Spirit—who are at the same time one God.

Question 3. What are the literal and symbolic meanings of the Greek word *ixthus?*
Answer. Ixthus literally means "fish," and it symbolized for early Christians their understanding of who Christ was. Each letter in the word begins a Greek word of the phrase "Jesus Christ, Son of God, Savior."

Question 4. What are the primary sources of information about the life of Jesus?
Answer. The New Testament Gospels (Matthew, Mark, Luke, and John).

Question 5. Briefly describe the political situation in Palestine during Jesus's lifetime.

Answer. When Jesus was a youth, most of Palestine, including Jerusalem, came under the direct rule of a procurator who reported to the Roman emperor. The northern region of Galilee was ruled by Herod Antipas, a puppet king who himself was also ultimately under the Roman emperor's rule.

Question 6. Name and briefly describe the varieties of Judaism at the time of Jesus, including their responses to Roman rule.

Answer. The Sadducees, wealthy aristocrats who controlled the Jerusalem Temple, generally remained on friendly terms with the Roman rulers. The Essenes chose to flee from the difficulties, leading lives of discipline and purity in desert communities. The Pharisees responded with moderation, obeying the traditional commandments of Judaism and developing the oral Torah. The Zealots believed the only way to achieve Jewish independence was through armed rebellion.

Question 7. Explain the meaning of apocalypticism.

Answer. Apocalypticism maintained that the world had come under the control of evil forces. The world's woes would become greater and greater until God would send the Messiah to conquer the forces of evil.

Question 8. Who was John the Baptist, and how was he important in Jesus's life?

Answer. John lived off the land and preached the imminent coming of the judgment of God. Jesus's ministry began shortly after he was baptized by John, whom Jesus apparently had followed as a disciple.

Question 9. What are parables? Name two well-known parables.

Answer. Parables are ingenious stories cast in language and settings familiar to listeners, but proclaiming radical lessons intended to disrupt conventional ways of thinking. Two well-known parables are the good Samaritan and the prodigal son. [Other well-known parables are also acceptable answers.]

Question 10. To what was Jesus likely referring when he spoke of the Kingdom of God?

Answer. God's intervention in history to right the wrongs of the world.

Question 11. What is Jesus's radical commandment on love?

Answer. "Love your enemies and pray for those who persecute you, so that you may be children of your Father in heaven" (Matt. 5:44–45).

Question 12. Why was Jesus crucified? Who ordered his execution?

Answer. The radical nature of Jesus's teachings and ministry, and the agitated crowds of followers he attracted, struck the authorities as troublesome. Jesus was crucified by order of the Roman procurator Pontius Pilate.

Question 13. What does the term *gospel* mean?

Answer. "Good news."

Question 14. What is the primary focus of the Gospel of Matthew?

Answer. Christ is the revealer of God's new Torah and calls for radical obedience to it.

Question 15. In what ways does the Gospel of Luke portray Jesus as reaching out to a diversity of people?

Answer. Jesus reaches out to help all segments of society. Women receive more attention here than in the other Gospels, and many of Luke's parables characterize outcasts in a favorable light.

Question 16. What is the doctrine of the Incarnation?

Answer. That God's Son became fully human in Jesus Christ while remaining fully divine.

Question 17. What is the focal point of the Gospel of John?

Answer. The Incarnation. Christ is presented as the Word, who from the beginning was with God and was God.

Question 18. According to his first epistle to the Corinthians, what is Paul's Gospel message?

Answer. "That Christ died for our sins in accordance with the scriptures, and that he was buried, and that he was raised on the third day in accordance with the scriptures" (15:3–4).

Question 19. What does Paul say will happen at the second coming?

Answer. Christ will return to the world, the dead will be raised, and all people—living and dead—will be judged. The good will be saved, and the evil condemned.

Question 20. What does Paul emphasize about salvation?

Answer. That it comes only through the grace of God.

Text Activities: Christ

Activity A

Apocalypticism continues to be an important perspective for many people. What are some ways that you have seen apocalypticism, as it is described here, manifested today?

Activity B

The lower strata of Jewish society in Jesus's day included prostitutes, tax collectors, and others whom the Bible calls sinners and outcasts. What kinds of people make up the lower strata of society today?

Activity C

How could you apply Jesus's commandment to love your enemies in your daily life?

Activity D

For Paul, God's giving of Christ marks the end of the era of Torah. This gift in no way releases humans from ethical responsibility. Now, however, good behavior is to be rooted in faith and the spiritual transformation it brings, rather than in obedience to the letter of the Law. Think about two or three ethical decisions you have faced. In those cases how might goodness rooted in the right spiritual perspective have differed from goodness based on rules of correct behavior?

Activity E

Read the Sermon on the Mount (see Matthew, chapters 5 through 7). Find three teachings (besides those mentioned in the textbook) that you think clearly illustrate Jesus's ethical message.

Activity F

Read the parable of the good Samaritan (see Luke 10:29–37). While keeping its basic message intact, how would you retell the parable to make it more relevant for modern society?

Additional Activities: Christ

Jesus on Stage and Screen

During your study of Christianity, you may wish to show the students one or more of the following productions, in full or in part:

- *Jesus of Nazareth* (directed by Franco Zeffirelli, 371 minutes, Artisan, VHS 1977, DVD 1999, not rated). Zeffirelli's epic covers Jesus's entire life and ministry. You probably will not be able to use the entire film; you will likely need to select one or more segments for class viewing. It would be wise to choose a variety of scenes so that the students see Jesus depicted in different contexts. For example, you might view the Sermon on the Mount, a conversation between Jesus and Mary Magdalene, and the Crucifixion.
- *Jesus Christ Superstar* (directed by Norman Jewison, 108 minutes, Universal Studios, VHS 1973, DVD 1999, rated G). This is a film version of the Broadway musical. Some of your students may have seen or appeared in stage productions of *Jesus Christ Superstar;* if so, you could invite them to use that experience as a basis for reflection.
- *Godspell* (directed by David Greene, 103 minutes, Columbia Pictures, VHS 1973, DVD 2000, rated G). Some students may have seen, or even acted in, amateur productions of the show *Godspell.*

It may benefit the students to read the sections of the Gospels covered in the film presentation before they view it. After showing a particular film or segment, engage the students in a discussion or assign them to write reactions to what they have seen. The following are some possible questions for discussion and writing:

- What is your impression of Jesus as he appeared in this piece? What type of human being does he seem to have been? How does this Jesus compare with the Jesus you have come to know through direct reading of the Bible, through your religious education, or through what you have heard believers say about him?
- How does the portrayal of Jesus in today's film compare with portrayals of him in other films or plays you have seen? In what ways are the depictions similar, and in what ways are they different? Do you find one depiction more appealing than another? Explain.
- What is the most important thing you learned about Jesus from this portrayal? Did you gain any new or surprising insights about Jesus? Were you in any way disappointed by the portrayal of Jesus? Explain.

The Temptation: Comparing *Jesus of Montreal* with the Gospels

The film used in this activity provides thought-provoking connections between the life of Jesus and the life of a young person today. Note that it is rated R and is available in French, with English subtitles. Preview the film, consider the needs of your students, and decide whether to use the film in its entirety or to play selected portions of it.

1. Show *Jesus of Montreal* (directed by Denys Arcand, 120 minutes, Max Films Productions Inc., VHS 1989; Koch Lorber Films, DVD 2004, rated R). This is a contemporary film about Daniel, a young actor who is hired to modernize a shrine's annual Passion play. Although his play is a critical and commercial success, the shrine feels that it is too unorthodox, and cancels all performances. The film draws parallels between the actor's experience and the life of Jesus.

2. After watching the movie, assign one half of the class to read Matthew 4:1–11 and the other half to read Luke 4:1–13 (both passages describe the temptation of Jesus). Ask the students to compare and contrast their Bible passage with the film scene in which Daniel and the man who wishes to become his lawyer are in a skyscraper. The young people could do this in small-group discussions or as a written homework assignment.

3. After the students have finished their comparisons, ask them to comment on the similarities and differences they found. Questions like these may help the discussion:

- Does the scene in *Jesus of Montreal* stay true to the spirit of the story in the Gospels?
- Does a viewer have to be familiar with the Gospel story to understand the scene? How might knowing the Gospel story add to a viewer's appreciation?
- What are the strengths and weaknesses of communicating truths about Jesus through different media—such as writing, film, visual art, and music? Is any one medium to be preferred over others?
- If you were writing a script for a new movie that included the temptation of Jesus, how would you portray that event?

Variation. Assign small groups to create their own scripted video productions of the temptation or of another scene from the Gospels. View the productions as a class, and discuss why the groups interpreted the story as they did.

Images of Jesus

1. As a homework assignment, direct the students each to find an artistic or photographic rendition of Jesus. Their images may range from classic paintings to depictions of Jesus from various cultures to greeting card pictures. (A page containing a variety of images of Jesus is located in the study aids section of *The Catholic Youth Bible, Revised,* edited by Brian Singer-Towns [Winona, MN: Saint Mary's Press, 2005]. This page is also available in poster form from Saint Mary's Press, at 800-533-8095 or *www.smp.org*.)

Handout 13–A

2. When the students have brought in their images, display them around the classroom. Assign each image its own number so that it can easily be identified. Distribute handout 13–A, "Images of Jesus." Give the following directions:

- This handout contains several phrases that the textbook uses to describe Jesus. Take a few minutes to study these phrases, and place a check mark next to the one or two that most closely match your own idea of Jesus. If you wish, add other phrases that express how you see Jesus.

  Then go around the room and slowly study the images of Jesus that have been brought in by your classmates. Choose one or two images that seem to bring out the characteristics of Jesus that you marked on the handout, and write the numbers of those images on the handout.

3. After the students have had ample time to study the characteristics of Jesus, survey the class to determine which image of Jesus was selected by the most students. Invite discussion about the qualities of that image and why it drew so many people to it. Follow this with a discussion of the images that were selected by the fewest students, trying to determine why they did not draw a positive response.

Bring the discussion to a close by pointing out that a multitude of images of Jesus have been created over the centuries. Jesus has been depicted as a member of numerous ethnic groups, in various styles of dress, as a "soft" person and as a "rough" person, and so on. This diversity of images is evidence of Jesus's universal appeal throughout many centuries and many lands.

Pages 230–232

Concept B: Creed

Review Questions: Creed

Question 21. What is the origin of the term *creed?*
Answer. It comes from the Latin word *credo,* which means "I believe."

Question 22. How does the Gospel of John emphasize both Jesus's divinity and humanity?
Answer. John emphasizes Jesus's divinity by identifying Christ as the Word, who from the beginning was with God and Was God (see John 1:1). He emphasizes Jesus's humanity by referring to such things as Jesus's hunger and thirst, and by pointing out that Jesus wept on occasion.

Question 23. What is Christ called in the first chapter of John's Gospel?
Answer. The Word (*Logos* in Greek).

Question 24. What two creeds were formulated by the year 325?
Answer. The Apostles' Creed and the Nicene Creed.

Question 25. Historically speaking, what was the most crucial point established at the Council of Nicaea?
Answer. That Jesus the Son and God the Father are "one in Being" (*homoousios* in Greek).

Question 26. What is the doctrine of the Trinity?
Answer. It is the centerpiece of Christian belief and theology. It states that the three Persons of God are distinct from one another and yet have the same essence or substance.

Additional Activities: Creed

Meditating on the Incarnation

Handout 13–B

Distribute handout 13–B, "'In the Beginning Was the Word.'" This handout contains the text of John 1:1–18 and an assignment that encourages the students to reflect on and write about the doctrine of the Incarnation. Instruct the students to complete the handout either as homework or as an in-class activity. Follow up with discussion.

Sculpting the Trinity

This activity attempts to engage the students' imagination as well as their rational understanding of the Trinity to help them further penetrate the mystery of the Trinity. You may wish to review the distinctive features of the Trinity before the exercise begins, or in a quiet, soothing voice during the reflection period.

Open the exercise by distributing one large lump of modeling clay to each student. Ask the students to close their eyes and imagine the Trinity. After allowing a minute or two for reflection, invite the students to open their eyes and fashion each Person of the Trinity out of the clay. When everyone has finished, invite them to take turns sharing their sculptures.

Pages 232–243

Concept C: Church

Review Questions: Church

Question 27. What did Paul say the Church is meant to be?
Answer. A unified body of Christians.

Question 28. What are heresies?
Answer. Sects whose theological opinions were denounced as erroneous by orthodox Christians.

Question 29. Describe how Paul came to be an Apostle of Christ.
Answer. While traveling on a road to Damascus, Paul experienced the risen Christ.

Question 30. What was decided at the Council of Jerusalem?
Answer. The Apostles and elders decided that Gentile Christians were virtually free from the requirements of Torah.

Question 31. Why did the early Christians settle on Sunday as their primary day of worship?
Answer. To commemorate the Resurrection of Christ and to distinguish the Church from Judaism, which celebrated the Sabbath on Saturday.

Question 32. What were the central rituals of the early Church?
Answer. The sacrament of the Eucharist, or Communion meal, patterned after the Last Supper, and baptism, the foundational sacrament of initiation.

Question 33. What were the three distinct offices in the Church by the early second century? Briefly describe the role of bishop in the early Church.
Answer. Bishops, presbyters, and deacons. Each bishop was the overseer of his church, and performed the chief task of administering the Eucharist.

Question 34. Why did worship on behalf of the Roman emporer bring Christians into conflict with the empire?
Answer. Roman worship of the emperor's genius, or guardian spirit, was primarily a display of loyalty toward the Roman state; when monotheistic Christians refused to worship on behalf of the emperor, they seemed to the Romans to be unpatriotic.

Question 35. Who was Augustine, and what great theological masterpiece did he write after the fall of Rome?
Answer. Augustine was the bishop of Hippo in North Africa. He wrote *The City of God.*

Question 36. What is the meaning of the Greek word from which we get the English word *catholic?*
Answer. "Universal."

Question 37. Identify the elements leading to the schism in the Church that divided the eastern and western parts of the Roman Empire.
Answer. Constantine established an eastern capital city, Constantinople, which quickly became a second center of the Church, along with Rome. The distance between Constantinople and Rome caused communication difficulties, which were compounded by a language barrier. Further strife resulted from a gradual loss of political unity when the western part of the empire fell, and the eastern part survived. Also, starting in the late fourth century, the Eastern Christians refused to accept the authority of the pope in Rome.

Question 38. What significant event occurred in the year 1054?
Answer. Pope Leo IX excommunicated the patriarch of Constantinople, who in turn excommunicated the pope. This marked the break of Eastern Orthodoxy from Roman Catholicism.

Question 39. Identify some achievements of Catholicism in the Middle Ages.
Answer. The Church continued to fortify itself as an organized institution with spiritual authority beyond that of any monarchs or other rulers. Great

cathedrals were constructed. Monasticism reached a new height of influence. Established communities of monks and nuns were reformed, and new ones were established. Medieval theology culminated in the work of Saint Thomas Aquinas.

Question 40. Where, and in what century, did the Protestant Reformation take place?
Answer. It swept across much of sixteenth-century Europe, most notably in Germany, Switzerland, and England.

Question 41. What did Luther's Ninety-five Theses protest against?
Answer. The selling of indulgences.

Question 42. What role did King Henry VIII play in the Protestant Reformation?
Answer. He broke with papal authority over his desire to remarry after divorcing his wife, and he declared himself head of the Church of England.

Question 43. Other than the establishment of Protestantism, what were two major effects of the Protestant Reformation?
Answer. It sparked the Catholic Reformation, which clarified Church doctrines and cleaned up many of the corrupt practices Luther had protested against. It also led to the Thirty Years' War, between Catholics and Protestants.

Question 44. What is one distinctive characteristic of Roman Catholicism?
Answer. Its dependence on both the Bible and Tradition as the means of God's revelation of Christ.

Question 45. Identify the seven sacraments of Catholicism and Eastern Orthodoxy.
Answer. Anointing, baptism, confirmation, the Eucharist (or Holy Communion), holy orders (ordination of deacons, priests, and bishops), matrimony, and reconciliation (or penance).

Question 46. When was the Second Vatican Council held, and what were its general aims?
Answer. It occurred from 1962 through 1965. Its general aims were to update Church teaching so that it would respond to the needs of the modern world, and to promote Christian unity.

Question 47. Name a distinctive practice of Eastern Orthodoxy and identify the tradition's theological focal point.
Answer. Its distinctive practices include a great emphasis on icons. Theologically, Eastern Orthodoxy tends to focus on the Incarnation, encouraging a kind of mystical union with God through faith in Christ, as emphasized in the Gospel of John.

Question 48. What challenges does Eastern Orthodoxy face as a result of recent changes in the world and in the Church?
Answer. The breakup of the former Soviet Union in 1991 threatened the Church's stability. In North America the ethnic makeup of the various Orthodox Churches is changing, with membership among traditional groups eroding and membership among other groups building.

Question 49. What has Protestantism historically tended to protest against?
Answer. Any form of authority that it perceives as false—anything that stands in the way of the Christian's relationship with God through Christ.

Question 50. What are the four main branches of Protestantism?
Answer. Lutheran, Calvinist, Baptist, and Anglican.

Question 51. What is ecumenism?
Answer. The promotion of worldwide Christian unity.

Text Activities: Church

Activity G

Before Emperor Constantine legitimized Christianity in the fourth century, many Christians died as martyrs for their faith. Do you think Christian martyrdom is still possible in today's society? If so, can you think of any modern Christian martyrs?

Activity H

Saint Francis of Assisi lived a Christian existence that has been admired through the ages. Imagine a modern Saint Francis. What sort of lifestyle, goals, and virtues would such a person have?

Activity I

Luther translated the Bible into German at about the same time the printing press was invented. Together these events greatly energized the Protestant Reformation by helping to make the Bible widely available in the language of the common people. List other technological innovations that have had a large impact on a religious tradition or traditions.

Activity J

Most of the sacraments of Catholicism and Eastern Orthodoxy function in part as rites of passage, marking divisions between one stage of life and the next. Given the nature of each sacrament, identify as many such divisions as you can. How might the sacraments celebrate the passage from one life stage to the next?

Additional Activities: Church

The Diversity of Christianity

This activity aims to show the students the diversity that exists among Christian denominations within their own communities. Before assigning this project, find out what Christian denominations are represented in your school's area. The number of different Churches may determine whether you make this an individual, paired, or small-group project.

Note: This activity is very similar to the chapter 15 exercise "An Interreligious Interview Project," on pages 224–225 in this manual. You may want to do one or the other, not both.

Explain to the students that they will be researching the various denominations of Christianity represented in their communities. They are to arrange to visit their assigned church and meet with someone on staff to learn more about its history and traditions, its style of worship, and what makes it unique among Christian churches today.

Assign a church to each individual, pair, or small group, providing the students with the address, phone number, and name of the minister, pastor, or other contact person. As much as possible, assign to the students churches they do not attend.

Direct the students to prepare for their interviews by formulating a list of questions to ask. You may wish to suggest and discuss the following questions as a class, adding others as the students offer them:

- What key principles distinguish your denomination from others?
- Describe the important figures and events in the history of your denomination.
- How would you characterize the relationship between the different denominations of Christianity?
- How do you feel about the diversity within the Christian tradition?

Once you have determined appropriate interview questions, go over other important details, such as making a phone call to arrange the interview, dressing for the interview, and writing thank-you letters.

Encourage the students to share their findings with the class using a presentation graphics program or other means. Suggest that they incorporate photographs, literature, posters, and so on, to accompany their verbal remarks.

Evaluate the students' projects on both content and presentation.

Learning About Ecumenism

The promotion of worldwide Christian unity, or ecumenism, is a major issue in Christian circles today. You may wish to expose the class to more depth on this topic by inviting a guest to talk about it. Contact your diocesan office on ecumenical affairs, or a regional cross-denominational action group, to locate a speaker.

To prepare for the guest speaker, the students could research the following historical aspects of the ecumenical movement:

- Changes in attitudes that have grown from World War II and Vatican II
- Cooperation between denominations and other religions in the civil rights movement
- The impact of John F. Kennedy's presidency
- Initiatives from Pope John XXIII
- Initiatives from Pope Paul VI
- Initiatives from Pope John Paul II
- Initiatives from Pope Benedict XVI

Variation. Help the class use the information it has gathered from its research, the guest speaker, and other sources such as interviews conducted for the preceding activity, "The Diversity of Christianity," to develop a Web site, poster, brochure, news article, videotaped advertisement, or other piece that can educate people about the importance and possibilities of ecumenism.

Additional Resources from Saint Mary's Press

See *Primary Source Readings in World Religions* (Saint Mary's Press, 2009) for *Declaration on the Relation of the Church to Non-Christian Religions (Nostra Aetate)* and "Meeting with Representatives of Other Religions: Address of His Holiness Benedict XVI" for readings about the Catholic Church's relationship to other religions. See also chapters 5–7 of Matthew's Gospel, excerpts from *Confessions* and *Concluding Unscientific Postscript to Philosophical Fragments,* as well as the accompanying leader's guide for suggestions about how to use these readings in your study of Christianity.

Images of Jesus

The chart below contains several phrases that the textbook uses to describe Jesus. Take a few minutes to study these phrases, and place a check mark to the left of the one or two that most closely match your own image of Jesus. If you wish, add other phrases that express how you see Jesus.

Then go around the room and slowly study the images of Jesus that have been brought in by your classmates. Choose one or two images that seem to bring out the characteristics of Jesus that you checkmarked, and write the numbers of those images on the line to the right of the respective characteristics of Jesus below.

Jesus was . . .		**Image Number**
_____	a peaceful rebel	________________
_____	a leader who remained within society	________________
_____	a storyteller who disrupted conventional ways of thinking	________________
_____	a person who reached out to the lower strata of society	________________
_____	charismatic	________________
_____	a healer	________________
_____	insightful	________________
_____	someone who practiced what he preached	________________
_____	radical	________________
_____	a role model for the way to live	________________
_____	fully human and fully divine	________________
_____	other: ____________________	________________
_____	other: ____________________	________________

"In the Beginning Was the Word"

The Incarnation, a core doctrine of Christianity, states that in Jesus Christ, God became fully human while remaining fully divine. In the Gospel of John, chapter 1, verses 1 through 18, we see one of the earliest expressions of that doctrine. Those verses are printed below. Read the passage carefully and meditatively, at least once. Then use a highlighter or underlining to mark parts of the passage that seem to describe Jesus Christ as being fully human. Use a different color of highlighter or a different style of underlining to mark parts of the passage that seem to describe Jesus Christ as being fully divine. After completing those tasks, read the passage once more. Finally, write a paragraph that explains your understanding of the doctrine of the Incarnation.

[1]In the beginning was the Word, and the Word was with God, and the Word
was God. [2]He was in the beginning with God. [3]All things came into being
through him, and without him not one thing came into being. What has
come into being [4]in him was life, and the life was the light of all people.
[5]The light shines in the darkness, and the darkness did not overcome it.

[6]There was a man sent from God, whose name was John. [7]He came as
a witness to testify to the light, so that all might believe through him. [8]He
himself was not the light, but he came to testify to the light. [9]The true light,
which enlightens everyone, was coming into the world.

[10]He was in the world, and the world came into being through him; yet
the world did not know him. [11]He came to what was his own, and his own
people did not accept him. [12]But to all who received him, who believed in
his name, he gave power to become children of God, [13]who were born, not
of blood or of the will of the flesh or of the will of man, but of God.

[14]And the Word became flesh and lived among us, and we have seen
his glory, the glory as of a father's only son, full of grace and truth. [15](John
testified to him and cried out, "This was he of whom I said, 'He who comes
after me ranks ahead of me because he was before me.'") [16]From his fullness
we have all received, grace upon grace. [17]The law indeed was given through
Moses; grace and truth came through Jesus Christ. [18]No one has ever seen
God. It is God the only Son, who is close to the Father's heart, who has
made him known.

CHAPTER 14

Islam

Major Concepts

A. **The Foundations of Islam.** Islam, the world's second-largest and fastest-growing religion, can be summarized in a simple phrase: submission to the one God, or Allah. The central teachings of Islam are derived from the Qur'an, the primary sacred text and Islam's earthly center, and from the life of Muhammad, the final prophet, who exemplifies human perfection. According to tradition, Muhammad's career as a prophet began when, in a dream, the archangel Gabriel commanded him to recite. Many citizens of Mecca were hostile to Muhammad's message, so he and his followers emigrated northward to Yathrib, later known as Medina. This emigration is known as the Hijra, an event on which Muslims base their system for assigning dates. Most of Arabia had converted to Islam by the time of Muhammad's death. Muhammad's own actions and teachings constitute the Sunna. Traditionally there are ninety-nine names for the one, transcendent, suprapersonal Allah. Prophets provide the link between Allah and human history. Muslims regard Abraham as father of the Arabs. Muslims also revere Moses and Jesus as great prophets. Islam teaches that human nature is essentially good, and people sin when they momentarily forget their basic goodness. It considers the natural world good as well, because it is another form of revelation of God's will. The Shari'a, or divine law, unites Muslims into one community known as the Umma.

B. **Basic Practices and Social Teachings.** Islam describes in detail the requirements and rewards of righteous living. The Five Pillars of Islam provide a basic framework for life. They are (1) confession of faith in one God and acknowledgment of Muhammad as a unique prophet, (2) prayer, (3) fasting, (4) wealth sharing, and (5) pilgrimage to Mecca. Islam has specific teachings on care of the body, including cleanliness, regulation of the diet, and proper enjoyment of sexuality. On the whole, Islam regards men and women as equals, but with different roles. *Jihad* refers to the struggle of individuals and society to act in accordance with the divine will. It is a principle that applies to all aspects of Islamic life, and is sometimes counted as the sixth pillar of Islam.

C. **The Expansion of Islam.** Within one century of Muhammad's death, Islamic civilization spread throughout the Middle East, Persia, North Africa, and almost all of Spain. It flourished until the era of European colonization. Currently the greatest concentration of Muslims is across the northern half of Africa, all of the Middle East, southwestern and South Asia, and the islands of Malaysia and Indonesia. Islam is the fastest-growing religion in the United States. All Muslims are unified by their belief that the Qur'an is the direct word of Allah, as well as by their ritual practices and regard for the Sunna of the Prophet. However, Islam has taken various forms. While the majority of Muslims practice the form of Islam called Sunnism, a small minority practice Shi'ism. Shi'ism holds that Ali, a cousin and a son-in-law of Muhammad's, was Muhammad's true successor. Shi'ism also emphasizes the Imam as an authority figure and believes that the twelfth and last Imam, Muhammad al-Mahdi, will return to restore Islam and bring on the Day of Judgment. Sufism is a mystical form of Islam in which individuals strive to experience Allah as immanent. Sufism draws both Sunni and Shi'i adherents and uses a variety of spiritual disciplines to experience union with the divine. Islam is distinctive among the world's religions for its all-encompassing nature that does not recognize a division between what is religious and what is secular.

Pages 248–253

Concept A: The Foundations of Islam

Review Questions: The Foundations of Islam

Question 1. What is the root meaning of the name *Islam?*
Answer. "Surrender" or "submission."

Question 2. Describe the Qur'an's size and structure, and identify its original language.
Answer. It is about four-fifths the size of the New Testament and is divided into 114 *surahs,* or chapters. It was originally written in Arabic.

Question 3. What is the literal meaning of the term *qur'an?*
Answer. "Reading" or "recitation."

Question 4. When and where was Muhammad born?
Answer. He was born about AD 570 in Mecca.

Question 5. Briefly describe the Night of Power and Excellence.
Answer. According to tradition, in AD 610, during one of Muhammad's visits to a cave on Mount Hira, the archangel Gabriel appeared to him in a dream and commanded, "Recite!" After Muhammad protested that he was not capable, twice more Gabriel issued his command, pressing hard on Muhammad's body. Then Gabriel told Muhammad what to recite.

Question 6. What is the Hijra, and why is it important?
Answer. It is the northward migration of Muhammad and his followers from Mecca to Yathrib in AD 622. It is important because Muslims base their system for assigning dates on it.

Question 7. Why is Muhammad referred to as the Seal of the Prophets?
Answer. Because Muslims believe he is the final prophet, revealing the will of Allah fully and precisely, and for all time.

Question 8. What is the Sunna of the Prophet?

Answer. Muhammad's actions and his own teachings (which he distinguished from the divine teachings of the Qur'an) together constitute the Sunna, or "custom," of the Prophet. It is the second most important authority for Islam.

Question 9. Why is Allah thought to be genderless?

Answer. Because maleness and femaleness seem to be human qualities and would thus limit God's nature.

Question 10. Identify at least two of Islam's prophets other than Muhammad.

Answer. [Any two of the following answers are correct:] Adam, Abraham, Moses, Jesus.

Question 11. Who is Ishmael, and what is his place in Islam?

Answer. Abraham's son. He moved to Mecca and became the ancestor of the Arabs.

Question 12. How do Muslims interpret the Fall from perfection in the Garden of Eden?

Answer. When Adam and Eve ate the forbidden fruit, they caused a state of forgetfulness to come upon them. When people momentarily forget their basic goodness, their passions can lead them to sin.

Question 13. Briefly describe what Muslims expect to happen before and on the Day of Judgment.

Answer. The Mahdi, a savior figure similar to Judaism's Messiah, will come to restore Islam and bring order on earth. After this, Jesus Christ will return to Jerusalem and usher in the Day of Judgment, at which time all humans will stand before Allah and be told their destiny.

Question 14. What is the Muslim view of the natural world?

Answer. Being Allah's creation, the natural world is good and worthy of reverence. Indeed it is another form of revelation of God's will, and is sometimes referred to as the cosmic Qur'an.

Question 15. What determines inclusion in the Umma?

Answer. Being Muslim.

Question 16. Identify two modern nations whose government is based on the Shari'a.

Answer. [Any two of the following answers are correct:] Saudi Arabia, Iran, Pakistan.

Text Activities: The Foundations of Islam

Activity A

Consider the following characteristics of the Prophet Muhammad. Discuss briefly how each one might have affected his role as the founder of Islam.

- He was illiterate.
- He was married.
- He was an able businessman and a brilliant administrator.

Activity B

Keeping in mind what you know about Muhammad and some of Islam's other prophets, describe in your own words the function of prophecy in Islam.

Activity C

The Cataclysm specifically describes the Day of Judgment. From that passage what can you infer about the Muslim perspective on Allah, on human nature, and on the role of Islam?

Activity D

Muslims embrace science because it fits perfectly with their religious perspective about the natural world. From your perspective how well do science and religion go together?

Activity E

Many Muslims live in countries governed by the Shari'a, or divine law, of Islam. Imagine what it would be like if your own country came to be ruled by a religion. What would be the most notable changes?

Additional Activities: The Foundations of Islam

The Bible and the Qur'an

Several of the familiar stories in the Bible also appear in the Qur'an, although often in a different form. By inviting the students to compare the Bible and Qur'an versions of the story of Noah and the Flood, this activity stresses the complementary relationship between the "religions of the Book"—Islam, Judaism, and Christianity.

1. Before class create the following chart on the board, leaving columns 2 and 3 blank (the answers are provided here for your reference):

Questions	*Answers from the Qur'an*	*Answers from the Bible*
Who is Noah?	A prophet or "warner."	A righteous man.
What is God's command to him?	Urge the people to repent.	Build an ark, save your family and animals.
Why is humanity punished?	They worship other gods.	Wickedness.
What are Noah's feelings?	He wants the unbelievers to be destroyed.	The passage doesn't say.
How does the destruction occur?	The people are drowned and made to enter fire.	Everyone is drowned.
Who survives?	Noah's family, believing men and women.	Noah's family and animals.

2. Introduce the activity by pointing out that biblical figures such as Adam, Abraham, Moses, and Jesus are also important figures in Islam, because they are considered prophets who changed humanity's relationship with God. Therefore it is natural that these individuals would also appear in the Qur'an. Review the common lineage shared by Jews, Christians, and Muslims through Abraham and his sons, Isaac and Ishmael.

Handout 14–A

3. Distribute handout 14–A, "The Story of Noah." Instruct the students to read both the selection on the handout and Genesis 6:5—9:17, either in class or for homework.

4. When the students have completed the reading, divide them into six small groups. Tell the groups to choose a recorder. Explain that the groups are each to create a chart like the one on the board, comparing the elements of the two stories. Clarify the questions if necessary.

5. After the groups have completed their charts, assign one question to each group and call the recorders up one at a time to write their group's answers on the board. Allow for a brief class discussion of each answer, working until the students reach a consensus. When the chart on the board is complete, discuss questions like these with everyone:

- Do the two accounts contradict each other? If not, how are they related?
- Would the Qur'an's version of the story make sense without the Bible's version?
- Does the Qur'an's account broaden your understanding of the Bible's account? Explain.

Variation. Assign other stories to compare and contrast, for extra credit or as small-group projects. The story of Yusuf in the Qur'an, *surah* 12, parallels the story of Joseph in Genesis, chapters 37 and 39–50. The story of Imran and Maryam in the Qur'an, *surahs* 3 and 19, can be used to examine the persons of Jesus (Isa) and Mary (Maryam) in Luke 1:1—2:21. Because both of these possibilities use long texts, you may want to assign specific passages to different groups or individuals.

The Ninety-nine Names of God

Handout 14–B

Distribute handout 14–B, "The Ninety-nine Names of God." Read the introduction and direct the students to follow the instructions. (If the first part of assignment is done in class, it will be helpful to make several dictionaries available.) After the students have completed the handout, invite them to explain why they chose the four names that they did. Then present them with the following choices:

- *Option 1.* For each name, write a paragraph that describes how it might apply to God. Then write a final paragraph reflecting on how all four names, or attributes, can accurately refer to the same God.
- *Option 2.* Illustrate each name, using colors, shapes, and abstract images. On the back of each depiction, write the name of God it embodies. [Consider providing the students with examples of Islamic art, and encouraging them to incorporate an Islamic style into their depictions.]

On the due date, you might break the class into small groups or pairs to share their work and discuss their reflections before they hand their pieces in to be evaluated.

Variation. To extend this activity, display the student art around the classroom. Allow the students time to view the pieces. Ask them to guess the name of God that is depicted, and to discuss the reasons for their choices.

Pages 253–257

Concept B: Basic Practices and Social Teachings

Review Questions: Basic Practices and Social Teachings

Question 17. What is the English translation of the Muslim confession of faith?
Answer. "There is no god except God. Muhammad is the messenger of God."

Question 18. Briefly describe the Muslim practice of daily prayer.
Answer. All Muslims are required to pray five times each day: early morning, noon, midafternoon, sunset, and evening. Muslim prayer requires ritual washing of the hands and face, prostration in the direction of Mecca, and other ritual movements. Usually the prayers are performed on a rug specifically designed for this purpose.

Question 19. What is Ramadan?
Answer. It is the Muslim month in which, from dawn to sunset, Muslims are to avoid eating, drinking, smoking, and sex.

Question 20. What is required of Muslims according to the fourth pillar, wealth sharing?
Answer. Muslims, except those who are poor, must contribute 2.5 percent of the value of their possessions to a public treasury.

Question 21. What is the *hajj,* and what is its religious significance?
Answer. It is the pilgrimage to Mecca. Its significance is that Allah forgives the sins of those who make the journey with reverence. Any pilgrim who dies on the journey to or from Mecca is a martyr, and enters Paradise.

Question 22. Summarize two Muslim teachings on the care of the body.
Answer. [Any two of the following teachings are correct:] The body is to be kept clean. The diet is regulated, with pork and alcoholic beverages forbidden. Sexuality is celebrated, but only within marriage.

Question 23. With regard to Muslim perspectives on women, what are the three specific points of contention commonly cited by Western critics?
Answer. Divorce, polygamy, and the wearing of the veil.

Question 24. Define the word *jihad.*
Answer. It means "exertion" or "struggle." On a personal level, *jihad* refers to the individual's spiritual struggle against anything that detracts from revering Allah and from acting in accordance with the divine will. Socially, *jihad* refers to the preservation of the order that Allah has willed for the world. In a narrow context, *jihad* refers to armed struggle.

Text Activities: Basic Practices and Social Teachings

Activity F

Islam places great emphasis on its primary pilgrimage, the *hajj*. Several features of that journey have great religious significance for Muslims. Try to identify at least three of those features. Does anything in your own life have symbolic meaning similar to that of the *hajj?*

Activity G

The Five Pillars of Islam provide a basic framework for life. State in your own words how they do so.

Activity H

Compare Islamic teachings on the care of the body with the teachings you have received from your own religion and culture.

Activity I

Very few Muslims practice polygamy, though it is technically allowed by the Qur'an. How do you interpret the Muslim teaching on this issue, as set forth in passage 4:3 of the Qur'an?

Additional Activities: Basic Practices and Social Teachings

Distractions from the Spiritual Path

The concept of *jihad* refers to Muslims' struggle against anything that detracts from revering Allah and from acting in accordance with the divine will. This exercise encourages the students to recognize potential distractions on the spiritual path.

1. By a random method, divide the class into groups of four or five. Give each group about fifteen 3-by-5-inch index cards, and about five 4-by-6-inch index cards. Direct the groups to brainstorm potential distractions from the spiritual path, writing each distraction an individual 3-by-5-inch card. Also tell them to write, underneath each distraction, at least one way they might "struggle" against the distraction. Make more index cards available if needed.

2. When the groups have had sufficient time to brainstorm, ask them to review the distractions they have named. Direct them to pile together distractions that seem similar. Then tell them to assign a category name to each pile of distractions and to write each category name on an individual 4-by-6-inch card.

3. Finally, call the groups to display and present the distractions and struggles they named. (You may wish to have them tape their index cards to the board or a wall, pin them on a bulletin board, or glue or tape them to newsprint.) Direct the groups to briefly explain why they organized the distractions as they did, and invite the entire class to discuss this question: "How do these ways of struggling spiritually correlate with the Five Pillars of Islam?"

An Essay on the Five Pillars

Direct the students each to choose one of the Five Pillars of Islam and to write a one-page essay comparing it with an analogous aspect of their own life. For example, one student might select the pilgrimage and write about a long-awaited trip to World Youth Day, the Olympics, or a major concert; another student might choose prayer and write about quiet time experienced on weekdays before anyone else gets home, or about fellowship experienced at weekly youth group meetings.

Be sure the students understand the assignment before they choose a pillar to write about. When the essays have been written and handed in, encourage class discussion about whether the assignment helped the students to better understand how Islam's Five Pillars provide a basic framework for Muslim life.

Pages 257–262

Concept C: The Expansion of Islam

Review Questions: The Expansion of Islam

14

Question 25. What was the extent of Islamic expansion one century after Muhammad's death?

Answer. It had expanded to the entire Middle East, Persia, North Africa, and almost all of Spain.

Question 26. What areas of the globe are presently populated with the greatest concentration of Muslims?

Answer. The northern half of Africa, all of the Middle East and southwestern Asia (including Turkey, Iraq, Iran, and Afghanistan), South Asia, and the islands of Malaysia and Indonesia.

Question 27. Why does Arabia enjoy a special status in Islam?

Answer. Because Arabic involvement in Islam goes back to the earliest history of Islam, Arabia is the location of Muslim sacred sites, and Arabic is the language of Islam.

Question 28. Why have some African Americans argued that Islam is better suited for their community than is Christianity?

Answer. Because nearly 20 percent of Africans brought to North America were Muslims, many African Americans can claim a Muslim heritage. Some African Americans regard Christianity as the religion of their white oppressors.

Question 29. What is Sunnism?

Answer. It is the form of Islam practiced by the majority (about 87 percent) of Muslims. The word *sunni* is drawn from a longer phrase referring to the people who follow the established custom, or sunna, meaning the Sunna of the Prophet.

Question 30. What is the meaning of the term *shi'i?*

Answer. The term *shi'i* comes from *shi'at 'Ali,* which means "partisans of Ali." Shi'i adherents consider Ali, a cousin and a son-in-law of Muhammad's, the true successor of Muhammad.

Question 31. Identify at least two modern nations that have a Shi'i majority or a significant Shi'i population.

Answer. The nations of Iraq and Iran have Shi'i majorities. Kuwait, Afghanistan, and Pakistan have significant Shi'i populations.

Question 32. Briefly describe the figure of the Imam in Shi'ism.

Answer. Though not a prophet, the Imam is believed to have special spiritual insight, and is revered as the true earthly authority.

Question 33. How does Sufism extend the first sentence of Islam's confession of faith?

Answer. It declares that there is nothing but God.

Question 34. Identify at least two Sufi methods, or disciplines.

Answer. Sufi groups known as orders are led by a master *(shaykh)* through a variety of spiritual disciplines to help them achieve union with God. Those disciplines include recitation of sacred names and phrases, breathing exercises, the chanting of odes, and a dance form best known in the West as the whirling dervish.

Text Activities: The Expansion of Islam

14

Activity J

What aspects of Islam have you observed in your own nation and community? What have your observations taught you about Muslims and their religion?

Activity K

Reconcile these two statements about Sufism:

- "The Sufi experience oneness with Allah."
- "Sufi's identify the aim of their disciplines as al-fana,or extinction of the person's sense of ego, of the notion of separate existence."

Additional Activity: The Expansion of Islam

Sufi Wisdom

In preparation for this activity, have the students conduct an Internet search for Sufi wise sayings and bring them to class.

1. Invite the students to share their research and allow them to pair up and discuss their impressions of the wisdom sayings. Also direct them to identify the saying that most impressed them and to tell their partner why it stood out for them. This informal conversation should last about 5 minutes.

2. Instruct the students to return to their own places, and to each choose one of the sayings and write about it. Explain that they may select the saying they just discussed with their partners, or one of their own, and they are also to select one of the following writing options:
- *Option 1.* Think of a friend or relative who is experiencing, or has experienced, some sort of distress for which she or he might seek your help or advice. Write the person a letter that centers on the Sufi wisdom saying that you have selected. (Avoid identifying the person you are writing to in the letter you hand in.)
- *Option 2.* Write a short story in which the Sufi wisdom saying that you have selected provides the turning point for a character in a conflict. The conflict may be an external one with another character, or it may be an internal one, such as a crisis of conscience.
- *Option 3.* Write an essay interpreting the Sufi wisdom saying that you have chosen. In the essay answer questions such as these: What does this saying mean to me? How might I apply this saying to my life and to the lives of people in my family and community?

3. Determine a due date for this assignment. On that date collect the papers and invite the students to discuss questions such as these:
- While you were working on your project, did your understanding of the Sufi saying change? Explain.
- Do you think wisdom such as that of the Sufis is useful in today's world? Why or why not?
- How might you apply Sufi wisdom in actual situations?
- If you could ask a Sufi master a question, what would it be?

Additional Resources from Saint Mary's Press

See *Primary Source Readings in World Religions* (Saint Mary's Press, 2009) for Sura 22 of The Qur'an, excerpts from *The Faith and Practice of Al Ghāzālī,* and "The Tagouris: One Family's Story," as well as the accompanying leader's guide for suggestions about how to use these readings in your study of Islam.

Teaching About Other Religions (Saint Mary's Press, 2006) offers guidelines and suggestions for creating a respectful and intellectually stimulating environment when studying world religions in the classroom. For ideas and strategies on teaching Islam, see chapter 3.

The Story of Noah

In the Name of God, the Compassionate, the Merciful
We sent forth Noah to his people, saying: "Give warning to your people before a woeful scourge overtakes them."

He said: "My people, I come to warn you plainly. Serve God and fear Him, and obey me. He will forgive you your sins and give you respite for an appointed term. When God's time arrives, none shall put it back. Would that you understood this!"

"Lord," said Noah, "night and day I have pleaded with my people, but my pleas have only aggravated their aversion. Each time I call on them to seek Your pardon, they thrust their fingers into their ears and draw their cloaks over their heads, persisting in sin and bearing themselves with insolent pride. I called out loud to them, and appealed to them in public and in private. 'Seek forgiveness of your Lord,' I said. 'He is ever ready to forgive. He sends down abundant water from the sky for you and bestows upon you wealth and children. He has provided you with gardens and with running brooks. Why do you deny the greatness of God when He created you in gradual stages? Can you not see how God created the seven heavens one above the other, placing in them the moon for a light and the sun for a lantern? God has brought you forth from the earth like a plant, and to the earth He will restore you. Then He will bring you back afresh. God has made the earth a vast expanse for you, so that you may roam its spacious paths.'"

And Noah said: "Lord, my people disobey me, and follow those whose wealth and offspring will only hasten their perdition. They have devised an outrageous plot, and said to each other: 'Do not renounce your gods. Do not forsake Wadd or Suwā' or Yaghūth or Ya'ūq or Naṣr.' They have led numerous men astray. You surely drive the wrongdoers to further error."

And because of their sins they were overwhelmed by the Flood and cast into the Fire. They found none besides God to help them.

And Noah said: "Lord, do not leave a single unbeliever on the earth. If You spare them, they will mislead Your servants and beget none but sinners and unbelievers. Forgive me, Lord, and forgive my parents and every true believer who seeks refuge in my house. Forgive all the faithful, men and women, and hasten to the destruction of the wrongdoers." (Qur'an 71:1–28; quoted in N. J. Dawood, translator, *The Koran,* fifth revised edition [London: Penguin Classics, 1990], pages 406–407. Copyright © 1956, 1959, 1966, 1968, 1974, 1990, by N. J. Dawood. Used with permission of Penguin Books, Ltd.)

The Ninety-nine Names of God

Islam insists that there is only one God. But God can be called on by many names, as the Qur'an says: "God has the Most Excellent Names. Call on Him by His Names" (7:180; quoted in N. J. Dawood, translator, *The Koran,* fifth revised edition [London: Penguin Classics, 1990], page 124; copyright © 1956, 1959, 1966, 1968, 1974, 1990 by N. J. Dawood. Used with permission of Penguin Books, Ltd.). Traditionally there are ninety-nine names for God, most of which are given in the Qur'an. The names are important in Muslim piety; each name is sometimes repeated dozens of times in prayer, and each of the ninety-nine beads on the Muslim rosary stands for one of the names. After reading the following list of the ninety-nine names of God, complete these tasks:

1. Check off any names whose meanings you do not know. Using a dictionary, look up the meanings of those names and write them below the names.
2. Circle all the names you have not previously thought of as applying to God.
3. From the names you just circled, star the four that you would be most likely to use for God.

____ 1. The Merciful
____ 2. The Compassionate
____ 3. The Sovereign
____ 4. The Holy
____ 5. The Consummate
____ 6. The Guardian
____ 7. The Masterful
____ 8. The Almighty
____ 9. The Compeller
____ 10. The Proud
____ 11. The Creator
____ 12. The Evolver
____ 13. The Fashioner
____ 14. The Oft-Forgiving
____ 15. The Vanquisher
____ 16. The Bestower
____ 17. The Donor of Livelihood
____ 18. The Revealer
____ 19. The All-Knowing
____ 20. The Constraining
____ 21. The Munificent
____ 22. The Degrading
____ 23. The Enhancing
____ 24. The Exalting
____ 25. The Abasing
____ 26. The All-Hearing
____ 27. The All-Seeing
____ 28. The Judge
____ 29. The Just
____ 30. The Subtle
____ 31. The All-Cognizant
____ 32. The Clement
____ 33. The Supreme
____ 34. The Remitter
____ 35. The Prodigal
____ 36. The Sublime
____ 37. The Great
____ 38. The Maintainer
____ 39. The Sustainer
____ 40. The Sufficer
____ 41. The Majestical
____ 42. The Bounteous
____ 43. The Vigilant
____ 44. The Responder
____ 45. The All-Embracing
____ 46. The All-Wise
____ 47. The Benevolent
____ 48. The Glorious
____ 49. The Resurrecter
____ 50. The Witness
____ 51. The Verity (or The Real)

____ 52. The Champion
____ 53. The All-Powerful
____ 54. The Puissant
____ 55. The Protector
____ 56. The Laudable
____ 57. The Reckoner
____ 58. The Originator
____ 59. The Restorer
____ 60. The Life-Giver
____ 61. The Life-Taker
____ 62. The Omniscient
____ 63. The Dominating
____ 64. The Entire
____ 65. The Illustrious
____ 66. The One
____ 67. The Sanctuary
____ 68. The Potent
____ 69. The Omnipotent
____ 70. The Advancer
____ 71. The Retarder
____ 72. The First
____ 73. The Last
____ 74. The Evident
____ 75. The Immanent
____ 76. The Lord
____ 77. The Transcendent
____ 78. The Benefactor
____ 79. Accepter of Repentance
____ 80. The Avenger
____ 81. The Oft-Pardoning
____ 82. The Most Kind
____ 83. The Owner of Sovereignty
____ 84. The Lord of All Glory and All Honour
____ 85. The Equitable
____ 86. The Congregator
____ 87. The Absolute
____ 88. The Endower
____ 89. The Averter
____ 90. The Harming
____ 91. The Useful
____ 92. The Enricher
____ 93. The Splendid
____ 94. The Guide
____ 95. The Superb
____ 96. The Sempiternal
____ 97. The Heir
____ 98. The All-Wise

____ 99. The Infinitely Patient

(Adapted from Jacques Jomier, *How to Understand Islam,*
translated from the French by John Bowden
[New York: Crossroad Publishing Company, 1989], page 42.

Wisdom from the Sufi Masters

El-Ghazali

A disciple had asked permission to take part in the "dance" of the Sufis.

The Sheikh said: "Fast completely for three days. Then have luscious dishes cooked. If you then prefer the 'dance,' you may take part in it." (Page 56)

A camel is stronger than a man; an elephant is larger; a lion has greater valour; cattle can eat more than man; birds are more virile. Man was made for the purpose of learning. (Page 57)

Attar of Nishapur

Some Israelites reviled Jesus one day as he was walking through their part of the town.

But he answered by repeating prayers in their name.
Someone said to him:
"You prayed for these men, did you not feel incensed against them?"
He answered:
"I could spend only of what I had in my purse." (Page 63)

Someone went up to a madman who was weeping in the bitterest possible way.

He said:
"Why do you cry?"
The madman answered:
"I am crying to attract the pity of His heart."
The other told him:
"Your words are nonsense, for He has no physical heart."
The madman answered:
"It is you who are wrong, for He is the owner of all the hearts which exist. Through the heart you can make your connection with God." (Page 63)

When an arrow is loosed from the bow, it may go straight, or it may not, according to what the archer does.

How strange, therefore, that when the arrow speeds without deviation, it is due to the skill of the archer: but when it goes out of true, it is the arrow which receives the maledictions! (Page 72)

Ibn el-Arabi

[Truth] has confused all the learned of Islam,
Everyone who has studied the Psalms,
Every Jewish Rabbi,
Every Christian priest.

(Page 78)

Saadi of Shiraz

If a gem falls into mud it is still valuable.
If dust ascends to heaven, it remains valueless.
(Page 83)

A thief entered the house of a Sufi, and found nothing there. As he was leaving, the dervish perceived his disappointment and threw him the blanket in which he was sleeping, so that he should not go away empty-handed. (Page 84)

In the eyes of the wise, the seeker of combat with an elephant is not really brave.
Brave is he who says nothing unbecoming in wrath.
A lout abused a man who patiently said:
"O you of bright prospects: I am worse even than you say.
I know all my faults, while you do not know them."
(Page 87)

Jalaludin Rumi

The Way has been marked out.
If you depart from it, you will perish.
If you try to interfere with the signs on the road, you will be an evil-doer.
(Page 103)

The Prophet said that Truth has declared:
"I am not hidden in what is high or low
Nor in the earth nor skies nor throne.
This is certainty, O beloved:
I am hidden in the heart of the faithful.
If you seek me, seek in these hearts."
(Page 108)

You have a duty to perform. Do anything else, do any number of things, occupy your time fully, and yet, if you do not do this task, all your time will have been wasted. (Page 110)

The people of Love are hidden within the populace;
Like a good man surrounded by the bad.
(Page 110)

CHAPTER 15

Religion in the Modern World

Major Concepts

A. **Modern Influences.** Modernization is the general process by which societies achieve increased literacy and education, enhanced technologies, self-sustaining economies, and more unified and participatory governments. The changes that accompany modernization affect religious traditions. Capitalism encourages a materialistic view of wealth, which is pervasive in the modern world. Because capitalism relies on large workforces amassed near manufacturing centers, as populations embrace it, they shift from rural settings to cities in a process known as urbanization. Technological advances in communications and transportation contribute to globalization, the linking and intermixing of cultures. Globalization gives rise to multiculturalism, the coexistence of different peoples and their cultures, which makes understanding other cultures and religions vitally important. Globalization has challenged traditional forms of inequality by introducing an egalitarian view of equality among groups, and over time religious traditions have tended to accommodate that view. Within religions traditionalists resist rapid change by maintaining older forms of belief and practice. Fundamentalism, an extreme form of traditionalism, can take two forms: it can insist on a literal interpretation of a religion's texts and teaching, or it can support a more general reaction against modern forces and reforms. At the opposite end of the spectrum, liberalism advocates adapting religious traditions to respond to the modern world. Those who regard all religious perspectives as valid may be said to have a universalist impulse. The Baha'i faith typifies this impulse in its emphasis on the unity of all religions and people. Interfaith dialogue is one attempt to promote harmony between religions. Postmodernism is a late-twentieth-century worldview that reflects a critical reaction to the trends of modernization and globalization.

B. **New Religious Movements.** New religions arise to fit the circumstances of the modern situation, and most of the world's established religions began as new religious movements. One effect of globalization has been the importation of religions into new cultures. The Vedanta Society was established in the nineteenth century, and bases its approach on the Hindu path of knowledge. The Hare Krishna movement, established in 1965, is another Hindu import, emphasizing the ritual dimension of the path of devotion. New religions also result from the mixing of two or more existing traditions: for example, Santeria combines elements of the Yoruba and

Catholic religions, and Voodoo joins various African religions with Catholicism. Mormonism began when its founder, Joseph Smith Jr., experienced a vision that led him to recover a set of lost prophecies that were eventually published as the Book of Mormon. Brigham Young later led the Mormons west to the Salt Lake Valley, in Utah. Because Mormons believe that we live in the "latter days," and await the Second Coming of Christ, they live by a strict code of ethics and rules. The Jehovah's Witnesses was founded during mid–nineteenth-century predictions of the end of the world. Its adherents discourage many aspects of contemporary life as being counter to their religious understanding. The New Age movement focuses on a rejuvenated future characterized by peace and harmony, and derives its doctrinal, ritual, experiential, and other dimensions from a variety of sources. In this movement the transformation of the world is linked to individual transformation and is achieved through various means. Although the New Age movement enjoys wide recognition, it faces several challenges. The worship of nature is common to many religious traditions. Neopaganism teaches that nature in its entirety is permeated by the divine, and thus emphasizes a basic ethic of doing no harm to others. Wicca also reveres nature, and involves practices and techniques that cause natural energy to conform to a witch's will. Pentecostalism is a form of Christianity in which the dominant feature is glossolalia, or the experience of speaking in tongues. It began in the twentieth century after individuals and an entire congregation experienced glossolalia. Partly because of the exposure available through television, Pentecostalism is a fast-growing form of Christianity.

C. **Religion and Science.** Science, as both a method for acquiring knowledge and the knowledge itself, makes certain assumptions about reality that generally challenge religious worldviews. Scientism holds that science is the only valid method for discovering truth. Evolutionary theory, known as Darwinism, is opposed by some religious views, and is accepted by others as part of the divine will. Science and religion are in tension over the question of whether a soul exists independently from a physical body. Neurotheology is a new scientific field that attempts to examine how the brain responds to religious experiences. Scientists and others acknowledge that brain activity may not reflect the entire phenomenon of religious experiences. The big bang theory is the accepted cosmology of science, although a new theory suggests an alternative. Scientific and religious worldviews may not agree, but they can be complementary. The cosmologies of both modern science and Christianity distinguish creation from the Creator. Quantum mechanics points out the uncertainty of the laws of nature, and invites harmony with religious ideas such as free will and moral choice. Both science and religion are permeated by mystery, and the inability to answer certain questions through a scientific method suggests that there is an essential place for religion.

Pages 268–275

Concept A: Modern Influences

Review Questions: Modern Influences

Question 1. Describe modernization. What is it? When did it begin?
Answer. Modernization stems mainly from the Industrial Revolution, which began in England in the eighteenth century. It is the general process by which societies achieve increased literacy and education, enhanced technologies, self-sustaining economies, greater national unity, and broader participation in politics and government.

Question 2. How do the changes brought on by modernization affect religion?
Answer. As the nation-state's authority rises, the traditional authority of religious institutions diminishes. Enhanced technology and education allow the common people access to sacred texts and religious teachings that previously tended to be controlled by the religious elite.

Question 3. What is materialism?
Answer. The perspective that private ownership of goods and wealth is a good in itself, and should be increased.

Question 4. What is urbanization, and how does it affect religion?
Answer. Urbanization is the shift of population centers from rural, agricultural settings to cities. This shift has created tension with religious traditions, which through the ages have typically conformed mainly to rural settings, often punctuated by festivals and holy days scheduled in accordance with agricultural seasons.

Question 5. Describe globalization, and explain how Tibet serves as an example of it.
Answer. Globalization is the linking and intermixing of cultures. Fifty years ago few Westerners had heard much about Tibetan Buddhism. Today, because of advances in transportation and communications, the Dalai Lama is known throughout the world, advocating freedom for his people and teaching about his tradition.

Question 6. What is multiculturalism, and how does it affect religions?
Answer. Multiculturalism is the coexistence of different peoples and their cultures. Multiculturalism makes it impossible for followers of a particular religious tradition to regard that tradition as the one and only, and makes it necessary for people of different religions to get along with one another.

Question 7. What is egalitarianism, and how does it challenge traditional religions?
Answer. Egalitarianism is a belief in equality between men and women, among racial and ethnic groups, and even among those who practice different religions. Over time the egalitarian ideal and the advocacy of equal rights have become integral to most religions.

Question 8. Describe traditionalism, and explain how Orthodox Judaism serves as an example of it.

Answer. Within religions, a common reaction to rapid changes in the surrounding world is traditionalism, in which adherents maintain older forms of belief and practice regardless of new social norms. For example, Orthodox Jews maintain Torah as the standard of truth despite changes in society.

Question 9. Briefly explain the two basic meanings of the term *fundamentalism.*

Answer. In its strictest sense, *fundamentalism* emphasizes a literal interpretation of a religion's sacred texts and primary teachings—thus getting back to the "fundamentals." In a more general sense, *fundamentalism* refers to an intensely traditionalist form of religion, reacting against modern forces and the religious reforms they encourage. It tends to reject a diversity of interpretations in favor of an authoritarian approach that insists on one "true" interpretation.

Question 10. Define *liberalism* and briefly explain three examples of it.

Answer. Liberalism is the opposite of *traditionalism.* For example: Reform Judaism holds that the religion should adapt to society's changes. Catholicism's Second Vatican Council updated Church teaching and responded to the needs of the modern world. Secular humanism holds that ultimate value is grounded entirely in the human realm, not in the divine or supernatural.

Question 11. Describe the universalist impulse, and cite three examples of religions that feature it.

Answer. The universalist impulse is to regard all religious perspectives as valid. It is a response to modernization, and especially to globalization. Three examples are Hinduism, Sikhism, and Baha'i.

Question 12. How does Baha'i embody the universalist impulse?

Answer. Baha'i teaches that all founders of the world's religions have been God's divine messengers, or prophets. It thus emphasizes the unity of all religions and of all people.

Question 13. Identify two leaders of Baha'i.

Answer. Mirza Husayn ali Nuri, who is known as Baha Allah in Arabic, or Bahaullah in Persian (both names mean "glory of God"), and the son of Baha Allah, Abbas Effendi, known as Abd al-Baha (whose name is Arabic for "the servant of the glory [of God]").

Question 14. Identify four main practices of Baha'i.

Answer. (1) A communal gathering every nineteenth day (called the Feast of the Nineteenth Day); (2) a period of fasting that lasts nineteen days (one month, according to the Baha'i calendar), corresponding to Islam's Ramadan; (3) complete avoidance of alcoholic beverages; (4) daily prayer.

Question 15. Describe the Parliament of the World's Religions, and explain why it was a milestone for interfaith dialogue.

Answer. The Parliament of the World's Religions was a gathering of hundreds of religious leaders from around the globe, held in Chicago in 1993. It was in part a celebration of the one hundredth anniversary of the first such parliament, which had been held in Chicago in 1893. The 1893 parliament had been a milestone for interfaith dialogue because it introduced the richness of the various traditions to a great number of people.

Question 16. What is postmodernism?
Answer. Postmodernism arose in the late twentieth century and reflects a critical reaction to the trends of the modern world.

Text Activities: Modern Influences

Activity A

Think about a technology that plays a significant role in your life—for example, the cell phone. Describe how this technology affects your daily routine and your outlook.

Activity B

Read Acts of the Apostles 2:43–47. In your own words, briefly describe the economic principles of the early Christian community. How compatible are those principles with the economic ways of today's society?

Activity C

Consider a religious tradition with which you are familiar. Do the various dimensions of that religious tradition (ethical, doctrinal, ritual, and so on) reflect a rural setting or an urban setting? Offer examples to support your observations.

Activity D

Briefly describe at least one personal experience or observation of how multiculturalism affects religion.

Activity E

Traditionalism can apply to many areas of life, not just religion. In what part of your life do you tend to be more traditional? Offer several specific examples of ways you try to maintain older beliefs and practices in that area.

Activity F

Reflect on the principles highlighted in the Declaration of a Global Ethic. Briefly describe the extent to which you see each principle being practiced in society.

Activity G

Would you describe yourself as a postmodernist? Why or why not?

Additional Activity: Modern Influences

Primary Source Reading

See *Primary Source Readings in World Religions* (Saint Mary's Press, 2009) for an excerpt from *Kitab-i-Aqdas,* as well as the accompanying leader's guide for suggestions about how to use this reading in your study of Baha'i.

Is Capitalism a Religion?

In this activity the students apply the seven dimensions of religion to the economic system of capitalism, and analyze whether capitalism might be a religion.

1. Before class write the seven dimensions of religion (experiential, mythic, doctrinal, ethical, ritual, social, and material) on the board. Begin class by covering the following points in your own words:

- Capitalism is an economic system based on individual rights, private ownership of property, and pursuit of wealth.
- In a capitalist system, free markets allow individuals to create wealth, make products available, and increase economic opportunity for themselves and for others. Theoretically this can raise the standard of living for everyone by giving everyone a chance to increase their own wealth and opportunities.

Ask the students to brainstorm all the ways that capitalism is at work in their lives, both as they observe its effects and as they participate in its process. Write their responses on a separate section of the board.

2. Break the class into seven groups and tell the groups each to choose a recorder. Assign each group one of the seven dimensions of religion. Ask the groups to consider how capitalism might manifest their assigned dimension. The following questions may be helpful starters:

- *Experiential.* What personal experiences make people "believers"?
- *Mythic.* What myths, stories, or historical figures help people make sense of capitalism and how it works?
- *Doctrinal.* What are some accepted doctrines or beliefs about capitalism?
- *Ethical.* What behaviors are acceptable in capitalism? What actions are considered wrong?
- *Ritual.* What are the formal ways people "practice" capitalism? What rites of passage or initiation exist?
- *Social.* How is capitalism organized? What are its communal aspects?
- *Material.* What are capitalism's structures of "worship"? What ritual objects are used in the practice of capitalism?

Allow the groups enough time for discussion. Tell the recorders each to summarize their group's responses on the board next to its dimension.

3. When all the groups have written their responses, bring the class back together and encourage the students to comment on the other groups' ideas. Conclude by discussing questions like the ones that follow:

- After today's evaluation do you think capitalism can be called a religion? Explain your answer.

- People have jokingly called football and other sports religions. What other phenomena in society manifest the different dimensions of religion?

Variations. Before class assign the students to keep for one day a journal of the ways they experience capitalism, either directly or indirectly. Then allow them to share what they have recorded as part of the brainstorming. Or ask the students to bring in news articles that highlight some aspect of capitalism.

For step 3 ask the students to complete the second question as a homework assignment. Consider allowing the students to create a collage or other visual that demonstrates how their selected phenomenon manifests the various dimensions.

Extend this activity by asking the students to consider nationalism in the same way as they considered capitalism. Appendix 5 of this manual, "Worldviews: Religions and Their Relatives," provides background for you as well as a comparison of nationalism's characteristics with the seven dimensions of religion.

Pages 275–285

Concept B: New Religious Movements

Review Questions: New Religious Movements

Question 17. Identify two new religious movements that are exports from India.

Answer. The Vedanta Society and ISKCON (International Society for Krishna Consciousness, popularly known as the Hare Krishna movement).

Question 18. What is the meaning of the name *Santeria,* and what does this name help explain?

Answer. Santeria means "the way of the saints." This name helps explain the basic nature of the religion, which identifies the Yoruba divine beings known as *orishas* with the various saints of Catholicism.

Question 19. Briefly describe at least three examples of Catholic influence on Voodoo.

Answer. Voodoo identifies traditional spirits with Catholic saints. Voodoo acknowledges, along with the many spirits, a high God, who is identified with the Christian God. Finally, Voodoo incorporates baptism, the Mass, confession, and Catholic prayers, some of them in Latin.

Question 20. Name the two prominent leaders of Mormonism, and briefly describe their roles.

Answer. Joseph Smith Jr. (1805 to 1844) founded Mormonism. Brigham Young (1801 to 1877) led the Church's migration to the Salt Lake Valley.

Question 21. Briefly describe Charles Taze Russell's prediction of a millennial age.

Answer. Charles Taze Russell (1852 to 1916) taught that in 1914 Christ would initiate a radical new era that would last one thousand years and would therefore be called the millennial age. Only the Witnesses would be saved when the millennial age began: 144,000 of them would rule with God and Christ in heaven, and the rest would enjoy physical immortality on earth, living peacefully with one another and with the animals.

Question 22. How do the expectations of the New Age movement differ from those of the Jehovah's Witnesses and the Latter-day Saints?

Answer. Like the Latter-day Saints and the Jehovah's Witnesses, New Agers focus on a dawning period of great significance. But for the New Age movement, this period is a rejuvenated future characterized by peace and harmony, not by the corruption of the "latter days," and no sudden end of history is anticipated.

Question 23. In one sentence, summarize Neopaganism.

Answer. Based on reverence for nature, the movement reacts against the technology of modernization and the patriarchal tradition of Christianity.

Question 24. Who participates in Wiccan rituals? When and where are those rituals typically practiced?

Answer. Witches practice Wiccan rituals in groups called covens, numbering from four to twenty, with thirteen considered optimal. Witches meet regularly, and also celebrate eight seasonal festivals, the most famous being Samhain (or Halloween). The sacred place is a circle nine feet in diameter.

Question 25. What is glossolalia, and what makes it a central element of Pentecostalism?

Answer. Glossolalia is the experience of speaking in other languages (or tongues). It is one of the "gifts of the Spirit" that Pentecostals regard as indications of direct experience of the Holy Spirit.

Text Activities: New Religious Movements

Activity H

Choose Buddhism, Christianity, or Islam, and think about its early years. What general features of new religious movements were present in that religion at its start?

Activity I

Briefly describe at least three reasons why Mormonism is an especially American religion.

Activity J

Think of a specific time when something you hoped for or expected did not take place. Describe similarities and differences between your experience and that of the Jehovah's Witnesses who expected the dawning of a millennial age that never came to pass.

Additional Activities: New Religious Movements

Primary Source Readings

See *Primary Source Readings in World Religions* (Saint Mary's Press, 2009) for excerpts from *The History of Joseph Smith, the Prophet; Awake!; Dianetics;* and *Dreaming the Dark: Magic, Sex and Politics,* as well as the accompanying leader's guide for suggestions about how to use these readings in your study of Mormonism, Jehovah's Witnesses, Scientology, and the Old Religion of the Goddess.

An Interreligious Interview Project

In this activity the students interview members of religions other than their own. They may conduct their interviews in person or through the mail, phone, Internet, or other means. Non-face-to-face interviews may be a necessity if your community lacks religious diversity.

Obviously, some caution is necessary before allowing the students to proceed with their interviews. Parents should be made aware of the nature of the project. If the students will be visiting interviewees, it would be prudent for a trusted adult such as a parent to accompany them. If the students decide to conduct interviews with people they do not know, especially over the Internet, review basic safety precautions, particularly points about not disclosing any personal information.

Note: This exercise is very similar to the chapter 13 activity "The Diversity of Christianity," on pages 196–197 in this manual. You may want to do one or the other, not both.

1. Give the students the following directions, perhaps in written form:

- For this project, you are going to choose a religion and interview a current, practicing member of it. Your goal during the interview is to become familiar with the experience of that person as a member of his or her particular religion.
- You will use data gathered from the interview to put together a formal, oral presentation to the class. Your presentation must be well organized, with a clear beginning, middle, and end. It also must have three parts: a brief introduction about your person, a detailed explanation of that person's experience as an adherent of her or his religion, and a personal reflection about what you have learned from this interreligious encounter. In addition, your presentation must contain two visual aids that relate to the interviewee and her or his faith. These may be photographs, maps, symbols, sayings, ritual objects, or other things relevant to the person's beliefs. You should create a written outline to use in giving your presentation.
- You will be evaluated on the three sections of the presentation (the brief biography, the explanation of the person's religious experience, and your personal reflection) and the visual aids. You must also turn in your written outline. This is a formal presentation, so appearance, attitude, and composure, as well as communication skills, will be taken into account.

2. Explain that the students should not interview someone from their own religion or from another religion with which they are very familiar. You may wish to make members of your school community (students, faculty members, administrators, and staffpeople) ineligible, to push the students out of their comfort zone, and also to save those individuals from being bombarded with requests (though they may be willing to help you and your students find prospective interviewees within their families or faith communities). If you have done the activity "The Diversity of Christianity," in chapter 13, you may wish to limit the students to religions other than Christianity.

Handout 15–A

3. Distribute handout 15–A, "An Interreligious Interview." Go over the handout with the students, clarifying points and answering questions as they arise. Allow the students time to begin the handout in class, and arrange for them to share with a partner the interview questions they develop. Also determine when the students' presentations will take place.

Handout 15–B

4. When the students present and turn in their work, evaluate it as described in step 1. You may wish to complete a copy of handout 15–B, "Teacher Evaluation: An Interreligious Interview," for each presentation.

When Old Was New

This section in the text makes the point that new religious traditions often arise to meet the needs of the modern situation. It explains that most of the world's established traditions began as new religious movements. Assign the students in pairs or groups to research one of the religions studied earlier, examining how it arose as a response to the situation of its time. The students should examine the presence or absence of charismatic figures, any mixing with other religious traditions, any new revelations, and any reinventions of older traditions. You may wish to ask them to share their findings with the class in an informal presentation, or to turn in written results.

Pages 285–291

Concept C: Religion and Science

Review Questions: Religion and Science

Question 26. How might science and religion complement and enrich each other?

Answer. Science and religion are two different ways of knowing, each best suited to helping us understand a different aspect of truth. Science is better able to explore how reality works, whereas religion is better able to explore the ultimate meaning of that reality.

Question 27. Identify three basic assumptions that science makes about reality.

Answer. Science assumes that the physical world is composed of matter and energy; truth is attained through objective experimentation rather than subjective experience; and nature, lacking anything akin to mind or spirit, is indifferent or even hostile toward humanity.

Question 28. What is scientism? What do its critics say are its limitations?

Answer. Scientism insists that science is the only valid method for acquiring knowledge. Critics fault scientism for pushing the reach of science too far and for losing sight of the bigger picture. They say that science is not equipped to deal with ethical issues or with questions of value and meaning.

Question 29. How does Darwinism challenge traditional religious perspectives on human origins?

Answer. Darwinism challenges many traditional religious perspectives on human origins because it does not involve a divine agent. No mind or ordering principle directs the evolutionary process, nor is any intentional purpose at work in it.

Question 30. What is neurotheology?

Answer. Neurotheology is a new scientific field for the psychological and biological study of religion.

Question 31. How is quantum mechanics significant for religion?

Answer. The general effect of quantum mechanics is the incorporation of such vital religious concepts as free will and moral choice within a scientific view of reality. Such circumstances invite harmony between religion and science, even as the latter forges ahead with new discoveries.

Text Activities: Religion and Science

Activity K

In a two-page essay, challenge or defend this statement: Scientific knowledge is the only truth.

Activity L

Read the account of Creation in the Book of Genesis, chapters 1 and 2. How might a liberal religious thinker find Darwinism to be at least somewhat compatible with the biblical account?

Activity M

From the material in this book, choose one religious cosmology and compare it with the scientific cosmology of the big bang theory. How are those cosmologies similar? How are they different? Do you think a follower of the religion could believe both are true? Explain your answer.

Activity N

Both science and religion explore the human experience of mystery. Use what you have learned from this book to write a two-page essay challenging or defending the following statement: Religion is essential to the human exploration of mystery, because some questions are unanswerable through science alone. Defend your argument with examples from the religions described in this book.

Additional Activities: Religion and Science

Knowing the "Truth"

In this exercise the students discuss various ways of categorizing knowledge, and how those ways help people arrive at the truth. By comparing and contrasting the various ways of knowing the truth, the students can come to appreciate that religious ideas and scientific theories can be complementary.

1. Before class write on the board the heads for columns 1, 2, and 3, and the entries for column 1 from the following chart (do not write the entries for columns 2 and 3). At the beginning of class, ask the students to define each way of categorizing knowledge and to provide an example for it (definitions and examples are given for your reference, in case the students have difficulty coming up with their own). Jot their ideas on the board. The finished chart should resemble this:

Categories of Knowledge	*Meaning*	*Examples*
Empirical or mathematical reality	Information that can be proved by mathematic principles (such as the transitive property) or experiments	1 + 1 = 2.
Scientific observation	Information that is supported by evidence but has not been proved conclusively	Water freezes at 0°C.
Scientific theory	A logical explanation drawn from all available evidence, and one that usually points to other implications or correlations	Evolution, the big bang.
History	Recorded names, dates, and occurrences that have been verified by witnesses	The Declaration of Independence was signed July 4, 1776.
Common knowledge, or knowledge widely accepted as true	Many people's common experience of something's effectiveness or ineffectiveness	Chicken soup helps cure a cold.
Revelation, or religious or mystical experience	An individual's personal experience of the divine that causes the individual or others to believe	Creation stories, such as those in Genesis.
Personal experience or personal testimony	A person's subjective experience and judgment about something	McDonald's has the best-tasting French fries.

2. Once the chart is complete, ask the students questions like these:

- Where and how do we use each of these categories of knowledge?
- Are some categories of knowledge more reliable than others? Why or why not?
- Do we tend to use one particular kind of knowledge more than others?
- Are all pieces of knowledge factual, or true? How do we determine whether a particular piece of knowledge is true?
- Are all the examples we have listed true? Might some people regard some or all of these examples as untrue? If so, which ones and why?

3. Call the students' attention to the words Galileo quotes in the student text on page 286: "The intention of the Holy Spirit is to teach us how one goes to heaven and not how heaven goes" (quoted in Finocchiaro, *The Galileo Affair,* p. 96). Point out that the statement suggests a complementary relationship between the scientific and religious ways of knowing. Assign the students to write a brief reflection paper that discusses what happens when one particular way of knowing is used to the exclusion of all others. The paper should incorporate issues raised in the class discussion.

Inherit the Wind

Show the 1960 film adaptation of the play *Inherit the Wind,* by Jerome Lawrence and Robert E. Lee. Directed by Stanley Kramer (127 minutes, MGM, VHS 1960, DVD 2001, rated PG). This production fictionalizes and dramatizes many aspects of the 1925 Scopes Monkey Trial, in which Tennessee schoolteacher Jonathan Scopes was arrested for teaching Darwin's theory of evolution. The trial pitted defense attorney Clarence Darrow against the fundamentalist former presidential candidate William Jennings Bryan. The film does a wonderful job of portraying the tension between the creationist and evolutionist belief systems, and showing how people struggle to find meaning in a constantly changing world. The question, "Who won the Scopes trial?" would make an interesting topic for debate at the conclusion of the film.

An Interreligious Interview

The Interview Process

1. Pick an interviewee. Ask yourself: What type of person do I wish to interview? an academic or a teacher? a student? a ritual or congregational leader? a convert? Will I feel more comfortable interviewing someone who is younger, or older? Does the gender of the person matter to me? All the factors mentioned in these questions also influence the interviewee's understanding of her or his religion.

If you do not personally know someone you would like to interview, you may check the phone book, church agencies such as the Catholic Church's diocesan office for ecumenical or interfaith affairs, and religious student groups at colleges and universities. In addition, the two-volume text *How to Be a Perfect Stranger: A Guide to Etiquette in Other People's Religious Ceremonies,* edited by Arthur J. Magida and Stuart M. Matlins (Woodstock, VT: SkyLight Paths Publishing, 1999), has contact information for many religions and denominations. The Internet can also be a tool for finding someone to interview, perhaps even someone from another country. You can start an Internet search by typing in the names of the religion and of the locale you are interested in.

If you choose to search out a stranger to interview, it is extremely important to be cautious. Not every religious person or organization has people's best interests at heart. Some may use manipulation to get individuals to join their church, and some may have other agendas.

Before you contact the person you have chosen to interview, check with your parents and teacher. Proceed only if they approve, and ask them to help you establish the contact and introduce yourself.

2. Ask for an interview. When you request an interview with someone, always be courteous and respectful. You are representing not only yourself but also your class and your school. Even asking for an interview is an important experience of interreligious encounter; remember, you never get a second chance to make a first impression! Be sure you are able to explain what the project is about and why you are interested in interviewing a member of the religion you have selected. Also be ready to arrange the nature, place, and time of the interview—for instance, you may want to schedule an in-person interview with a local pastor in his office at three o'clock next Thursday. If you will be contacting someone in person, over the phone, or in a real-time electronic exchange, you may want to write out what you will say, or practice with someone else, beforehand.

Give the potential interviewee only as much information about you and your project as necessary or appropriate, depending on the nature of the contact and how well you know the person. *Never* give out personal information to a stranger, especially over the Internet. If anyone asks you inappropriate questions, immediately terminate your contact and report that person to your parents and teacher.

3. Prepare and conduct the interview. Formulating questions ahead of time is essential to a good interview. Ask yourself what you want to learn from your interviewee. Whereas some questions may focus on biographical information, most should be aimed at getting the interviewee to open up and share his or her faith story. Personal stories tend to make an interview rich, opening a window onto the rituals, family practices, and important faith experiences of the person.

4. Follow up after the interview. Be sure to thank the interviewee at the conclusion of your time together. Also send her or him a thank-you note or thank-you e-mail. If other people helped set up the interview, it might be appropriate to thank them as well.

Preparation for the Interview

1. Below are several statements to help you begin the process of preparing for your interview. Complete each statement.

   a. The religion I have selected is __________________________. I am interested in this religious tradition because . . .

   b. I would like to interview someone who . . .

   c. Some things I want to learn from the person I interview are . . .

2. In the remaining space or on a separate sheet of paper, write several questions you would like to ask during your interview. Then share your questions with a partner. Use your partner's feedback to help you improve or add to your interview questions.

Teacher Evaluation: An Interreligious Interview

Student's name or names: ______________________________

Date: ________________

The following ratings identify your scores on a scale from **1** (poor) to **10** (excellent).

The **organization** of the presentation was good, providing a clear beginning, middle, and end.

1 2 3 4 5 6 7 8 9 10

The **brief biography** presented meaningful information about the life of the interviewee.

1 2 3 4 5 6 7 8 9 10

The presentation clearly detailed the **interviewee's experience** as a member of the religion.

1 2 3 4 5 6 7 8 9 10

The **personal reflection** clearly described the educational value of this experience for the interviewer.

1 2 3 4 5 6 7 8 9 10

The **visual aids** highlighted relevant information.

1 2 3 4 5 6 7 8 9 10

The **visual aids** were legible, neat, and creative.

1 2 3 4 5 6 7 8 9 10

The presenter's **appearance, attitude, and body language** engaged the class.

1 2 3 4 5 6 7 8 9 10

The presenter's **communication** was clear and incorporated the appropriate volume, speed, diction, and eye contact.

1 2 3 4 5 6 7 8 9 10

Appendices

APPENDIX 1

Sample Test Questions

Chapter 1: Studying the World's Religions

True or False

t 1. Religions offer responses to fundamental questions concerning human existence.
f 2. Anyone who is spiritual is also considered religious.
f 3. All religions provide answers to the question of where we are ultimately going.
f 4. Monotheism is the belief that the divine reality exists in everything.
t 5. In nontheistic religions, religious experience usually takes the form of mysticism.
f 6. All religious traditions emphasize the seven dimensions of religion equally.
f 7. The world's religious traditions do not have anything in common.

Multiple Choice

Write the letter of the single *best* answer in the blank before each question.

d 1. The basic dimensions of a religious tradition include
  a. doctrines
  b. sacred stories
  c. rituals
  d. all of the above

c 2. The understanding of the nature of the universe is called
  a. astrology
  b. universalism
  c. cosmology
  d. psychology

b 3. Religion and science
  a. are totally contradictory
  b. often approach the same types of questions about the world's nature
  c. should never be studied together
  d. both *a* and *c*

_b_ 4. A religion that does not hold a belief in a personal god or gods is
- a. theistic
- b. nontheistic
- c. invalid
- d. better described as a myth

_c_ 5. The experience of the holy other is often characterized by
- a. fear
- b. fascination
- c. both *a* and *b*
- d. neither *a* nor *b*

_a_ 6. Friedrich Max Müller noted that to know just one religion is to know
- a. none
- b. all
- c. the truth
- d. God

Matching

Write the letter of each word in the blank before the word's definition.

_h_ 1. The belief that God is in all
_e_ 2. The dimension of religion that deals with how we are to act while living in the world
_f_ 3. A formal worship practice, often re-enacting a myth
_a_ 4. The transmission of the divine will or knowledge to human beings
_g_ 5. The capacity for seeing things from another's perspective
_d_ 6. The belief in many gods
_b_ 7. A type of religious experience characterized by union with the divine through inward contemplation
_c_ 8. The overcoming of the limitations imposed by the human condition

- a. revelation
- b. mysticism
- c. transcendence
- d. polytheism
- e. ethical
- f. ritual
- g. empathy
- h. pantheism

Essay

1. Name three of the primary religious questions. Choose one and describe some of the issues that might be part of the answers offered by religions. What religious question concerns you most at this stage of your life? Why?
2. What is religious transcendence, and how does it relate to the quest for spiritual perfection?
3. Give three specific examples of how human beings learn about the ultimate, or divine, reality.
4. Define myth and give an example of one.
5. What is the challenge of the study of world religions for those who are religious themselves? What is the biggest challenge for you as you begin studying world religions, and how do you expect to overcome that challenge?
6. Name at least five dimensions of religion. Give concrete examples of two of those dimensions.

Chapter 2: Primal Religious Traditions

True or False

_t_ 1. All religions stem, more or less directly, from primal beginnings.
_f_ 2. The Aborigines are the native people of Africa.
_t_ 3. According to Aboriginal belief, the world was originally formless.
_t_ 4. Behind every Aboriginal ritual lies a myth that tells of certain Ancestors' actions during the Dreaming.
_t_ 5. In Aboriginal religion both boys and girls undergo initiation rituals.
_f_ 6. The Yoruba prefer to live in rural areas.
_f_ 7. Esu, who mediates between heaven and earth, has an entirely good nature.
_t_ 8. Divination is an extremely important aspect of Yoruba religion.
_t_ 9. The religion of the North American Plains Indians serves as the model of pan-Indian religion.
_t_ 10. The Lakota believe that four souls depart from a person at death.
_f_ 11. The vision quest is supervised by a close family member, such as a father or a brother.
_f_ 12. The Sun Dance is always presided over by a male sacred leader.
_t_ 13. For all tribes, the major task in preparing for the Sun Dance is constructing the lodge.
_f_ 14. The Sun Dance has always been legal in the United States.
_t_ 15. Native American languages have no words for religion.
_f_ 16. The Aztecs were a relatively small group of people whose civilization was very remote.
_t_ 17. The Aztecs believed that Teotihuacan was the origin of the cosmos.
_t_ 18. The Aztecs believed that the only way of delaying the end of the Age of the Fifth Sun was to nourish the sun through human sacrifice.
_f_ 19. Aztec "knowers of things" used divination to communicate with the gods.
_f_ 20. Nothing of Aztec culture has survived in today's world.

Multiple Choice

Write the letter of the single *best* answer in the blank before each question.

_d_ 1. Primal religions tend to be the traditions of
- a. tribal peoples
- b. nonliterate peoples
- c. the most elite communities
- d. both *a* and *b*

_b_ 2. The foundation of Aboriginal religion is the
- a. *axis mundi*
- b. concept of the Dreaming
- c. Wakan Tanka
- d. both *a* and *b*

_d_ 3. The Aborigines believe that the spiritual essence of the Ancestors
- a. remains in various symbols the Ancestors left behind
- b. resides within each individual
- c. can be known only in the afterlife
- d. both *a* and *b*

_d_ 4. All primal traditions include basic features such as
a. myth
b. ritual to re-enact myth
c. animal and, on rare occasions, human sacrifices
d. both *a* and *b*

_d_ 5. The purpose of the Yoruba religion is to
a. guard against the evil deeds of sorcerers and witches
b. maintain the balance between the human beings of earth and the gods and ancestors of heaven
c. relive the early days of creation
d. both *a* and *b*

_a_ 6. Most primal religions believe that the boundaries between the human and supernatural realms are
a. easily crossed over
b. crossed over only rarely and with great difficulty
c. impenetrable
d. interchangeable

_b_ 7. Wakan Tanka is
a. the one supreme god of the Lakota
b. sixteen separate deities
c. the afterlife
d. the best way to live

_b_ 8. The Plains Indians often go for ritual purification to a
a. deep lake
b. sweat lodge
c. bathtub
d. church

_a_ 9. In a vision quest, the vision arrives in the form of
a. an animal or some other natural object or force
b. a living friend or family member
c. a written message
d. both *a* and *b*

_c_ 10. The Sun Dance is a ritual that
a. celebrates the new year
b. prepares the tribe for the annual buffalo hunt
c. both *a* and *b*
d. none of the above

_d_ 11. Mesoamerica included the present-day countries of
a. Mexico
b. Costa Rica
c. El Salvador
d. both *a* and *b*

_c_ 12. Aztecs attributed the creation and ordering of the world to
a. Olmec
b. Toltec
c. Quetzalcoatl
d. Topiltzin Quetzalcoatl

_c_ 13. The Aztec understanding of the *axis mundi* extended to
a. human beings
b. Serpent Mountain
c. both *a* and *b*
d. none of the above

_a_ 14. Tenochtitlan fell to the Spanish partly because Hernán Cortés was mistaken for
a. Topiltzin Quetzalcoatl
b. Quetzalcoatl
c. Moctezuma
d. Nahuatl

Matching

Write the letter of each word in the blank before the word's definition.

_j_ 1. According to Aboriginal religion, something that could be charged with sacred power
_f_ 2. A natural form, such as an animal or rock, that symbolizes an Ancestor
_c_ 3. A system that dictates that certain sacred things and activities are set aside for specific members of a group and are forbidden to other members
_k_ 4. The capital city of the Aztec empire, believed to be the center of the world
_e_ 5. The supreme god of the Yoruba
_l_ 6. The hundreds of deities worshiped by the Yoruba
_a_ 7. A sort of mischievous supernatural being who tends to disrupt the normal course of life
_i_ 8. Yoruba priests who help people learn their future
_g_ 9. The Mesoamerican creator god worshiped by the Toltecs
_d_ 10. The Lakota name for the supreme reality
_b_ 11. The Lakota trickster figure
_h_ 12. A mountain, tree, or pole that is believed to connect heaven and earth, and is sometimes regarded as the world's center

a. trickster figure
b. Inktomi
c. taboo
d. Wakan Tanka
e. Olorun
f. totem
g. Quetzalcoatl
h. *axis mundi*
i. diviners
j. cave
k. Tenochtitlan
l. *orisha*

Essay

1. Briefly explain the concept of the Dreaming. How does this period live on today, and what part do rituals play in it? Among which three aspects of reality does Aboriginal religious life seek to maintain harmony?
2. What is the purpose of Aboriginal initiation rituals? Give a specific example of such a ritual and explain its symbolism.
3. Briefly describe the supernatural beings, including Olorun, worshiped by the Yoruba. By what means are these heavenly beings connected to the earthly world?
4. Explain two rituals that are common to all Plains Indians.
5. Describe the concept of the *axis mundi* and explain its importance in Aztec cosmology.
6. Describe the role of religion in primal societies. What understandings do most primal religions share?

Chapter 3: Hinduism

True or False

t 1. Holy man Shri Ramakrishna became a Muslim and a Christian but remained a Hindu throughout his life.
f 2. Brahman is personal and is easily perceived by humans.
t 3. Brahman is Atman.
f 4. Hindus believe that a person dies only once before *moksha* is achieved.
t 5. Hindus worship as many as 330 million gods and goddesses.
f 6. *Karma* is delivered by Hindu deities to reward good behavior and to punish bad behavior.
t 7. *Dharma* has much in common with the Christian ethical principle of unconditional love.
f 8. Hinduism's three paths to *moksha* are mutually exclusive.
t 9. In *samadhi* the knower becomes that which is known.
f 10. Millions of Hindus still worship Brahma.
t 11. The Bhagavad-Gita is a small section of the epic poem *Mahabharata.*
t 12. Hindus consider the Ganges River sacred enough to purify all sins.
f 13. Hinduism has had a very large influence on the religious tradition of Muslims.
t 14. Swami Vivekananda, who lived from 1863 to 1902, was the first Hindu missionary.

Multiple Choice

Write the letter of the single *best* answer in the blank before each question.

c 1. The doctrine of monism holds that
a. one personal God created all things
b. money reigns supreme
c. all reality is ultimately one
d. animals have no afterlife

d 2. Brahman is the
a. eternal essence of reality
b. highest of the four classes
c. source of the universe
d. both *a* and *c*

a 3. One of the most frequently cited passages in Hindu literature is
a. "That art thou."
b. "That is the truth."
c. "Love is the answer."
d. "All is illusion."

_a_ 4. Krishna compares reincarnation to
- **a.** getting undressed at night and putting on a different set of clothes in the morning
- **b.** putting on a mask
- **c.** enjoying an endless banquet
- **d.** climbing a tower that goes on forever

_b_ 5. Hinduism's closest equivalent to the Western term *religion* is
- **a.** *maya*
- **b.** *dharma*
- **c.** *brahmin*
- **d.** *artha*

_d_ 6. A person's particular *dharma* is determined by his or her
- **a.** gender
- **b.** class
- **c.** stage of life
- **d.** all of the above

_b_ 7. A wandering ascetic who has advanced to the fourth and highest stage of life is called a
- **a.** *samadhi*
- **b.** *sannyasin*
- **c.** forest dweller
- **d.** *brahmin*

_c_ 8. Which of the following concepts is *not* one of Hinduism's four goals of life?
- **a.** *kama*
- **b.** *artha*
- **c.** *maya*
- **d.** *dharma*

_c_ 9. Which of these Hindu gods is known for destruction and is worshiped by millions?
- **a.** Brahma
- **b.** Vishnu
- **c.** Shiva
- **d.** Rama

_d_ 10. Which of the following entities is an *avatar* of Vishnu?
- **a.** Krishna
- **b.** Rama
- **c.** Kali
- **d.** both *a* and *b*

_d_ 11. Hindu worship includes
- **a.** household and village rituals
- **b.** pilgrimages to holy places
- **c.** veneration of cows
- **d.** all of the above

_c_ 12. Which of the following events occurred in 1948?
- **a.** Mohandas K. (Mahatma) Gandhi was assassinated.
- **b.** The Indian government officially forbade discrimination against outcastes.
- **c.** both *a* and *b*
- **d.** none of the above

Identification

Listed below are Hinduism's three paths to liberation, and examples and descriptions of those paths. Write the letter of each path in the blanks before the examples and descriptions that fit it.

a. *karma marga*
b. *jnana marga*
c. *bhakti marga*

_b_ 1. Meditating and studying
_c_ 2. The path that the Bhagavad-Gita is most closely associated with
_a_ 3. The path that was advocated by Mahatma Gandhi and that is marked by an attitude of unselfishness in all its aspects
_b_ 4. The predominant path a yogi would follow
_a_ 5. Helping out in a homeless shelter or soup kitchen
_c_ 6. Worshiping at a temple or a household shrine

Identification

Listed below are three schools of Hindu philosophy within the path of knowledge, and descriptions of those schools. Write the letter of each school in the blanks before the descriptions that fit it.

a. Vedanta
b. Yoga
c. Sankhya

_b_ 1. Emphasizes physical and psychological practices
_c_ 2. Asserts that reality comprises two distinct categories: matter, and an infinite number of eternal selves
_a_ 3. Is most faithful to the predominant monism of Hinduism, and embraced by the majority of Hindus who traverse the path of knowledge
_a_ 4. Teaches that the world and all finite beings within it are the stuff of *maya*
_c_ 5. Offers basic teachings that are important for Jainism and Buddhism
_b_ 6. In its most famous version, sets forth eight steps that culminate in *samadhi*
_a_ 7. Is the approach whose most notable advocate was the medieval Hindu philosopher Shankara

Matching

Write the letter of each word in the blank before the word's definition.

_c_ 1. Hinduism's earliest sacred text
_f_ 2. The Hindu term for liberation
_i_ 3. Ancient philosophical texts that form the basis of Hindu doctrines
_d_ 4. The eternal self

a 5. The wheel of rebirth
e 6. Hinduism's most popular sacred text
k 7. The moral law of cause and effect of actions
b 8. Ethical duty based on the divine order of reality
o 9. The group of people whom Mahatma Gandhi renamed Harijan, "God's children"
g 10. The highest of the four classes, made up of priests
m 11. The lowest class, made up of servants and laborers
l 12. Cosmic illusion
j 13. A trancelike state in which self-consciousness is lost, and the mind is absorbed into the ultimate reality
h 14. An incarnation, or living embodiment, of a deity (generally Vishnu), who is sent to earth to accomplish a divine purpose
n 15. The traditional practice of burning a widow on her husband's funeral pyre, outlawed since 1829 though it still occurs rarely

a. *samsara*
b. *dharma*
c. Rig Veda
d. Atman
e. Bhagavad-Gita
f. *moksha*
g. *brahmin*
h. *avatar*
i. Upanishads
j. *samadhi*
k. *karma*
l. *maya*
m. *shudra*
n. *sati*
o. the Untouchables

Essay

1. How does the image of many rivers flowing into one ocean characterize Hinduism?
2. Define Brahman and Atman, and explain their relationship.
3. Describe two cyclical patterns in Hinduism.
4. Explain the two Hindu principles that connect the divine with this world and provide a basis for moral life.
5. Describe the Hindu caste system. Build a case stating why it is fair or unfair.
6. Name and briefly explain each of Hinduism's four goals in life. Compare them with goals that are considered worthwhile in your society today.
7. If you were Hindu, what path to liberation would you choose? Explain your choice and include examples of what following your path would entail.
8. In discussing his thoughts on the "complications" of Hinduism, Shuvo, a Hindu student, says, "One who quarrels about the ways but forgets about the destination is nothing but a fool." Do you agree with his statement? Why or why not?
9. Give two examples of the modern challenges that traditional Hinduism faces.
10. Explain how Mohandas K. Gandhi "forever changed the nature of India, and of Hinduism." How is he regarded by Hindus today?

Chapter 4: Buddhism

True or False

t 1. The life of Gautama is known more through legend than through verifiable fact.
f 2. Gautama remained an ascetic all his life.
t 3. One of the Three Jewels is the Buddha.
f 4. *Dharma* in Buddhism is exactly the same as the Hindu doctrine of *dharma*.
f 5. Like many religions Buddhism depends on a revelation from the divine for its truths.
t 6. Both Buddhism and Hinduism teach the doctrine of *samsara.*
f 7. In Buddhist morality the emphasis is on the actual outcome of an act, not the intention behind the act.
f 8. The Five Precepts apply only to Buddhist monks and nuns.
t 9. The Buddha severely condemned attachments, even between family members.
f 10. The heart of Buddhist practice lies specifically in wisdom.
t 11. *Nirvana* cannot be understood until it is experienced.
t 12. The Buddha specifically refused to say whether or not a person exists in *nirvana.*

Multiple Choice

Write the letter of the single *best* answer in the blank before each question.

a 1. Buddha was a
- **a.** man
- **b.** god
- **c.** supernatural being
- **d.** both *a* and *c*

d 2. Siddhartha Gautama was born into
- **a.** poverty
- **b.** luxury
- **c.** the warrior class
- **d.** both *b* and *c*

b 3. Which of the Four Passing Sights filled Gautama with hope?
- **a.** the decrepit old man
- **b.** the ascetic
- **c.** the corpse
- **d.** the diseased man

b 4. Gautama finally attained enlightenment when he
- **a.** perceived his previous lifetimes
- **b.** discovered the Four Noble Truths
- **c.** acquired the "divine eye"
- **d.** accepted a simple meal

a 5. Taking refuge in the Three Jewels means being
- **a.** a Buddhist
- **b.** loath to accept asceticism
- **c.** mired in Mara's realm
- **d.** distracted by worldly charms

_c_ 6. For Buddhists, Gautama the Buddha is
- **a.** the first Buddha
- **b.** the only Buddha
- **c.** not the first or only Buddha
- **d.** the most superior deity

_b_ 7. Buddhism holds that salvation must be won through
- **a.** the gods
- **b.** efforts of the human mind
- **c.** the intervention of *arhats*
- **d.** both *a* and *c*

_c_ 8. When Gautama looked deeply within himself, he discovered
- **a.** Atman
- **b.** the eternal self
- **c.** change
- **d.** both *a* and *b*

_c_ 9. Which of the following concepts is *not* one of the Three Marks of Existence?
- **a.** no-self *(anatta)*
- **b.** impermanence *(anicca)*
- **c.** action *(karma)*
- **d.** suffering *(dukkha)*

_c_ 10. The Noble Eightfold Path sets forth
- **a.** extreme religious practices
- **b.** stages to be mastered and left behind
- **c.** a life of moderation and ongoing practices
- **d.** both *a* and *b*

_a_ 11. Which of the following ideas is *not* a primary focal point of Buddhist training, embraced by the Noble Eightfold Path?
- **a.** unconditional love
- **b.** wisdom
- **c.** morality
- **d.** concentration

_d_ 12. The *arhat* is
- **a.** free from *tanha*
- **b.** free from *dukkha*
- **c.** perfectly compassionate toward all living things
- **d.** all of the above

Identification

Listed below are Buddhism's three great "vehicles," and characteristics of those vehicles. Write the letter of each vehicle in the blanks before the characteristics that fit it.

- **a.** Theravada
- **b.** Mahayana
- **c.** Vajrayana

_b_ 1. Is called the Great Vehicle, and its adherents revere *bodhisattvas* and consider compassion the supreme virtue

_a_ 2. Is also known by the somewhat derisive name *Hinayana* (the Lesser Vehicle), and is the prevalent form of Buddhism in Cambodia, Myanmar (formerly Burma), Sri Lanka, and Thailand

_c_ 3. Is referred to as the Vehicle of the Diamond

__a__ 4. Follows the earliest texts, focuses on the teachings of Buddhism, and emphasizes the monastic life
__b__ 5. Is the largest division of Buddhism and the dominant form of Buddhism in China, Korea, and Japan
__b__ 6. Focuses on the Buddha, celebrating him as a divine savior
__c__ 7. Is the prevalent form of Buddhism in Tibet
__c__ 8. Harnesses sensual energies to propel individuals toward enlightenment

Matching

Write the letter of each word in the blank before the word's definition.

__g__ 1. Rigorous self-denial
__c__ 2. "Awakened one"
__d__ 3. The state of eternal bliss that is ultimate salvation
__h__ 4. A saint, or one who has become enlightened
__a__ 5. The Buddhist community of monks, nuns, and laity
__f__ 6. The teachings of the Buddha
__j__ 7. An ancient language of India, spoken by the common people
__b__ 8. The force that determines the nature of one's rebirth
__m__ 9. Selfish desire; the second noble truth
__k__ 10. A "Buddha in the making," the ideal type for Mahayana Buddhists
__i__ 11. Patterned icons that visually excite and are used in Vajrayana Buddhism
__l__ 12. Choreographed hand movements used in Vajrayana Buddhist rituals
__e__ 13. Resonating chants used especially in Vajrayana Buddhism
__n__ 14. Head of the hierarchy of the Vajrayana Buddhist clergy

a. *sangha*
b. *karma*
c. Buddha
d. *nirvana*
e. mantras
f. Dharma
g. asceticism
h. *arhat*
i. mandalas
j. Pali
k. *bodhisattva*
l. mudras
m. *tanha*
n. Dalai Lama

Essay

1. How did Siddhartha Gautama learn about the reality of suffering and the impermanence of life's pleasures? What did he do in response to that discovery? What would you have done if you had been in his position?
2. Define the Middle Way. Compare that doctrine with another religion's perspective on what constitutes a healthy spiritual life.
3. Describe two ways that Buddhism and Hinduism are alike, and two ways that they are different.
4. According to the student text, "to examine completely the inner realm of self leads to the discovery that the self *does not exist.*" Explain how a Buddhist might make sense of that paradox. Then describe briefly how a Hindu might respond to such a statement.
5. Contrast the Buddhist and Hindu views of what is reborn after death.

6. What are Buddhism's central teachings called? List them and tell whether you agree with each one, and why or why not.
7. Do you think Buddhism is a pessimistic religion? Explain your answer.
8. Briefly recall, in writing, the story of the Buddha and the tigress. Propose an argument either for or against the degree of compassion being held up as the ideal.
9. Which of the three great rafts, or "vehicles," of Buddhism most appeals to you? Why?

Chapter 5: Jainism

True or False

_t_ 1. Jainism shares many basic doctrines with Hinduism and Buddhism.
_f_ 2. According to Jain belief, only five people in the present turning of the world cycle have established a "river crossing."
_t_ 3. Jainism rejected the Hindu caste system, but replaced it with a Jain caste system.
_f_ 4. Like Gautama, Mahavira learned the true practices of Jainism on his own, not from others.
_t_ 5. Jains understand the universe to be vast yet finite.
_t_ 6. Many of the gods and goddesses of Hinduism are also acknowledged by Jains.
_t_ 7. The Jain universe passes through cycles that are depicted as turnings of a wheel.
_f_ 8. Jains believe that the soul of an elephant differs from the soul of a human.
_t_ 9. Jains believe that even some microbes have the potential for spiritual advancement.
_f_ 10. Salvation is attainable for Jains of this world, despite this era's being one of continuing decline.
_f_ 11. Nearly half of the three million Jains in the world today are ascetics.
_t_ 12. Today Jain ascetics tend to wander in groups, rather than setting out alone.
_f_ 13. The Jain principle of nonviolence implies complete pacifism.
_t_ 14. Jains universally practice vegetarianism.
_t_ 15. Jains often use statues in their worship.

Multiple Choice

Write the letter of the single *best* answer in the blank before each question.

_d_ 1. Which of these religions originated in India?
a. Hinduism
b. Buddhism
c. Jainism
d. all of the above

d 2. What are the defining characteristics of Jainism?
- **a.** *ahimsa*
- **b.** asceticism
- **c.** service
- **d.** both *a* and *b*

a 3. In Jainism, spiritual conquerors who have attained salvation are called
- **a.** *tirthankaras*
- **b.** *bodhisattvas*
- **c.** *rajahs*
- **d.** *lokas*

b 4. Mahavira practiced
- **a.** mild asceticism
- **b.** extreme asceticism
- **c.** the Middle Way
- **d.** hedonism

a 5. Knowing the makeup of the universe was
- **a.** unimportant to Gautama, important to Mahavira
- **b.** important to Gautama, unimportant to Mahavira
- **c.** important to both Gautama and Mahavira
- **d.** unimportant to both Gautama and Mahavira

c 6. In Jainism, both deities and hell beings
- **a.** stay in their condition eternally
- **b.** are liberated souls
- **c.** are destined to experience rebirth
- **d.** both *a* and *b*

a 7. *Jivas* are
- **a.** perfectly pure
- **b.** impure
- **c.** known for their large size
- **d.** all destined to become *tirthankaras*

b 8. Jainism understands reality to be
- **a.** essentially one thing
- **b.** ultimately many things
- **c.** impure
- **d.** both *b* and *c*

b 9. Jains believe that complete purification of the soul can be achieved only through
- **a.** divine assistance
- **b.** an ascetic life
- **c.** the direct assistance of *tirthankaras* who have passed from material existence
- **d.** both *a* and *c*

b 10. If a Jain nun is carefully sweeping a path and steps on a bug, she has
- **a.** violated the vow of *ahimsa*
- **b.** not violated the vow of *ahimsa*
- **c.** taken a significant step toward liberation
- **d.** effectively eliminated herself from the ascetic life

b 11. The central Jain ritual is that of
- **a.** eating (communion)
- **b.** repentance
- **c.** meditation
- **d.** prayer

_a_ 12. The ideal method of dying for Jains is
- **a.** voluntarily starving
- **b.** going to sleep
- **c.** succumbing to disease
- **d.** being sacrificed by an ascetic

_b_ 13. Jain laypeople regard achieving the ultimate aim of salvation as
- **a.** guaranteed
- **b.** a distant possibility
- **c.** limited to those who are prosperous
- **d.** both *b* and *c*

_c_ 14. Which of the following assertions is *not* one of the Five Lesser Vows taken by Jain laity?
- **a.** Avoid lying.
- **b.** Do not take what has not been given.
- **c.** Renounce sexual activity.
- **d.** Avoid greed.

_a_ 15. The proportion of Jains among India's population is about
- **a.** 2 percent
- **b.** 25 percent
- **c.** 50 percent
- **d.** 75 percent

Matching

Write the letter of each word in the blank before the word's definition.

_d_ 1. The root of the name *Jainism;* a word that means "conqueror" and is synonymous with the term *tirthankara*

_f_ 2. The twenty-third *tirthankara,* who continues to be a popular object of Jain devotion

_j_ 3. The perfect and complete knowledge that is Jain enlightenment

_a_ 4. The Jain universe, often depicted as having the shape of a giant man

_h_ 5. Souls

_i_ 6. The nonliving components of the universe, such as space, time, motion, rest, and all forms of matter

_b_ 7. What Jain monks and nuns are collectively known as

_g_ 8. The principle of nonviolence and the central standard of conduct for all Jains

_c_ 9. The largest Jain sect, whose monks and nuns wear white robes

_e_ 10. The second-largest Jain sect, whose monks go about naked, or "sky-clad"

- **a.** *loka*
- **b.** ascetics
- **c.** Shvetambaras
- **d.** *jina*
- **e.** Digambaras
- **f.** Parshva
- **g.** *ahimsa*
- **h.** *jivas*
- **i.** *ajiva*
- **j.** *kevala*

Essay

1. Who was Mahavira, when did he live, and what role does he play in Jainism? Compare his legendary biography with that of Gautama. How did Mahavira's manner of death reflect his beliefs?
2. Why do Jains consider all life-forms worthy of great respect and care? Give two examples of how nonhuman life-forms participate in Jain religious life. How do those life-forms attain salvation? What is your perspective on these ideas?
3. How is the Jain understanding of *karma* similar to and different from the Hindu and Buddhist understandings of *karma?*
4. How does the central principle of *ahimsa* relate to the Five Great Vows?

Chapter 6: Sikhism

True or False

_f_ 1. Sikh communities are rarely found outside India.
_t_ 2. Sikhism has acquired a reputation for being a militant religion.
_f_ 3. The ten historical Gurus of Sikhism were divine incarnations of God.
_t_ 4. Guru Nanak sat on a special seat while teaching in his community.
_f_ 5. To this day only a small minority of Sikhs belong to the Khalsa.
_t_ 6. The poet Kabir contributed to the Adi Granth.
_f_ 7. Sikhism did not adopt the concept of *samsara* from Hinduism.
_f_ 8. Like Hindus, Sikhs are opposed to eating meat.
_t_ 9. Guru Nanak rejected much of the traditional religious life of Hinduism and Islam.
_t_ 10. The primary purpose of the Five Ks in the Khalsa initiation ceremony is to strengthen Sikh identity.
_f_ 11. Sikhism's commitment to justice is secondary to its militant aspect.

Multiple Choice

Write the letter of the single *best* answer in the blank before each question.

_c_ 1. Sikhism tries to reconcile the differences between
- **a.** Hinduism and Buddhism
- **b.** Hinduism and Jainism
- **c.** Hinduism and Islam
- **d.** Buddhism and Jainism

_b_ 2. Sikhism is
- **a.** polytheistic
- **b.** monotheistic
- **c.** dualistic
- **d.** monistic

d 3. Over the centuries Sikhs have occasionally engaged in violent confrontations with
a. Muslims
b. Hindus
c. Christians
d. both *a* and *b*

d 4. Sikhism's most important sacred text is called the
a. Adi Granth
b. Guru Granth Sahib
c. Khalsa
d. both *a* and *b*

b 5. Shortly after Guru Nanak received God's revelation, he
a. became a hermit
b. traveled widely
c. died
d. got married and started a family

c 6. Which of the following changes was *not* one of the effects of Guru Arjan's leadership in Sikhism?
a. Sikhism took on a military dimension.
b. Sikhism became more political.
c. Arjan installed the Adi Granth as Guru.
d. Arjan provided Sikhs with a geographical center.

b 7. Sikhism teaches that the ultimate purpose of life is to
a. serve others
b. attain complete union with God
c. enjoy life to the fullest
d. detach oneself from all desire

c 8. Sikh theology maintains that God
a. is totally transcendent
b. is impersonal and unapproachable
c. dwells within creation
d. both *a* and *b*

d 9. *Haumai*
a. is the human inclination to be self-centered
b. is the human inclination to be God-centered
c. increases the distance between individuals and God
d. both *a* and *c*

b 10. To symbolize the Sikh community's unity, worship in the *gurdwara* generally ends with
a. a hymn and a prayer
b. a sharing of a wheat and honey cake
c. a ritual dance
d. a reading from the Adi Granth

Matching

Write the letter of each word in the blank before the word's definition.

c 1. The literal meaning of the word *sikh*
f 2. A special building for Sikh worship that is the central structure of any Sikh community
a 3. The township where the Guru Nanak and his followers formed the first Sikh community and whose name means "abode of the creator"
h 4. The Guru who compiled the Adi Granth and constructed the Temple of God
j 5. The Guru who was revered as the greatest Guru after Nanak, and who instituted the Khalsa and installed the Adi Granth as Guru
b 6. Literally "first book"
e 7. An order within Sikhism, also called the Pure Ones
i 8. A name that Sikhs sometimes use for God
d 9. Indwelling
g 10. The divine order of the universe

a. Kartarpur
b. Adi Granth
c. learner
d. immanent
e. Khalsa
f. *gurdwara*
g. *hukam*
h. Arjan
i. Guru
j. Gobind Singh

Essay

1. Who was Guru Nanak? How did he contribute to the development of Sikhism?
2. Explain the three ways Sikhs use the capitalized term *Guru.*
3. Describe the Khalsa and its place within Sikhism. How was it established, and why?
4. What do some say is Sikhism's greatest attraction? Why? Explain what *you* consider its greatest attraction.
5. Compare Sikhism's understanding of God's nature with Hinduism's understanding of God's nature.
6. Describe the Sikh perspective on human nature and on what constitutes salvation. How does the Sikh view of human nature compare with your own view?
7. What is the purpose of the male Sikhs' turbans and beards? What are the advantages and disadvantages of being easily recognized as adherents of a particular religion?

Chapter 7: Confucianism

True or False

_t_ 1. Confucius was an apparent failure when he died in 479 BC.
_f_ 2. Confucius argued that love, not justice, should be the primary response when dealing with an enemy.
_f_ 3. Confucius offered extensive teachings on life after death.
_t_ 4. Confucius advocated the continuation of ancestor worship.
_f_ 5. Confucianism can be equated only with the teachings of Confucius.
_f_ 6. Mencius claimed that human beings are naturally evil, and that assertion became a basic Confucian teaching.
_t_ 7. The Tao is basic to all forms of Chinese religion.
_t_ 8. Good government is a primary goal of Confucianism.
_t_ 9. Three of the Five Constant Relationships involve family.
_f_ 10. According to Confucius it is more important to correct one's parents when they are wrong than it is to be filial.
_f_ 11. Confucians, like people in modern Western society, tend to regard old age negatively.

Multiple Choice

Write the letter of the single *best* answer in the blank before each question.

_a_ 1. Confucianism's central project is learning
- **a.** to be human
- **b.** to overcome one's humanity
- **c.** all the sacred scriptures by heart
- **d.** to care for others more than for oneself

_c_ 2. At one point Confucius was a
- **a.** chef
- **b.** soldier
- **c.** government official
- **d.** doctor

_d_ 3. Confucius seems most of all to have been a
- **a.** stern disciplinarian
- **b.** eager student
- **c.** diligent teacher
- **d.** both *b* and *c*

_a_ 4. Confucius was most concerned with
- **a.** transmitting traditional ways
- **b.** inventing new theories
- **c.** punishing those who made mistakes
- **d.** both *a* and *c*

_c_ 5. Neo-Confucianism was largely a response to
- **a.** Confucius's relatively few erroneous ideas
- **b.** challenges from Christianity
- **c.** challenges from Taoism and Buddhism
- **d.** the general apathy that had taken hold of most Confucians

_c_ 6. How many Confucian texts are to this day considered most important?
- a. one
- b. two
- c. four
- d. six

_d_ 7. Confucius viewed nobility as being bestowed by
- a. birth
- b. merit
- c. steadfast learning
- d. both *b* and *c*

_b_ 8. The supreme virtue in Confucianism is
- a. courage
- b. benevolence
- c. uprightness
- d. wisdom

_d_ 9. *Li* means
- a. "rite," or "sacred ritual"
- b. "propriety"
- c. "deceit"
- d. both *a* and *b*

_a_ 10. A significant aspect of *li* is that proper behavior is largely dependent on one's place in society. Confucians refer to this as
- a. the rectification of names
- b. poetic justice
- c. reciprocity
- d. *wen*

_a_ 11. Confucius believed that good government comes about through
- a. the cultivation of *te*
- b. edicts
- c. punishments
- d. both *b* and *c*

_c_ 12. A Confucian doctrine summarizing the proper ethical principle for each basic human relationship is the
- a. Neo-Confucian Analect
- b. Five Great Vows
- c. Five Constant Relationships
- d. Way of Righteousness

_b_ 13. Confucianism emphasizes the
- a. individuality of the self
- b. self as primarily a center of human relationships
- c. unchanging self
- d. both *a* and *c*

Matching

Write the letter of each word in the blank before the word's definition.

_c_ 1. A name by which Confucius was known
_g_ 2. The collection of Confucius's sayings
_i_ 3. The person who was revered as the second founder of Confucianism and whose teachings are set forth in one of Confucianism's central texts
_a_ 4. Neo-Confucianism's most important figure
_j_ 5. In Confucianism, generally the moral order that permeates the universe, the Way that should be followed
_e_ 6. An ideal human being with perfect moral character
_b_ 7. The supreme human virtue; doing one's best to treat others as one would wish to be treated
_h_ 8. A basic Confucian ethical principle that says not to do to others what you would not want them to do to you
_f_ 9. The cultural arts and skills of behavior valued by Confucius as being of moral benefit
_d_ 10. Virtue as shown through the power of example

a. Chu Hsi
b. *jen*
c. Master K'ung
d. *te*
e. *chun-tzu*
f. *wen*
g. Analects
h. *shu*
i. Mencius
j. Tao

Essay

1. What is the focus of Confucianism? Explain how it is possible to be a Confucian at the same time as being a Buddhist, Muslim, Christian, or Taoist.
2. Name two reasons that Confucius has been influential in East Asia for over two thousand years. Describe how his teachings have differed from at least one other approach to solving China's problems during that time.
3. What did Confucius seek to learn? Why? How does his view of learning compare with the central life concerns of another Asian religion, Taoism?
4. What was Confucius's vision of the ideal human being? Did he think ideal humans were born or made that way? Explain your answer. Then describe your own perspective on the question.
5. Which is more important in Confucianism: behaving properly or having the right moral perspective? Explain.
6. Name three skills included in the broad category *wen*. What part does Confucianism consider *wen* to play in improving society? Do you agree or disagree with that perspective? Why?
7. Briefly describe the Five Constant Relationships, and how they all relate to one another.
8. Explain Confucius's understanding of Heaven, comparing it with your own understanding of heaven.
9. Describe some ways Confucian ideas could lead to improvements in your society.
10. "Do not worry because you have no official position. Worry about your qualifications. Do not worry because no one appreciates your abilities. Seek to be worthy of appreciation" (Analects 4.14). How does this passage illuminate the life and teachings of Confucius?

Chapter 8: Taoism

True or False

t 1. It is uncertain whether Lao Tzu ever existed.
t 2. Confucius is said to have sought Lao Tzu's advice.
t 3. The teachings of Taoism, like those of many mystical religious traditions, contain many paradoxes.
f 4. Tao is immense and complex, yet comprehensible.
f 5. Tao is not immanent.
t 6. Taoism emphasizes the need to embrace the yin.
t 7. Males are made up of both yang and yin.
t 8. For a Taoist, there is no such thing as absolute goodness.
f 9. The *Tao Te Ching* says that personal souls continue to exist in the afterlife.
f 10. Human beings are not a part of the grand harmony of nature in Taoism.
f 11. Taoists advocate simply doing nothing in order to achieve *wu-wei.*
t 12. Taoist naturalism, unlike some forms of environmentalism, is always a hands-off approach.
t 13. Taoists believe that a good ruler takes a passive approach to governing.
f 14. For over two thousand years, Taoism has been a central part of the religious life of India.
t 15. From a Taoist perspective, the West is fixated on the yang.

Multiple Choice

Write the letter of the single *best* answer in the blank before each question.

b 1. The original name of the *Tao Te Ching* was the
   a. *Chuang Tzu*
   b. *Lao Tzu*
   c. *Yin-Yang*
   d. *Chun-tzu*

d 2. The *Chuang Tzu* is
   a. just as famous as the *Tao Te Ching*
   b. the second foundational text of Taoism
   c. equally important to Taoism as the *Tao Te Ching*
   d. both *b* and *c*

a 3. One of the central themes of the *Chuang Tzu* is the
   a. relativity of things
   b. evils of overeating
   c. joys of the afterlife
   d. nature of the Godhead

b 4. The power or virtue an individual acquires through living in harmony with Tao is
   a. *ching*
   b. *te*
   c. yin
   d. *karma*

_d_ 5. Tao is the
- **a.** ultimate source of the universe
- **b.** principle of order in the universe
- **c.** Way of nature
- **d.** all of the above

_c_ 6. Taoism regards moral values as
- **a.** unimportant
- **b.** absolute
- **c.** relative
- **d.** masculine

_b_ 7. In Taoism life and death are
- **a.** polar opposites
- **b.** two harmonious parts of the same whole
- **c.** considered the most significant issues to study
- **d.** none of the above

_d_ 8. The sage attains oneness with Tao through insight regarding its
- **a.** complexity
- **b.** simplicity
- **c.** natural unity
- **d.** both *b* and *c*

_a_ 9. When a sage chooses not to compete,
- **a.** he emerges victorious
- **b.** it is the same as giving up the fight
- **c.** he loses his status as sage
- **d.** both *b* and *c*

_d_ 10. Taoism
- **a.** admits that warfare is sometimes necessary
- **b.** encourages pacifism
- **c.** advocates fighting for one's beliefs at all costs
- **d.** both *a* and *b*

Matching

Write the letter of each word in the blank before the word's definition.

_e_ 1. A statement that seems illogical on the surface and yet contains deeper truth

_b_ 2. Taoism's foundational text, traditionally thought to have been authored by Lao Tzu

_c_ 3. The negative, passive, feminine, earthly component of the universe, characterized by darkness and weakness

_f_ 4. The positive, active, masculine, heavenly component of the universe, characterized by light and strength

_a_ 5. What a perfectly balanced individual is called in Taoism

_d_ 6. The virtue that when practiced leads the individual to be so perfectly in harmony with nature that nature's energy infuses and empowers the individual

- **a.** sage
- **b.** *Tao Te Ching*
- **c.** yin
- **d.** *wu-wei*
- **e.** paradox
- **f.** yang

Essay

1. What is the overall aim of Taoism? Briefly describe the tradition's two strands.
2. Who was Lao Tzu, and what was his contribution to Taoism?
3. Explain the meaning of Tao. In what way can Tao be compared to magnetism?
4. What is the relationship between yin and yang? Which is more valued in your society, and why? Describe the balance of yin and yang in your own life.
5. "No value could exist if it were not for its opposite." Explain why that statement is in either agreement or disagreement with Taoism. Then write your own response to the statement.
6. Explain why Lao Tzu believed that despite the simplicity of his doctrines, no one can understand or practice them.
7. Name the primary virtue of Taoism, and describe how to practice it. Do you think it is possible to achieve that virtue? Explain your answer.
8. Lao Tzu and Chuang Tzu insisted that Tao would prevail if it were left alone. Explain how two Taoist virtues each illustrate this point.
9. Using the concepts of yin and yang, compare Taoism with Confucianism.

Chapter 9: Zen Buddhism

True or False

t 1. The Zen tradition can be traced back to the Buddha.
t 2. Zen can be described as a mixture of Indian Buddhism and Chinese Taoism.
f 3. Ch'an continues to this day to be a major religious tradition in China.
f 4. The Soto sect focuses on the crowning achievement of *satori.*
f 5. One of Zen's main emphases is speculation on the nature of reality.
t 6. The insight of Zen cannot be expressed completely in words.
f 7. *Satori,* like *nirvana,* is a permanent state.
f 8. Most Zen students must correctly answer at least half of the approximately seventeen hundred *koans* before their training is finished.
f 9. Zen denies the world and sees everyday reality as irrelevant.
t 10. Zen neither affirms nor denies the existence of an afterlife.
f 11. Women are excluded from Zen monastic life.
t 12. Zen's concern for social justice lies at the heart of its teachings.
t 13. According to Zen, the Buddha is still engaged in Zen training, still deepening his insight.
f 14. Zen affirms the existence of God.

Multiple Choice

Write the letter of the single *best* answer in the blank before each question.

_a_ 1. Zen Buddhism developed within
- **a.** Mahayana Buddhism
- **b.** Vajrayana Buddhism
- **c.** Theravada Buddhism
- **d.** none of the above

_c_ 2. Zen focuses on
- **a.** devotion to Buddhas
- **b.** the history of its tradition
- **c.** the experience of enlightenment
- **d.** philosophical elaboration on Buddhist scripture

_b_ 3. The word *zen* means
- **a.** "enlightenment"
- **b.** "meditation"
- **c.** "puzzle"
- **d.** "insight"

_a_ 4. One of Hui-neng's contributions to Ch'an was
- **a.** ending the traditional position of patriarchs by refusing to name a successor
- **b.** affirming the existence of an afterlife
- **c.** starting an interreligious dialogue with Muslims
- **d.** emphasizing the necessity of social justice

_b_ 5. Rinzai contends that Zen training really begins
- **a.** as soon as one starts the day-to-day practice of Zen
- **b.** only after one's first *satori*
- **c.** once one has read all the Zen scriptures
- **d.** both *a* and *c*

_d_ 6. Zen is *not*
- **a.** experiential
- **b.** beyond words
- **c.** beyond logical thinking
- **d.** theological

_c_ 7. According to Zen Buddhists the primary means of attaining enlightenment is
- **a.** scientific study
- **b.** living in community
- **c.** meditation
- **d.** devotion to Buddhas

_d_ 8. Ultimately Zen
- **a.** can be taught
- **b.** cannot be taught
- **c.** depends on direct experience of the truth
- **d.** both *b* and *c*

_b_ 9. In Rinzai Zen, *satori* is
- **a.** less important than daily meditation practice
- **b.** both the beginning and the end of Zen practice
- **c.** reached through logical thinking
- **d.** synonymous with *dokusan*

_c_ 10. *Koans* can be answered only through
- **a.** logical thinking
- **b.** library research
- **c.** direct insight into reality
- **d.** both *a* and *b*

_a_ 11. In *sumie,* landscape gardening, and flower arranging, this element is very significant:
a. empty space
b. variety of color
c. geometric shapes
d. keeping down the expense

_c_ 12. Physical arts, such as swordplay and archery, have been practiced in Zen primarily as
a. tools for warfare
b. tools for bodybuilding
c. a means of gaining Zen insight
d. both *a* and *b*

_b_ 13. Zen's influence on literature can be recognized particularly in the form of the
a. novella
b. haiku
c. limerick
d. sonnet

Matching

Write the letter of each word in the blank before the word's definition.

_f_ 1. The Chinese sect of Buddhism that emphasizes meditation as the primary means to enlightenment

_b_ 2. The person under whose direction Chinese Zen began to flourish in the seventh century AD

_e_ 3. Zen masters who are considered competent to teach others

_d_ 4. Known as the school of sudden awakening, the sect that was brought to Japan by Eisai in the twelfth century AD

_a_ 5. Known as the school of gradual awakening, the sect that was brought to Japan by Dogen in the thirteenth century AD

_h_ 6. The basic method of Zen meditation, traditionally practiced while seated

_c_ 7. The person most responsible for explaining Zen to the West

_j_ 8. The Zen experience of enlightenment, in which the true nature of one's being is known directly

_g_ 9. A verbal puzzle designed to short-circuit the workings of the rational, logical mind

_i_ 10. The periodic meeting with the master during which the disciple offers an answer to the assigned *koan*

a. Soto
b. Hui-neng
c. D. T. Suzuki
d. Rinzai
e. *roshis*
f. Ch'an
g. *koan*
h. *zazen*
i. *dokusan*
j. *satori*

Essay

1. Briefly explain the history of the Zen tradition. Name the two sects of Japanese Zen and describe the difference in emphasis between them.
2. Suzuki said, "Zen in its essence is the art of seeing into the nature of one's own being." According to Zen why is that not simple to do? Explain why you agree or disagree with Zen's perspective on the problem.
3. Explain why a textbook explanation is inadequate for imparting a full understanding of Zen. How does one learn the truth in Zen, and what part does Zen consider words to play in gaining insight into the truth?
4. Why is it often said that a Zen mind is a beginner's mind?
5. Offer an example of a *koan* and explain the purpose of *koans* in Zen training.
6. Someone who has not studied world religions claims that Zen is a negative, world-denying religion. Explain why you agree or disagree with that statement.
7. Briefly describe Zen monastic life. How is Zen practiced outside the monastery? What appeals to you most about Zen practice?
8. Describe Zen's influence on East Asian cultural arts. Describe or create your own example of one of those arts.
9. List both the Buddhist and the Zen words for enlightenment, and tell how the concepts that they represent differ from each other.

Chapter 10: Shinto

True or False

_f_ 1. Shinto exists independently of other East Asian religious traditions.
_t_ 2. Shinto emphasizes ritual over theological and ethical teachings.
_t_ 3. Shinto has no sacred scripture.
_t_ 4. The Japanese have traditionally regarded their emperors as *kami.*
_f_ 5. The *kami* number eight million.
_t_ 6. The *kami* body is a highly sacred object, rarely seen even by priests.
_t_ 7. Shinto has always been closely tied to the agricultural life of Japan.
_f_ 8. Shinto regards humans as naturally impure.
_f_ 9. Shinto fueled Japanese aggression in World War II.
_f_ 10. Shinto is a rural religion that is not faring well in modern Japan.

Multiple Choice

Write the letter of the single *best* answer in the blank before each question.

_b_ 1. Shinto is the native religious tradition of
a. China
b. Japan
c. India
d. Indonesia

c 2. Which of the following contributions is *not* made by an aspect of Shinto?
- **a.** veneration of nature
- **b.** help securing good crops and homes
- **c.** meditation in order to escape *samsara*
- **d.** vehicle for patriotism

d 3. The Shinto myth
- **a.** tells of the divine ancestry of Japan and its people
- **b.** illustrates that the *kami* are always present and always close to Japan's land and people
- **c.** tells what will happen after death
- **d.** both *a* and *b*

a 4. Shinto's most important deity is
- **a.** Amaterasu
- **b.** Shintazi
- **c.** Izanami
- **d.** Buddha

b 5. Shinto regards nature as
- **a.** impure and in need of redemption
- **b.** sacred
- **c.** insignificant
- **d.** frightening

c 6. Which of the following items would *not* be found on a *kami* shelf?
- **a.** names of deceased ancestors
- **b.** objects brought back from shrines
- **c.** Shinto scriptures
- **d.** statues of favorite deities

a 7. In ceremonial worship the *kami* of the shrine is believed to
- **a.** descend into the *kami* body
- **b.** appear to all worshipers
- **c.** speak to the priests
- **d.** both *b* and *c*

c 8. The *torii* is formed by
- **a.** timber soaked and bent into a semicircle
- **b.** mud bricks stacked on top of one another
- **c.** two upright pillars and a cross beam
- **d.** none of the above

d 9. The Grand Imperial Shrine at Ise is
- **a.** dedicated to the sun goddess Amaterasu
- **b.** the grandest and most famous of all Shinto shrines
- **c.** rebuilt every twenty years to ensure purity
- **d.** all of the above

b 10. In the medieval Japanese tale "The Forty-seven *Ronin*," the *ronin* were
- **a.** considered bad examples
- **b.** revered for having perfectly embodied *bushido*
- **c.** all made princes and sent to live in a luxurious castle for the rest of their long lives
- **d.** banished to a forest for ten years before resuming their normal lives

Identification

Listed below are the three main types of Shinto, and descriptions of those types. Write the letter of each type of Shinto in the blanks before the descriptions that fit it.

a. Shrine Shinto
b. sect Shinto
c. popular Shinto

_a_ 1. Was officially recognized as the state religion by 1882
_c_ 2. Lacks any formal organization
_b_ 3. Includes women as leaders
_c_ 4. Is best understood as a Japanese folk religion
_c_ 5. Does not require a priest or a formal shrine
_b_ 6. Calls its places of worship churches

Matching

Write the letter of each word in the blank before the word's definition.

_b_ 1. "Way of the *kami*"
_e_ 2. Basically any people or things that are regarded as sacred and have evoked the wonder of the Japanese, including deities, certain humans, natural objects, and animals
_c_ 3. A small altar that is the focal point of Shinto worship in the home
_a_ 4. Shinto's most recognized symbol, an archway marking the entrance to a Shinto shrine
_f_ 5. Japan's medieval knights
_d_ 6. Ritual suicide prescribed by *bushido* for samurai who have committed crimes or acts of dishonor
_g_ 7. "Way of the warrior"

a. *torii*
b. Shinto
c. *kamidana*
d. *seppuku*
e. *kami*
f. samurai
g. *bushido*

Essay

1. Define the *kami* and describe their role in Shinto.
2. What is the focus of Shinto worship? Describe typical Shinto worship, both in the home and at shrines. How does Shinto worship compare with the form of worship you are most familiar with?
3. Give three examples of the part purification plays in Shinto.
4. Explain the significance of festivals in Shinto. Describe one Shinto seasonal festival and compare it with a seasonal festival celebrated in your society.
5. Trace the history of Shrine Shinto from its origin to the present.
6. Explain what *bushido* is, including the different religious elements that contribute to it. How do samurai differ from European knights?
7. East Asian religions have typically involved a variety of traditions that form an interwoven fabric. This fabric, rather than any particular tradition, has typically provided for the religion of the individual. Which traditions form the fabric of East Asian religion, and what is the main contribution of each one?

Chapter 11: Ancestors of the West

True or False

t 1. Zoroastrianism in ancient times exerted a strong influence on the formation of Judaism and Christianity.
t 2. Ethical dualism is Zoroastrianism's most distinctive feature.
f 3. In Zoroastrianism a person's choices during earthly life do not have eternal consequences.
t 4. Zoroastrians believe in a final bodily resurrection of everyone, good and evil alike.
t 5. The traditional life of Zoroastrianism is centered on agriculture.
f 6. Most of the world's Zoroastrians today still live in Iran.
f 7. The Parsis encourage conversion to Zoroastrianism.
t 8. Alexander the Great imported classical Greek culture to the region stretching from Egypt in the West to India in the East.
t 9. The Greek dramatists contributed new ideas to Homeric religion.
f 10. The Greek deities discouraged mortals from making sacrificial gifts to them.
f 11. The Olympic Games have been held continuously every four years since they were founded in 776 BC.
t 12. The Olympic Games were primarily a religious festival in honor of Zeus.
f 13. Homer believed that most mortals enter the Elysian fields, finding joy after death.
t 14. Mystery religions were typically based on a myth celebrating the theme of new life arising from death.
t 15. The Orphics believed in reincarnation of the soul.
f 16. Like Homer, the early Romans thought of their gods in human terms.
t 17. The names of seven of the nine planets in our solar system are derived from Roman deities.
t 18. Around the beginning of the first century BC, it was common for Romans (except Jews) to be initiates of more than one mystery religion.
t 19. Some Roman emperors openly declared that they were divine.
f 20. Roman Christians worshiped the emperor as well as God.

Multiple Choice

Write the letter of the single *best* answer in the blank before each question.

c 1. The region surrounding the eastern part of the Mediterranean Sea is commonly referred to as the
   a. Fertile Crescent
   b. East European Empire
   c. cradle of the West
   d. Communist bloc

b 2. Zoroastrianism arose and flourished in
   a. India
   b. ancient Iran, or Persia
   c. the Iberian Peninsula
   d. west Africa

_d_ 3. Before Zoroastrianism was founded, Iran's traditional religion was
- **a.** polytheistic
- **b.** monotheistic
- **c.** closely related to Hinduism
- **d.** both *a* and *c*

_b_ 4. Ahura Mazda is
- **a.** a combination of good and evil
- **b.** eternal and universal goodness
- **c.** allied with "the Lie"
- **d.** not considered divine

_c_ 5. In the fire ritual, Zoroastrians worship
- **a.** fire itself
- **b.** Zarathustra
- **c.** Ahura Mazda's perfect purity
- **d.** the Avesta

_d_ 6. Zoroastrians are supposed to pray how many times a day?
- **a.** one
- **b.** two
- **c.** three
- **d.** five

_a_ 7. Parsis dispose of the dead by
- **a.** placing the corpse on a hilltop for vultures to eat
- **b.** burying the corpse
- **c.** cremating the corpse
- **d.** none of the above

_b_ 8. Homer composed the *Iliad* and the *Odyssey* in the
- **a.** fourteenth century BC
- **b.** eighth century BC
- **c.** first century BC
- **d.** twentieth century AD

_c_ 9. The gods in the Greek pantheon are
- **a.** all-powerful
- **b.** all-knowing
- **c.** like humans, with shortcomings
- **d.** both *a* and *b*

_a_ 10. Aeschylus and Sophocles emphasized the ______ of Zeus
- **a.** justice
- **b.** anger
- **c.** kindness
- **d.** joyfulness

_d_ 11. Toward the end of the fourth century AD, Roman emperor Theodosius I abolished
- **a.** Orphism
- **b.** the Olympic Games
- **c.** the oracle at Delphi
- **d.** both *b* and *c*

_d_ 12. Apollo is credited with having pronounced,
- **a.** "Know thyself."
- **b.** "Nothing to excess."
- **c.** "Cleanliness is godliness."
- **d.** both *a* and *b*

_b_ 13. Ancient Greek and Roman religion were oriented toward achieving
- **a.** a blessed afterlife
- **b.** things in this world
- **c.** a status equal to that of the deities
- **d.** all of the above

_d_ 14. *Numina*
- **a.** could be transferred from one thing to another
- **b.** were believed to inhabit a wide variety of things and places
- **c.** were possessed in abundance by the gods
- **d.** all of the above

_d_ 15. Mithraism
- **a.** was the favored cult of the Roman army
- **b.** was one of the two main rivals to Christianity in the late Roman Empire
- **c.** allowed only men to join
- **d.** all of the above

_d_ 16. Emperor Augustus encouraged worship of
- **a.** the Roman state
- **b.** himself personally
- **c.** his own genius, or guardian spirit
- **d.** both *a* and *c*

Identification

Listed below are the names of Greek and Roman gods and goddesses, and descriptions of those deities. Write the letter of each deity in the blank before the description that fits.

a. Demeter	**e.** Zeus
b. Hades	**f.** Dionysus
c. Venus	**g.** Jupiter
d. Asclepius	**h.** Poseidon

_e_ 1. The father of the gods in the Olympian pantheon
_h_ 2. The god of the ocean
_b_ 3. In Homer's works the ruler of the underworld with his queen, Persephone
_a_ 4. The Greek grain goddess honored by the Eleusinian mysteries
_f_ 5. The Greek god of fertility and vegetation, often depicted with vines and grapes
_d_ 6. Described by Homer as a mortal physician, a man who came to be regarded by the Greeks (as well as the Romans) as a god
_c_ 7. The Roman goddess of love (identified with the Greek goddess Aphrodite)
_g_ 8. The Roman sky god and most powerful of all Roman deities (identified with the Greek god Zeus)

Matching

Write the letter of each word in the blank before the word's definition.

_f_ 1. The Wise Lord, recognized by Zarathustra and later by Zoroastrians as the one true God
_c_ 2. Zarathustra's hymns; the oldest material in the Avesta
_b_ 3. The entire sacred text of Zoroastrianism

g 4. The belief in universal forces of good and evil
a 5. The most famous form of Zoroastrian worship
j 6. The Zoroastrians who live in India today
i 7. A group of gods recognized by a society
l 8. Of human form
k 9. A sanctuary at which revelations of a god are received
h 10. In Greek mythology a legendary musician and singer after whom an ancient Greek religion is named
d 11. What the Romans called the attitude of reverence toward the divine powers
e 12. Supernatural powers, each in charge of a very specific function

a. fire ritual
b. Avesta
c. Gathas
d. *pietas*
e. *numina*
f. Ahura Mazda
g. ethical dualism
h. Orpheus
i. pantheon
j. Parsis
k. oracle
l. anthropomorphic

Essay

1. Who was Zarathustra? Explain why his teaching was radical in the context of ancient Iranian society.
2. According to Zarathustra how did the forces of good and evil come to be?
3. Name at least two ways Zoroastrianism influenced Judaism, Christianity, and Islam.
4. How does the Zoroastrian description of heaven and hell compare with the description you are familiar with?
5. What are the *Iliad* and the *Odyssey?* Describe their religious contributions, noting two ways that Homeric religion differs from Judaism and Christianity.
6. Name a well-known oracle and tell which god's wisdom was sought there. How does the way the god communicated at the oracle and the sorts of messages the god sent compare with the way God is believed to communicate with Christians today?
7. Compare and contrast Homer's perspective on death and afterlife with the perspectives of the mystery religions and of Orphism. Then explain why Christianity appeared to the ancient Romans to be a mystery religion (be sure to include all three basic aspects of mystery religions in your explanation).
8. Explain the differences between the ways the mystery religion cult and Orphism worshiped Dionysus.
9. Describe two ways that Orphism influenced Plato's philosophy. Then define Platonic dualism and describe its influence on Christianity.
10. For what was Asclepius known, and what did he have in common with Jesus?
11. How does the Roman pantheon compare with the Greek pantheon?
12. Summarize the myth of Isis and Osiris, highlighting the theme that is central to the cult of Isis. In what way did this cult influence early Christianity?

Chapter 12: Judaism

True or False

_t_ 1. Judaism places great emphasis on group identity.
_t_ 2. Observant Jews avoid speaking God's name, out of reverence.
_f_ 3. The Mishnah is based directly on the Talmud.
_t_ 4. The Pharisees focused on Torah, rather than on the Temple.
_f_ 5. Judaism became the official religion of the Roman Empire in the fourth century.
_t_ 6. Jews lived in relative peace and prosperity in Muslim Spain and Poland during the medieval period.
_f_ 7. The Kabbalah does not observe the basic forms of Jewish practice, such as keeping the commandments of the Torah.
_f_ 8. Jewish mystics are more focused on the ultimate transcendence of God than on the immanence of God.
_t_ 9. Large Hasidic communities still exist today in North America and elsewhere.
_t_ 10. Fewer than half of the world's Jews live in Israel.
_f_ 11. Orthodox Judaism rejects all aspects of modernity.
_f_ 12. Conservative Judaism is relatively relaxed regarding observance of traditional Jewish practices.
_t_ 13. Judaism is far more concerned with correct practice than with correct belief.
_t_ 14. In Judaism males alone are required to wear certain ritual accessories during prayer.
_f_ 15. The Sabbath, for all but some Reform Jews, begins at sunset on Saturday and lasts until sunset on Sunday.
_t_ 16. With only about fourteen million adherents worldwide, Judaism is among the smallest of the world's major religions.

Multiple Choice

Write the letter of the single *best* answer in the blank before each question.

_b_ 1. God's name appears in the Bible in the Hebrew equivalents of the letters
- a. *INRI*
- b. *YHWH*
- c. *TNK*
- d. *TOR*

_d_ 2. The five books of the Torah are
- a. traditionally believed to have been revealed directly by God to Moses
- b. the central statement of Judaism's religious laws
- c. a summary of the entire Hebrew Bible
- d. both *a* and *b*

_a_ 3. Jews refer to the Hebrew Bible as the
- a. Tanakh
- b. Old Testament
- c. Talmud
- d. both *a* and *b*

_c_ 4. He received the Law at Mount Sinai and is regarded as the Torah's author:
- a. Abraham
- b. Jacob
- c. Moses
- d. David

_b_ 5. It is most accurate to think of the Jews as
- a. a single "race" of genetically related people
- b. an ethnic group that shares a common history and religion
- c. adherents of the first official religion in history
- d. both *a* and *c*

_a_ 6. Jews believe that God is
- a. directly involved in history
- b. completely uninvolved in history
- c. at times subject to humans
- d. none of the above

_d_ 7. The second large-scale revolt the Jews waged against Romans ended in AD 135 when the Romans
- a. leveled Jerusalem
- b. decreed that Jews could no longer inhabit Palestine
- c. agreed to allow Jewish representatives in the Roman government
- d. both *a* and *b*

_d_ 8. The most important events in Israelite history were
- a. the Exodus from Egypt and the revelation on Mount Sinai
- b. the fall of the northern kingdom (Israel) and the revelation on Mount Sinai
- c. fall of the southern kingdom (Judah) and the revelation on Mount Sinai
- d. none of the above

_c_ 9. Israel was granted statehood in
- a. 1933
- b. 1941
- c. 1948
- d. 1958

_c_ 10. Torah defines
- a. worship
- b. ethical conduct
- c. both *a* and *b*
- d. none of the above

Matching

Write the letter of each word in the blank before the word's definition.

_f_ 1. The people who conquered Palestine and the surrounding area in the seventh century AD

_i_ 2. The man God called to be the father of a great nation; the first patriarch

_d_ 3. Abraham's grandson, also known as Israel

_a_ 4. The person who helped free the Israelites from slavery in Egypt

_e_ 5. The Israelite king whom Jews have always regarded as a prototype of the Messiah

_c_ 6. The person who built the Temple in Jerusalem

_j_ 7. The people who conquered the northern kingdom, Israel, in 722 BC

_g_ 8. The people who conquered the southern kingdom, Judah, in about 587 BC

_b_ 9. The people who destroyed the Jerusalem Temple for the second time in AD 70

_h_ 10. A Jewish philosopher who lived in Muslim Spain during the medieval period and who applied the philosophy of Plato and Aristotle to the biblical tradition and contributed Judaism's most famous statement of beliefs

a. Moses
b. Romans
c. Solomon
d. Jacob
e. David
f. Muslims
g. Babylonians
h. Moses Maimonides
i. Abraham
j. Assyrians

Matching

Write the letter of each word in the blank before the word's definition.

_p_ 1. Literally "instruction"; the will of God as it is revealed to humankind

_b_ 2. Greek for "five books"; the Torah

_h_ 3. The most famous of the 613 laws in the Torah, found in chapter 20 of Exodus

_e_ 4. A building for Jewish worship

_r_ 5. Someone who is called to speak for God

_q_ 6. The starting point for rabbinic study of the oral Torah; a collection of sacred traditions that was written down in about AD 200 and contains teachings of the rabbis of the preceding four centuries

_j_ 7. The vast depository blending together the oral and written forms of Torah, based on the Mishnah with extensive rabbinic commentary

_m_ 8. The situation of Jews living away from their homeland, a circumstance that has been true for most Jews since the classical period

_k_ 9. The most famous text of Jewish mysticism

_f_ 10. Jewish mysticism, which teaches that God can best be known with the heart

_l_ 11. A form of Judaism that arose in eighteenth-century eastern Europe and emphasizes mysticism, a personal relationship with God and the community, and the leadership of the *zaddik*

a. kaddish
b. Pentateuch
c. repentance
d. the Holocaust
e. synagogue
f. Kabbalah
g. Seder
h. the Ten Commandments
i. circumcision
j. Talmud
k. the Zohar
l. Hasidism
m. Diaspora
n. rabbi
o. Zionism
p. Torah
q. Mishnah
r. prophet
s. bat mitzvah

o 12. A movement that was originally committed to the re-establishment of a Jewish homeland; since 1948, generally the support of Israel
d 13. The persecution of the Jews by German Nazis from 1938 to 1945, resulting in the murder of nearly six million Jews; sometimes called Shoah
n 14. A teacher of Torah and leader of Jewish worship
g 15. The high point of the Passover festival
c 16. What Yom Kippur emphasizes
i 17. A physical feature that distinguished the Israelites from people of other nations
s 18. A coming-of-age ritual for a Jewish girl
a 19. A prayer of mourning

Essay

1. What is the Covenant, and what significance does it have for Jews?
2. What is the Shema, and why was it considered a radical statement when it was first formulated? What else did the Jews believe about God's nature?
3. Name the major sections of the Hebrew Bible, and specify at least one unique thing about each section, such as its author or an item associated with it.
4. Judaism sees God's will revealed outward in a series of concentric circles, like the rings of a tree trunk. Briefly describe each ring.
5. Explain why Judaism can be thought of as the interpretation of the history of the Jewish people.
6. Who ruled the Jews between the end of the Exile and the destruction of the second Temple in AD 70? How did the Temple's destruction affect Judaism?
7. Explain the Babylonian Exile's significance for Jews.
8. Compare Jewish life in the medieval period with Jewish life in the modern period.
9. Define anti-Semitism. Name at least two instances of persecution of Jews through the centuries, and explain the reasons for the persecution.How do you think such a history of persecution has affected Jews and their beliefs?
10. Name and describe two traditions in Judaism that emphasize mysticism.
11. Name the three most prominent forms of Judaism in North America, and explain the differences between them.
12. Consider the following statement from the textbook, and explain its implications for Jewish life: "Traditionally, a Jew is not a 'believer' so much as an 'observer of the commandments.'" Also explain the role of Torah in Jewish daily life.
13. Name and briefly describe each of the three most important Jewish holy days.
14. Describe in detail one rite of passage prescribed by Judaism. Compare it with a similar but different rite of passage that you celebrate or are familiar with. What do you think are the benefits of celebrating rites of passage?

Chapter 13: Christianity

True or False

_t_ 1. Christianity is the world's largest religion.
_f_ 2. Much is known about Jesus's early life.
_t_ 3. Jesus remained a practicing Jew his entire life.
_f_ 4. During Jesus's lifetime, Palestine was ruled by the Greeks.
_f_ 5. Jesus's ministry lasted about seven years.
_t_ 6. Jesus, unlike the Pharisees and other religious figures of his day, constantly reached out to the lower strata of Jewish society.
_f_ 7. Jesus was crucified by order of King Herod Antipas.
_f_ 8. Jesus taught that God's original revelation of the Torah to the Israelites was to be disregarded.
_t_ 9. Paul emphasized that salvation comes only through the grace of God.
_t_ 10. The doctrine of the Trinity states that the three Persons are distinct from one another and yet of the same substance.
_t_ 11. Some of Paul's epistles are the earliest New Testament books.
_f_ 12. Paul proclaimed the Gospel primarily to Jews.
_t_ 13. The canon of the New Testament consists of twenty-seven writings.
_f_ 14. By the end of the fourth century, only about 10 percent of the Roman Empire was Christian.
_t_ 15. Martin Luther translated the Bible into German to help make it accessible to Christians.
_f_ 16. Eastern Orthodoxy is doctrinally closer to most forms of Protestantism than it is to Catholicism.
_t_ 17. Pope John XXIII convened the Second Vatican Council to update Church teaching so that it would respond to the modern world's needs, and to promote Christian unity.

Multiple Choice

Write the letter of the single *best* answer in the blank before each question.

_d_ 1. Christianity is the dominant religious tradition in
- **a.** the Americas
- **b.** Europe
- **c.** Australia
- **d.** all of the above

_b_ 2. Early Christians used a symbol on their doors to indicate they were Christians. It was a
- **a.** fig tree
- **b.** fish
- **c.** dove
- **d.** butterfly

_a_ 3. The primary sources of information about Jesus's life are
- **a.** the New Testament Gospels
- **b.** the Pauline epistles
- **c.** the Torah and the prophets
- **d.** the writings of the saints

_d_ 4. The Gospel authors strove mainly to
- **a.** present Christ's teachings
- **b.** express the meaning of the events of Christ's life
- **c.** assemble a factual record
- **d.** both *a* and *b*

_c_ 5. A primary example of apocalyptic writing is the
- **a.** Gospel of John
- **b.** Letter to the Hebrews
- **c.** Book of Revelation
- **d.** Book of Exodus

_b_ 6. Jesus was baptized by
- **a.** a rabbi in his local synagogue
- **b.** John the Baptist
- **c.** Joseph and Mary
- **d.** himself

_d_ 7. All the Gospels portray Jesus as
- **a.** an exorcist
- **b.** a healer
- **c.** a political activist
- **d.** both *a* and *b*

_b_ 8. The heart of Jesus's ethical teachings can be found in
- **a.** the Ten Commandments
- **b.** his radical commandment to love one's enemies
- **c.** his commandment to obey the Torah only to the letter of the Law
- **d.** both *a* and *c*

_a_ 9. For Paul, salvation is
- **a.** overcoming sin and death
- **b.** detachment from worldly things
- **c.** achieved only by doing good works
- **d.** gained by both good people and evil people

_d_ 10. What will happen at the Second Coming?
- **a.** The dead will be raised.
- **b.** All people, living and dead, will be judged.
- **c.** Christ will return to the world.
- **d.** all of the above

_b_ 11. Which offers the more elaborate, precise statement of the doctrine of the Incarnation?
- **a.** the Apostles' Creed
- **b.** the Nicene Creed
- **c.** the Lord's Prayer
- **d.** the Beatitudes

_d_ 12. To be a Christian means to
- **a.** accept Christ as one's savior
- **b.** believe in the Christian doctrines
- **c.** belong to the Church
- **d.** all of the above

_b_ 13. Paul believed Gentile Christians should
- **a.** observe Torah just like Jewish Christians
- **b.** be exempt from most requirements of Torah
- **c.** be required to convert to Judaism
- **d.** both *a* and *c*

_d_ 14. What symbolized the unity and equality of Christians?
a. baptism
b. the shared meal of the Eucharist
c. the doctrine of predestination
d. both *a* and *b*

_d_ 15. Who assisted bishops in the early Christian Church?
a. presbyters
b. deacons
c. rabbis
d. both *a* and *b*

_d_ 16. Which of the following acts did the emperor Constantine perform?
a. issued the Edict of Milan, which ended persecution of Christians
b. convened the Council of Nicaea
c. wrote the Apostles' Creed
d. both *a* and *b*

_b_ 17. Eastern Orthodoxy and Roman Catholicism have been independent of each other since
a. the fourth century
b. 1054
c. 1225
d. 1483

_a_ 18. Which of the following events did *not* happen during the Middle Ages?
a. Constantine declared Christianity a legitimate religion.
b. Great cathedrals were constructed.
c. Christian monasticism reached a new height of influence.
d. Christians fought in the Crusades.

_b_ 19. The Protestant Reformation sparked the
a. Crusades
b. Thirty Years' War, between Catholics and Protestants
c. First Vatican Council
d. both *a* and *b*

_d_ 20. In Roman Catholicism, Tradition
a. is a primary means of God's revelation of Christ
b. began with the Apostles
c. is carried on as bishops and popes clarify anew in every age the Tradition passed on to them
d. all of the above

_a_ 21. The four main branches of Protestantism are Lutheran, Calvinist,
a. Baptist, and Anglican
b. Presbyterian, and Methodist
c. Mormon, and United Church of Christ
d. Unitarian Universalist, and Baptist

Identification

Listed below are three Gospels (each of which has a different emphasis), and descriptions of those writings. Write the letter of each Gospel in the blanks before the descriptions that fit it.

a. Matthew
b. Luke
c. John

_b_ 1. Particularly emphasizes Jesus as a role model of the perfect way to live
_c_ 2. Particularly emphasizes that salvation comes through knowing Christ and believing in who he is
_b_ 3. Gives women more attention than do the other Gospels
_a_ 4. Presents Christ as the revealer of God's new Torah
_c_ 5. Focuses on the Incarnation and presents Christ as the Word
_a_ 6. Contains the Sermon on the Mount

Identification

Listed below are well-known figures in the history of Christianity, and descriptions of those people. Write the letter of each person in the blank before the description that fits him.

a. Saint Augustine
b. Saint Francis of Assisi
c. Saint Thomas Aquinas
d. Martin Luther
e. King Henry VIII
f. John Calvin

_a_ 1. The bishop of Hippo in North Africa who wrote the theological masterpiece *City of God*
_c_ 2. The Dominican whose final and greatest work, the *Summa Theologiae,* remains important today
_b_ 3. Founder of the Franciscan order, a man who loved nature and cared for poor people
_d_ 4. Originally a devoted monk, the man who wrote the Ninety-five Theses and led the Protestant Reformation
_f_ 5. In Switzerland the man who played a very important role in the Protestant Reformation, emphasizing humanity's original sin and the doctrine of predestination
_e_ 6. The man who broke with papal authority because of his desire to remarry after divorcing his wife, and then declared himself head of the Church of England

Matching

Write the letter of each word in the blank before the word's definition.

b 1. The region where Jesus's ministry was mainly carried out

j 2. Stories cast in language and circumstances familiar to common people, used by Jesus to teach moral lessons

o 3. "Good news"; the name often used to refer to the Christian message

d 4. The doctrine that states that God's Son became fully human in Jesus Christ while remaining fully divine

a 5. God's presence freely given, which helps humans overcome sin

m 6. The gathering that established as its most crucial point that Jesus the Son and God the Father are "one in Being"

h 7. From the Greek *ekklesia;* the community of all Christian believers

p 8. Literally "right doctrine"

i 9. Sects whose theological opinions were denounced as erroneous by orthodox Christians

c 10. From the Greek word that means "messenger"; an early follower of Christ who had authority to preach the Gospel

n 11. The Communion meal, patterned after the Last Supper, which was shared by Jesus and his Apostles

e 12. The bishop of Rome, considered by Catholics to be the direct successor of the Apostle Peter

l 13. From the Greek word meaning "witness"; one who chooses to die rather than violate her or his religious convictions

s 14. From the Greek word for "universal"; the largest of the three major divisions of Christianity

r 15. Pardons or reductions in the punishment due for sins committed; commonly bought and sold in medieval Catholicism

q 16. Humanity's state of moral and spiritual corruption, inherited from Adam and Eve

k 17. The doctrine stating that God has already chosen those who will be saved from sin

t 18. A movement begun in 1545 that clarified Church doctrines and cleaned up corrupt practices

g 19. Christians for whom the Bible must be read literally as the direct word of God

f 20. The promotion of worldwide Christian unity

a. grace
b. Galilee
c. Apostle
d. Incarnation
e. pope
f. ecumenism
g. fundamentalists
h. Church
i. heresies
j. parables
k. predestination
l. martyr
m. Council of Nicaea
n. the Eucharist
o. Gospel
p. orthodox
q. original sin
r. indulgences
s. Catholic
t. Catholic Reformation

Essay

1. Explain what Christians believe about Jesus. How do Christians today come to know Jesus?
2. Explain the various ways that Jews responded to Roman rule in Jesus's time. How did Jesus respond?
3. Define apocalypticism, and then build a case to support the contention that Jesus's religious perspective was apocalyptic.
4. Explain the two interrelated themes that Jesus focused on in his teachings.
5. Why was Jesus crucified, and what do Christians believe happened afterward?
6. According to Paul how are people saved in this life and in the next life? In Paul's view what part did observing the Law play in attaining salvation?
7. Name one of Christianity's most important statements of belief and tell why it is considered important. Be sure you describe Christianity's two core doctrines in your answer.
8. Describe the distinctive features of each of the three Persons of the Trinity. How does the belief that God is trinitarian compare with the Jewish belief about God's nature?
9. What was Paul's role in the early Church?
10. Compare early Christian worship with Jewish worship practices. Include the two central early Christian rituals in your answer.
11. Why were Christians persecuted by the Romans, and how and why did that change during the fourth century?
12. Why did Christianity split into three major divisions? Briefly describe the distinctive characteristics of each division.
13. What did Martin Luther protest against? Describe at least one other religious reform movement that was taking place around the time of the Protestant Reformation.

Chapter 14: Islam

True or False

t 1. Islam is the world's fastest-growing and second-largest religion.
f 2. Muslims believe that Muhammad had a divine nature.
t 3. Muslims believe that Muhammad ascended to heaven.
t 4. In Muslim tradition there are ninety-nine names for Allah.
f 5. Allah did not come to be worshiped in Arabia until Muhammad founded Islam.
t 6. Muslims regard Abraham as the father of the Arab people.
f 7. Muslims generally regard science as being in conflict with their faith.
t 8. The Shari'a is the basis of government in some countries with Muslim majorities today.
f 9. The Five Pillars demonstrate Islam's emphasis on correct belief.
f 10. Ramadan occurs at the same time each year.
t 11. It is believed that Abraham built the Ka'ba.
t 12. Washing is part of the Muslim prayer ritual.

_t_ 13. Veiling was a pre-Islamic practice in Arabia that is no longer universal among Muslim women.

_t_ 14. Within one century of Muhammad's death, Islam was the religion of the entire Middle East, Persia, North Africa, and almost all of Spain.

_t_ 15. About 40 percent of Muslims in the United States are African Americans.

_f_ 16. Most Muslims regard the Nation of Islam as an authentic part of their religion.

_t_ 17. Islam, as practiced by most Muslims, emphasizes the transcendence and suprapersonal nature of Allah.

Multiple Choice

Write the letter of the single *best* answer in the blank before each question.

_d_ 1. Islam
  a. is deeply rooted in the biblical tradition
  b. reveres Jesus Christ and Judaism's great prophets
  c. has played a crucial role in shaping Western culture, especially during the Middle Ages
  d. all of the above

_b_ 2. The name *Muslim* means
  a. "wrapped in cotton cloth"
  b. "one who submits"
  c. "Muhammad's friend"
  d. all of the above

_a_ 3. Who appeared to Muhammad in a dream on the Night of Power and Excellence?
  a. the archangel Gabriel
  b. Abraham
  c. Jesus
  d. Imam

_c_ 4. Muslims consider Muhammad to be the Seal of the Prophets because they believe that he is
  a. the sacred presence in the world
  b. a prophet like Abraham, Moses, and Jesus, revealing God's will only partially
  c. the final prophet, revealing the will of Allah fully and precisely, and for all time
  d. both *a* and *c*

_a_ 5. Islam is
  a. monotheistic
  b. polytheistic
  c. pantheistic
  d. solipsistic

_c_ 6. What do Muslims believe leads to sin?
  a. humanity's essentially evil nature
  b. the devil's temptations
  c. forgetfulness
  d. both *a* and *b*

_d_ 7. In Islam the natural world is
- **a.** seen as good and worthy of reverence
- **b.** another form of revelation of God's will
- **c.** sometimes referred to as the cosmic Qur'an
- **d.** all of the above

_c_ 8. All Muslims are required to pray how often a day?
- **a.** one time
- **b.** two times
- **c.** five times
- **d.** hourly except while sleeping

_d_ 9. Fasting during Ramadan helps Muslims
- **a.** focus attention on moral and religious concerns and thus develop spiritual fortitude
- **b.** gain insight into the situations of less fortunate people
- **c.** become more aware of their own mortality
- **d.** all of the above

_b_ 10. What proportion of their possessions' value are Muslims required to contribute to a public treasury?
- **a.** 1 percent
- **b.** 2.5 percent
- **c.** 5 percent
- **d.** 10 percent

_c_ 11. Islam holds that the body ultimately belongs to
- **a.** the individual
- **b.** the individual's spouse
- **c.** God
- **d.** the evil forces

_d_ 12. Islamic dietary regulations forbid
- **a.** eating pork
- **b.** drinking alcoholic beverages
- **c.** eating leavened bread
- **d.** both *a* and *b*

_d_ 13. Which areas presently have the greatest concentration of Muslims?
- **a.** all of the Middle East and southwestern Asia
- **b.** South Asia and the northern half of Africa
- **c.** the islands of Malaysia and Indonesia
- **d.** all of the above

_d_ 14. Why does Arabia enjoy a special status in Islam?
- **a.** Arabs currently make up over 50 percent of the entire Muslim population
- **b.** Muslim sacred sites are located in Arabia, and Arabic is the language of Islam
- **c.** Arabic involvement in Islam goes back to Islam's earliest history
- **d.** both *b* and *c*

_c_ 15. What has made Shi'ism more politically volatile than Sunnism?
- **a.** the belief in the return of Muhammad al-Mahdi
- **b.** the general emphasis on the Imam as an authority figure
- **c.** both *a* and *b*
- **d.** none of the above

_a_ 16. Sufism
- **a.** draws its adherents from both Sunnism and Shi'ism
- **b.** is one of the two major historical divisions of Islam
- **c.** shuns mysticism
- **d.** both *b* and *c*

Matching

Write the letter of each word in the blank before the word's definition.

_c_ 1. Literally "reading" or "recitation"
_g_ 2. The emigration of Muhammad and his followers from Mecca to Yathrib (later called Medina) in AD 622
_i_ 3. Muhammad's own teachings and actions; Islam's second most important authority after the Qur'an
_b_ 4. The community of all Muslims
_e_ 5. The divine law, derived from the Qur'an and the Sunna, encompassing all and setting forth in detail how Muslims are to live
_d_ 6. The first pillar of Islam; the tradition's central creedal statement
_k_ 7. The Muslim place of worship, traditionally a structure that includes a prayer hall and an enclosed courtyard, with towers called minarets at the corners
_h_ 8. The leader of the Friday worship service who also delivers a sermon
_a_ 9. The month-long period during which Muslims fast from dawn until sunset each day
_o_ 10. The pilgrimage to Mecca that all Muslims are to make at least once in their lifetime, if they can afford it and are physically able
_l_ 11. The stone cubical structure in the courtyard of Mecca's Great Mosque that is regarded by Muslims as the sacred center of the Earth
_n_ 12. Arabic for "exertion" or "struggle"
_j_ 13. The military and political leaders of the Muslim community who succeeded Muhammad after his death
_m_ 14. A master and teacher in Islam, such as the leader of an order in Sufism
_f_ 15. The aim of Sufi mystics; the extinction of one's sense of separate existence before achieving union with Allah

a. Ramadan
b. Umma
c. *qur'an*
d. Shahada
e. Shari'a
f. *al-fana*
g. Hijra
h. *imam*
i. Sunna
j. caliphs
k. mosque
l. Ka'ba
m. *shaykh*
n. *jihad*
o. *hajj*

Essay

1. What is the Qur'an? Compare its role in Islam with Jesus Christ's role in Christianity.
2. Briefly describe Muhammad's life story, including how he came to be a prophet. How did his fellow Meccans react to his teachings?
3. Describe what Islam teaches about the nature of God, human nature, and the world.
4. How does the Muslim view of human destiny and the Day of Judgment compare with the Christian view?
5. Explain the purpose of the Five Pillars of Islam and briefly describe each pillar.

6. Western critics have accused Islam of denying basic rights to women. Build a case either agreeing or disagreeing with them.
7. Define and explain the principle of *jihad*. Why, do you think, is it sometimes counted as the sixth pillar of Islam? Does the Qur'an support the concept of *jihad* as armed struggle?
8. Explain how Islam can also be said to be Islamic civilization. Name some of its contributions.
9. What unites all Muslims? Tell what distinguishes Shi'i from Sunni Islam.
10. What is the guiding principle of Sufism, and how does it sometimes land Sufis in trouble with orthodox Muslims? Compare Sufism with Christian monasticism or Hinduism.
11. Can a religion, like Islam, that understands itself as embracing the totality of life truly be tolerant of other religions?

Chapter 15: Religion in the Modern World

True or False

_f_ 1. Although many religious movements have emerged in modern times, few have become firmly established.
_t_ 2. Modernization affects society and religions at different times.
_f_ 3. Religions tend to prevent egalitarian ideals from being incorporated into their traditions.
_f_ 4. The Baha'i religion is characterized by strict fundamentalist beliefs.
_t_ 5. New religious movements often arise in response to modern situations.
_f_ 6. Elements of other religious traditions are never incorporated into new religious movements.
_f_ 7. Reverence for nature is uncommon in many of the world's religious traditions.
_f_ 8. Scientific methods and knowledge have generally supported traditional religious worldviews.
_f_ 9. Most religious groups have rejected Darwinism as completely incompatible with their perspectives of human origins.
_f_ 10. Research has indicated that the human brain does not react differently during religious experiences or events.

Multiple Choice

Write the letter of the single *best* answer in the blank before each question.

_c_ 1. The economic system based on private ownership and the pursuit of wealth is
a. modernization
b. materialism
c. capitalism
d. urbanization

_a_ 2. Religious traditions have generally been shaped to conform to
- **a.** rural settings
- **b.** urban settings
- **c.** religious communities
- **d.** a combination of rural and urban settings

_b_ 3. Which of the following institutions is an example of liberalism within an established religious tradition?
- **a.** Orthodox Judaism
- **b.** Catholicism's Second Vatican Council
- **c.** both *a* and *b*
- **d.** none of the above

_c_ 4. The tendency to regard all religious perspectives as equal is
- **a.** liberalism
- **b.** secular humanism
- **c.** the universalist impulse
- **d.** Baha'i

_d_ 5. Baha'i teaches that the founders of the world's religions
- **a.** are inferior to Baha Allah
- **b.** are false prophets
- **c.** were brilliant, but misguided, individuals
- **d.** have all been God's divine messengers

_a_ 6. The Vedanta Society and ISKCON are based on which religious tradition?
- **a.** Hinduism
- **b.** Islam
- **c.** Baha'i
- **d.** Zen Buddhism

_b_ 7. Mormonism began with which of these events?
- **a.** the birth of its founder
- **b.** the Restoration
- **c.** the Great Migration
- **d.** the establishment of Deseret

_a_ 8. A practice that is no longer common in Mormonism is
- **a.** polygamy
- **b.** the prohibition of alcohol
- **c.** missionary work
- **d.** both *b* and *c*

_b_ 9. Jehovah's Witnesses are awaiting
- **a.** the birth of a new savior
- **b.** the millennial age
- **c.** both *a* and *b*
- **d.** none of the above

_d_ 10. Jehovah's Witnesses believe that other forms of Christianity
- **a.** are compatible with their beliefs
- **b.** are controlled by the government
- **c.** will also be saved at the end of the world
- **d.** should be avoided

_b_ 11. The New Age movement believes that the transformation of the world is vitally linked to
- **a.** the coming of a great teacher
- **b.** individual transformation
- **c.** vegetarianism
- **d.** the harnessing of the world's energy

_b_ 12. Neopaganism embraces
- a. monotheism
- b. polytheism
- c. monism
- d. atheism

_a_ 13. A central element of Pentecostalism is
- a. glossolalia
- b. missionary work
- c. meditation practices
- d. none of the above

_c_ 14. Which of the following statements is *not* an assumption science makes about reality?
- a. Nature is indifferent to humanity.
- b. The physical world is composed of matter and energy.
- c. The truth can be known through subjective experience.
- d. *a* and *b* only

_b_ 15. Which of the following statements is *not* part of the big bang theory?
- a. The universe has no special reason for its existence.
- b. The universe relies on divine action or intention.
- c. The earth will eventually be engulfed by the sun.
- d. The universe is constantly, endlessly expanding.

Identification

Listed below are founders of modern religious or scientific movements, and descriptions of those people. Write the letter of each founder in the blank before the description that fits him or her.

a. Baha Allah	e. Charles Taze Russell
b. Charles Darwin	f. Joseph Smith Jr.
c. Charles Fox Parham	g. Swami Vivekananda
d. Swami Prabhupada	h. Brigham Young

_d_ 1. The founder of the International Society for Krishna Consciousness, who also wrote *The Bhagavad-Gita As It Is*

_f_ 2. The young visionary who found and translated the lost prophetic writings of Mormon

_b_ 3. The author of *Origin of Species*, whose scientific theory of evolution challenges many religious perspectives on the origin of human beings

_e_ 4. The successful businessman from Pennsylvania who founded the Jehovah's Witnesses and made several predictions of the end of the world

_g_ 5. The man who, after attending the World's Parliament of Religions in 1893, went on to establish the Vedanta Society in New York, the first Hindu organization in the United States

_h_ 6. The Mormon leader who in 1847 led his followers west to the Salt Lake Valley, creating a community that quickly grew to over one hundred thousand people

_c_ 7. The man who founded and presided over Bethel Bible College, from which the Pentecostal movement was launched

_a_ 8. The man who was imprisoned and exiled by Muslim authorities after he claimed in 1863 to be a prophet

Matching

Write the letter of each word in the blank before the word's definition.

_d_ 1. The evolutionary theory that human life originates in the simplest of forms, that each generation of life passes on the best traits for survival, and that over time this process leads to a variety of more complex life-forms

_a_ 2. The worldview that science is the only valid method of acquiring knowledge

_e_ 3. A religious group in which membership is voluntary, and that generally opposes the ordinary ways of society

_f_ 4. The field that incorporates the psychological and biological study of religion, focusing on the brain's responses to experience and ritual

_i_ 5. An emphasis on a literal interpretation of a religion's sacred texts, or an intensely traditionalist form of religion impelled by reaction against modern forces and the religious reforms they encourage

_h_ 6. The coexistence of different peoples and their cultures

_k_ 7. A late-twentieth-century perspective that reflects a critical reaction to the trends of the modern world

_o_ 8. A "gift of the spirit"; the ability to speak in tongues

_n_ 9. The linking and intermixing of cultures

_c_ 10. The counterpart to traditionalism, holding that a religion should adapt to society's changes

_m_ 11. Within religious traditions, a reaction to rapid changes in the world, involving the maintenance of older forms of belief and practice regardless of new social norms

_g_ 12. The worldview that ultimate value is grounded entirely in the human realm, not in the supernatural

_j_ 13. Groups that are somewhat distinctive, yet are generally accepted by society at large and by its predominant religion or religions

_b_ 14. The general process by which societies transform economically, socially, and culturally to conform with the standards set by industrialized Europe

_l_ 15. A theory of physics that holds that the laws of nature are not entirely certain

a. scientism
b. modernization
c. liberalism
d. Darwinism
e. sect
f. neurotheology
g. secular humanism
h. multiculturalism
i. fundamentalism
j. cults
k. postmodernism
l. quantum mechanics
m. traditionalism
n. globalization
o. glossolalia

Essay

1. Discuss the positive and negative effects of modernization on religious traditions. How has modernization altered your own religious tradition or worldview? Do you believe its influence has been positive or negative? Why?
2. Choose two of the new religious movements described in this chapter and explain how each one manifests the seven dimensions of religion.
3. Briefly explain how the expectations of the New Age movement differ from those of the Latter-day Saints and the of Jehovah's Witnesses.
4. What is interfaith dialogue? How might interfaith dialogue positively influence the process of globalization?
5. Describe the universalist impulse and give an example of a religion that features it. What are the pros and cons of adopting such a belief system?
6. Build a case either agreeing or disagreeing with this statement: Science is not equipped to address ethical issues or questions of value and meaning.
7. Explain how science and religion might complement each other.
8. How has your study of the world's religions changed the way you see other traditions? How has it affected your own set of beliefs or worldview?

APPENDIX 2

Audiovisual Recommendations

The following is a listing of audiovisuals that may be shown to your class. The list is divided into selections that are of general interest in the study of world religions, and selections that are particularly pertinent to the topics of each chapter—though for some chapters there are no readily available, appropriate selections.

General Interest

On the Trails of World Religions (seven parts, 57 minutes each, Cambridge Educational, VHS and DVD 1999)

Over the course of this illuminating series, the outspoken yet sincere Hans Küng—arguably one of the world's best-known living theologians—exercises his talent for transforming the complex into the comprehensible as he presents an overview of the emergence and historical development of religion.

Religion: A World History (ten parts, 51–59 minutes each, Cambridge Educational, VHS and DVD 1998)

This series examines religion from spiritual, historical, social, and political viewpoints. From the roots of various belief systems to "Religion on Demand," each program outlines a particular aspect of humankind's quest for spiritual fulfillment.

Religions of the Book: Holy Places and Pilgrimages (29 minutes, Films for the Humanities and Sciences, 1991)

Judaism, Christianity, and Islam have much in common, but also each has its own special history, rituals, holy places, personal interpretations, and definition of holiness. This video explores what holiness means in each of those traditions, and how it is born of people, places, and events within the religions. The program also explores the importance of pilgrimages to believers who seek to be closer to God.

Religions of the Book: The Great Religions and the Poor (29 minutes, Films for the Humanities and Sciences, 1991)

As the number of people living in poverty worldwide continues to swell, concern about them occupies an important place in religious and social thought. This video compares the traditional concept of the poor in the beliefs of Judaism, Christianity, and Islam. The program also explains the theological basis for identifying those who are poor, as well as modern means for the world's religions to provide relief.

The Wisdom of Faith with Huston Smith (290 minutes on five discs, Films for the Humanities and Sciences, VHS 1996, DVD 2003)

Bill Moyers talks with scholar Huston Smith, author of *The World Religions,* about Hinduism, Buddhism, Confucianism, Christianity, Judaism, and Islam. Smith highlights their similarities and differences. The final episode contains Smith's discussion of his own philosophy of religion. The film is enriched by art, architecture, music, and poetry. Smith interprets the meaning of prayer in Western religions and the difficulty of achieving spirituality today.

Chapter 1: Studying the World's Religions

Money and Culture: Jacob Needleman (30 minutes, Films for the Humanities and Sciences, 1990)

Jacob Needleman, author and professor of philosophy and comparative religion, says he writes for people like himself who want to return to the basic questions: Who am I? Why am I on earth? How do I make a living and still keep my soul? In this video Bill Moyers and Needleman discuss the role of money in our society and its power to shape our culture and our soul. This is an excellent mind-opening introduction to the study of world religions. It emphasizes the universal human need for meaning, for a sense of the sacred in life.

Chapter 2: Primal Religious Traditions

Sitting Bull: Chief of the Lakota Nation (60 minutes, A&E Home Video, VHS 1995, DVD 2005, rated A-I)

Sitting Bull was one of the last great leaders of Native American resistance, earning his place in legend with the stunning defeat of General George Custer's expedition at the Battle of the Little Big Horn. But his life embraced much more than that one battle. This biography journeys back to the fading days of the Old West and takes a comprehensive look at this Sioux medicine man's many struggles with the settlers and his modification of the Native American strategies, which enables his people to become more effective fighters.

Chapter 3: Hinduism

City of Joy (132 minutes, Columbia Tristar, VHS 1992, DVD 2006, rated A-II and PG-13)

Disillusioned with the red tape of American medical practice, an American doctor travels to India on a journey of self-discovery. Soon after he arrives, he is attacked and robbed. He is befriended by an impoverished rickshaw driver who takes him to a medical clinic where he is persuaded by a missionary sister to use his medical skills to help the poor people of the city.

Gandhi (188 minutes, Sony Pictures, VHS 1982, DVD 2008, rated A-II and PG)

This epic film spans fifty-five years of Gandhi's life as he practices nonviolence in his advocacy for justice, from his work in South Africa to his promotion of independent self-rule in India.

Hindu Ascetics (44 minutes, Films for the Humanities and Sciences, 1989)

This video examines the practices of some of India's ascetics—*sadhus* (penitents), *fakirs,* and *yogi.* The practices range from the itinerant life of a *sannyasin* to ritual piercing of the skin. The video acknowledges that there are charlatans among the ascetics, and attempts to maintain the distinction between genuine and false asceticism and to connect genuine asceticism with ancient beliefs and practices.

Warning: The last 15 minutes of the video document some practices that may be too gruesome for some students. Preview the video so that you can decide whether to show it in its entirety.

Hinduism (27 minutes, Cambridge Educational, VHS and DVD 2007)

In this program, Dennis Wholey engages in a conversation about Hinduism with Sadhvi Vrnda Chaitanya of Arsha Vijnana Mandiram. Topics of discussion include the history of Hinduism; the Vedas, which are typically committed to memory; the meaning of the words *karma, samsara,* and *moksha* and their relationship to one another; the concept that everything is God and that secular and sacred are therefore one; and the individual rather than communal nature of Hindu prayer.

Hinduism: Faith, Festivals, and Rituals (51 minutes, Cambridge Educational, VHS and DVD 1995)

This program examines India's multifaceted majority religion. Devotional ceremonies and observances of Hinduism and sacred Hindu literature, such as the *Ramayana* and the *Mahabharata,* are explored, as are some of the region's ornate temples. The Hindu emphasis on right living, or *dharma,* is also examined.

Water (117 minutes, 20th Century Fox, DVD 2006, rated A-III and PG-13)

Set against the backdrop of a temple in the holy city of Varanasi, this film examines the plight of a group of widows forced into poverty. It focuses on a relationship between one of the widows, who wants to escape the social restrictions imposed on her as a widow, and a man who is from the highest caste and a follower of Mahatma Gandhi.

Chapter 4: Buddhism

Becoming the Buddha in L.A. (57 minutes, WGBH Boston Video, 1993)

Narrated by Diana Eck, professor of world religions at Harvard, this film explores the experiences of individual Buddhists and their communities in Southern California. Families, teenagers, monks, and converts are portrayed well in an interview format.

Compassion in Exile: The Story of the Fourteenth Dalai Lama (60 minutes, Lemle Pictures, 2005)

Through interviews with the Dalai Lama, this documentary provides an intimate glimpse into the sacred leader's life and family. It contains helpful background about the Chinese invasion of Tibet and subsequent genocide of the Tibetan people, as well as an interview with U.S. State Department personnel.

The Dalai Lama: The Four Noble Truths (360 minutes, Mystic Fire Video, DVD 2002)

This series of lectures on the Four Noble Truths represents the first time the Dalai Lama had given these teachings in the West. It was also the first time His Holiness had been invited to give a major teaching on such a wide spectrum of Buddhist traditions. This two-disc set captures the Dalai Lama addressing the central questions of Buddhism, exploring what are known as the Noble Truths: the truth of suffering, the truth of the origin of suffering, the truth of the cessation of suffering, and the path that leads to the cessation of suffering.

Kundun (135 minutes, Touchstone Video, 1998, rated PG-13 and A-II)

This biographical film directed by Martin Scorsese progresses through the Dalai Lama's early childhood, his recognition as spiritual leader, and finally his escape over the Himalaya Mountains to India. The production provides good coverage of important historical and religious events: the monastic training of the Dalai Lama, Tibetan ceremonies, the Chinese invasion, and a meeting with Chairman Mao. Dream sequences and visions may be confusing for some students. Please preview, as some of the more violent scenes may not be appropriate.

Walking with Buddha (29 minutes, Films for the Humanities and Sciences, 1996)

The Buddhist emphasis on compassion based on meditation offers an example and challenge to all. This video, filmed in Bangkok, Thailand, looks at the life of the Buddha and how Buddha's present-day Thai followers live their beliefs. It depicts the daily life of Buddhist monks as they teach, counsel, beg for alms, and meditate. The result is a basic introduction to Theravada Buddhism, the school of Buddhism likely to be encountered by North Americans as the number of emigrants from Southeast Asia increases.

Chapter 7: Confucianism

A Confucian Life in America: Tu Wei-Ming (30 minutes, Films for the Humanities and Sciences, 1990)

This video presents an interview with Tu Wei-ming, a Chinese-born and Western-educated scholar. As a Confucian, Tu Wei-ming believes that ancient Confucian humanism can help solve contemporary problems. With Bill Moyers, he discusses how Confucian philosophy is relevant today. To follow some portions of the conversation, the students will probably need some background on the 1989 student uprising in China and massacre in Tiananmen Square.

Confucius: Words of Wisdom (50 minutes, A&E Home Video, VHS 1998, DVD 2005)

Confucius's name is synonymous with ageless wisdom. His teachings are credited with helping spur East Asia's current "economic miracle." In this biography, we travel to China's troubled feudal era to learn Confucius's dramatic story, from his childhood in poverty, through his long road to enlightenment, to his years as a celebrated teacher. Leading scholars reveal why his message of five virtues was not always accepted by the leaders of the day. Interviews with a direct descendant provide a personal glimpse into the legend of Confucius.

Chapter 9: Zen Buddhism

Dream Window (57 minutes, Freer Sackler of Art / Arthur M. Sackler Gallery, VHS and DVD 1992)

For more than a thousand years, Japanese gardens, renowned for their beauty, have been retreats enabling people to rediscover the natural world and themselves. The film reveals the secrets of both classical and contemporary Japanese gardens, including those of the legendary Moss Temple of Saiho-ji, Shugaku-in and Katsura Imperial Villas, and Sogetsu Hall. Prominent Japanese personalities add commentary, shedding light on the role of gardens in Japanese society today.

Thich Nhat Hanh's Mindful Movements: Gentle Contemplative Exercises with the Monks and Nuns of Plum Village (38 minutes, Sounds True Video, VHS 1998)

This introduction to mindful meditation is led by Zen master Thich Nhat Hanh, who guides viewers through a series of gentle exercises created specifically to cultivate a joyful awareness of the body and breath. These are the same meditations-in-motion the monks and nuns of Plum Village Monastery use daily as a complement to their practice of seated meditation. These ten unique exercises combine simple stretching and graceful gestures with mindful meditation.

Zen Buddhism: In Search of Self (65 minutes, Turtle Press, DVD 2007)

Following a tradition dating back over a thousand years, two dozen Buddhist nuns gather for a ninety-day period of meditation, fasting, and contemplation deep in the mountains of South Korea. With the singular goal of attaining enlightenment, the women undertake a rigorous schedule of meditation, at one point sitting for seven days without sleep. In this first-ever documentary on the practice of *Dong Ahn Geo* (Winter Zen Retreat), the Baek Hung Buddhist Temple provides the setting for the nuns' daily lives, which entail not only a deep spiritual discipline that involves a strict practice of meditation but also an almost childlike joy and simplicity.

Chapter 10: Shinto

Buddha in the Land of the Kami (Seventh–Twelfth Centuries) (53 minutes, Films for the Humanities and Sciences, 1989)

The history of Japan is the story of the *kami,* the supernatural beings who created the Japanese islands at the beginning of time. This video, from the *Japan Past and Present* series, presents the creation myth of Japan and explains the origin and scope of the *kami* concept. The video also describes how Japan was influenced by the arrival of Buddhism, and how Buddhism and the *kami* were assimilated. Finally, the program discusses the role of Chinese culture, style, and writing in Japanese culture. The Japanese values of creativity, patience, harmonious order, and self-effacement of the individual within the collective whole shine through in this presentation.

Chapter 11: Ancestors of the West

Applying the Lessons of Ancient Greece: Martha Nussbaum (30 minutes, Films for the Humanities and Sciences, 1994)

Imagine being told that the only way to save your entire fleet from shipwreck is to sacrifice your own daughter. Wrenching predicaments like this were the stuff of Greek tragedy nearly twenty-five hundred years ago; surely we do not face dilemmas so difficult in real life today—or do we? Human goodness is a fragile achievement, says Martha Nussbaum, and leading a moral life sometimes requires more luck than anything else. A tenured professor of philosophy and classics at Brown University, and member of the faculty at the University of Chicago Law School, Nussbaum finds lessons for modern Americans in what the ancient Greeks thought about virtue and tragedy. Her thought-provoking discussion with Bill Moyers might best be used as a teacher resource or with students who have a background in the literature of the ancient Greeks.

Chapter 13: Christianity

An Empire Conquered (52 minutes, Vision Video, 1992)

This film about the early centuries of Christianity combines an interesting narrative with a walk through many of the sites in Rome where Christians gathered or were persecuted. The drama aspect of this docudrama consists of re-enactments of the lives of several Christian martyrs during the terrible persecutions before Constantine made Christianity legal in 313. Although these segments are mostly based on legend, care is taken to convey accurate historical data. A study guide comes with the video.

From Jesus to Christ: The First Christians (four parts, 60 minutes each, PBS Home Video, 1998)

This four-part series traces the origins of Christianity from the time of Jesus's life and death until the beginning of the fourth century. Theologians, archaeologists, and historians address several key issues, controversies, and critical problems relating to the life of Jesus and the evolution of Christianity. The discussion revolves around the question of whether a historical approach to the Bible can be reconciled with Christian faith.

Godspell (103 minutes, Columbia Pictures, VHS 1973, DVD 2000, rated A-I and G)

Based on the Gospel of Matthew, *Godspell* uses music and dance to provide a modern-day retelling of the parables set against the backdrop of New York City.

Jesus Christ Superstar (108 minutes, Universal Studios, VHS 1973, DVD 1999, rated A-III and G)

Employing an artistic blend of the modern and the ancient, Andrew Lloyd Webber and Tim Rice's rock opera focuses on the last week in Jesus's life, from his entry into Jerusalem to his Crucifixion at Calvary. Particularly poignant are the creative depictions of the inner struggles and interpersonal relationships of the characters of Jesus, Mary Magdalene, and Judas.

Jesus of Montreal (120 minutes, Max Films Productions Inc., VHS 1989, rated L and R; 120 minutes, Koch Lorber Films, DVD 2004, rated L and R)

A group of young actors is commissioned to put on a modernized interpretation of a church's annual Passion play. Though the depiction meets with rave reviews from the public, it is eventually cancelled by church leadership for being too unorthodox. The film contains many parallels, some overt and others more subtle, between the actors' lives and the Gospels. Due to the film's R rating, some scenes may not be appropriate to show in the classroom.

Jesus of Nazareth (371 minutes, Artisan, VHS 1977, DVD 2005)

Based on the Gospel of John, *Jesus of Nazareth* tells the story of Jesus from his birth through his Passion, death, and Resurrection. The movie is set within the historical and cultural background of first-century Palestine.

Chapter 14: Islam

I Am a Sufi, I Am a Muslim (52 minutes, Films for the Humanities and Sciences, 1996)

This video introduces Sufism, a branch of Islam not well known in the West. Sufism respects outward elements of Islam, but also has its own practices that oppose orthodox Islam. For example, music and veneration of saints are key elements of Sufism, but are not part of orthodox Islamic practice. The program explores exactly what Sufism is and observes how it is practiced in modern India, Pakistan, Turkey, and Macedonia. Among the aspects of Sufism featured are the whirling Dervishes of Turkey, who find God through ecstasy; ecstatic *fakirs* in Macedonia; and the vital role of music in Sufism in India and Pakistan. Be aware that the program introduces concepts and vocabulary not covered in chapter 14 of the text. Also, the video shows graphic images of body piercing during a *zikr,* or religious ceremony.

Inside Mecca (60 minutes, National Geographic, VHS and DVD 2003)

This story presents a three-dimensional documentation of the annual pilgrimage to Mecca and sheds light on the universal principles of Islam during the days of the Hajj. This documentary examines the historical significance of the city of Mecca to Muslim and non-Muslim populations alike. It follows the personal stories of the pilgrims and the mental preparation, physical strain, and spiritual ecstasy they encounter on their life-altering pilgrimage of faith.

Islam: The Faith and the People (22 minutes, Harcourt Religion Publishers, 1991)

This video provides a brief overview of Islamic faith. Topics covered include the Prophet Muhammad, Islamic art and architecture, and Islam in the world today.

The Islamic Mind: Seyyed Hossein Nasr (30 minutes, Films for the Humanities and Sciences, 1994)

It is estimated that by the year 2020, one-quarter of the world's population will be Muslim. This rapid growth makes understanding Islam all the more imperative. Seyyed Hossein Nasr, a scholar of Islamic studies at George Washington University, has written extensively on Islamic science, philosophy, and art. In this discussion with Bill Moyers, Nasr comments on the roots of Islam's attitude toward the West, how Islam and the West can coexist, and the presence of the West in the Middle East. Nasr makes three key points about Islam: (1) that Islam is based on faith in God and peace among people, (2) that Islam wants to coexist peacefully with other religions, and (3) that Islam wants to maintain its own identity.

Chapter 15: Religion in the Modern World

Faith and Reason (seven parts, 60 minutes each, PBS Home Video, DVD 2006)

Are fear and violence the inevitable consequences of clashing beliefs, or is a more tolerant world possible? Bill Moyers explores this question with leading thinkers on the topic of the relationships between religious fundamentalism and democracy, equality, and human rights.

Inherit the Wind (127 minutes, MGM, VHS 1960, DVD 2001, rated A-III and PG)

This film production of Jerome Lawrence and Robert E. Lee's play presents a fictionalized and dramatic interpretation of the 1925 Scopes Monkey Trial, in which Tennessee schoolteacher Jonathan Scopes was arrested for teaching Darwin's theory of evolution. The trial pitted defense attorney Clarence Darrow against the fundamentalist former presidential candidate William Jennings Bryan. The film portrays the tension between the creationist and evolutionist belief systems, and demonstrates how people struggle to find meaning in a constantly changing world.

When Faith Meets Physics (29 minutes, Films for the Humanities and Sciences, 1997)

Are religion and science in conflict, or are they compatible? This film briefly examines some historical conflicts between faith and science. It then moves into a discussion of how the heated arguments between the scientific and religious communities, which were somewhat quiet for a time, have reignited in recent years.

APPENDIX 3

For Further Reading

General Interest

Ashton, John, and Tom Whyte. *The Quest for Paradise: Visions of Heaven and Eternity in the World's Myths and Religions.* San Francisco: HarperSanFrancisco, 2001.

Carmody, Denise Lardner. *Women and World Religions.* Nashville, TN: Abingdon Press, 1979.

Carmody, Denise Lardner, and John Tully Carmody. *Prayer in World Religions.* Maryknoll, NY: Orbis Books, 1990.

de Mello, Anthony. *Sadhana, A Way to God: Christian Exercises in Eastern Form.* New York: Doubleday, 1978.

DiNoia, J. A. *The Diversity of Religions: A Christian Perspective.* Washington, DC: Catholic University of America, 1992.

Dulles, Avery. "Christ Among the Religions." *America.* February 4, 2002. Pp. 8–15.

Earhart, H. Byron, ed. *Religious Traditions of the World: A Journey Through Africa, Mesoamerica, North America, Judaism, Christianity, Islam, Hinduism, Buddhism, China, and Japan.* San Francisco: HarperSanFrancisco, 1993.

Eastman, Roger, ed. *The Ways of Religion: An Introduction to the Major Traditions.* 3d ed. New York: Oxford University Press, 1999.

Eck, Diana L. *Encountering God: A Spiritual Journey from Bozeman to Banaras.* Boston: Beacon Press, 1993.

———, ed. *On Common Ground: World Religions in America.* New York: Columbia University Press, 1997. CD-ROM.

Eliade, Mircea, ed. *The Encyclopedia of Religion.* 16 vols. New York: Macmillan, 1987.

———, ed. *From Primitives to Zen: A Thematic Sourcebook of the History of Religions.* New York: Harper and Row, 1967.

Endo, Shusaku. *Deep River.* Trans. Van C. Gessel. New York: New Directions, 1994.

Fisher, Mary Pat. *Living Religions.* 4th ed. Upper Saddle River, NJ: Prentice-Hall, 1999.

Hesse, Hermann. *Siddhartha.* Trans. Hilda Rosner. New York: Bantam Books, 1951.

Noss, John B., and David S. Noss. *A History of the World's Religions.* 9th ed. New York: Macmillan, 1994.

Richard, Lucien. *What Are They Saying About Christ and World Religions?* New York: Paulist Press, 1981.

Sharma, Arvind, ed. *Our Religions.* San Francisco: HarperSanFrancisco, 1993.

———, ed. *Women in World Religions.* Albany, NY: State University of New York, 1987.

Sherwin, Byron, and Harold Kasimow, eds. *John Paul II and Interreligious Dialogue.* New York: Orbis Books, 1999.
Smart, Ninian. *The World's Religions: Old Traditions and Modern Transformations.* 2d ed. Cambridge, England: Cambridge University Press, 1998.
Smart, Ninian, and Richard D. Hecht, eds. *Sacred Texts of the World: A Universal Anthology.* New York: Crossroad Publishing, 1982.
Smith, Huston. *The World's Religions.* San Francisco: HarperSanFrancisco, 1991.
Smith, Jonathan Z., ed. *The HarperCollins Dictionary of Religion.* San Francisco: HarperSanFrancisco, 1995.
Viladesau, Richard, and Mark Massa, eds. *World Religions: A Sourcebook for Students of Christian Theology.* New York: Paulist Press, 1994.

Chapter 1: Studying the World's Religions

Capps, Walter H. *Religious Studies: The Making of a Discipline.* Minneapolis: Fortress Press, 1995.
Eliade, Mircea. *Myth and Reality.* New York: Harper and Row, 1963.
———. *The Sacred and the Profane: The Nature of Religion.* New York: Harper and Row, 1961.
Hall, T. William, Richard B. Pilgrim, and Ronald R. Cavanagh. *Religion: An Introduction.* San Francisco: HarperSanFrancisco, 1986.
Jurgensmeyer, Mark, ed. *Teaching the Introductory Course in Religious Studies: A Sourcebook.* Atlanta: Scholars Press, 1991.
Leeuw, Gerardus van der. *Sacred and Profane Beauty: The Holy in Art.* New York: Holt, Rinehart, and Winston, 1963.
Otto, Rudolf. *The Idea of the Holy: An Inquiry into the Non-rational Factor in the Idea of the Divine and Its Relation to the Rational.* New York: Oxford University Press, 1958.
Sharpe, Eric. *Comparative Religion: A History.* New York: Scribner's, 1976.
Smart, Ninian. *Worldviews: Crosscultural Explorations of Human Beliefs.* New York: Scribner's, 1983.

Chapter 2: Primal Religious Traditions

Berndt, Ronald M. *Australian Aboriginal Religion.* Leiden, Netherlands: Brill Academic Publishers, 1974.
Brown, Joseph Epes. *The Spiritual Legacy of the American Indian.* New York: Crossroad Publishing, 1989.
Carrasco, Davíd. *Religions of Mesoamerica: Cosmovision and Ceremonial Centers.* Prospect Heights, IL: Waveland Press, 1998.
Drewal, Henry John. *Yoruba: Nine Centuries of African Art and Thought.* New York: Center for African Art in association with H. N. Abrams, 1989.
Gill, Sam D. *Native American Religions: An Introduction.* The Religious Life of Man Series. Belmont, CA: Wadsworth Publishing, 1982.
Hultkrantz, Ake. *The Religions of American Indians.* Berkeley, CA: University of California Press, 1979.
Lawson, E. Thomas. *Religions of Africa: Traditions in Transformation.* San Francisco: HarperSanFrancisco, 1985.
Mails, Thomas E. *Secret Native American Pathways: A Guide to Inner Peace.* Tulsa, OK: Council Oak Books, 1988.
Mbiti, John. *Introduction to African Religion.* New York: Praeger, 1975.

Mol, J. J. *The Firm and the Formless: Religion and Identity in Aboriginal Australia.* Waterloo, Ontario: Wilfred Laurier University Press, 1982.
Nabokov, Peter, ed. *Native American Testimony: A Chronicle of Indian-White Relations from Prophecy to the Present, 1492–2000.* New York: Viking Press, 1999.
Parrinder, Edward Geoffrey. *West African Religion: A Study of the Beliefs and Practices of Akan, Ewe, Yoruba, Ibo, and Kindred Peoples.* 2d ed. London: Epworth Press, 1961.
Ray, Benjamin C. *African Religions: Symbol, Ritual, and Community.* London: Heinemann Educational, 1972.

Chapter 3: Hinduism

Basham, A. L. *The Wonder That Was India: A Survey of the Culture of the Indian Sub-continent Before the Coming of the Muslims.* New York: Grove Press, 1954.
Doniger O'Flaherty, Wendy, trans. *The Rig Veda.* New York: Penguin Books, 1981.
Eck, Diana L. *Darsan: Seeing the Divine in India.* 2d ed. New York: Columbia University Press, 1985.
Eliade, Mircea. *Yoga: Immortality and Freedom.* 2d ed. Princeton, NJ: Princeton University Press, 1969.
Ellsberg, Robert, ed. *Gandhi on Christianity.* Maryknoll, NY: Orbis Books, 1991.
Hopkins, Thomas J. *The Hindu Religious Tradition.* The Religious Life of Man Series. Belmont, CA: Wadsworth Publishing, 1971.
Kinsley, David T. *Hinduism: A Cultural Perspective.* 2d ed. Prentice-Hall Series in World Religions. Englewood Cliffs, NJ: Prentice-Hall, 1993.
Knipe, David M. *Hinduism: Experiments in the Sacred.* San Francisco: HarperSanFrancisco, 1991.
Mascaro, Juan, trans. *The Upanishads.* New York: Penguin Books, 1965.
Miller, Barbara Stoler, trans. *The Bhagavad-Gita: Krishna's Counsel in Time of War.* New York: Bantam Books, 1986.
Mitter, Sara S. *Dharma's Daughters: Contemporary Indian Women and Hindu Culture.* New Brunswick, NJ: Rutgers University Press, 1991.
Nikhilananda, Swami, trans. *The Bhagavad-Gita.* New York: Ramakrishna-Vivekananda Center, 1944.
———, trans. *The Upanishads.* 4 vols. New York: Ramakrishna-Vivekananda Center, 1975–1979.
Prabhavananda, Swami. *The Spiritual Heritage of India.* Hollywood, CA: Vedanta Press, 1963.
Prabhavananda, Swami, and Christopher Isherwood, trans. *The Song of God: Bhagavad-Gita.* Hollywood, CA: Vedanta Press, 1944.
Prabhavananda, Swami, and Frederick Manchester, eds. and trans. *The Upanishads: Breath of the Eternal.* New York: New American Library, 1957.
Radhakrishnan, Sarvepalli. *The Hindu View of Life.* San Francisco: HarperSanFrancisco, 1988.
Radhakrishnan, Sarvepalli, and Charles A. Moore, eds. *A Source Book in Indian Philosophy.* Princeton, NJ: Princeton University Press, 1957.
Renou, Louis, ed. *Hinduism.* New York: George Braziller, 1962.
Zaehner, Robert Charles. *Hinduism.* New York: Oxford University Press, 1962.
Zimmer, Heinrich. *Myths and Symbols in Indian Art and Civilization.* Princeton, NJ: Princeton University Press, 1972.
———. *The Philosophies of India.* Princeton, NJ: Princeton University Press, 1969.

Chapter 4: Buddhism

Ch'en, Kenneth K. S. *Buddhism: The Light of Asia.* Woodbury, NY: Barron's Educational Series, 1968.

———. *Buddhism in China.* Princeton, NJ: Princeton University Press, 1973.

Chödron, Pema. *When Things Fall Apart.* Boston: Shambhala Publications, 1997.

Conze, Edward. *Buddhism: Its Essence and Development.* New York: Harper Torchbooks, 1959.

———, trans. *Buddhist Scriptures.* New York: Penguin Books, 1959.

Fernando, Antony. *Buddhism Made Plain: An Introduction for Christians and Jews.* Maryknoll, NY: Orbis Books, 1985.

Gyatso, Tenzin. *Freedom in Exile: The Autobiography of the Dalai Lama.* San Francisco: HarperSanFrancisco, 1990.

Ling, Trevor. *The Buddha: Buddhist Civilization in India and Ceylon.* New York: Scribner's, 1973.

Lopez, Donald S., Jr. *Prisoners of Shangri-La: Tibetan Buddhism and the West.* Chicago: University of Chicago Press, 1998.

Martin, Rafe. *The Hungry Tigress: Buddhist Myths, Legends, and Jataka Tales.* Completely rev. and expanded ed. Cambridge, MA: Yellow Moon Press, 1999.

Nakamura, Hajime. *Gotama Buddha.* Kyoto, Japan: Hozokan, 1965.

Nhat Hanh, Thich. *The Miracle of Mindfulness.* Boston: Beacon Press, 1976.

———. *Old Path White Clouds: Walking in the Footsteps of the Buddha.* Berkeley, CA: Parallax Press, 1991.

Powers, John. *Introduction to Tibetan Buddhism.* Ithaca, NY: Snow Lion Publications, 1995.

Radhakrishnan, Sarvepalli, and Charles A. Moore, eds. *A Source Book in Indian Philosophy.* Princeton, NJ: Princeton University Press, 1957.

Rahula, Walpola. *What the Buddha Taught.* Rev. ed. New York: Grove Press, 1974.

Robinson, Richard H., and Willard L. Johnson. *The Buddhist Religion: A Historical Introduction.* 4th ed. The Religious Life of Man Series. Belmont, CA: Wadsworth Publishing, 1997.

Thurman, Robert A. F., trans. *The Tibetan Book of the Dead: Liberation Through Understanding in the Between.* New York: Bantam Books, 1994.

Tucci, Giuseppe. *The Religions of Tibet.* Trans. Geoffrey Samuel. London: Routledge and Kegan Paul, 1980.

Warren, Henry Clarke, trans. *Buddhism in Translations.* New York: Atheneum, 1962.

Wilson Ross, Nancy. *Buddhism: A Way of Life and Thought.* New York: Vintage Books, 1981.

Zimmer, Heinrich. *The Philosophies of India.* Princeton, NJ: Princeton University Press, 1969.

Chapter 5: Jainism

Dundas, Paul. *The Jains.* London: Routledge, 1992.

Jain, Shri Satish Kumar, and Kamal Chand Sogani, eds. *Perspectives in Jaina Philosophy and Culture.* New Delhi, India: Ahimsa International, 1985.

Jaini, Padmanabh S. *The Jaina Path of Purification.* Berkeley, CA: University of California Press, 1979.

Mehta, M. L. *Jaina Culture.* Varanasi, India: P. V. Research Institute, 1969.

———. *Jaina Philosophy.* Varanasi, India: P. V. Research Institute, 1971.

Radhakrishnan, Sarvepalli, and Charles A. Moore, eds. *A Source Book in Indian Philosophy*. Princeton, NJ: Princeton University Press, 1957.
Zimmer, Heinrich. *The Philosophies of India*. Princeton, NJ: Princeton University Press, 1969.

Chapter 6: Sikhism

Cole, W. Owen, and Piara Singh Sambhi. *The Sikhs: Their Religious Beliefs and Practices*. 2d, rev. ed. Brighton, United Kingdom: Sussex Academic Press, 1995.
McLeod, W. Hew. *The Evolution of the Sikh Community*. Oxford, England: Clarendon Press, 1976.
———. *Guru Nanak and the Sikh Religion*. London: Oxford University Press, 1968.
———. *Sikhism*. London: Penguin Books, 1997.
———. *The Sikhs: History, Religion, and Society*. New York: Oxford University Press, 1989.
Singh, Harbans. *The Heritage of the Sikhs*. New Delhi, India: Manohar Publications, 1969.
Singh, Khushwant. *A History of the Sikhs*. 2 vols. Princeton, NJ: Princeton University Press, 1963–1966.
———, trans. *Hymns of Guru Nanak*. New Delhi, India: Orient Longman, 1969.
Singh, Trilochan, Jodh Singh, Kapur Singh, Bawa Harishen Singh, and Khushwant Singh, trans. *The Sacred Writings of the Sikhs*. London: George Allen and Unwin, 1960.

Chapter 7: Confucianism

Chan, Wing-tsit, trans. and comp. *A Source Book in Chinese Philosophy*. Princeton, NJ: Princeton University Press, 1963.
Confucius. *The Analects of Confucius*. Trans. Arthur Waley. New York: Vintage, 1938.
———. *Confucius: The Analects*. Trans. D. C. Lau. New York: Penguin Books, 1979.
Creel, H. G. *Chinese Thought: From Confucius to Mao Tse-Tung*. Chicago: University of Chicago Press, 1953.
———. *Confucius and the Chinese Way*. New York: Harper and Row, 1960.
Fingarette, Herbert. *Confucius: The Secular as Sacred*. New York: Harper and Row, 1972.
Graham, A. C. *Disputers of the Tao*. La Salle, IL: Open Court, 1989.
Liu, Wu-Chi. *Confucius: His Life and Time*. New York: Philosophical Library, 1955.
Mencius. *Mencius*. Trans. W. A. C. H. Dobson. Toronto: University of Toronto Press, 1963.
———. *Mencius*. Trans. D. C. Lau. New York: Penguin Books, 1970.
Smith, D. Howard. *Chinese Religions*. New York: Holt, Rinehart, and Winston, 1968.
Thompson, Laurence G. *Chinese Religion: An Introduction*. 5th ed. The Religious Life of Man Series. Belmont, CA: Wadsworth Publishing, 1996.
Tu Wei-ming. *Confucian Thought: Selfhood as Creative Transformation*. Albany, NY: State University of New York Press, 1985.
Waley, Arthur. *Three Ways of Thought in Ancient China*. Stanford, CA: Stanford University Press, 1939.

Chapter 8: Taoism

Chan, Wing-tsit, trans. and comp. *A Source Book in Chinese Philosophy*. Princeton, NJ: Princeton University Press, 1963.

Chuang Tzu. *Chuang Tzu: Basic Writings*. Trans. Burton Watson. New York: Columbia University Press, 1964.

———. *The Complete Works of Chuang Tzu*. Trans. Burton Watson. New York: Columbia University Press, 1968.

———. *The Way of Chuang Tzu*. Trans. Thomas Merton. New York: New Directions, 1965.

Graham, A. C. *Disputers of the Tao*. La Salle, IL: Open Court, 1989.

Kaltenmark, Max. *Lao Tzu and Taoism*. Trans. Roger Greaves. Stanford, CA: Stanford University Press, 1969.

Lao Tzu. *Tao Te Ching*. Trans. Gia-fu Feng and Jane English. New York: Alfred A. Knopf, 1974.

———. *Tao Te Ching*. Trans. D. C. Lau. New York: Penguin Books, 1963.

———. *The Way and Its Power*. Trans. Arthur Waley. New York: Grove-Atlantic, 1958.

———. *The Way of Lao Tzu (Tao-te-Ching)*. Trans. Wing-tsit Chan. Indianapolis: Bobbs-Merrill, 1963.

———. *The Way of Life: Lao Tzu*. Trans. R. B. Blakney. New York: Mentor, 1955.

Smith, D. Howard. *Chinese Religions*. New York: Holt, Rinehart, and Winston, 1968.

Thompson, Laurence G. *Chinese Religion: An Introduction*. 5th ed. The Religious Life of Man Series. Belmont, CA: Wadsworth Publishing, 1996.

Waley, Arthur. *Three Ways of Thought in Ancient China*. London: George Allen and Unwin, 1939.

Welch, Holmes. *Taoism: The Parting of the Way*. Rev. ed. Boston: Beacon Press, 1966.

Welch, Holmes, and Ann Siedel, eds. *Facets of Taoism: Essays in Chinese Religion*. New Haven, CT: Yale University Press, 1979.

Chapter 9: Zen Buddhism

Aitken, Robert. *Taking the Path of Zen*. San Francisco: North Point Press, 1982.

Dumoulin, Heinrich. *A History of Zen Buddhism*. New York: Pantheon Books, 1963.

Earhart, H. Byron. *Japanese Religion: Unity and Diversity*. 3d ed. The Religious Life of Man Series. Belmont, CA: Wadsworth Publishing, 1982.

Kapleau, Philip. *The Three Pillars of Zen*. New York: Anchor Books, 1989.

O'Halloran, Maura. *Pure Heart Enlightened Mind: The Zen Journal and Letters of Maura "Soshin" O'Halloran*. Boston: Charles E. Tuttle, 1994.

Reps, Paul. *Zen Flesh, Zen Bones: A Collection of Zen and Pre-Zen Writings*. Boston: Charles E. Tuttle, 1957.

Sekida, Katsuki. *Zen Training: Methods and Philosophy*. New York: Weatherhill, 1983.

Suzuki, D. T. *An Introduction to Zen Buddhism*. New York: Grove Press, 1964.

Suzuki, Shunryu. *Zen Mind, Beginner's Mind*. New York: Weatherhill, 1970.

Watts, Alan. *The Way of Zen*. New York: Pantheon Books, 1957.

Chapter 10: Shinto

Earhart, H. Byron. *Japanese Religion: Unity and Diversity.* 3d ed. The Religious Life of Man Series. Belmont, CA: Wadsworth Publishing, 1982.

———, ed. *Religion in the Japanese Experience: Sources and Interpretations.* 2d ed. The Religious Life of Man Series. Belmont, CA: Wadsworth Publishing, 1997.

Kitagawa, Joseph M. *On Understanding Japanese Religion.* Princeton, NJ: Princeton University Press, 1987.

———. *Religion in Japanese History.* New York: Columbia University Press, 1966.

Nelson, John K. *A Year in the Life of a Shinto Shrine.* Seattle: University of Washington Press, 1996.

Ono, Sokyo. *Shinto: The Kami Way.* Boston: Charles E. Tuttle, 1962.

Tsunoda, Ryusaku, William Theodore de Bary, and Donald Keene, eds. *Sources of Japanese Tradition.* New York: Columbia University Press, 1958.

Chapter 11: Ancestors of the West

Beard, Mary, John A. North, John North, Simon Price, and S. R. F. Price. *Religions of Rome.* Vol. 1, *A History.* Cambridge: Cambridge University Press, 1998.

———. *Religions of Rome.* Vol. 2, *A Sourcebook.* Cambridge: Cambridge University Press, 1998.

Boyce, Mary. *A History of Zoroastrianism.* 2 vols. Leiden, Netherlands: Brill Academic Publishers, 1975, 1982.

———. *Zoroastrians: Their Religious Beliefs and Practices.* London: Routledge and Kegan Paul, 1979.

———, ed. and trans. *Textual Sources for the Study of Zoroastrianism.* Textual Sources for the Study of Religion. Manchester, England: Manchester University Press, 1984.

Brown, Peter. *The Making of Late Antiquity.* Cambridge, MA: Harvard University Press, 1979.

Burkert, Walter. *Greek Religion.* Cambridge, MA: Harvard University Press, 1985.

Cumont, Franz. *The Oriental Religions in Roman Paganism.* New York: Dover, 1956.

Duchesne-Guillemin, Jacques. *Religion of Ancient Iran.* Bombay, India: Tata Press, 1973.

———. *Symbols and Values in Zoroastrianism.* New York: Harper and Row, 1966.

Dumezil, Georges. *Archaic Roman Religion.* 2 vols. Trans. Philip Krapp. Chicago: University of Chicago Press, 1970.

Ferguson, John. *The Religions of the Roman Empire.* Aspects of Greek and Roman Life. Ithaca, NY: Cornell University Press, 1970.

Festugiere, A. J. *Personal Religion Among the Greeks.* Berkeley, CA: University of California Press, 1954.

Grant, Frederick C. *Hellenistic Religions: The Age of Syncretism.* Indianapolis: Bobbs-Merrill Educational Publishing, 1953.

Guthrie, W. K. C. *The Greeks and Their Gods.* London: Methuen, 1962.

Hinnells, John R. *Zoroastrianism and the Parsees.* London: Ward Lock Educational, 1981.

Martin, Luther H. *Hellenistic Religions.* New York: Oxford University Press, 1987.

Meyer, Marvin W., ed. *The Ancient Mysteries, a Sourcebook: Sacred Texts of the Mystery Religions of the Ancient Mediterranean World.* Philadelphia: University of Pennsylvania Press, 1999.

Nilsson, Martin P. *A History of Greek Religion.* New York: W. W. Norton, 1964.
Nock, Arthur Darby. *Conversion: The Old and the New in Religion from Alexander the Great to Augustine of Hippo.* Oxford, England: Oxford University Press, 1933.
Rice, David G., and John E. Stambaugh. *Sources for the Study of Greek Religion.* Atlanta: Scholars Press, 1979.
Vermaseren, M. J. *Cybele and Attis: The Myth and the Cult.* London: Thames and Hudson, 1977.
Zaehner, Robert Charles. *The Dawn and Twilight of Zoroastrianism.* New York: Putnam, 1961.

Chapter 12: Judaism

Buber, Martin. *Tales of the Hasidim.* 2 vols. New York: Schocken Books, 1947–1948.
Danby, Herbert, ed and trans. *The Mishnah.* Oxford, England: Oxford University Press, 1933.
Dawidowicz, Lucy S., ed. *A Holocaust Reader.* New York: Behrman House, 1975.
Encyclopædia Judaica. 16 vols. New York: Macmillan, 1971.
Falk, Marcia. *The Book of Blessings: A New Prayer Book for the Weekdays, the Sabbath, and the New Moon Festival.* Boston: Beacon Press, 1999.
Finkelstein, Louis. *The Jews: Their History, Culture, and Religion.* 2 vols. New York: Harper and Row, 1960.
Fishbane, Michael A. *Judaism: Revelation and Traditions.* San Francisco: Harper and Row, 1987.
Guttmann, Julius. *Philosophies of Judaism: The History of Jewish Philosophy from Biblical Times to Franz Rosenzweig.* New York: Holt, Rinehart, and Winston, 1964.
Hallie, Philip. *Lest Innocent Blood Be Shed: The Story of the Village of Le Chambon and How Goodness Happened There.* New York: HarperCollins, 1980.
Heschel, Abraham J. *God in Search of Man: A Philosophy of Judaism.* New York: Farrar, Straus and Giroux, 1976.
———. *The Sabbath: Its Meaning for Modern Man.* New York: Farrar, Straus and Giroux, 1951.
Hilbert, Raul. *The Destruction of the European Jews.* Chicago: Quadrangle, 1961.
Levin, Nora. *The Holocaust.* New York: Schocken Books, 1973.
Matt, Daniel Charan, trans. *Zohar: The Book of Enlightenment.* New York: Paulist Press, 1983.
Montefiore, C. G., and H. J. Lowe, eds. *A Rabbinic Anthology.* New York: Schocken Books, 1974.
Neusner, Jacob. *The Way of Torah: An Introduction to Judaism.* 6th ed. The Religious Life of Man Series. Belmont, CA: Wadsworth Publishing, 1997.
———, ed. *The Life of Torah: Readings in the Jewish Religious Experience.* The Religious Life of Man Series. Belmont, CA: Wadsworth Publishing, 1974.
Potok, Chaim. *The Chosen.* New York: Simon and Schuster, 1967.
———. *My Name Is Asher Lev.* New York: Ballantine Books, 1972.
Rabinowicz, Harry M. *The World of Hasidism.* Hartford, CT: Hartmore House, 1970.
Roth, Cecil. *A History of the Jews: From Earliest Times Through the Six-Day War.* Rev. ed. New York: Schocken Books, 1970.
Ruether, Rosemary Radford, and Eleanor McLaughlin. *Women of the Spirit: Female Leadership in the Jewish and Christian Traditions.* New York: Simon and Schuster, 1979.
Rush, Barbara. *The Jewish Year: Celebrating the Holidays.* New York: Stewart, Tabori, and Chang, 2001.

Scholem, Gershon. *Major Trends in Jewish Mysticism.* 3d rev. ed. New York: Schocken Books, 1964.

Schwartz, Howard. *Gabriel's Palace: Jewish Mystical Tales.* New York: Oxford University Press, 1993.

Seltzer, Robert M. *Jewish People, Jewish Thought: The Jewish Experience in History.* New York: Macmillan, 1980.

Spiegelman, Art. *The Complete Maus: A Survivor's Tale.* New York: Pantheon, 1996.

Steinsaltz, Adin. *The Essential Talmud.* New York: Basic Books, 1976.

Tanakh: A New Translation of the Holy Scriptures According to the Traditional Hebrew Text. Philadelphia: Jewish Publication Society, 1985.

Ten Boom, Corrie, John Sherrill, and Elizabeth Sherrill. *The Hiding Place.* New York: Bantam Books, 1971.

Wiesel, Elie. *Night.* New York: Bantam Books, 1982.

Wouk, Herman. *This Is My God.* New York: Doubleday, 1959.

Chapter 13: Christianity

Ahlstrom, Sidney. *Religious History of the American People.* New Haven, CT: Yale University Press, 1972.

Albanese, Catherine. *America: Religion and Religions.* Belmont, CA: Wadsworth Publishing, 1981.

Augustine, Saint. *Confessions.* Trans. R. S. Pine-Coffin. New York: Penguin Books, 1961.

Barrett, C. K., ed. *The New Testament Background: Selected Documents.* Rev. ed. San Francisco: Harper and Row, 1989.

Brown, Peter. *Augustine of Hippo: A Biography.* Berkeley, CA: University of California Press, 1967.

Brown, Robert McAfee. *The Spirit of Protestantism.* New York: Oxford University Press, 1965.

Carmody, Denise Lardner, and John Tully Carmody. *Roman Catholicism: An Introduction.* New York: Macmillan, 1990.

Epp, Eldon, and George W. MacRae, eds. *The New Testament and Its Modern Interpreters.* Minneapolis: Augsburg Fortress, 1987.

Forell, George W. *The Protestant Faith.* Columbus, OH: Augsburg Fortress Publications, 1975.

Frend, W. H. C. *The Early Church.* Philadelphia: Fortress Press, 1976.

Gutierrez, Gustavo. *A Theology of Liberation.* Rev. ed. Maryknoll, NY: Orbis Books, 1988.

Hudleston, Dom Roger, ed. and trans. *Little Flowers of Saint Francis of Assisi.* Springfield, IL: Templegate, 1988.

Johnson, Paul. *A History of Christianity.* New York: Atheneum, 1976.

Knitter, Paul F. *No Other Name? A Critical Survey of Christian Attitudes Toward World Religions.* Maryknoll, NY: Orbis Books, 1985.

Koch, Carl. *A Popular History of the Catholic Church.* Winona, MN: Saint Mary's Press, 1997.

Kung, Hans. *On Being a Christian.* Garden City, NY: Doubleday, 1976.

Libreria Editrice Vaticana. *Catechism of the Catholic Church.* 2d ed. Trans. United States Conference of Catholic Bishops (USCCB). Washington, DC: USCCB, 1997.

Metzger, Bruce M., and Roland E. Murphy. *The New Oxford Annotated Bible with the Apocryphal/Deuterocanonical Books.* New Revised Standard Version. New York: Oxford University Press, 1991.

Pearson, Birger A. *The Emergence of the Christian Religion: Essays on Early Christianity.* Harrisburg, PA: Trinity Press International, 1997.
Pelikan, Jaoslav. *Jesus Through the Centuries: His Place in the History of Culture.* New Haven, CT: Yale University Press, 1985.
Perrin, Norman, and Dennis C. Duling. *The New Testament, an Introduction: Proclamation and Parenesis, Myth and History.* 2d ed. San Diego: Harcourt Brace Jovanovich, 1982.
Reynolds, Stephen. *The Christian Religious Tradition.* The Religious Life of Man Series. Belmont, CA: Wadsworth Publishing, 1977.
Robinson, John M. *A New Quest for the Historical Jesus.* London: SCM Press, 1961.
Ruether, Rosemary Radford, and Eleanor McLaughlin. *Women of the Spirit: Female Leadership in the Jewish and Christian Traditions.* New York: Simon and Schuster, 1979.
Schweitzer, Albert. *The Quest of the Historical Jesus.* New York: Macmillan, 1968.
Ware, Timothy. *The Orthodox Church.* New York: Penguin Books, 1963.

Chapter 14: Islam

Alavi, Karima Diane. "Turning to the Islamic Faith." *America.* March 4, 2002. Pp. 18–20.
Arberry, A. J., trans. *The Koran Interpreted: A Translation.* New York: Macmillan, 1955.
Burckhardt, Titus. *An Introduction to Sufism.* Wellingborough, England: Crucible, 1990.
Cragg, Kenneth. *The House of Islam.* The Religious Life of Man Series. 3d ed. Belmont, CA: Wadsworth Publishing, 1988.
Cragg, Kenneth, and R. Marston Speight. *Islam from Within: Anthology of a Religion.* The Religious Life of Man Series. Belmont, CA: Wadsworth Publishing, 1980.
Dawood, N. J., trans. *The Koran.* Rev. ed. New York: Penguin Books, 1990.
Denny, Frederick Mathewson. *An Introduction to Islam.* New York: Macmillan, 1985.
———. *Islam and the Muslim Community.* Religious Traditions of the World. San Francisco: HarperSanFrancisco, 1987.
Esposito, John L. *Islam: The Straight Path.* Expanded ed. New York: Oxford University Press, 1991.
Geertz, Clifford. *Islam Observed: Religious Development in Morocco and Indonesia.* New Haven, CT: Yale University Press, 1976.
Haddad, Yvonne Yazbeck, ed. *The Muslims of America.* New York: Oxford University Press, 1991.
Jomier, Jacques. *How to Understand Islam.* New York: Crossroad Publishing, 1989.
Kritzeck, James, ed. *Anthology of Islamic Literature: From the Rise of Islam to Modern Times.* New York: Holt, Rinehart, and Winston, 1964.
Lings, Martin. *Muhammad: His Life Based on the Earliest Sources.* Chicago: Kazi Publications, 1996.
———. *What Is Sufism?* New York: Routledge, Chapman, Hall, 1988.
Martin, Richard C. *Islam: A Cultural Perspective.* Englewood Cliffs, NJ: Prentice-Hall, 1982.
Nasr, Hossein. *Ideals and Realities of Islam.* Chicago: Kazi Publications, 1996.
———, ed. *Islamic Spirituality.* 2 vols. London: Routledge and Kegan Paul, 1987, 1991.

Pickthall, Mohammed Marmaduke, trans. *The Meaning of the Glorious Koran*. New York: New American Library, 1953.
Rahman, Fazlur. *Islam*. 2d ed. Chicago: University of Chicago Press, 1979.
Rumi, Jalal al-Din. *Mystical Poems of Rumi*. Trans. A. J. Arberry. Chicago: University of Chicago Press, 1968.
———. *The Sufi Path of Love: The Spiritual Teachings of Rumi*. Trans. William C. Chittick. Albany, NY: State University of New York, 1983.
Schimmel, Annemarie. *Mystical Dimensions of Islam*. Chapel Hill, NC: University of North Carolina Press, 1975.
Schuon, Frithjof. *Understanding Islam*. Chicago: Kazi Publications, 1996.
Shah, Idries. *Tales of the Dervishes*. New York: E. P. Dutton, 1970.
———. *The Way of the Sufi*. New York: E. P. Dutton, 1969.
Smith, Jane I. *Women in Contemporary Muslim Societies*. Lewisburg, PA: Bucknell University Press, 1979.

Chapter 15: Religion in the Modern World

Barker, Eileen. *New Religious Movements: A Practical Introduction*. London: Her Majesty's Stationery Office, 1989.
Book of Mormon: Another Testament of Jesus Christ. 1830. Reprint, Salt Lake City: Church of Jesus Christ of Latter-day Saints, 1981.
Braybrooke, Marcus. *Faith and Interfaith in a Global Age*. Grand Rapids, MI: CoNexus Press; Oxford, England: Braybrooke Press, 1998.
Fisher, Mary Pat. *Religion in the Twenty-first Century*. Upper Saddle River, NJ: Prentice-Hall, 1998.
Gaver, Jessyca Russell. *The Baha'i Faith: Dawn of a New Day*. New York: Hawthorn Books, 1967.
Gilbert, James Burkhart. *Redeeming Culture: American Religion in an Age of Science, 1925–1962*. Chicago: University of Chicago Press, 1998.
Gonzalez-Wippler, Migene. *Santeria: The Religion*. 2d ed. Saint Paul, MN: Llewellyn Publications, 1996.
Larson, Edward J. *Summer for the Gods: The Scopes Trial and America's Continuing Debate over Science and Religion*. New York: Basic Books, 1997.
Magida, Arthur J., and Stuart M. Matlins, eds. *How to Be a Perfect Stranger: A Guide to Etiquette in Other People's Religious Ceremonies*. Vols. 1 and 2. Woodstock, VT: SkyLight Paths Publishing, 1999.
Melton, J. Gordon. *Encyclopedia of American Religions*. 5th ed. Detroit: Gale Research, 1996.
———. *New Age Encyclopedia*. Detroit: Gale Research, 1990.
Starhawk. *The Spiral Dance: A Rebirth of the Ancient Religion of the Great Goddess*. San Francisco: Harper and Row, 1979.
Wuthnow, Robert. *The Struggle for America's Soul: Evangelicals, Liberals, and Secularism*. Grand Rapids, MI: W. B. Eerdmans, 1989.

APPENDIX 4

The Comparative Study of Religions

World Religions: A Voyage of Discovery considers one religion at a time, chapter by chapter. An alternative approach is to select central themes of inquiry and to investigate how the religions engage with each theme. This approach is known as comparative religion. Chapter 1 of the student text isolates appropriate themes for comparative study: the religious questions that the traditions answer. The seven dimensions of religion presented in the student text are conducive to a different type of comparative study, and a brief analysis of the ethical dimension is included at the end of this essay. However, our main purpose here will be to consider the religious questions. In addition to investigating each religious question in turn, we can conclude by asking (and attempting to answer) another question: Do the religions ultimately agree or disagree?

Why Compare Religions?

At its beginning the student text notes the dictum of Friedrich Max Müller, one of the nineteenth-century founders of comparative religion: to know just one religion is to know none. This statement may seem a bit extreme—certainly there is much that can be known merely by learning about one religion. But Müller is making an important epistemological point. Given the generally subjective nature of religion, the question of *how* we know a religion—especially our own—is of concern. We might "know" perfectly well what faith is, or what God is, or what a particular ritual means, and that knowledge might be satisfactory for our own understanding of religion. But what meaning does such knowledge have for anyone else? Could it ever amount to *shared* knowledge? Could it hold up to an objective standard of truth?

For many people, subjective knowledge regarding religion is adequate—it fulfills their personal religious needs. But for Müller, and for many others who endeavor to be not only religious individuals but also students of religion, subjective knowledge is not adequate. We need to share our knowledge. We need to strive toward objectivity (even if total objectivity with regard to religion—or to any other subject matter—is not possible). Otherwise our claims of truth regarding religion are not valid for anyone but us.

The comparative approach offers a potent means of gaining a more objective perspective on religions. Knowing many religions, not just one, allows us to map out the terrain and thereby to situate each religion relative to the others.

Of course the desire to gain academic understanding is not the only reason people study the world's religions. Personal understanding is also important, and on that level, too, the comparative approach has much to offer. Our own religion can become more intelligible and meaningful when we reflect on it in the light of other religions. For some people, the religious quest extends across the boundaries of traditions, where alternative features are explored, some to be adopted and others to be left behind.

Methods and Challenges of Comparing Religions

When we attempt to understand other cultures, we necessarily do so from the perspective of our own culture. This poses the risks of bias and of misunderstanding due to barriers of language and other cultural differences. Comparing religions is therefore a difficult task, and it demands attention to certain methodological issues.

Chapter 1 of the student text notes the importance of empathy in the study of world religions. Empathy is especially important when comparing religions across cultures, and not just for the sake of respecting other people. Empathy is essential for maintaining academic integrity. Only through seeing the phenomena of a religion from the perspective of those within that religion are we able to understand it with any degree of accuracy.

Obviously religions do not stand still, but continue to grow and change through history. Thus to describe a tradition comprehensively, it is necessary to proceed historically to some extent. This need further complicates the task of comparative studies, because it means we are comparing moving pictures rather than still photographs.

One common tendency—sometimes taking the form of a religious perspective—is to see all religions as ultimately saying the same thing. This possibility will be the focus in the concluding section of this article. For now it is important methodologically that we not lose sight of the distinctive aspects of each religion. This is only fair to the traditions, and mandatory if our study is to be of any use.

Other difficulties have sometimes plagued the comparative study of religions: the sloppy use (and overuse) of certain terms, such as *mysticism;* the varying dependability of accounts from inside participants; and bias, both positive and negative, in the accounts of outside observers. There is also the basic theoretical challenge of comparing across cultures: how can that be done when almost every means of comparison is culture specific?

Comparative religion is an imperfect science. But the same can be said of almost any human endeavor to understand human phenomena. (As we have noted, perfect objectivity in such matters seems impossible.) Still, the comparative study of religions is vital, and it becomes increasingly so as our global community becomes ever more tightly knit. As for its difficulties, we can add intellectual challenge as another compelling reason for undertaking the comparative task.

The Catholic Approach to the Study of Other Religions

Especially since the time of the Second Vatican Council, the Catholic Church has sought to foster an atmosphere of mutual understanding and cooperation among people of different religions through open, respectful dialogue. In his *Declaration on the Relation of the Church to Non-Christian Religions (Nostra Aetate,* 1965), Pope Paul VI clearly states that while acknowledging the differences between various faith traditions, the Catholic Church recognizes and affirms what is true and holy in other religions, treating them with reverence and respect.

At the same time, however, Pope John Paul II, in his encyclical *On the Mission of the Redeemer (Redemptoris Missio,* 1990), voices the Church's caution to avoid "a religious relativism which leads to the belief that 'one religion is as good as another'" (no. 36). While promoting an atmosphere of respect and collaboration between various religions, the Church must also remain true to its own belief and conviction that salvation comes through Jesus Christ and in the Church as the continued presence of Jesus in the world. Though seeking common ground between belief systems, authentic discourse must also acknowledge the very real differences that exist between religions. Denying this diversity fails to respect the uniqueness of another's beliefs as well as the uniqueness of our own, rendering such dialogue meaningless.

Even when there is substantial disagreement over beliefs, the Catholic Church upholds a respect for the sincerity, goodwill, and dignity of believers within other faiths. Furthermore, by virtue of the dignity possessed by all, the Catholic Church condemns any and all discrimination against members of other faith traditions as being incompatible with the Gospel (see *Nostra Aetate,* no. 5). Unfortunately, it must also be admitted that the language employed in Church documents can often come off in an exclusivist or harsh tone, obscuring the spirit of respect and cooperation they contain.

Essential to all of this is that although the Church maintains the unique role of Christ and the Catholic Church in the economy of salvation, the Church also promotes respectful dialogue with other faith traditions. It is hoped that through open communication and collaboration, people of differing faiths might come together to work toward the spiritual and material common good of all the world's people (see *Nostra Aetate,* no. 2). Twenty-five years after *Nostra Aetate,* the Pontifical Council for Inter-Religious Dialogue expressed the conviction that such open communication can also be a catalyst allowing one to grow in one's own faith:

> While keeping their identity intact, Christians must be prepared to learn and to receive from and through others the positive values of their traditions. Through dialogue they may be moved to give up ingrained prejudices, to revise preconceived ideas, and even sometimes to allow the understanding of their faith to be purified. *(Dialogue and Proclamation: Reflections and Orientations on Interreligious Dialogue and the Proclamation of the Gospel of Jesus Christ,* no. 49)

Rather than being viewed with an air of suspicion or an attitude of fear, interreligious dialogue should be embraced as an opportunity to not only grow in our understanding of others but also develop a deeper self-awareness and an appreciation of our own faith tradition. It is by studying other religions that we hope to eliminate those misunderstandings and biases that form obstacles to authentic dialogue and acceptance.

Though much progress has been made in recent decades to foster open dialogue and understanding among various faith traditions, it is essential that the leaders and believers within the world's various faith traditions remain steadfast in their dedication to a spirit of collaboration and authentic communication. In the April 2005 "Address of His Holiness Benedict XVI to the Delegates of Other Churches and Ecclesial Communities and of Other Religious Traditions," the newly elected Pope Benedict XVI applauds the strides made by Pope John Paul II toward interreligious dialogue and expresses his own commitment to promoting a spirit of ecumenism and cooperation.

Comparing Religious Answers

Chapter 1 of the student text offers an overview of the questions commonly asked of the religions. Here we compare various answers.

What Is the Human Condition?

Religions are perhaps most famous for describing God. But they also tell us a great deal about what it is to be *human*. Because answers regarding the human condition are generally closer to home, so to speak, than typical theological descriptions of God, this is a good place to begin our comparative study.

What Is a Human Being?

Western culture has long tended to regard a human being as being made up of both body and soul. To a great extent, Plato is responsible for shaping this perspective. According to Platonic dualism, reality consists of the material realm, which includes physical bodies, and the realm of Ideas, or Forms, which are entirely intellectual constructs knowable by the mind (or soul). The realm of Ideas is eternal and divine, whereas the realm of matter is temporary and not of lasting worth. With Platonic dualism as a guiding influence, most of Western culture came to conceive of the soul as eternal, created in each individual by God. The body, while also part of God's creation, is regarded as separate from the soul and doomed to die, even as the soul continues to exist.

How very normal, even obvious, has this conception of the human being been to most Westerners! Only recently has this dualism come under serious scrutiny, in part because of advances in neurophysiology, which tend to argue that the material brain is the primary seat of the mind (or soul). But in the light of our survey of world religions, we see that this Western conception is not so normal or obvious after all. Let us recall some Eastern perspectives.

First, let us look at the Confucian conception of self. Far from emphasizing the uniqueness or importance of the individual, Confucianism regards the self as part of a network of human relationships. Self-identity is based on a person's place within this network. There is no "soul" in the Western sense—that is, there is no immaterial essence individually fashioned by God. (For that matter, no "God" exists.)

Second, let us recall the predominant South Asian perspective, that the individual is but one part of a greater, even universal, reality. This is most apparent in the dominant form of Hinduism (including the school of Vedanta), which holds a monistic understanding of reality. The individual atman is part of the eternal Atman (or Brahman), a drop of water from the infinite ocean, destined to return to its source. This monistic perspective on the human being is very different from Western dualism.

We can cite other distinctive perspectives on the makeup of the human being: the Buddhist concept of *anatta* (no-self), the Jain pluralism of eternal souls *(jivas)* and matter *(ajiva),* the shared divine ancestry of Shinto, and so on. Let us continue to explore this issue by considering the closely related question of the basic disposition of human nature.

Are We Good or Are We Evil?

Some religions assert that human beings are by nature entirely and inevitably good. This became a basic teaching of Confucianism owing to the influence of Mencius, who taught that humans are naturally good, and that we commit evil actions only in violation of our true nature. Shinto emphasizes the basic goodness of human nature with its myth of divine ancestry. Born with a divine essence, people cannot actually be sinful. The Shinto focus on purification assures that the light of this divine essence will continue to shine.

The major Western religions also espouse the notion of a divine essence, without attributing it to a descent from gods or goddesses. (In the ancient West, however, this was a well-known motif; Homeric heroes, for example, have divine ancestors.) As God-given and eternal, the soul is commonly regarded as something of a divine essence. But does this imply that human nature is essentially good? The details vary from religion to religion (and from faction to faction within each religion), and to some extent the answers depend on semantics (for example, what is meant by *essentially?*). But in general, Western religions understand human nature to be good in a qualified sense. For Christianity, humanity's original goodness is qualified owing to the "fall" from innocence, all of which is symbolized by Adam and Eve and the original sin against God. Islam holds a different perspective on the qualified goodness of human nature, asserting that people are subject to *forgetfulness* regarding their original goodness. Muslims have their own interpretation of Adam and Eve to symbolize this perspective. This propensity to forget leads to sin; it is overcome through the practice of Islam.

In South Asian religion, this question of the basic goodness of human nature is quite complex due to the general tendency to distinguish the realm of ultimate reality from the this-worldly realm of *samsara.* Simply put, the distinction between good and evil has relevance only in *samsara.* It would hardly make sense, then, to assert that the atman is "good," when ultimately the atman is part of the realm that lies beyond any such qualification. Buddhism accentuates the point, asserting with its doctrine of *anatta* that "human nature" itself is but an illusion, and that in truth we have no individual essence. And yet ethics plays a central role in both Hinduism and Buddhism.

What Is Spiritual Perfection?

The human quest for spiritual perfection lies at the heart of all religious traditions. It is even plausible to assert that religions exist *because* of our need for spiritual perfection. The existence of religion, after all, does not depend on the existence of God or of heaven or hell. Religion is a human phenomenon, born of such human needs as conceptualizing ultimate reality or finding meaning in the face of death—in other words, seeking answers to life's most profound questions. At the center of those needs is our need for attaining spiritual perfection.

For most religions, spiritual perfection extends beyond this lifetime. We will consider this phenomenon shortly under the category of destiny. But typically some form of it is also attainable in this lifetime. We can categorize this type of spiritual perfection as transcendence. In fact, transcendence is commonly regarded as the distinguishing mark of religion. First and foremost, a religion serves to connect individuals to that which they perceive as being beyond the normal or mundane sphere of things. For the Western monotheistic religions, God is understood to be the ultimate manifestation of the transcendence. For some other religions, however, the transcendent is not necessarily understood as being above or outside of the individual or the world. As we will now explore, Buddhism and other Asian traditions offer clear examples of such forms of transcendence.

Experiences of Religious Transcendence

Some of the primary challenges of our human condition are classically expressed in the Buddha's experience of the Four Passing Sights: we get ill, we grow old, and we die. To meet these challenges adequately, the Buddha sought enlightenment. And in that state of perfect wisdom, he led a long life of joy and tranquillity, even as he grew old, and even as he died of illness.

Buddhist enlightenment is a clear-cut example of transcendence—of spiritual perfection in this life. So is its Jain counterpart, *kevala.* So is Hindu *samadhi,* the eighth and final stage of Yoga, in which the mind of the yogi is absorbed into the ultimate reality. South Asian religions also tend to emphasize such absorption into, or union with, ultimate reality, which generally is said to happen in this life. In East Asia, too, a similar form of transcendence is prevalent. For Taoism, it is being one with Tao, the manner of living perfected by the sage and characterized by simplicity and naturalness. For Zen, it is *satori,* the experience of enlightenment that sets one free from the bondage of ego.

Asian religions characteristically emphasize experiences of transcendence. Not coincidentally, they also tend to be oriented more toward mystical experiences in which ultimate reality is encountered within oneself or within nature.

What about the Western monotheistic religions? For one thing, they also sometimes manifest a mystical approach. Sufism, for example, is Islamic mysticism. It teaches a form of transcendence known as *al-fana,* the "extinction" of the person's sense of ego, triggering union with God. (A similar sort of union is experienced in Sikhism, which, like Sufism, combines monotheism with mysticism.) Certain forms of Judaism, the Kabbalah and Hasidism, teach a mystical approach to God, leading to similar types of experience. Mysticism has also been important to Christianity. Saint Teresa of Ávila and Saint John of the Cross were famous Christian mystics. But spiritual perfection for the living is not confined to the mystical strands of monotheistic religions. In Christianity, for example, the power of sin and death—basic challenges of the human condition—are overcome through faith in Christ. Christians are free to live in joy and peace, and to look forward to resurrection and the afterlife.

Transcendence of this last type, while perhaps not as dramatic or as experientially intense as *samadhi, satori,* or *al-fana,* is clearly a form of spiritual perfection attainable in this life. All religions, by virtue of providing answers to life's most problematic questions, offer some degree of transcendence. One of the most pressing of these questions involves a person's destiny after this life, and here the teachings on spiritual perfection take on new features.

What Is Our Destiny?

For Jews, Christians, and Muslims, the question of destiny is relatively straightforward. Death is followed by an afterlife, which will consist either of salvation or of condemnation. Time in the West is generally regarded as being linear, and human existence proceeds accordingly. People have one life to live, one death to die, one afterlife.

Generally speaking, then, Western religions teach of an afterlife, which is the final destiny of all. Even Homer believed this much, although his concept of the realm of Hades left little room for optimism in the face of death. The afterlife was the subject of much greater attention in Zoroastrianism, which established early on the distinction between heaven and hell, and introduced the concept of a judgment of the soul. Jewish, Christian, and Muslim perspectives on destiny illustrate further development of these ideas. Islam, with the Qur'an's vivid descriptions of both Paradise and Hell, and its great emphasis on the Day of Judgment, is especially concerned with the afterlife.

When we consider the cyclical time scheme prevalent in the East, the question of destiny gets much more complicated. Hindus and Buddhists believe that there are many lives to live, many deaths to die, many afterlives—and then, finally, an ultimate destiny. In Hinduism this is *moksha,* "liberation" from the realm of *samsara.* The Buddhist counterpart, *nirvana,* is quite similar. In both cases the ultimate destiny is a realm qualitatively removed from this realm of *samsara,* such that it is impossible to describe adequately. Does a person continue to "live" in *moksha?* Does *nirvana* even entail "existence" as we know it in this life? The traditions themselves admit that such questions cannot be answered. One thing, however, is made clear: individual existence vanishes upon entering *moksha* or *nirvana.* This is a crucial distinction from Western notions of destiny.

The question of destiny gets more complicated still. We can cite an example from American Indian religion. The Lakota believe in four souls. One of them is judged after death, either to be allowed to journey to the otherworld of the ancestors, or to be condemned to exist as a ghost on earth. Meanwhile the other three souls are reincarnated. East meets West, and in a religious system that likely predates any meaningful distinction between these two geographical categories!

Finally, it is notable that some religions simply do not concern themselves with what happens after death. Confucius, when one of his followers asked him about death, responded: "'You do not understand even life. How can you understand death?'" (Analects 11.12). For Taoism, death is simply a return to the primal unity of Tao, the counterbalance to life in this grand harmony of nature. (This is true of philosophical Taoism, the main subject of the textbook's chapter; religious, or popular, Taoism includes elaborate teachings on the afterlife, along with directives for attaining physical immortality in this life.) Zen, its focus fully on the present, neither affirms nor denies an afterlife. It holds that to distinguish between life and death would be to construct a false duality, when in truth there is only the simple unity of the here and now.

What Is the Nature of the World?

Thus far we have considered issues about human beings: the human condition, the quest for spiritual perfection, and human destiny. Another major question that we ask of the religions involves the world. What is its origin? Is the world real, ultimately, or is it illusory? Is it sacred and alive, or is it material and inert? And is the world a help or a hindrance to our religious quest? These are all questions of cosmology: the understanding of the nature of the cosmos (the word *cosmos* is Greek for "world" or "universe").

The Origin and Significance of the World

The Genesis account of Creation underlies the Jewish, Christian, and Muslim perspective on both the origin and the significance of the world. In just two chapters, Genesis sets forth an array of fundamental teachings: the world is created by God; it exists independently of God; there is only one inhabited Earth, populated by God's creations; the world is cherished by God as being "very good."

This last teaching has especially strong ramifications with respect to religion. For although the world is material (rather than living), it is sanctioned by God's blessing. Islam emphasizes this point by referring to the world as the cosmic Qur'an, a revelation of God's will.

The concept of a divinely created world that is good without qualification has a clear parallel in Shinto. Japan is believed to have been created by a primordial pair of *kami,* Izanagi and Izanami. Japan is inhabited by a great many other *kami,* such that the natural world is imbued with their sacred presence. In this respect the world of Shinto tends to be a living, sacred world, in contrast with the material world of Western monotheism.

A different cosmology is prevalent in South Asian religions, which understand the world as being of the realm of *samsara,* the wheel of rebirth. These traditions believe that the universe undergoes endlessly recurring cycles of creation and destruction. Within this cyclical time scheme, many worlds exist, with heavens, hells, earths, and other inhabited spheres. This realm of *samsara* is characterized by what the Hindus call *maya,* or cosmic illusion. That is to say, the realm of *samsara* is not ultimately real. Buddhism expresses the same general perspective with its second mark of existence, *anicca* (impermanence). According to this principle, all things are continually changing; there is no underlying reality, no permanent essence. Jainism sets forth some interesting (though slight) modifications to the general South Asian cosmology. It refers to the universe as the *loka,* an immeasurably vast, yet finite, space depicted as having the shape of a giant man. The *loka* is eternal, never having been created and never to cease existing. And yet the realms of existence within the *loka* are in a constant cyclical process of creation and improvement, and decay and destruction. The Jains carefully chart the stages of these cycles; presently we are in the next-to-the-last stage of decay.

What is the origin of this "unreal" world of South Asian religions? That is a difficult question. Jainism simply asserts that the *loka* has existed forever. The Buddha dismissed this sort of question as not tending toward edification—he believed that people need to overcome the immediate problem of their own suffering, not to decipher the mysteries of the universe. Hinduism tends to regard the universe as a great mystery, somehow the result of the creative energies of Brahman, the ultimate reality, which is itself a mystery. Farther east, the Taoists, while not dismissing the universe as somehow unreal, similarly consider its existence a mystery. The Tao, entirely unfathomable, is the "mother" of the universe.

We can see how straightforward, detailed, and revealing the first two chapters of Genesis are, compared with Eastern cosmology in general. The basic distinctive patterns carry through to views regarding humanity's place in the world.

Our Place in the World

South Asia offers a rather stunning perspective on our place in this world: it is not our rightful place. We need to leave it, to be released from the bondage of *samsara*. But in the meantime, we are here and need to make the most of it. Hinduism explicitly teaches an attitude of patience with respect to living in *samsara*. It assumes that for most people, *moksha* will not occur for many lifetimes. Hinduism sets forth *kama, artha,* and *dharma* as legitimate goals of life, appropriate for everyone who is not genuinely ready for the rigors of the goal of *moksha*. But in spite of this, Hinduism and the other South Asian religions do not embrace this world as something sacred, nor do they celebrate humanity's place in it. They see the world as a temporary vessel, transitory and impermanent, destined eventually to be destroyed.

For Jews, Christians, and Muslims, God has not only created this world—a unique and very good world—but has also given us "dominion" over the plants and animals. This principle of having dominion, commonly known as stewardship, continues to shape the basic Western perspective on our place in the world, whether that perspective is still recognized as religious or not. It is our responsibility to care for the world, and, in turn, the world is here to provide for us. We are its superiors, spiritually speaking.

East Asian religions offer yet another perspective. They revere the world as a spiritual entity, permeated with the divine. For Shinto, the world is inhabited by innumerable *kami,* and human beings dwell humbly among them. For Taoism, nature itself is primary, the unfathomed reservoir of Tao. The best we can do is to live in perfect harmony with the way of nature; we can never be its superiors. It is instructive to compare this hands-off perspective of Taoist naturalism with Western environmentalism. Having tampered with nature, the West typically strives to fix things through technology, in keeping with the principle of stewardship. The *Tao Te Ching* at times seems to have anticipated a modern Western readership:

> Do you think you can take over the universe and improve it?
> I do not believe it can be done.
>
> (Chapter 29)

What Is Ultimate Reality, and How Is It Revealed?

Perhaps the most famous of all questions to be asked of the religions is, What is God? Of course, to study world religions comprehensively, we need to be more inclusive than this, and so we ask, What is the divine, or the ultimate reality? A second question, arguably just as relevant, asks how this ultimate reality is revealed to human beings.

Various Conceptions of the Divine

We can begin by charting the categories of theism, which is the general belief in the existence of a god or gods.

Polytheism, the belief in multiple gods, is exemplified in the religions of ancient Greece and Rome. The gods are anthropomorphic—depicted as male and female, as subject to typically human emotions, as falling in love and marrying. They are known to involve themselves with human beings, sometimes having children with them (such is the ancestry of Achilles and some of the other Homeric heroes). These anthropomorphic gods are not all-powerful, although most polytheistic pantheons have a clear leader, such as the Greek

Zeus or the Roman Jupiter. Among ancient religions, polytheism tended to be the norm. Today polytheism is most evident in Hinduism, which is emphatically polytheistic (with its 330 million gods). Because most Hindus are at the same time monistic, this form of polytheism is rather distinct from that of the ancient West. (It is notable that Neoplatonism, a later development combining Greek philosophy and religion, bears striking resemblances in this respect to Hinduism.)

Given this prevalence of polytheism in the ancient world, it is not surprising that the monotheistic religions have tended to place great emphasis on their conception of divinity, thus distinguishing themselves from their polytheistic neighbors. When Zarathustra asserted that Ahura Mazda was the one and only God, he was departing radically from the norm (which resembled the polytheism of Hinduism). The central theological statement of Judaism is the Shema: "Hear, O Israel! The LORD is our God, the LORD alone" (Deut. 6:4, Tanakh). Islam's Shahada, which sets forth the oneness of Allah (the God), is similarly central. In general, the God of monotheism is believed to be omnipotent, omniscient, and omnipresent. This God is also usually thought of as personal but aloof—as wholly other, completely distinct from human beings. Some religions such as Sikhism, however, believe God to be immanent, or indwelling. A similar form of immanent monotheism is prevalent among the mystical strands of Judaism, Christianity, and Islam.

A third category of theism is pantheism, which conceives of the divine as being present throughout creation, and includes a broad spectrum of beliefs. Examples are Shinto, with its ubiquitous *kami,* and the early Roman religion, for which the *numina* were supernatural powers inhabiting the gods, humans and their possessions, and a wide variety of natural entities. Primal religions are commonly pantheistic. For example, the ultimate reality of the Lakota, Wakan Tanka, comprises sixteen separate deities, related to the four compass directions. Such an intimate connection with nature is typical of pantheism.

Some religions conceive of ultimate reality as other than a god or gods. Their belief system is called nontheism (which is not necessarily atheism—the outright denial of belief in a god or gods). Hindu monism is clearly nontheistic. It makes no sense to describe Brahman as a monotheist would describe God, because by definition Brahman is indescribable. Besides, monism understands all reality to be ultimately one. Theism, by contrast, conceives of the divine as being somehow distinct from humans and creation. Buddhism denies even the monistic claim that reality is one, insisting instead that there is no real essence of things or of human beings—no Brahman or Atman. Sometimes *nirvana* is identified as the divine or the ultimate reality of Buddhism. Even so, Buddhism remains nontheistic. For like Brahman, *nirvana* is indescribable. Furthermore, *nirvana* cannot be distinguished from the individual who experiences it—*nirvana* is the experience, and in this experience individuality ceases to be.

The religions Taoism and Confucianism also hold nontheistic conceptions of divinity. According to the *Tao Te Ching,* Tao is the ultimate source of reality, an unseen force that is both the origin and the order of the universe. Like Brahman, Tao is ultimately beyond human understanding. But unlike Hindu monism, Taoism does not assert that all reality essentially is Tao. This is nontheism of a different sort, one that is more difficult to categorize.

Tao is also of basic significance for Confucianism, although here the meaning is confined to the moral order of the universe, the Way that people ought to follow. Confucius also referred to Heaven, a concept similar, and perhaps even identical, to Tao. It is the universal moral force. Because Confucius seems not to have conceived of Tao or Heaven as having any metaphysical import, his conception of ultimate reality is not altogether clear. It can be said that the grand harmony of moral relationships, which includes Heaven, is at the very least the foundation of Confucian life.

Forms of Revelation

Ultimate reality is revealed in a wide variety of ways, although in general those ways are patterned after the two basic categories we have been considering: theism and nontheism.

Revelation in theistic religions includes the dramatic events in which human beings find themselves in the presence of the deity. Examples abound: Guru Nanak being escorted from his morning bath to the court of God; Zarathustra being brought as a disembodied soul to Ahura Mazda; Moses standing before the burning bush; Jeremiah receiving a call to be a prophet; Paul experiencing conversion on a road to Damascus; Muhammad ascending from Jerusalem to heaven, into the presence of Allah.

These are well-known examples, some of them marking the beginnings of new religions. But more mundane versions of the same sort occur rather commonly. German theologian Rudolf Otto, in his book *The Idea of the Holy* (1917), classified this type of religious experience in terms that have become famous. Otto describes an encounter with the divine, which he calls the Holy, as a numinous (from the Latin *numen*) experience. It is characterized by inspiring *mysterium tremendum et fascinans:* "a feeling of mystery, both fearful (to be trembled at) and fascinating." The Holy thus repels even as it attracts.

Encountering God in such a numinous experience is perhaps the most notable form of revelation in theism. But several other forms are also of great importance: prophetic revelation, a central motif in Israelite religion and in Western monotheism generally, especially Islam; oracles, common in ancient Greece and Rome; and providence, the concept that God is directly involved in guiding and caring for creation, always a focus of Judaism. Divine revelation is also believed to be contained in myth, or sacred stories, some of which have been written down over time in the form of scriptures.

Ultimate reality is also revealed when God takes human form, and in a manner quite distinct from the anthropomorphism characteristic of, for example, Greek polytheism. God in human form becomes a paradigm for people to revere and to follow. Of course, the Incarnation of God is the heart of Christianity. Other religions also revere the divine in human form. Hinduism has its *avatars,* the most popular of whom are Krishna and Rama; they are worshiped by millions. Whereas Christianity believes that Jesus Christ is unique, Hinduism reveres a great many incarnations of the divine. In fact, the number is steadily growing. Mahatma Gandhi, for example, is now regarded by some as an *avatar.*

These various forms of revelation are also experienced in another manner through the sacred narratives that relate the events and divine figures to ordinary worshipers. The means of transmitting scared narratives has varied through the ages and across cultures, from oral storytelling to scriptures, to popular literature, and, recently, to the array of electronic forms of communication. Whatever the means of transmission, sacred narratives have the power to inspire and transform individuals through their accounts of revered figures and events.

For nontheistic religions, the ultimate reality is revealed (if *revealed* is even the appropriate word) experientially, specifically, in mystical experience. This contrasts sharply with the numinous experience of the Holy as described by Otto. Rather than being a fearful encounter with the "wholly other" (as Otto refers to the Holy), the mystical experience is generally characterized as being tranquil. It is also typically an experience of oneness, devoid of any distinction between self and the rest of reality. In Hindu *moksha* the individual atman is dispersed in the infinite ocean of Atman, the eternal essence. In Buddhist *nirvana,* self-awareness disappears; all that remains is the experience.

Are all mystical experiences ultimately the same? This is the subject of much debate. To a great extent, their ineffable nature prevents us from knowing. People who have had mystical experiences inevitably lack the words to describe them fully. In any event, certain basic distinctions seem to exist among such experiences, depending on the religion. For example, mystical experiences within monotheistic religions do tend to involve encountering God, who remains distinct from the individual. Sufis, for instance, however much their experience of *al-fana* is one of union with ultimate reality, still understand Allah in monotheistic terms.

Comparative mysticism, a major component of the comparative study of religions, illustrates the usefulness but also the difficulties of this field. The intensely subjective nature of the mystical experience to some extent belies meaningful analysis. Still, the most effective means of knowing about these experiences is to compare them.

Conclusion: Do All Religions Say the Same Thing?

This introduction to comparative religion merely touches the surface. It is hoped that it at least illustrates the intriguing and compelling potential of comparative religion, while also bringing to light its complexity and some of its challenges. We can perhaps emphasize all these points by concluding with a final question: Do the religions ultimately agree or disagree?

Many people assert that religions, while differing on the surface owing to unique cultural and historical settings, essentially say the same thing. This perennial philosophy, as it is sometimes called, would say, for example, that we share the same basic human condition and that there is really only one ultimate reality. But can we then conclude that all religions ultimately agree?

One useful approach to this basic question is to consider the analogy of ascending a mountain. The mountain represents the challenges that each person faces given the human condition. Do we all share the same human condition? It does not matter (for the sake of the analogy, at least); the mountain has different sides, each with a potentially different set of challenges. The summit represents ultimate reality, and the ascent toward the summit is the quest for spiritual perfection. Are we all heading for the same summit? We cannot know, because we have not all finished our ascent. The summit (or summits) is in fact veiled in clouds. Its true nature cannot be known fully from here below. About all we can do is depend on the reports of others who we believe have reached the top. As for the religions, they are represented by the various means by which we make the ascent: choosing a path, donning the proper gear, honing the required skills, and putting forth the necessary effort. These means are fashioned in large part by those who have made the ascent before us.

Do these means—the religions—deliver us to the same summit? The mountain analogy does not reveal that. It maps out the mystery, but leaves the mystery unanswered. Here we have an analogy for comparative religion itself. While not able—nor intended—to answer once and for all the deepest questions about religions, it maps out the terrain. In doing so it helps foster understanding not only of the religions but also of the people who adhere to them.

Comparative Religion and the Ethical Dimension: An Example

What follows is an example showing how a comparative study of the ethical dimension of the religions in this text might look. It is hoped that this brief examination will provide a framework from which your students can begin their conversation about the world's religions.

Religions have much to offer regarding ethics: how we are to act while living in this world. Along with providing detailed guidelines for behavior, ethical teachings also tend to be closely linked with the issue of spiritual perfection and the related issue of salvation. The destiny of the Buddhist, for example, is tied to *karma,* the moral law of cause and effect. *Karma* brings about rebirth and determines the basic dispositions of the new person. Enlightenment and *nirvana* can be attained only when *karma* is overcome and the chain reaction of worldly desires and deeds is extinguished.

A religion's ethical teachings are also closely linked with its basic perspective on human nature—whether we are good or evil. Most religions consider us good, or at least redeemable. For these religions, ethical ideals and paradigms of ethical perfection are potent means of inspiring good behavior.

Ideals and Models of Ethical Perfection

Jesus Christ taught that we should love even our enemies. His actions, reaching out to society's outcasts and caring for the sick and downtrodden, teach this ideal perhaps even more powerfully than his words. The Buddhist ideal of compassion is practically an identical teaching. Stories abound of the compassion of the Buddha, both in his life as Gautama and in previous lives. The *bodhisattvas,* those who have vowed not to enter *nirvana* until "the last blade of grass" becomes enlightened, provide additional paradigms of the perfect practice of compassion. Jainism teaches *ahimsa* (nonviolence) as its ethical ideal. Mahavira and the other *tirthankaras* are models of nonviolent living. So too are the Jain ascetics, who wander the roads and paths of India as living paradigms for the laity to admire and aspire to.

Ethical perfection in Hinduism is regarded as one of four legitimate goals of life. *Dharma* involves the observance of traditional Hindu laws and customs, along with an ongoing concern for the world. *Dharma* has been exemplified most recently by Mahatma Gandhi, for whom religion and social service were inextricably linked. Are Hindus who pursue the other goals of life somehow released from ethical responsibility? Not at all. In its more general meaning, *dharma* is "ethical duty," and it applies to all Hindus. In Hinduism, as in Buddhism, *karma* is an integral aspect of the quest for salvation, and *karma* is based in *dharma.* When ethical perfection is embraced as the primary goal of life, however, *dharma* is no longer regarded as a mere duty. It becomes an opportunity and is carried out with joy.

Ethics is the central aspect of Confucianism, the means by which social harmony is maintained. Little wonder, then, that it elaborates on the ideal of ethical perfection by setting forth multiple teachings. *Jen,* the supreme virtue of benevolence, is similar to Christian love and Buddhist compassion. A primary component of *jen* is *shu,* reciprocity, which corresponds to the Golden Rule. It is notable that Confucius did not go so far as to advocate loving one's enemy (which was the teaching of another ancient Chinese philosopher, Mo

Tzu). Virtue, Confucius said, should be repaid with virtue, but hatred with uprightness (see Analects 14.36). Confucius also emphasized the power of moral example. The *chun-tzu,* the "mature person" or "gentleman," is the paradigm of ethical perfection, embodying the ideals of *jen* and *shu.* The *chun-tzu* leads through manifesting *te,* virtue as shown through the power of moral example.

The religions we have considered so far seem to be quite similar with respect to ideals and models of ethical perfection. Even Hindu *dharma,* though grounded more thoroughly in customs specific to one culture, aspires ultimately toward a universal perspective of love and concern similar to Confucian *jen,* Buddhist compassion, and Christian love. (One of Gandhi's favorite spiritual texts was the Sermon on the Mount, in which Jesus teaches love of one's enemy.) Are there any exceptions to this general agreement on ethical perfection?

Taoism, while not necessarily rejecting the ideal of ethical perfection, certainly approaches it in a unique way. In its insistence on the relativity of values, Taoism rejects the notion of absolute goodness. Good and evil exist, says the *Tao Te Ching,* only insofar as we recognize them as opposites. Ethical perfection for Taoism is a matter not of doing "good," but rather of living in accord with nature. The supreme virtue of Taoism is *wu-wei,* "nonaction"—hardly an injunction to go forth and do good deeds. Does it therefore follow that the Taoist sage, when judged by the standards of other religions, would come across as being less than ethical? Not necessarily. After all, living in accord with nature—in harmony with Tao—might indeed inspire the same degree of ethical perfection as loving perfectly, or practicing infinite compassion. This issue gets us to the heart of comparing religions and seems to extend beyond the limits of human understanding.

Rules of Ethical Behavior

Along with ideals and models of ethical perfection, religions usually provide rules of ethical behavior. Again, Taoism tends to be an exception—the way of nature is too spontaneous for rules and the social contrivances used to enforce them.

Typically a tension exists between ethical ideals and the ethical rules that apply to the specific circumstances of life. Christianity teaches people to love their neighbor as themselves. But how exactly are they to apply this ideal? To a great extent, love is an attitude or disposition rather than an applied rule of behavior. Islam, while revering Christ and his teachings, argues that humans require more specific guidelines in order to act according to the will of God. Islam sees the Qur'an and the Sunna as providing the applied ethical rules that the New Testament lacks. The Shari'a, or divine law, is an all-encompassing collection of rules that sets forth in detail how a Muslim is to live.

Underlying both Christianity and Islam are the ethical teachings of Judaism. Most famous among its rules for behavior are the Ten Commandments, with such injunctions as honoring one's parents, and not killing, stealing, or committing adultery. Rules like these are condoned by most religions; they tend to be universal in scope. We can name other sets of similar ethical teachings: the five forbidden acts of Hindu Yoga; the Five Precepts of Buddhism; the Five Lesser Vows of Jainism (the laity's version of the more rigorous Five Great Vows, which apply only for ascetics).

Are all important ethical teachings universal? Great philosophers like Immanuel Kant have argued that they ought to be, based on our common human faculty of reason. But a comparative study of religions illustrates that they are not. The ethical teachings of Hinduism, for example, are grounded in *dharma,* a deeply traditional set of norms thought to have been delivered by ancient sages (the *rishis*). *Dharma* instructs women to maintain obedience to men. It divides Hindu society into castes, and carefully governs the relationships between their members. Obviously such ethical teachings are not universal. Examples of such culturally specific norms could surely be found in every tradition. Confucianism, for instance, sets forth the Five Constant Relationships, fortifying the superior position of elders and of men, and emphasizing the virtue of being "filial." Confucius based his teachings regarding *li*—proper behavior as sacred ritual—on his own understanding of ancient Chinese customs. Confucius's teachings about *li* are intentionally specific to that culture; they are not universal.

And that is how a comparison of the ethical dimension works. Though it may take your students some time to begin to think in terms of comparative analysis, by the end of the course, they should be able to easily discuss similarities and differences between the religions covered in the student text.

APPENDIX 5

Worldviews: Religions and Their Relatives

World Religions: A Voyage of Discovery considers—appropriately enough—"religions." But exactly what is it about those many traditions that make them religions? As we outlined in chapter 1 of the student text (and dealt with at length in appendix 4 of this manual), each tradition provides its own answers to a common set of questions. And all traditions are composed of the same dimensions. It is therefore reasonable to group the traditions together in a single category.

On close analysis, however, we can see that this category has fuzzy boundaries. Other traditions and systems usually not regarded as religions provide answers to the same set of questions, and are composed of similar dimensions. To avoid the ambiguities resulting from this fuzziness, let us employ a label more inclusive than *religion* for our category. A popular choice is *worldview.*

Ninian Smart is a leading scholar in the field of world religions. He has been instrumental in establishing widespread use both of the dimensional approach and of the term *worldview.* He understands worldviews to include both religions and "secular ideologies" like nationalism, Marxism, and humanism. His reasoning for including such ideologies is twofold:

> In undertaking a voyage into the world's religions we should not define religion too narrowly. It is important for us to recognize secular ideologies as part of the story of human worldviews. It is artificial to divide them too sharply from religions, partly because they sometimes function in society like religions, and partly because the distinction between religious and secular beliefs and practices is a modern Western one and does not represent the way in which other cultures categorize human values. (*The World's Religions,* p. 9)

In this appendix we will explore two examples of prevalent modern worldviews: nationalism and humanism. Along with closely resembling the traditional religions, these worldviews compete with them to varying degrees. But they can also function hand in hand with the traditional religions. Nationalism, for example, has at times served as a potent vehicle for religions, and vice versa. And humanism clearly illustrates the ambiguous distinction between religions and secular ideologies mentioned by Smart. Most religious traditions would agree wholeheartedly with humanism's great emphasis on ethics, among other qualities.

See *Primary Source Readings in World Religions* (Saint Mary's Press, 2009) for the selection titled "Parable of a Madman," as well as the accompanying leader's guide for suggestions about how to use this reading in your study of secular humanism.

Nationalism: Living and Dying for *La Patrie*

Nationalism is a bond shared by a group of people who are attached to a particular land and to such things as language, history, and culture. It is characterized by a sense of devotion to the nation on the part of the citizenry, to the extent of providing them a cause for which to live and to die.

Today we tend to take nationalism for granted; a nation's self-identity and its citizens' relationship with that identity are simply facts of life. But nationalism is actually a recent phenomenon. Based philosophically on the ideas of Jean-Jacques Rousseau (1712–1778) concerning the organic nature of a people, nationalism took concrete political form during the French Revolution in 1789. Having suddenly cast aside the ruling system of monarchy, the leaders of the revolution embraced the idea of each citizen's living and dying for *la patrie,* "the fatherland."

As a worldview, nationalism has much in common with religions. In the United States, for example, various nationalistic features are now commonly considered part of a civil religion (a concept developed by sociologists Phillip Hammond and Robert Bellah). Influenced by Christianity and Judaism, this civil religion is a tradition all its own, with unique religious aspects. Its myths include stories of the founding of the country. George Washington, Abraham Lincoln, and Martin Luther King Jr. are among its saints. Holy days include the Fourth of July and Memorial Day, and civil religion's many rituals are especially apparent on these occasions. With these and many other religious aspects, civil religion has the power to unify the populace.

Nationalism's Answers to Religious Questions

As a worldview, nationalism provides answers to the various religious questions considered in the student text and in appendix 4 of this manual. This section outlines some of nationalism's answers to those questions.

There are many forms of nationalism—in fact, as many forms as there are nations. (In this respect nationalism as a category is not exactly correlative with an individual religion like Buddhism or Islam.) We will focus somewhat on the civil religion of the United States. To a large extent, however, the examples given here have counterparts in most other varieties of nationalism.

What Is the Human Condition?

Generally speaking, nationalism does not set out to explain what it is to be a human being—it does not offer philosophical descriptions of the self or the soul. But to some extent, nationalism defines the meaning of the individual's existence in terms of the national cause. Self-identity is shaped by such things as war efforts and nationwide attempts to preserve energy. Great achievements of the nation tend to enhance self-esteem. For example, when the U.S. hockey team accomplished its "miracle on ice" at the 1980 Winter Olympics by defeating the Soviet Union and going on to win the gold medal, the nation erupted in celebration. Individuals just seemed to feel good about being Americans.

What Is Spiritual Perfection?

For nationalism, spiritual perfection is achieving a degree of patriotism such that one is ready to sacrifice individual interests for the sake of the national cause. Sometimes this means the "ultimate sacrifice" of dying for one's country; the national cause transcends one's individual interest in self-preservation. National cemeteries are filled with the graves of martyrs—soldier-heroes who have given their lives for the nation.

The quest for spiritual perfection typically does not require sacrificing one's life. The essential thing is a commitment to the nation beyond the concerns of self. This quest may best be summed up in the famous words of President John F. Kennedy, "Ask not what your country can do for you—ask what you can do for your country."

What Is Our Destiny?

Nationalism does not promise the individual an afterlife in the typically religious sense. But to die for one's country is to gain a sort of symbolic immortality. Thousands of Americans pay respects every day at the Tomb of the Unknowns. Many Americans also feel compelled to honor or memorialize the innocent people killed in the terrorist attacks of September 11, 2001. Those martyrs may not be known by their individual identities, but they will be remembered for their ultimate sacrifice.

Sometimes the perception of a collective destiny of the nation is significant. The Manifest Destiny of the United States is a concept based on the belief that God has ordained that the nation thrive as a rightful home for freedom and justice. Such a perception further strengthens commitment to the national cause, thus encouraging sacrifice to the nation. The individual's destiny comes to be identified with the nation's.

What Is the Nature of the World?

Each nation has its own environmental policy. Should the environment be protected at all costs, even if slow economic expansion results? Or is it appropriate to exploit the nation's natural resources for the sake of economic well-being? These are fundamental questions. The ways that nations answer them reveal to some extent national perspectives on the nature of the world.

Whatever the environmental policy, nationalism tends to foster the belief that a nation's own land is somehow special. In some cases—Japan, for example—the land is regarded as sacred. Environmentalism itself generally has patriotic overtones. In the United States, many are committed to protecting "America the Beautiful" for future generations of Americans. Environmentalism is an important part of the national cause.

What Is Ultimate Reality, and How Is It Revealed?

As we have seen, nationalism does not attempt to explain philosophically the nature of the self. Nor does it set forth doctrines explicitly intended to describe ultimate reality. It would be a stretch to ascribe to nationalism such terms as *theistic* or *monistic*.

Still, in some ways nationalism seems to involve itself with conceptions of ultimate reality. Some examples serve as interesting analogies to the perspectives of traditional religions. The Marxism-Leninism practiced by the Soviet Union and other nations throughout most of the twentieth century seems to have had its gods, namely, Marx and Lenin. In the People's Republic of China, the same can be said of Chairman Mao. These men are revered as creators of new nations, as founts of sacred wisdom, and as saints whose significance lives on long after their death. Mao's Red Book is an established sacred text of China. For decades Lenin's embalmed body lay in Red Square to be worshiped by throngs of passersby.

It could be argued that a national cause for which one is expected to die is itself the ultimate reality. As we saw in appendix 4, even with respect to the traditional religions, the category of ultimate reality admits a wide variety of concepts.

The Seven Dimensions of Nationalism

Now we take a slightly different tack and consider how nationalism compares with the religions with respect to the seven dimensions.

The Experiential Dimension

Nationalism evokes a wide range of emotions. People feel pride in the history and achievements of the nation. Scenic beauty and symbolic monuments inspire love. When troubles beset the nation, citizens feel pained and sometimes ashamed. On the other hand, victory in war or in sporting events causes spirits to soar in joyous celebration. When Brazil won soccer's World Cup in 1994, some people believed that the great positive effect on the emotions of the populace would improve the nation's economic productivity. With the success of the United States in the Persian Gulf War in 1991, President George Bush's approval ratings soared to record heights, and many Americans took great pride in the nation's achievement. Not much later, however, the nation's mood and priorities changed, and the year after the war, Bush was defeated in the presidential election.

The Mythic Dimension

Myths—sacred stories answering questions of origins and serving as sources of sacred truth—are common and important aspects of nationalism. They help bond people of a nation together by conveying a shared history of origins and of collective achievements. In the United States, history textbooks tell of the country's founders and their noble and daring deeds. Sometimes the factual nature of those accounts is questioned. Nevertheless, the stories of the founders present values that are fundamental to the nation.

Other nations have their own myths, many of which are set in the distant past. Germans, for example, possess a reservoir of ancient Teutonic myths, some of which were put to music by Richard Wagner in his mid-nineteenth-century operatic cycle *The Ring of the Nibelung*. In the early nineteenth century, Jacob and Wilhelm Grimm collected German fairy tales, such as "Snow White" and "Little Red Riding Hood," to record the spirit of the people.

All such myths unify a nation's populace and strengthen ties to land, history, language, and culture.

The Doctrinal Dimension

Each nation has chosen one or more ideologies, such as democracy or communism or capitalism, on which it bases its government and way of life.

Specific beliefs and teachings are spelled out in important doctrinal statements. The United States has the Declaration of Independence, the Constitution, and the Bill of Rights (to name but a few). Like Christianity's Nicene Creed or Buddhism's Four Noble Truths, these teachings are foundational to the very nature of the nation.

The Ethical Dimension

In their laws nations answer the basic ethical question, What is right and what is wrong? National legal codes often provide specific ethical instruction that goes well beyond that of traditional religions.

Nations also tend to hold general ethical values, such as patriotism. For example, even if it is not against the law to burn the nation's flag, it is usually considered unethical to do so. Taxes are to be paid, and military and other service is to be given when appropriate. Depending on the nation, specific ethical values are deeply cherished. In the United States and other Western countries, those values include freedom and justice.

The Ritual Dimension

The ongoing celebration of the nation is punctuated with numerous rituals. Saluting and caring for the flag, singing the national anthem, traveling to national shrines—all are performed in the manner of religious rituals. Nations also have their holy days (or holidays). In the United States, Memorial Day, the Fourth of July, Veterans Day, and Thanksgiving are especially sacred. Certain events involving the president or other officials are marked by formal ceremony and protocol. Even voting, considered the responsibility of a patriotic citizen, is in some ways a ritual.

The Social Dimension

Nations are communities based on a shared history and culture. Citizens feel themselves to be part of the larger group.

In various ways nations establish and maintain communal organizations. For instance, governments are hierarchical, the public sector is distinguished from the private, and citizenship status is usually not granted to everyone.

The Material Dimension

With the material dimension, as with most of the other dimensions, examples are almost too abundant to count. The many material aspects—sacred entities, art, and architecture—of nationalism include national parks, the flag, historic buildings, monuments, national cemeteries, patriotic paintings and sculptures, and the national anthem and other musical compositions.

Humanism: Spirituality Without the Supernatural

The worldview of humanism understands the good of humanity on earth to be the highest purpose of life. Human beings, then, along with the natural world they inhabit, are understood to be the ultimate reality. There is no belief in a god or an afterlife. Instead, life is believed to be significant and entirely worth living in the here and now, as judged by human standards of goodness. Humanists are committed to the ongoing improvement of the human situation, especially in the realm of ethics. Reason and the scientific method are the primary tools for ascertaining ethical truth and for making the world a better place.

Humanism dates back to Athens in the fifth century BC, and the dictum of the philosopher Protagoras: "Man is the measure of all things." The humanist tradition flowered in the European Renaissance and in the Enlightenment. Today it enjoys a rather large following, as evinced by organizations like the American Humanist Association, and journals such as the *Humanist* and *Religious Humanism.*

Humanism is primarily a Western tradition, and in fact has drawn much from the ethical teachings of Judaism and Christianity. But it is a very broad phenomenon, with various roots and a wide array of forms (Confucianism, for example, is considered by some to be a form of humanism).

To narrow our scope to a more manageable one, we will draw on one of these forms—humanistic psychology—as our primary example. Two of its main figures are Erich Fromm and Abraham Maslow. These men of Jewish heritage had both become thoroughgoing humanists who denied the need for believing in God, an afterlife, or anything else commonly regarded as the supernatural. However, they believed strongly in the human need for spiritual fulfillment. Fromm advocated a "humanistic religion," which aimed at overcoming the ego, loving others, and living life to its fullest capacity, in order to realize our highest potential. Maslow also advocated religion in its healthy sense, which he believed was centered in the "peak-experience," an intense and illuminating event common to mystics and prophets, and to human beings generally.

Humanism's Answers to Religious Questions

Humanism uses reason and scientific method in its quest for truth. It rejects religious revelation and the claims to authority made by religious traditions. Still, this does not eliminate religion from the realm of humanist inquiry or interest. Indeed, as Maslow pointed out, religious questions are entirely appropriate for scientific inquiry:

> What the more sophisticated scientist is now in the process of learning is that though he must disagree with most of the answers to the religious questions which have been given by organized religion, it is increasingly clear that the religious questions themselves—and religious quests, the religious yearnings, the religious needs themselves—are perfectly respectable scientifically, that they are rooted deep in human nature, that they can be studied, described, examined in a scientific way, and that the churches were trying to answer perfectly sound human questions. Though the answers were not acceptable, the questions themselves were and are perfectly acceptable, and perfectly legitimate. (*Religions, Values, and Peak-Experiences,* p. 18)

Let us see how Maslow, Fromm, and humanism in general answer the basic religious—and basically human—questions that we have been examining in this manual and in the student text.

What Is the Human Condition?

Humanists generally embrace the theory of evolution (and reject creationism) and therefore understand humans as being part of the greater whole that is the natural world. This in no way devalues humanity. In fact, according to

Maslow, evolution has provided human beings with a higher nature that is part of their biological makeup. This higher, transcendent nature, said Maslow, is our human essence. We have the potential to realize, or actualize, this higher nature. This, according to Maslow, is the task that confronts us in our human condition: to make actual that which is for most of us merely potential.

Fromm similarly believed that the true task of human life is to realize our highest potential. True to his existentialist leanings, Fromm described our human condition as characterized by inescapable dichotomies. We have both an animal nature and a rational, imaginative mind, and we thus are trapped between fundamental limitations and abundant possibilities. To deal with this predicament, Fromm believed, we need a frame of orientation and an object of devotion. That is to say, we need religion, and more precisely, humanistic religion. This is the pathway to salvation.

What Is Spiritual Perfection?

Like Fromm and Maslow, humanists in general believe that spiritual perfection lies in realizing our human potential, and thereby in living life to its fullest. They do not anticipate an afterlife. Spiritual perfection, for them, is to be achieved in the here and now, in this world.

As we have seen, for Fromm, spiritual perfection was achieved through humanistic religion (*humanistic religion* is one of his terms for the humanist worldview). Humanistic religion is based in humankind and its strengths, such as rationality and artistic creativity. People face a choice between this path and the path of "authoritarian religion," an unhealthy surrender to an imagined power that transcends humankind, such as the god or gods of traditional forms of theism. Casting this choice in other terminology, Fromm wrote of the "being" mode of existence versus the "having" mode. The being mode is characterized by wisdom, love and care for others, and a profound respect for nature. The having mode is marked by possessiveness—of material things, of status, of knowledge, and of other people. Spiritual perfection, for Fromm, is being human in the deepest and fullest sense, which is an experience suffused with love and contentment.

For Maslow, self-actualization is the fulfillment of our human potential. That is to say, self-actualization is spiritual perfection, given Maslow's humanism. The peak-experience is also a form of spiritual perfection, and is to some extent correlated with the process of self-actualization. But even people who have not attained self-actualization sometimes have the peak-experience, "so great and high an experience that it justifies not only itself but even living itself" (Maslow, *Religions, Values, and Peak-Experiences,* p. 62).

We will explore the peak-experience in more detail later as we consider the experiential dimension of humanism. For now we can note that this event applies here because it involves transcendence of the ordinary limitations of our human condition. Fromm's humanistic religion, otherwise described as the being mode of existence, is also characterized by transcendence. It infuses life with contentment and joy, and thus overcomes the sorrows that typify our inescapable predicament of being human.

What Is Our Destiny?

Humanists do not believe in an afterlife. For them, whatever destiny is in store for the individual can be derived only from the ongoing effects of the individual's actions while here on earth. A good reputation and a positive legacy for future generations are the extent of an individual's destiny. But an individual's destiny is intertwined with the destiny of the world and humanity at large. And in this respect humanism is indeed concerned with our destiny. Humanism is in constant pursuit of a better society, and is therefore intent on overcoming such present problems as overpopulation, environmental damage, and the threat of nuclear or chemical warfare. A world free of such problems would approximate a sort of humanistic heaven.

What Is the Nature of the World?

To the extent that humanity is of ultimate concern for humanists, so too is our home, planet Earth. Humanism therefore tends to be highly environmentally minded. Concern for the future of humanity naturally implies that the ecosystem be cared for.

Fromm elaborated most interestingly on humanism's environmentalist perspective through an analysis of the Sabbath. This special day, Fromm wrote, symbolizes the perfect relationship both between humans and between humans and the world. Work is avoided on the Sabbath in order not to violate our original peace with nature. Fromm's great interest in Taoism and Zen Buddhism also bespoke his environmentalist concerns.

What Is Ultimate Reality, and How Is It Revealed?

For humanism, there is no ultimate reality beyond humanity and the natural world we inhabit. There is no god who has created us. There is no Brahman that underlies reality, nor is there an Atman at the root of our existence. Atomic structure could be the "essence" of reality. The human "soul" consists of the personality, along with our hidden potential—our higher nature, as Maslow would say. This higher nature is revealed through self-actualization and during the moments of the peak-experience.

In a similar manner, Fromm described achieving our human potential as self-realization. To realize the self is to become fully human. Interestingly, Fromm acknowledged a theistic form of humanistic religion, for which God is a symbol of our human potential, or of the higher self that we should all strive to realize. In this respect God is the symbolic manifestation of ultimate reality.

The Seven Dimensions of Humanism

We now consider the extent to which humanism draws from the seven dimensions of religious traditions. As we might expect, some of these dimensions, such as the mythic and ritual dimensions, are not so relevant for humanism. Others, like the experiential, are surprisingly so.

The Experiential Dimension

When we picture the typical humanist maneuvering through life by means of rational decisions and scientific investigations, we may not envision moments of heightened experiential intensity. But, according to Maslow, the peak-experience (which Maslow sometimes refers to as a core-religious experience) is common to almost everyone—including scientifically minded humanists. During the peak-experience, wrote Maslow, one's perception becomes "relatively ego-transcending, self-forgetful, egoless, unselfish" (*Religion, Values, and Peak-Experiences,* p. 62). It is no coincidence that this sounds similar to the religious experiences of Hinduism, Buddhism, and other traditions. For Maslow, they are all basically the same experience. Far from regarding them as the possessions of only the traditional religions, Maslow advocated that peak-experiences be encouraged and thus made more accessible to all.

Fromm also advocated an experiential dimension of humanism. The being mode of existence amounts to a special type of experience, similar to the faith experience as described by some religious writers. It is characterized by contentment and joy.

The Mythic Dimension

Owing to its scientific orientation, humanism tends to place less importance on myths than do some religions. Still, some humanists value myths as symbolic representations of basic truths. For example, Fromm, in his book *You Shall Be as Gods: A Radical Interpretation of the Old Testament and Its Tradition* (1966), offered a most intriguing analysis. The Hebrew Bible, Fromm wrote, is "a *revolutionary* book; its theme is the liberation of man from the incestuous ties to blood and soil, from the submission to idols, from slavery, from powerful masters, to freedom for the individual, for the nation, and for all of mankind" (pp. 9–10). The sacred stories of the Bible are pervaded with humanist values.

The Doctrinal Dimension

While humanism rejects religious revelation and traditional authority as sources of truth, it nevertheless embraces a complex set of beliefs. These beliefs are derived primarily from rational thinking and scientific investigation. They are therefore malleable, as dictated by further thinking and new scientific discovery. Certain deep-seated beliefs seem to be constants, however. Liberalism and democracy, for example, are basic to humanism. Freedom of inquiry, a fundamental tenet of humanism, depends on them.

The Ethical Dimension

Ethics is an area of central concern for humanism. Indeed the worldview is sometimes referred to as ethical humanism. Humanists generally agree on some basic values: treating others with justice and tolerance, advancing political freedom, increasing human rights, eliminating hunger, and opposing violence and racism.

Fromm specifically advocated a global perspective that emphasizes the oneness of humanity. His book *The Art of Loving* (1956) focuses on the basic ethical teachings of love, truth, and justice.

The Ritual Dimension

Fromm and others have considered rituals, like myths, to have a symbolic significance. But for the most part, humanism gets along without formal worship practices. In fact, Maslow regarded as secondary to the spiritually central peak-experience all such "paraphernalia of organized religion—buildings and specialized personnel, rituals, dogmas, ceremonials, and the like" (*Religions, Values, and Peak-Experiences,* p. 28).

The Social Dimension

The ideal of a harmonious society, including all human beings regardless of nation, race, or culture, is highly valued by most humanists. It is fundamental to Fromm's humanistic religion.

Focusing on another form of community, Maslow believed that peak-experiencers tend to group together in close friendships, bonding as a result of their spiritual kinship.

The Material Dimension

One of the things humanists most celebrate is the human capacity for artistic creation. Therefore humanists regard virtually every work of art and architecture as a token of human potential and thus worthy of reverence. Given their environmental concerns and kinship with nature, they also characteristically appreciate scenic wonders and the harmonious workings of the natural world.

Competing with the Traditional Religions

The ability to categorize together the traditional religions and such modern worldviews as nationalism and humanism has a far-reaching practical implication: at least to some extent, all of these perspectives compete for adherents.

This competition can become severe. Some nationalist regimes, such as Hitler's National Socialism, explicitly clash with religion. The political and economic doctrines of Marxist-Leninist nations and Maoist China did so as well. On a less drastic note, many nations maintain a legal separation of church and state, which has significant consequences. In the United States, for example, formal prayer sessions are generally prohibited in public schools, while the Pledge of Allegiance is routinely recited in them (though various groups debate the constitutionality of the pledge's phrase "one nation under God").

Humanism, by its very nature, is nontheistic (and often atheistic). Maslow opposed the typical trappings of religious traditions as hindering universal accessibility to the peak-experience. Even Fromm, who had a deep appreciation for some religious symbolism and for religions that focus on nature, such as Taoism and Zen, was harshly critical of much that is commonplace in traditional religion. His humanistic religion, moreover, like Maslow's project of achieving self-actualization, is a functional alternative to traditional religion. It purports that one need not be a member of a church or synagogue—or a Zen monastery, for that matter—to realize one's highest potential. Indeed it deems reliance on religious revelation or traditional authority detrimental to the task.

Perhaps the clash between these modern worldviews and the established religions is most insurmountable precisely on the points where they are most in agreement. Humanism advocates spiritual growth, the fulfillment of human beings' potential to be loving, creative individuals. Nationalism advocates devotion to a higher cause, even to the extent of being willing to die for it. Religions tend to advocate the same things. Responding to the same fundamental questions, constituted of the same dimensions, advocating similar tasks—it is little wonder that nationalism and humanism compete with the traditional religions.

The prevalence of secular ideologies among the other worldviews illustrates the deep-seated human need for seeking spiritual contentment. Traditional religions may be rejected, but their functions are carried out in other forms. God-fearing or atheistic, traditionalist or New Age, the needs and tendencies of the spirit perhaps do not differ so very much among human beings.

Acknowledgments

The scriptural quotations marked Tanakh are reprinted from *Tanakh: The Holy Scriptures: The New JPS Translation to the Traditional Hebrew Text* (Philadelphia: The Jewish Publication Society, 1985). Copyright © 1985 by the Jewish Publication Society. All rights reserved. Used with permission of the Jewish Publication Society.

All other scriptural quotations contained herein are from the New Revised Standard Version of the Bible, Catholic Edition. Copyright © 1993 and 1989 by the Division of Christian Education of the National Council of the Churches of Christ in the United States of America. All rights reserved.

The excerpt on handout 2–A is from *The Old North Trail, or Life, Legends and Religion of the Blackfeet Indians*, by Walter McClintock (Lincoln, NE: University of Nebraska Press, Bison Books, 1968), page 508. Copyright © in the United States. Used with permission of the University of Nebraska Press.

The activity "Bhakti Marga and Puja," on pages 55–56, is adapted from one developed by John Reine, Newton Country Day School of the Sacred Heart, Newton, Massachusetts. Used with permission.

The meditation on pages 56–57 is from *Sadhana, a Way to God: Christian Exercises in Eastern Form*, complete and unabridged, by Anthony de Mello, SJ (New York: Doubleday, Image Books by special arrangement with Center for Spiritual Exchange, 1984), pages 13–15. Copyright © 1978 by Anthony de Mello, SJ, Poona, India. Used with permission of Doubleday, a division of Random House.

The excerpt on handout 3–A is from *The Upanishads: Breath of the Eternal*, selected and translated from the original Sanskrit by Swami Prabhavananda and Frederick Manchester (Hollywood, CA: Vedanta Society of Southern California, 1948; reprint, New York: New American Library, Mentor Books, 1957), pages 69–70. Copyright © 1948, 1957 by the Vedanta Society of Southern California. Used with permission of Vedanta Press.

The excerpts on handout 3–D are from *The Bhagavad-Gita: Krishna's Counsel in Time of War*, translated by Barbara Stoler Miller (New York: Bantam Books, 1986), pages 36 and 46. English translation copyright © 1986 by Barbara Stoler Miller.

The excerpt on handout 3–E is adapted from *The Spiritual Heritage of India*, by Swami Prabhavananda with the assistance of Frederick Manchester (Hollywood, CA: Vedanta Press, 1969), pages 281–282. Copyright © under the Berne Convention.

Handout 3–G is based on "The Dance of Love," in *Myths of the Hindus and Buddhists*, by Ananda K. Coomaraswamy and Sister Nivedita (1913; unabridged republication, New York: Dover Publications by special arrangement with George G. Harrap and Company, 1967), pages 232–235.

The meditations and quotation on pages 73–74 are from *The Miracle of Mindfulness: An Introduction to the Practice of Meditation*, by Thich Nhat Hanh, translated by Mobi Ho (Boston: Beacon Press, 1987), pages 83, 28, and 84, respectively. Copyright © 1975, 1976 by Thich Nhat Hanh; preface and English translation copyright © 1975, 1976, 1987 by Mobi Ho. Used with permission of Beacon Press, Boston.

The excerpts and quotations on pages 79–80 and the story on handout 4–B are from *The Hungry Tigress: Buddhist Myths, Legends, and Jataka Tales*, completely revised and expanded edition, by Rafe Martin (Cambridge, MA: Yellow Moon Press, 1999), pages xv, xvi, xvi, xviii, xx, xxi, xxiv, xxiv, 224, and 224; and 113–114; respectively. Copyright © 1999 by Rafe Martin. Used with permission of the author.

The excerpts and quotations about Buddhism's "neglect" of God on pages 81–83 are from *Buddhism Made Plain: An Introduction for Christians and Jews*, revised edition of *Buddhism and Christianity: Their Inner Affinity* (Colombo, Sri Lanka: Ecumenical Institute for Study and Dialogue, 1981), by Antony Fernando with Leonard Swidler (Maryknoll, NY: Orbis Books, 1985), pages 104, 104, 104–105, 105, 105, 105, 106, 107, 107, 108, 108, 109, and 109, respectively. Copyright © 1985 by Antony Fernando. Used with permission of Orbis Books.

The story on handout 4–A is from *Old Path White Clouds: Walking in the Footsteps of the Buddha,* by Thich Nhat Hanh (Berkeley, CA: Parallax Press, 1991), pages 146–148. Copyright © 1991 by Thich Nhat Hanh. Used with permission of Parallax Press, Berkeley, California, *www.parallax.org.*

Handout 4–D is based on *The World's Religions,* revised and updated edition of *The Religions of Man,* by Huston Smith (San Francisco: HarperSanFrancisco, 1991), pages 106–107. Copyright © 1991 by Huston Smith. Original copyright © 1958 by Huston Smith; copyright © renewed 1986 by Huston Smith.

The description of the fasting Siddhartha on handout 4–E is adapted from *Buddhism: A Religion of Infinite Compassion,* by Clarence H. Hamilton (1952; reprint, New York: Liberal Arts Press, 1954), pages 14–15.

The excerpts of Colette Caillat on page 97 and the summary of her words on handout 5–A are from *The Encyclopedia of Religion,* volume 14, edited by Mircea Eliade (New York: Macmillan Library Reference, 1987), pages 535 and 536. Copyright © 1986 by Gale, a part of Cengage Learning, Inc. Used with permission of Cengage Learning, *www.cengage.com/permissions.*

The passages from *The Analects* on pages 119, 120, 255, 311, and handout 7–A are from *The Analects,* by Confucius, translated by D. C. Lau (London: Penguin Classics, 1979), pages 65, 66, 64; 63, 64; 74; 107; and 73, 80, 76, and 74; respectively. Copyright © 1979 by D. C. Lau. Used with permission of Penguin Books, Ltd.

The passage from the *Book of Mencius* on page 122 is from *Mencius,* translated by D. C. Lau (Harmondsworth, England: Penguin Books, 1970), page 102. Copyright © 1970 by D. C. Lau.

The passage from the Great Learning on page 123 is from *Chinese Religion: An Introduction,* fifth edition, by Laurence G. Thompson (Belmont, CA: Wadsworth Publishing Company, 1996), page 12. Copyright © 1996 by Wadsworth Publishing Company.

The quotations of Wordsworth on page 130, Oscar Wilde on page 130, John F. Kennedy on page 322, and Protagoras on page 325 are from *The Oxford Dictionary of Quotations,* fourth edition, edited by Angela Partington (Oxford, England: Oxford University Press, 1992), pages 745, 735, 394, and 530, respectively. Selection and arrangement copyright © 1979 by Oxford University Press.

The passage from the Tao Te Ching on page 134 is from *The Way of Lao Tzu,* translated by Wing-tsit Chan (Indianapolis: Bobbs-Merrill Company, Library of Liberal Arts Press, 1963), page 101. Copyright © 1963 by the Liberal Arts Press, a division of Bobbs-Merrill Company.

The koans on handout 9–B are from *The Gateless Gate,* by Ekai, called Mu-mon, translated by Nyogen Senzaki and Paul Reps (Los Angeles: J. Murray, 1934).

The story on handout 9–C is from *Zen Flesh, Zen Bones: A Collection of Zen and Pre-Zen Writings,* compiled by Paul Reps (Garden City, NY: Doubleday and Company, Anchor Books by arrangement with Charles E. Tuttle Company of Boston and Tokyo, 1957), pages 24–26. Copyright © 1957 by Charles E. Tuttle Company. Used with permission of Tuttle Publishing, a member of the Periplus Publishing Group.

Matsuo Basho's haiku on handout 9–D are from *Japanese Haiku: Two Hundred Twenty Examples of Seventeen-Syllable Poems,* by Basho, Buson, Issa, Shiki, Sokan, Kikaku, and others; translated by Peter Beilenson (Mount Vernon, NY: The Peter Pauper Press), pages 9–13. Copyright © 1956 by the Peter Pauper Press.

Annie Dillard's description of holiness as a theme in literature on page 151 is from her book *Holy the Firm* (New York: Harper and Row, 1977), page 11. Copyright © 1977 by Annie Dillard.

Wilfred Pelletier and Ted Poole's description of holiness as a theme in literature on page 151 is from *No Foreign Land: The Biography of a North American Indian,* by Wilfred Pelletier and Ted Poole (New York: Pantheon Books, 1974), page 209. Copyright © 1973 by Wilfred Pelletier and Ted Poole.

The other brief examples of holiness as a theme in literature on page 151 are from *Earth Prayers from Around the World: 365 Prayers, Poems, and Invocations for Honoring the Earth,* edited by Elizabeth Roberts and Elias Amidon (San Francisco: HarperSanFrancisco, 1991), pages 41, 56, 57, 61, 362, and 363, respectively. Copyright © 1991 by Elizabeth Roberts and Elias Amidon.

The excerpt from Saint Francis of Assisi's "Canticle of Brother Sun" on handout 10–A is from *Francis and Clare: The Complete Works,* translated by Regis J. Armstrong, OFM, and Ignatius C. Brady, OFM (New York: Paulist Press, 1982), pages 38–39. Copyright © 1982 by Paulist Press. Paulist Press, Inc., New York/Mahwah, NJ. Used with permission of Paulist Press, *www.paulistpress.com.*

The quotation on page 176 is from *Man's Quest for God: Studies in Prayer and Symbolism,* by Abraham Joshua Heschel (New York: Charles Scribner's Sons, 1954), page 45. Copyright © 1954 by Abraham Joshua Heschel.

The activity "Miriam's Shabbat" on page 180 and handout 12–C is adapted from an activity and handout developed by John Reine, Newton Country Day School of the Sacred Heart, Newton, Massachusetts. Used with permission.